DIVIDING THE NILE

DIVIDING THE NILE

Egypt's Economic Nationalists in the Sudan 1918–56

David E. Mills

The American University in Cairo Press
Cairo New York

First published in 2014 by
The American University in Cairo Press
113 Sharia Kasr el Aini, Cairo, Egypt
420 Fifth Avenue, New York, NY 10018
www.aucpress.com

Exclusive distribution outside Egypt and North America by I.B.Tauris & Co Ltd.,
6 Salem Road, London, W2 4BU

Dar el Kutub No. 14519/13
ISBN 978 977 416 638 9

Dar el Kutub Cataloging-in-Publication Data
Mills, David E.
Dividing the Nile: Egypt's Economic Nationalists in the Sudan, 1918–1956 /David E. Mills.—Cairo: The American University in Cairo Press, 2014
p. cm.
ISBN: 978 977 416 638 9
1.Sudan—History—
to 1821
962.403

1 2 3 4 5 18 17 16 15 14

Designed by Jon W. Stoy
Printed in Egypt

Contents

This book is dedicated
to the memory of my mother,
Jean Barbara Mills

Tables

Acknowledgments

This book is the product of many years of research and writing, during which time I have benefited tremendously from the assistance and encouragement of numerous family members, friends, and colleagues. I am certain to inadvertently omit some who aided me in the creation of this book, and I can only ask the forgiveness of those I forget to mention.

Unquestionably, the most instrumental scholarly guidance behind this work came from Dr. Byron Canon, who chaired my supervisory committee at the University of Utah. His roles as scholar, mentor, taskmaster, and friend were absolutely critical to my graduate studies, my research in Egypt, and my efforts to find employment in this field. Although I have tried over the years, I have never adequately expressed my appreciation for all Byron's efforts on my behalf. Additionally, Dr. Peter von Sivers and other members of my supervisory committee at Utah contributed tremendously to my scholarly progression. Finally, the financial and educational support of the University of Utah's Department of History and Middle East Center were vital to my work during this period.

Critical financial assistance for research conducted in Egypt was provided initially by a Fulbright doctoral dissertation research grant from the U.S. Department of Education and later through a research fellowship from the West Virginia Humanities Council. Thanking all those Egyptians who have assisted me over the years is well-nigh impossible. Instead of omitting some individuals, I would like to thank every scholar and staff member of the Binational Fulbright Commission of Egypt, the Institute of African Research and Studies at Cairo University, the American University in Cairo libraries, and, especially, the Egyptian National Archives and

National Library. I would be remiss not to thank Dr. Muhammad Gamal al-Din al-Massady of Cairo University for his assistance in gaining access to various Egyptian archival repositories and introducing me to colleagues. Finally, the friendly advice and conversations with Alaa al-Din Arafat, Mine Ener, and many others made my work in Egypt so much more enjoyable.

Much of the writing and revising of this book has occurred over the past three to four years, with assistance from different sources. My colleague from Marshall University's Department of Geography, Dr. Jamie Leonard, was gracious enough to spend some of his valuable time creating the map included in this book. Many of my Department of History colleagues critiqued sections of this work, most notably Drs. David Kenley, Montserrat Miller, Dan Holbrook, and Kevin Barksdale. Furthermore, the critical comments of the anonymous readers were very much appreciated and instrumental in my revision process. Finally, the editors and staff of the American University in Cairo Press have been consistently helpful and a pleasure to work with on this project. I would like to express my gratitude especially to Nadia Naqib, Randi Danforth, and Johanna Baboukis. Your patience with my delays, questions, and communication difficulties has made the final stages of this publication a much easier process.

All of the individuals noted above have provided invaluable assistance in the completion of this project, but all responsibility for any errors, omissions, or other shortcomings of this book rests on my shoulders alone.

My family—Phil, Jean, Allison, and Alan—have always been supportive of my academic and professional pursuits, for which I am extremely thankful. Finally, my wife, Stephanie, and my son, Riley, will always have my deepest love and appreciation. They have had to endure my long nights of working on this book and have listened patiently over the years as I voiced my plans, difficulties, and concerns about this project.

The Nile and surrounding countries, 1918–1956

INTRODUCTION

In 1955, Sudanese parliamentary leaders chose an independent existence for their country. Their decision disappointed many Egyptian nationalists who had been extolling the unity of the Nile Valley for decades. The Sudanese decision may have been the inevitable outcome of Britain's efforts to isolate the Sudan since 1899, but there were other factors that critically inhibited unification. This study focuses on the economic initiatives of Egyptian nationalists, who sought to connect the Sudan and Egypt through commerce, investment, water sharing, infrastructural developments, and more. The study argues that Egyptian economic efforts in the Sudan were too little, too late, and constituted a missed opportunity reflective of a lack of political willpower. In other words, the lack of sustained economic contact between Egypt and the Sudan during the first half of the twentieth century confirmed broader trends that made the Egyptian dream of Nile Valley unity untenable.

The Sudanese ended Egyptian dreams of a unified nation in 1955, and scholars have traditionally taken two broad approaches in explaining why the Sudanese chose independence. One group of authors, including Peter Woodward, Heather Sharkey, Tim Niblock, and others, has described the path to independence through analysis of the composition and activities of local Sudanese leaders, political groupings, native officials, and the educated urban elite.[1] Most of these scholars emphasized the role of the prominent Sudanese sectarian rivals, Sayyid 'Abd al-Rahman al-Mahdi and Sayyid Ali al-Mirghani, and the Graduates Congress.[2] Heather Sharkey's work is unique in its analysis of those Sudanese working within the Condominium administration and the dilemma they faced—assisting in foreign control of their country, while also desiring to see it undone. The eventual Sudanese choice of a separate independent existence may have resulted from a history of

Egyptian mistreatment or British encouragement of their independence, but these studies argue that it was ultimately the Sudanese who chose their future.

In contrast to those emphasizing Sudanese agency, scholars such as M.W. Daly, Gabriel Warburg, and Muddathir Abdel Rahim give much greater prominence to British and Egyptian activities, Condominium policies and personnel, or Anglo–Egyptian negotiations in deciding the Sudan's fate.[3] These studies do not entirely ignore the Sudanese, but emphasizing the centrality of external factors or actors in modern Sudanese history is only logical, considering that British and Egyptian officials largely denied the Sudanese any political role until the 1950s. Still, histories emphasizing Sudanese agency and those stressing external factors behind developments are not mutually exclusive.

However, what neither group includes in the history of eventual Sudanese independence is the role played by Egyptians. These scholars have not entirely omitted Egyptians, but typically the latter have more of a supporting role behind the 'true' players in this historical drama—the British and Sudanese. Yes, Egyptians are part of negotiations, but they are only the irrational, stubborn diplomats attempting to subvert British-led Sudanese progress. Yes, they have been an actual physical presence in Sudanese history, but throughout this history they have uniformly viewed the Sudan as a colonial possession to be exploited to the fullest extent possible.[4] Irrespective of how negatively—or not—scholars have portrayed Egyptians, they have consistently treated them as definitively less influential actors in twentieth-century Sudanese history. Egyptians may have had a small role in the story of Sudanese independence, but efforts to unite the Nile Valley were a central component of the Egyptian nationalist movement.

This study is ultimately a history of Egyptians—one that examines their intentions and actions in respect to the Sudan. The breadth of historical works on the Egyptian nationalist movement is vast, considering that the possible chronological restraints on the subject might range from Muhammad Ali's era to Gamal Abdel Nasser's eviction of the last British forces from Egypt in 1956, and beyond. Even a review of only histories of the first half of the twentieth century reveals a wide-ranging body of literature. Early works by scholars such as Alexander Scholch, Afaf Lutfi Sayyid-Marsot, Charles Wendell, Jacques Berque, Mahmud Zayid, and others tended to focus on the motivation and actions of Egyptian elites.[5] They did not intentionally neglect the Egyptian masses, but extensive reliance on official correspondence and western documentation resulted in their focus on the elite groupings and the latter's interactions with external actors in Egyptian history. These studies are excellent, comprehensive histories in respect to their stated objectives, but primarily emphasizing Egyptian leaders' interactions with foreign elements provides only a partial picture of the nationalist movement.

More recent works by Eve Troutt Powell, Joel Beinin, Lisa Pollard, Beth Baron, Donald Reid, and others have rectified the perceived shortcomings of earlier histories of the Egyptian nationalist movement significantly, through examination of different sources and social groups.[6] Women, workers, peasants, students, and other non-elites—all of them local inhabitants—have assumed center stage in these histories. Personal memoirs, non-governmental organization records, literary forms, various visual arts, demographic data, and so forth have all helped illuminate the narrative of Egypt's nationalist movement. These scholars do not deny a foreign role or the importance of local leaders in Egypt's march toward independence, but they have demonstrated that the masses were active and influential.

Finally, this study's emphasis on the economic motives and initiatives of Egyptians in the Sudan expands our understanding of twentieth-century Egyptian economic development. Charles Issawi, Marius Deeb, Robert Tignor, Eric Davis, Robert Vitalis, and others have examined the interactions of both local and foreign businessmen, landowners, government officials, and others and the role of such interactions in Egyptian economic progress.[7] These studies differ in their characterization of economic results—the development of a neocolonial or dependency position for the local economy and its leaders. They differ in identifying the critical 'actors' in this economic history, ranging from groups of local landowners or aspiring industrialists to Egyptian government officials or foreign economic interests—frequently some combination of these elements. With their emphasis on the socioeconomic elite and heavy reliance on official documentation, these economic studies are actually a subgroup of the Egyptian nationalist movement histories mentioned above. Like the broader nationalist movement studies, these scholars of Egyptian economic development emphasized the post–First World War era and its nation-building preoccupation.[8]

These histories and economic studies share one major problem. From start to finish of their investigations, the Sudan and Egypt are two separate entities. As stated earlier, in histories of Sudanese development Egyptians play a relatively minor role—and a patently negative, exploitative, and malicious one at that. In studies of the Egyptian nationalist movement, Sudanese play an equally superfluous part. Sudanese affairs intrude on the story of Egypt's road to independence only when Nile water concerns are raised, disturbances in Egypt are mirrored in the Sudan, or the issue of Sudanese sovereignty derails diplomatic efforts to end the British occupation—of

Egypt. One work that more concretely links Egypt and the Sudan is Eve Troutt Powell's *A Different Shade of Colonialism*, and even this study links the two regions as a means of arguing that Egyptian nationalists defined their own identity and own nationalist movement through contrasting themselves with the Sudanese.[9] One of the most prolific scholars on the involvement of the Egyptian elite in Sudanese affairs would be Yunan Labib Rizq. Much of his scholarship examines the domestic political utility of Sudanese issues or relationships for Egyptian leaders.[10] Finally, the only study of economic developments in the region that does not specifically conceive of the Nile Valley as two separate entities is Terence Walz's *Trade between Egypt and Bilad as-Sudan, 1700–1820*, which is confined to an earlier century.[11] Therefore, one could legitimately claim that to this point virtually all histories of the modern Nile Valley begin with the assumption that 'normally' Egypt and the Sudan are and have always been independent of one another. Interestingly, as will be demonstrated in this work, virtually all Egyptians have claimed that 'normally' Egypt and the Sudan form a single nation.[12]

Studying Egyptian claims of a united Nile Valley nation and their efforts to achieve such invites comparison with all sorts of works on nationalism and nationalist movements. For centuries now, scholars from a wide range of disciplines have vigorously debated the phenomenon of nationalism without reaching consensus on the central issues. There is great diversity of topical and analytical emphasis among scholars of nationalism, but they could be loosely grouped under the labels 'modernists' and 'perennialists.'[13] Modernists argue that the rise of nations is connected to the Enlightenment, industrialization, scientific progress, secular educational systems, military advancements, and expansion of the modern state apparatus. Ernest Gellner, undoubtedly among the foremost theorists on the subject, wrote that "nationalism is rooted in modernity."[14] Many of Gellner's modernist colleagues view the nation as a distinctly political or physical entity—yet there are also those modernists who emphasize less tangible, more amorphous aspects of nations.[15] Perennialists, such as Anthony Smith or John Armstrong, argue for the primacy of culture or ethnicity in the composition of a nation. However, they also stress that nations—Smith labeled them 'ethnies'—are not modern creations but rather have existed for centuries.[16] These ethnies may not have always enjoyed administrative/political structures reflective of their distinctiveness, but this does not mean that they constituted any less of a nation.

The modern history of Egypt can provide evidence supportive of either the modernist or the perennialist argument concerning nation formation. The modernists, stressing the centrality of the state and its administrative functions as the critical element in claiming a nation, would naturally focus on the nineteenth-century activities of Muhammad Ali and his heirs. The timing and activities of this 'founder' of modern Egypt correspond precisely with post-French Revolution-era developments studied by Eric Hobsbawm, Elie Keddourie, Max Weber, Gellner, and other modernists. At the same time, the cultural continuity of the Nile Valley since the earliest pre-pharaonic societies provides plenty of fodder for perennialist arguments. Egyptian nationalists in the twentieth century certainly claimed that the Sudan and Egypt had constituted a single nation for millenia. Besides dating the emergence of nations, scholars have researched extensively the various institutions and societal groupings that have led to successful nationalist movements. Typically, some combination of a local vernacular press, a public education system, a conscripted national army, or other development is linked to successful nationalist movements.

Meanwhile, scholars have relegated analysis of economic interests and activities of a nation, or at least of its leadership, to studies of nation *building*—a process that occurs only after independence. Certainly, buttressing political liberation with domestic economic development is a logical course of action after independence is achieved. However, equally logical is the idea that economic interests—just as readily as other unifying characteristics—could be the glue that unites a nationalist movement from its infancy. Emphasizing material interests, however, indirectly attacks the selfless motives of national leaders. For instance, shared economic and financial concerns may have been the true bond of America's founding fathers, but only after a century of existence could Charles Beard attribute such base motives to the United States' revolutionary-era leaders.[17] The point is that financial interests or strong economic linkages between regions may be just as important in the process of nation formation as a common history, language, and religion, or opposition to foreign control. The shared economic interests of nationalist movements have received little scholarly attention.[18]

In Egypt's case, some scholars have linked the history of economic development and the early twentieth-century nationalist movement. Most concretely, Robert Tignor, Eric Davis, and Robert Vitalis have argued for the central role played by various Egyptian politicians, local landowners, and both foreign and local entrepreneurial elements in the emergence of a national economy. Generally, these authors agree that local economic and political groupings had a tremendous impact on the liberation of Egypt from foreign control and the Egyptian nation's socioeconomic make-up. They acknowledge the rivalries between foreign and local interests, between landowners and industrialists, and between multiple groups seeking state support of their undertakings, but also that these groups with different specific economic concerns generally wanted and worked toward the nationalist goal of true independence. Like the works of Tignor, Davis, and Vitalis—and others—this study examines various Egyptian economic interest groups and their nationalist efforts. Unlike those works, this study broadens the territorial range of Egyptian economic efforts, looking at the economic nationalism of the entire Nile Valley.

In examining the economic efforts of Egyptian nationalists hoping to bind the Sudan to their country, this work is organized around a 'rough' chronology, addressing water resources, land ownership, investment, trade, and so forth as these issues moved to the forefront of debates among Egyptians and Sudanese officials. However, the earliest and most consistently expressed claims of a united Nile Valley were not of an economic nature. Egyptians had maintained since the late nineteenth century that Egypt and the Sudan shared a common history, language, religion, ethnicity, and so forth. Chapter one examines these and other cultural attributes of the nation, as well as twentieth-century Egyptian initiatives to solidify such cultural bonds. Foreshadowing the later analysis of economic efforts, Egyptian activities to expand educational, religious, and other cultural bonds with the Sudan were started too late, were poorly organized, and were insufficiently supported by their government. Still, the nationalist leadership considered these cultural bonds clearly to favor unity of the Nile Valley.

The Egyptian leadership proclaimed the certainty of Nile Valley unity because of these historic, cultural bonds—and the unifying nature of the Nile River. Egyptians claimed not only that the river constituted unquestioned geographic evidence for Nile Valley unity but also that it economically united Egyptian and Sudanese regions—the subject of chapter two. With the inauguration of perennial irrigation and the cultivation of cotton in the nineteenth century, Egypt's elite became extremely concerned with obtaining sufficient water for its agricultural undertakings. After the turn of the twentieth century, British and Egyptian officials studied, planned, and completed major hydraulic projects in Sudanese territories, most importantly the construction of the Sennar and Jabal Awliya' dams along the Blue and White Niles south of Khartoum. Because of British administrative dominance in the Sudan, Egyptians feared officials there might withhold water to force Egyptian acquiescence to British imperial objectives. Even when Egypt's allotment of water was assured, there was still criticism of the actual utility of Sudanese projects, the costs of such, and the possible international cotton market competition created. By 1929, British and Egyptian officials reached agreement on a distribution of Nile waters that clearly favored Egyptian interests. Moreover, this splitting of water resources inherently undermined nationalists' claims that the Nile united the two regions. Roughly a decade after their agreement on Nile water distribution, Egyptian and British officials agreed also on Sudanese repayment of Egyptian loans. Debt repayment analysis concludes this chapter on Nile River developments because arrangements in both fields implied the same thing, namely the separation of Egypt and the Sudan.

Beyond Nile River concerns and the provision of developmental loans, there was little Egyptian economic interaction with the Sudan. This finally changed in the mid-1930s. Much of the initial Egyptian effort to improve economic relations with the Sudan centered on support structures, especially administrative institutions and transportation linkages between the two regions. Chapter three examines the flurry of pre–First World War institutional developments, ranging from the creation of government agencies and commercial exhibitions to the dispatch of economic missions and experts to the Sudan. Among the most pressing concerns addressed by these groups and individuals was the improvement of transportation between Egypt and the Sudan. Chapter four explores all means, methods, and costs of moving men, material, and manufactured goods between the Nile neighbors. Although the chapter briefly examines the early establishment of rail, road, and ship services, the emphasis is on Egyptian attempts to improve services during the latter 1930s. Egyptian businessmen enjoyed no advantages over foreign competitors along the Red Sea maritime route, so they were most concerned with improving the combination of rail and river transportation along the Nile. Still, Egyptians were disinclined to utilize the Nile route because of the vast number of technical and bureaucratic difficulties encountered there. Most importantly, the lack of a direct railroad link between the two regions was a flagrant physical symbol of the separation of Egypt and the Sudan.

Beginning with chapter five, the analytical focus of this study shifts from infrastructure and institutional arrangements to the actual activities of Egyptian merchants, industrialists, landowners, and other interested parties. The specific topic analyzed in this chapter is Egyptian investment objectives and undertakings in the Sudan. Investing in commercial ventures is addressed in later chapters, and industrial opportunities were few, so this chapter concentrates on Egyptian efforts to acquire and develop Sudanese agricultural lands. There had been some minimal interest in Sudanese agricultural lands to possibly alleviate Egyptian population pressure, but after the 1936 Anglo–Egyptian treaty acknowledged the permissibility of acquiring property there, Egyptian investment efforts intensified.

Furthermore, Egypt's entrepreneurial elite was most experienced, capable, and desirous of investment in agricultural undertakings. However, British officials imposed such restrictive conditions on the purchase or lease of lands that no significant investment took place prior to Sudanese independence in 1956. From examination of Egyptian areas of interest and their criticism of British obstructionism, one can conclude that such investment might have assisted some Sudanese, thereby garnering popular support for union. However, assessing the benefits of land investments depends on one's perspective. In Egyptian eyes, the development of an irrigated agricultural scheme helped their Sudanese brothers, but British officials feared Egyptian land speculation and exploitation of the Sudanese peasantry.

Similar contrasting interpretations could be offered for commercial activities along the Nile Valley. Does increased trade between Egypt and the Sudan, and lessening the role of foreign trading partners, translate to commercial interdependence and greater likelihood of union? Or does such commerce mean the unnecessary exploitation of a population through restricting foreign competition? The examination of Nile Valley trade in chapters six and seven addresses these and other questions. In these chapters, particular attention is given to the period from the mid-1930s through the Second World War because these years witnessed restricted foreign competition, sufficient local production for commercial exchange, and concerted Egyptian efforts from 1935 onward. Both chapters utilize statistical evidence for specific exports, selecting this evidence to highlight causes of commercial difficulties and because they were the commodities Egyptian and Sudanese traders were promoting. Although there were some temporary or specific commodity successes, the general record of Nile Valley commercial exchange was fairly dismal from start to finish.

The explanations for the failure to increase either Egyptian exports to or Egyptian imports from the Sudan are similar. Foreign competition, administrative indifference or opposition, deficient infrastructural and institutional support, and simple supply and demand variables all contributed to the poor results. Chapter six demonstrates that only with fixed administrative arrangements (refined sugar) or in minor, specific niches (hand-woven cotton–artificial silk mixed textiles) were Egyptian exporters able to capture a significant market share. In the most lucrative Sudanese market, cotton textiles, Egyptians made no headway whatsoever. Chapter seven claims that increased Sudanese exports to Egypt were equally absent. Sudanese exports were largely confined to agricultural produce and livestock, neither of which enjoyed governmental encouragement and both of which tended to fluctuate in response to supply and demand levels. No significant, sustained commercial exchange meant there was little tangible benefit for the local population or for an entrepreneurial merchant class, groups that then might have more forcefully called for Nile Valley unity.

Egyptian leaders had certainly expected eventual Nile Valley unity, claiming that the dual Anglo–Egyptian Condominium administration established in 1899 after the reconquest was only a temporary measure. Years of diplomatic wrangling with British representatives to end this administrative division of the valley proved fruitless. Since Egypt was occupied by British forces in the later nineteenth century and enjoyed only limited independence prior to the 1950s, diplomatic efforts may have been destined to fail. Yet Egyptians apparently believed that their claims of historical, religious, linguistic, ethnic, and cultural bonds with the Sudan were so solidly established that strengthening them was unnecessary. However, Egyptian leaders would also assert that an economic unity of the Nile Valley existed. In 1947, before the United Nations Security Council, the Egyptian prime minister, Mahmud Fahmi al-Nuqrashi, claimed that his country and the Sudan "are so closely interdependent that any policy pursued separately to further local interests may stifle the progress of the whole Valley. This economic unity, based on agricultural, industrial and commercial interests, is further enhanced by the complete dependence of both sections of the Valley on the waters of the Nile."[19] Mutual dependence on Nile waters did unite the northern and southern halves of the valley, but Egyptians made virtually no progress in strengthening any other economic bond.

Scholars' explanation for the division of the Nile Valley have ranged from Sudanese ill will because of nineteenth-century rule to British imperial opposition to union, but no study addresses economic development as a factor in the eventual separation of Egypt and the Sudan. This work does that—it examines the Egyptian failure to develop economic bonds with the Sudan. Although all manner of causes for this failure will be explored, a critical general factor was the absence of any concerted, supported, and sustained effort—or even expressed interest—in developing economic ties until just prior to the Second World War. Yes, Egyptians had studied, planned, and executed hydraulic works that assisted all inhabitants of the valley—but they had also agreed to 'divide' this common resource. Yes, in the early decades of Condominium rule over the Sudan, Egypt provided significant funds for infrastructure, military defense, or simply to balance the budget, but it also demanded and eventually agreed to the repayment of these loans. In the early years of the twentieth century Egyptians initiated almost no 'unifying' economic projects in the Sudan. One must conclude that little effort to promote economic unity during the first forty years of Condominium rule certainly did not help the Egyptian cause. Or, conversely, forty years of British-dominated Sudanese development had already divided the Nile Valley economy. Subsequently, Egyptian claims of strong historical, cultural, and geographic bonds mattered little. The separation of Egypt and the Sudan occurred swiftly and painlessly in 1956 and was merely a political reflection of the independent economic development during the preceding decades.

1 The 'Natural' Unity of the Nile Valley

This is our situation in respect to the Sudan: We spend money there, we shed blood there, we endure hardships there, and our fathers endured such before us, and we draw life from that river which pours forth from the highest reaches of the Sudan. In any case, it is impossible, unless we were a lifeless people, that we leave one speck of the Sudan for others.[1]

—Sa'd Zaghlul, Egyptian Chamber of Deputies, 28 June 1924

Among the greatest occasions for satisfaction is that I see steady progress in the Sudan, and my government will spare no effort in strengthening connections, especially cultural and progressive, with its people, to whom we are bound by unbreakable bonds.[2]

—'Ali Mahir, Egyptian Chamber of Deputies, 18 November 1939

Reflective of domestic popular opinion during the interwar era, all Egyptian politicians believed in the indisputable unity of the Nile Valley. Comments from Egyptian leaders about the unbreakable unity of the Nile Valley were normally just their introductory remarks before addressing the latest British 'imperialist' machinations in the Sudan. The natural unity of Egyptians and Sudanese was never questioned by any political party or interest group. When describing the claimed unity of the Nile Valley, Egyptian nationalists referenced some combination of historical, geographical, or cultural bonds—and, less frequently, economic ties. For instance, in Egypt's Chamber of Deputies on 6 February 1945, Muhammad

Mahmud Jalal of the Watani Party joined the raucous debate caused by the Sudanese government's failure to follow certain clauses of the 1936 Anglo–Egyptian treaty. This deputy stated:

> I always hold that the Nile Valley is an indivisible union, persistently remonstrate against every instance which cuts the cords of the single nation, just as [other] deputies in the chambers tirelessly hold to this guiding principle, viewing always as an established fact that a single people inhabit the Nile Valley, bound together by a nationalist, geographic, economic, and historical union that has no fissure.[3]

Egyptian nationalists mentioned Nile Valley unity frequently, but their activities focused on ending the British occupation. There was virtually no effort directed toward strengthening various cultural, geographic, or historical bonds with the Sudan. Admittedly, little could be accomplished to actually improve historical or geographic bonds, but did Egyptians effectively emphasize these 'unifying' features of the Nile Valley?

A Geographically United Nation?

The geographical or topographical features of the Nile Valley constitute some of the strongest evidence for the union of Egyptians and Sudanese. The dominant feature of northeastern Africa is undoubtedly the Nile River. Flowing northward from the Great Lakes of Central Africa to the Mediterranean Sea, the Nile has been almost the sole source of livelihood for peoples in the region for millennia. The oft-quoted phrase of the Greek historian Herodotus that "Egypt is the gift of the Nile" applies equally well to northern Sudanese regions. After various tributaries inch through the swampy Sudd regions of southern Sudan, the White Nile flows steadily by Khartoum, Atbara, Wadi Halfa, and Aswan through Upper Egypt to Cairo and the northern delta before emptying into the sea. Over these hundreds and hundreds of miles the river flows through desert regions, forcing settled civilizations into the valley. The Blue Nile, rising from the Ethiopian highlands to join the White Nile at Khartoum (thereafter referred to as simply the Nile), produces the annual flood and silt deposits upon which peasants to the north depend. For millennia, the peasants of the valley from Khartoum northward relied on traditional irrigation methods for their sustenance. In the nineteenth century, Egyptian leaders, with European assistance, began to construct hydraulic works and to implement perennial irrigation methods, tactics that would be employed in the Sudan later. The river valley is a relatively homogeneous environment bordered by the sea in the north, deserts to the west and east, and a combination of mountainous highlands and swamp-like regions to the south.

Egyptian nationalists wholeheartedly endorsed this conception of a uniform, bordered, united Nile Valley, stretching from central Sudanese regions to the Mediterranean Sea. 'Abd al-Rahman al-Rafi'i Bey proclaimed to the Egyptian Senate in August 1945 that

> there is no doubt that the essential foundation in forming nations is that there is unity of climate, geography and history linking the parts of the country. And there is not found in the world a stronger unity of climate, geography and history than the unity of the Nile Valley, because [this unity] links together all the lands through which the Nile passes. The existing unity between Egypt and the Sudan is a natural unity, and it is not possible that any other country participates in it with us.[4]

Israel Gershoni wrote about the Egyptian official most qualified to describe the natural unity of the valley—Sulayman Huzayin. Huzayin, a geographer by training, was clearly in line with the Egyptian nationalists' goals, later being employed by the government to formulate arguments for the unity of the Nile Valley. Gershoni wrote of Huzayin that "as a geographer, . . . his entire aim is to impart the 'geographical dimension' to the national discourse and the political struggle, in order to endow them with 'scientific force' and to base them, as far as possible, on solid historical and geographical realities. He complained that the political discussion was ignoring 'solid geographical facts.'"[5] Huzayin described these solid facts of a united valley in the following manner:

> The Nile River carved a unique topographical and climatic belt into an arid desert. The geographical autonomy of this belt's environment is complete because it was the Nile that created it from its waters: from the water itself and the silt it brought with it that shaped the features of the soil and the landscape of the valley. The flow of the Nile and its rhythm dictated the structure of the valley. Over tens of thousands of years they created a rigid and permanent pattern of landscape. The absolute dependence on the Nile ensured symmetry, stability, and continuity. The relative isolation created by the deserts surrounding the valley preserved its independence as a self-contained ecological entity.[6]

Huzayin dissected the entire Nile Valley watershed into three regions—valley, heights, and basin—but stated, "It is only in the valley that identical topographical and ecological conditions exist, making it one integrative geographical unit. Here the effect of the Nile on the physical environment is *exclusive and absolute*."[7] The absolutely integrated valley he was describing included all of Egypt and the northern/central regions of the Sudan. Sulayman Huzayin's description of an integrated valley seems to be 'scientific' evidence in favor of unity, but if one examines his united valley closely, and considers other topographical features and developments of the modern era, the claimed integration is less absolute.

First, the Nile River, although often described by historians as facilitating irrigation and transportation, is actually not so easily and constantly utilized. It flows through six cataracts north of Khartoum, making transport via the river difficult during periods of the year, and forming a 'natural' border for Egypt just south of Aswan. The geographic division of the valley caused by the cataracts was reinforced by the construction of the Aswan Dam in 1902. Despite difficulties arising from the cataracts and subsequent dams constructed at Aswan, men, material, and information had successfully traversed this region of the valley by various means historically—timely river transport, later road development, or the traditional routes through the surrounding deserts.

Besides the Nile River not absolutely binding the regions together, both Egypt and the Sudan had strong geographical linkages to other regions. Egypt had significant historical, commercial, and cultural connections to the Mediterranean and Levantine worlds. Meanwhile, the Sudan had historical linkages to neighbors other than Egypt. Although there were some connections between western and southern Sudanese regions and their sub-Saharan neighbors, the strongest of these non-Egyptian ties was with the Red Sea/Indian Ocean communities. Stephen Serels, in his 2012 article on Sudanese grain trade and difficulties arising in the late nineteenth century, argues convincingly that eastern Sudanese regions were bound to the Red Sea, not the Nile Valley.[8] Later, British policies in the Sudan would reinforce these connections to the Red Sea, the Indian Ocean, and the international community, largely through the construction of Port Sudan and the establishment of rail service connecting it to the Nile Valley. Such modern facilities are not, strictly speaking, geographic features, but they clearly were developments that undermined claims of a naturally united Nile Valley. Still, Egyptians could and did make a strong case that the Nile River, and its centrality to the people of the region, naturally united the valley.

An Ethnically United Nation?

As with their claims of geographic unity, Egyptians argued that they and the Sudanese had been ethnically or racially united for millennia. The obvious difficulty with such claims was the population of the southerly Sudanese regions. The people living among the various tributaries of the White Nile, in a region bordering Congo, Uganda, Kenya, and other neighbors, clearly differed from northern Sudanese—and Egyptians. The southern Sudanese were racially different, maintained different customs, sustained themselves in different occupational pursuits, professed different faiths, spoke different languages, and so forth. Historically, Egyptians and northern Sudanese had treated them differently—and harshly. Northerners had exploited the southern regions for centuries, most frequently through slave-raiding activities. During the modern era, southern Sudan retained this 'separate' status, as British administrators restricted all access to the southern districts. British officials maintained their policies were "designed to prevent unscrupulous foreigners from exploiting the simple inhabitants of these regions," but Egyptians feared British imperial designs on the region, potentially adding these areas to Britain's East African possessions.[9] Whether under British, Egyptian, or local control, it is difficult to claim an ethnic/racial unity between the southern and northern regions of the Sudan.

Egyptian leaders were reluctant to exclude southern Sudan from their claimed nation. Still, without the south a better case can be made for the ethnic unity of the Nile Valley. This ethnic homogeneity was based on common Arab ancestry and centuries of intermarriage of local inhabitants with Arab conquerors/migrants. Arab armies conquered Egypt just a few short decades after the death of the prophet Muhammad, and Arabs began to settle along the Nile Valley, gradually extending their presence and control toward the Sudan. In addition to Arab rule over much of the northern valley and melding with the local population, migrants from the Arabian Peninsula also came via the Red Sea to settle in Sudanese territories. After generations of these invaders, migrants, and natives inhabiting the same lands, Egyptians in the twentieth century maintained that the Sudanese were fellow Arabs. 'Ali Talib Allah emphasized in an article for the Egyptian daily, *al-Ahram*, that it was a common 'Arab' ethnicity that linked Sudanese and Egyptians. He wrote, "The cultured man understands that the history of the Nile Valley dictates a union of the brotherly countries. Time cannot weaken the bonds that connect the two parts of the valley. And when the Arabs of the Sudan have dreamed of a future that binds them to Iraq and the Najd, they feel nothing but love and friendship toward brotherly Egypt, the leader of the Arab East."[10]

Secondary sources also note the Arab ancestry of both sedentary and nomadic Sudanese tribes, such as the Kababish, Shukriya, or Shaiqiya. For instance, Gabriel Warburg wrote that Egyptian historians analyzing the conquest of the Sudan concluded that Egyptians and Sudanese were both descendants of Arabs, so "to accuse Egypt of an invasion or conquest was absurd, since there were no borders between the two regions."[11] In 1937 'Ali Yahya Bey, president of the Alexandria Chamber of Commerce, also mentioned common Arab origins in a speech welcoming a Sudanese delegation to Egypt. He described the unity of the Nile Valley as "a result of those enduring, natural, spiritual ties, rooted in the land of the fertile Nile—from its sources to its outlet—making one body, its arteries pulsing from one heart, in which flows one blood, from you to us, with the soul of one community—a community of *Arab* character, religion, language, kinship, and neighbors."[12] Egyptian nationalists would claim an ethnic homogeneity, not only based on a common Arab-Egyptian heritage but also African ethnic elements of the south.

This inclusion of both Arabic and African ethnicities into a single 'Egyptian-ness' was critical for nationalists' claiming that all of the Sudan should make up their nation. Claiming southern Sudan necessitated that Egyptians address apparent racial and ethnic diversity—and their history of less than cordial relations. In late 1939, 'Abd al-Majid Ibrahim Salih described a history of racial intermixing in the Nile Valley, maintaining that this Egyptian–Arab–African racial mixture was a natural, positive fact that his countrymen should embrace and utilize in efforts to liberate the Nile Valley. This deputy stated:

> When I mention the Nile Valley I do not have in mind the link that is the great principle economic artery, the spine between the two regions. No, gentlemen, this artery is not enough to make Egypt and the Sudan one, but rather there are other ties, like the ties of blood. . . .
>
> When the slave trade was widespread, a great number of Sudanese slaves were brought to Egypt. Throughout all time the Egyptians have believed that they are themselves Sudanese, and they have not considered them [the latter] as a low or vulgar race. The proof of that is that there is not a family in Egypt that has not had children from slave girls and concubines. If you were to research various centuries and eras you would find that there is blood of a Sudanese in the sons of most Egyptian families. . . . And I do not hesitate to state that this is well established historically and that it is a reality.

> The disgrace is that we look to the Sudan as a colony, and this is a serious danger, and it must be eliminated from our minds. In fact, we must treat this subject like the French have handled the subject of Alsace-Lorraine and like the English have handled the subject of Scotland and Wales.[13]

Acknowledging a history of slave raiding, trading, and utilization may be a first step, but truly incorporating different ethnicities into the claimed nation necessitated more work. Clearly during the interwar era Egyptians did not work hard enough on this issue. In 1947, an article on Sudanese government censorship of Egyptian films encouraged filmmakers to portray the Sudanese in a more favorable light. Among the specific recommendations were advising that not all doormen and servants in films need be of "Sudanese ethnicity" and that heroic figures in the movies be permitted to marry "cultured Sudanese."[14] The belittling portrayal of Sudanese within Egyptian culture was acknowledged by scholars and leaders of that era, as well as contemporary historians.[15] Racial or ethnic divisions alone do not undermine claims of Nile Valley unity. But relations between an Arabic-Egyptian northern region and the African populations of the south were not improved during the twentieth century. Nationalists' claims of ethnic homogeneity stand on firmer foundations when central and northern Sudanese regions remain the primary focus.[16]

A Linguistically United Nile Valley

The fact that the overwhelming majority of residents between the Nile delta and central Sudan professed the same faith, spoke the same language, and were enveloped by the same cultural milieu buttressed shakier claims of ethnic uniformity in the Nile Valley. As the early Arab armies conquered Egypt and expanded their control both across North Africa and up the Nile, they also spread Islam, the Arabic language, educational practices, and literary and other cultural trends. Abd el-Fattah Ibrahim el-Sayed Baddour wrote in his work on the legal intricacies of Egyptian–Sudanese relations that "the middle of the seventh century A.D. witnessed a new religion, Islam, spreading all over the Nile Valley, and a new tongue, Arabic, was beginning to find its way among the people. Thus, the foundation for cultural unity was provided."[17] The precise timing and territorial extent of the spread of Islam to the Sudan are really immaterial to this study because, by the Funj sultanate period of the sixteenth century, the Nile Valley was overwhelmingly Islamic and Arabic-speaking.

The spread of Arabic and Islam occurred simultaneously, and one facilitator of their extension was the development of education throughout the valley. Educational practices in the Sudan followed a trajectory similar to that in Egypt and the rest of the Islamic world. Learning was closely tied to reading the Qur'an, often rote memorization of *suras* or portions of such, and organized by the ulama and located at local mosque schools. In the Sudan the ulama and mosque schools were largely replaced by the local *faki* (Sufi order leader) and *khalwa* school, but the methods, language, and religious objectives were largely the same.[18] Egyptian rulers of the Sudan in the nineteenth century instituted educational reforms and began constructing state-controlled schools—like the modernization efforts in Egypt. The steady progress of educational development in the Sudan continued in the twentieth century under British supervision—but with Arabic-speaking, Muslim Egyptians playing a key role. The centrality of Egyptians in Sudanese education is attested by the British director of education during the first decade of British control. James Currie glowingly praised the work of Egyptians during this period and feared an end in educational improvements with the dismissal of many Egyptians after 1924. Currie wrote:

> To the best of the writer's knowledge, no Egyptian school-master was guilty of disloyalty to the Government that he served, and he desires to pay tribute to the fine work they did, and to put on record his conviction that without Egyptian aid in the early days, educational work—to say nothing of the general administrative work—in the Sudan would have been impossible.[19]

Currie also hinted at the territorial extent of Egyptian work in the Sudan, stating, "All the pioneer work would have been impossible but for the help given by a corps of well-trained Egyptian school-masters, whose work in all corners of the Sudan it is impossible to praise too highly. Without them, steady progress would have been unattainable."[20]

"All corners of the Sudan" did not include Upper Nile regions, where British policy had attempted to forbid the introduction of Egyptian teachers, the Arabic language, and Islam—instead facilitating various Christian missionary groups' educational and proselytization efforts. In the northern and central regions of the Sudan British officials struggled to undermine the traditional linguistic and religious homogeneity of the Nile Valley. Still, they inhibited Egypt's ability to sustain or augment this unifying characteristic. Mohamed Omer Beshir wrote in his survey of Sudanese education that the 1924 events had led to official preference for traditional schooling, since modern educational establishments had become "infected" by Egyptian nationalist ideals. Plus, the unrest resulted in "the loss by the department of education of all its Egyptian teachers working in the Gordon Memorial College and many of those in the primary schools."[21] Additionally, Beshir points out that the British goal of reducing the number of Egyptian civil servants preceded the events of 1924. He claims the military school attached to Gordon College in Khartoum and the sub-*mamur* school—both constructed before the First World War—"represented another step in the policy of employing Sudanese and replacing the Egyptian personnel."[22] Despite British efforts to undermine Egypt's presence in Sudanese education, Egyptians had been and continued to be extensively involved in this field, one that seemed to aid in unifying the valley's population.

Unfortunately for their nationalist goals, Egyptians made little effort to improve their role within Sudanese educational development. One could explain this failure by various means—financial constraints, political obstacles, regional or international affairs—but, other than protests in response to the dismissal of Egyptian teachers and other officials after 1924, there were not even expressions of interest or concern until the latter 1930s. With the years of financial difficulties passing and better relations with British officials since the signing of an Anglo–Egyptian treaty in 1936, there was increased potential for educational work in the Sudan. In 1939, *Al-Ahram* reported a Ministry of Education plan to fund a secondary school in Khartoum.

> There is no doubt that this proposal comes at an appropriate time in consolidating relations between Egypt and the Sudan. Many of the older restrictions have disappeared. It is becoming incumbent upon us to firmly augment our ties with the Sudan, to improve the Sudanese knowledge of Egypt and to improve the Egyptian knowledge of the Sudan. Undoubtedly, education is one of the methods leading to this understanding, perhaps even the most powerful since collaboration in culture has always preceded true friendship and fruitful cooperation, and these are what is needed in our relations with the Sudan.[23]

At virtually the same time, the Sudanese were including educational progress among the list of their demands to the British-led government. The Sudanese Graduates Congress' note on education stated:

> In numerous aspects of our life we have much in common with the Arab countries of the Islamic Orient which is due to our akin descent. We therefore consider that education in this country should take an

> Islamic Oriental character and not a pagan African one, or in other words that the Arabic Language and Religious Instructions should receive the greatest possible care in all stages of education.[24]

The Arabic-Islamic educational program envisioned here would likely entail greater Egyptian involvement, with possible political benefits. Beshir wrote that while Britain continued to oppose committing funds to new schools, Egyptians increasingly believed that "the provision of education for the Sudanese would . . . create an educated and public opinion favourable to its political interests in the Sudan."[25] The Second World War disrupted Egyptian plans to build a new secondary school in Khartoum, and post-war diplomatic rows with British officials undermined efforts in the last years before independence. Still, some Egyptian leaders reminded fellow nationalists of the potential political windfalls from educational development in the Sudan. Makram 'Ubayd did this indirectly when criticizing British opposition to educational progress in the Sudan. This Egyptian leader stated on 20 Jaunary 1947:

> The English have not established schools in the Sudan throughout the period of their occupation, only Gordon College and an industrial school in Atbara and nine other primary schools. I have been informed by a Sudanese delegation that the Sudanese congress founded fifty schools and requested the establishment of other schools, but the governor-general for the Sudan refused. He did not permit their opening, and schools there are not opened without his approval, and why did he refuse? Because he knows that knowledge generates an enlightened spirit, and this spirit begets freedom and freedom begets revolution. This, then, is the imperial policy that is determined to kill spirits for the sake of imperialism.[26]

Whatever their motivation, British antipathy toward educational progress did not undermine the Arabic-Islamic homogeneity maintained by the more numerous local, traditional schools of the Sudan. However, these widely dispersed traditional schools were less useful avenues for an increased Egyptian presence in the Sudan. Still, Egyptians might have taken advantage of the governor-general's refusal to construct additional schools by facilitating the admission of Sudanese to schools in Egypt. Immediately following the 1936 treaty, some advocates of Nile Valley unity worked at admitting Sudanese students to Egyptian schools. 'Ali al-Barir was a Sudanese trader, residing in Egypt, serving on the Cairo Chamber of Commerce's board of directors, and intimately involved in unity efforts of the latter 1930s. The chamber's journal reported in April 1937 that "Mr. 'Ali al-Barir spoke at great length on the cultural responsibility of Egypt concerning the Sudan and the necessity of opening its schools' doors to various Sudanese applicants."[27] Despite such hopes, the number of Sudanese students in Egypt did not quickly increase. *Al-Ahram* reported in 1939 that "the Wafd ministry was the first to open the door to the desire of Sudanese to enter Egyptian schools" and that the Wafd Party's newspaper was calling upon the current Ministry of Education to "eliminate the restrictions which it has decreed for the admission of the Sudanese youth in our colleges and schools, prior to the beginning of the upcoming school year. Restrictions like this arouse in a new generation distaste for Egypt."[28] Beshir again provided greater detail about these Sudanese educational activities. He wrote that student missions arranged by 'Ali al-Barir in 1937 and 1938 were largely composed of Sudanese sons of merchants residing in Egypt or from families in the extreme north of the Sudan—all of whom had to pay their own way. Still, with the Egyptian government ending restrictions on the admission of Sudanese students to Egyptian schools, the numerical progress continued. Beshir wrote that by 1943 "the number of Sudanese students attending Egyptian educational institutions in Egypt was 594, of whom 36 were following university courses, 95 in secondary schools, and the majority of the rest in al-Azhar. In 1945 a Sudan House was established in Cairo by the Egyptian Government for the residence of Sudanese students in Cairo."[29]

Sudanese educational missions and attendance at Egyptian schools might make a new generation more inclined to a union of the Nile Valley. Similarly, the recovery of a prominent role for Egyptian teachers in Sudanese schools could aid the nationalists' cause. The works of Currie, Beshir, and others note the vital role Egyptian teachers played in early Sudanese educational development,[30] but British officials did not universally share this positive opinion of the Egyptian presence. The aftermath of the events of 1924 in the Sudan and the onset of financial constraints with the Depression in the 1930s allowed Sudanese officials practically to eliminate Egyptian educators from the Sudan by the mid-1930s, after which time they successfully thwarted any increase of Egyptians in Sudanese schools. Primarily this was done through employment of greater numbers of Sudanese teachers, augmented by reliance on Syrians/Levantines in secondary schools. Even after the 1936 treaty, provisions of which gave preference to Egyptian and British applicants after the Sudanese, the government still avoided hiring Egyptian teachers. Egyptians were angered by the Sudanese government purportedly advertising only in Britain and by its requiring applicants to hold British diplomas. In 1939, *al-Ahram* reported extensively on these British transgressions.

> The Ministry of Education reported that the government of the Sudan does not precisely implement this article [of the 1936 treaty] because it advertises teaching positions in London only.
>
> This issue arose last year at the time of the governor-general's visit to Egypt, and his Excellency promised to pay attention to the matter in the future.
>
> But last May it occurred that the government of the Sudan announced in the *Times* seven vacant positions in the Sudan for teaching the subjects of history, natural science, law, and other subjects for which suitable Egyptians are found. . . .
>
> And it was stipulated that applicants hold British citizenship and that they have obtained a university degree from an English university.[31]

'Abd al-'Aziz al-Sufani, a critic of the government that year, mentioned the same grievances and lamented the damage done to Nile Valley unity. He stated,

> So, we read in the newspapers recently that diplomas of Egyptian schools are not recognized in the Sudan, and this is also an astonishing matter because our diplomas are accepted in England itself, where they are valued. You may wonder why the government of the Sudan does not recognize our diplomas? This is in order to prevent Egyptians from teaching in Egyptian schools [located in the Sudan] and from residing or working in the Sudan. It is a policy designed to cut every connection between us and them and to terminate every bond, growing or diminishing, between us and the Sudanese.[32]

After the early interwar elimination of most teachers from the Sudan, there was little Egyptian educational presence capable of strengthening bonds between the regions. Added to the lack of Egyptian teachers in the Sudan was the Egyptian government's failure to provide general assistance to Sudanese education. Certainly there was some financial assistance, although more of this was directed to transportation and other noneducational sectors. The Egyptian government would eventually establish some schools in the Sudan, but in 1931 only four schools in the Sudan had clear Egyptian ties, and these were Coptic Church–controlled schools that did not admit Sudanese pupils.[33] Success in constructing schools came for Egypt only after the Second World War and only in secondary and intermediate education, not the much more numerous traditional primary schools. By 1954, there were seventeen Egyptian secondary and intermediate schools for boys and three for girls, with admission of both resident Egyptians and Sudanese possible.[34] Undoubtedly, these numbers were an improvement and could have won some Sudanese support, but one decade of 'improvement' must be weighed against five decades of virtually nothing—at least in respect to schools established.

Equally valid would be the claim that the Sudanese government had worked consistently against Egyptian educational efforts in the Sudan. But, even where Sudanese officials could not stop their efforts—namely, in Egypt itself—Egyptians had done little to facilitate education throughout the Nile Valley. As noted above, students had been admitted to Egyptian schools, but only in limited numbers—and most going to al-Azhar—and starting only about a decade prior to Sudanese independence. Other than delegations of Sudanese students, the most celebrated educational initiative to promote Egyptian–Sudanese unity was the establishment of a research institute in Egypt for studying the Sudan. On 17 June 1947, the Chamber of Deputies approved the recommendation outlining the objectives, organization, and funding of this institute, including an initial budget of LE5,000. The recommendation stated, "The committee is pleased by the government's concern and effort in strengthening the connection between Egypt and the Sudan through various means. In consideration of cultural relations between Egypt and the Sudan the committee formed a subcommittee for the establishment of an institute attached to Fuad I University and dedicated to higher studies of Sudanese affairs."[35] During the following parliamentary session, Prime Minister Mahmud Fahmi al-Nuqrashi declared,

> My government has directed great concern toward cultural affairs in the Sudan. For that it established a special administration in the Ministry of Education to supervise encouraging educational opportunities for Sudanese students in Egyptian institutes, dispatching delegations of [these students] abroad, and Fuad I University is making preparations for the establishment of a higher institute for specialized studies of Sudanese affairs, endeavoring to find scholars specializing in these affairs.[36]

The Institute of Sudanese Studies was established in 1947. The parliamentary report recommending this institute had emphasized the "practical application" of the center's work, encouraging research in the Sudan, with Sudanese, at Egyptian facilities there. However, the most important aspect of this institute is the date of its establishment. Within six years of 1947, Egyptians would sign documents that eventually ended their dream of a united Nile Valley.

The critical factor in Egyptian failure to develop stronger educational bonds with the Sudan was the belated initiation of these efforts. The Institute of Sudanese Studies, the delegations of pupils sent to either region, and the efforts to employ Egyptian teachers or build Egyptian schools in the Sudan were all generally undertaken only in the last decade before Sudanese independence. The most dramatic development of the entire period of this study—in respect to educational bonds—was the dismissal of most Egyptian teachers in the Sudan after 1924. Obviously, this was not a positive development for the hopes of Egyptian nationalists. Yet they could still claim that the schools, teachers, curriculum, and language used were culturally 'unifying.' Egyptians and Sudanese clearly shared a common language and educational traditions—components of a broader claimed cultural unity.

Linked to their shared language and educational practices was the gradual development of a literate Sudanese public, with common literary traditions. Egypt was the model and conduit for literary and artistic trends in the Sudan. With the historical presence of Egyptian teachers, the utilization of the Arabic language in Sudanese schools, and the eventual establishment of a local press, a literate Sudanese class emerged—an educated elite mentored extensively by Egyptians, speaking and reading Arabic. The first Arabic newspaper in the Sudan was established in 1903 by the same publishers that produced *al-Muqattam* in Egypt. Profitability for newspapers in the Sudan was difficult, largely due to a small reading public, but in the 1920s a series of often short-lived newpapers was produced, most founded by publishers with Levantine or Greek backgrounds.[37] With the spread of higher education, there emerged literary groups, reading clubs, and the first Sudanese authors. The Egyptian literary milieu greatly influenced all of these activities. In his study on Sudanese nationalism and literary development, Eiman el-Nour wrote of Egyptian influences on Sudanese literary circles in the 1920s and 1930s. He stated that "in these activities, the cultural movements in Egypt influenced the intellectuals. The popular and serious writings of Taha Husayn, 'Abbas Mahmud al-'Aqqad, Muhammad Husayn Haykal, and Ibrahim 'Abd al-Qadir al-Mazini were windows through which the educated looked at the outside world including Europe."[38] Virtually all the writers noted by Eiman el-Nour were educated, lived, and wrote in Egypt at some point in their careers. He explained this Egyptian influence as being due to "the fact that Egyptian writings had been the first available source to the Sudanese writers, and trying to imitate Egyptian styles and techniques of writing was a natural step towards developing and finding their own way of writing."[39] When investigating this potentially positive literary/cultural bond of the Nile Valley, one must recognize the absence of any Egyptian efforts to strengthen such bonds.

Like their work in education, organized efforts to ensure that literary developments in the Sudan supported Nile Valley unity were late and ineffective. Egyptians did not attend closely to Sudanese literature and focused instead on means of communicating nationalist objectives to larger audiences—through radio, film, or lectures. For instance, from the mid-1930s forward, the Egyptian press occasionally reported radio broadcast deficiencies, usually limited broadcast range or an insufficiently nationalist "message" being transmitted. The comments of 'Abdallah Fakri Abaza, who previously served in the Sudan, neatly summarize the sort of problems highlighted for over a decade. *Al-Jarida al-tijariya al-misriya* reported,

> Mr. 'Abdallah Abaza Bey spoke frankly to the financial committee on the gravity of the situation in the Sudan. He requested that it dedicate large amounts for propaganda favoring Egypt in the Sudan and that the Telephone department work on strengthening the Egyptian broadcast station so that every Sudanese can listen to our station clearly, considering the multiple complaints about the lack of receiving the Egyptian broadcast with clarity, and [the Sudanese] listen to the Arab broadcast of London.[40]

During the Second World War, the Egyptian economic expert in the Sudan organized a series of lectures in the Sudan, presented at the Egypt Club in Khartoum and emphasizing Arabic history. These took place in March 1943, and *al-Ahram* noted that "the Sudanese were greatly interested in the lectures delivered by Drs. Ibrahim Khalil and Muhammad 'Ali Mustafa, and they view these as a pleasing start to the spread of Egyptian culture in the Sudan."[41] Considering the history of linguistic, educational, and literary influences on the Sudan, labeling a lecture series as a "start" may be inappropriate. Still, that the Sudanese considered it such is telling. There had been a historical sense of linguistic, literary, and educational unity in the Nile Valley, but Egyptians failed to initiate any new culturally unifying measures until it was simply too late.

The Islamic Nile Valley

Mirroring linguistic, literary, and educational unity within the Nile Valley, the religious similarity of the inhabitants was a result of history—not an initiative of Egyptian leaders. Arab conquests and centuries of gradual settlement in the valley facilitated the simultaneous spread and dominance of the Islamic faith. Other than a small Coptic minority and the varied, non-Islamic faiths limited to Upper Nile regions, the valley was almost wholly Islamic. Islam was undoubtedly a potential unifier of Egyptians and Sudanese, but there have always been important differences among Muslims.

The primary religious difference between Egyptian and Sudanese regions was the greater significance of Sufi orders in the latter. The most important Sufi orders of the Sudan were a modern development. Orders with more extensive territorial and demographic scope arose in the Sudan around the seventeenth century, especially the Qadiriya and Shadhiliya. Such early Islamic mysticism in the Sudan tended to be widespread but was normally not structured or centralized in its organization. Instead, local orders were associated with a particular 'holy' family, possessing *baraka* and engendering saintly worship/pilgrimage practices around the order's founder. In the early nineteenth century, reformist Islamic impulses sweeping the Middle East and North Africa, including groups such as the Wahhabi and Sanussi, led to new, more centralized and influential Sufi orders in the Sudan. Specifically, the Khatmiya and the Samaniya orders found homes in the Sudan. One leader of the Samaniya, Muhammad Ahmad al-Mahdi, would establish an independent reformist movement that temporarily achieved independence from Egyptian rule and functioned thereafter much like an independent Sufi order, variously labeled as the Mahdiya or the Ansar.[42] Although there certainly were others, twentieth-century Sudanese history was dominated by leaders of the two main rival Sufi orders, the Mahdiya and the Khatmiya.

Adherents of the Khatmiya and other Sufi orders existed in Egypt, but association with a particular order was vastly less significant in Egyptian than in Sudanese society. Egyptian leaders were well aware of the utility of Sudanese Sufi leaders' support, however, as were Egypt's British occupiers in the nineteenth century. Frederick de Jong notes that British imperial interests in Egypt and the Middle East used Egyptian funds to make regular payments to Sufi leaders in order to garner their support. For instance, they paid the head of the Mirghani family in Egypt to ensure support from the Mirghani-led Khatmiya order in the Sudan. But when British reliance shifted to the Mahdiya, these payments "were reduced and finally suspended in accordance with the decreasing political utility of the members of the Mirghani family in Egypt for British policy in the Sudan, notwithstanding 'the excellent and loyal conduct of the Mirghani family during the time of the British occupation,' as was noted in Foreign Office correspondence."[43] Egyptian nationalists would later support the Mirghani family and the Khatmiya order as a means of undermining British control in the Sudan—not because of any Khatmiya or Sufi 'unity' of the Nile Valley.[44] In fact, both Egyptian and subsequently British authorities in the Sudan implemented religious policies that sought to weaken Sufi influence. Gabriel Warburg noted that Egyptian officials "attempted to undermine the supremacy of the sufi orders in the Sudan first by importing Egyptian 'ulama from al-Azhar and later by training sons of Sudanese tribal and sufi shaykhs in al-Azhar and appointing them as qadis or teachers in Kuttabs," while the British "regarded sufis as ignorant and hence prone to fanatic Mahdist propaganda," necessitating continued reliance on "orthodox 'ulama."[45] Despite this initial antipathy toward Sufi orders, British officials claimed their religious policies had engendered the greatest confidence in the local population.[46]

Regardless of how much confidence the Sudanese had in British rule, Egyptian nationalists, as the co-religionists of the Sudanese that the British were not, believed Islamic identity was inevitably favorable to Nile Valley unity. Sudanese scholar Fadwa Abd al-Rahman Ali Taha wrote of Egyptian calls for Islamic unity that "it was natural for the Sudan Government to fear this slogan as the unity of the Muslims in general and those in Egypt and the Sudan in particular had always been hostile to British interests and policies. . . . The motto of Islamic unity was incompatible with the consistent British claim that the Sudan had a separate identity from that of Egypt."[47] Al-Azhar ulama and the offices of the Muslim Brotherhood appealing to Islamic unity had heightened British officials' concerns. Yet these religious appeals began in earnest only in the early 1940s, and, as in education and other cultural fields, efforts to strengthen religious bonds were late, half-hearted, and ineffectual.

Probably the strongest Egyptian–Sudanese religious bond during the early twentieth century was between the Sudanese and al-Azhar. Gabriel Warburg and others have noted the reliance on ulama from al-Azhar for numerous judicial and teaching positions—a reliance maintained even during the patently anti-Egyptian Mahdiya period.[48] During the 1930s and 1940s these connections were furthered through Egyptian efforts to associate higher religious education in the Sudan with al-Azhar, especially in respect to the Ma'had al-'Ilmi of Omdurman. British officials had established this institute in the early 1900s for the training of Sudanese ulama—hoping to replace the 'politically unreliable' Egyptians. Now, Egyptians hoped to add it to al-Azhar's educational network. *Al-Ahram* reported in November 1939 that "there is no Islamic religious institute in the Sudan, except the Omdurman institute, and it is bereft of resources," but that discussions to rectify this problem were taking place between the governor-general of the Sudan and the rector of al-Azhar.[49] Early the following year, Egypt's prime minister traveled to the Sudan and intended to press the governor-general on the right to establish al-Azhar religious institutes in Omdurman.[50] Ultimately, the Sudan government prevented al-Azhar's attempt to take control of religious education at the institute. Even with this failure, Egyptian religious connections were not necessarily diminished. Fadwa Abd al-Rahman Ali Taha summarizes the results of this Egyptian failure, noting the possible positive impact for Egypt's nationalist hopes: "Nevertheless, Egypt's benevolent attitude towards al-Ma'had, whatever its motive was, had impressed the Sudanese in general. Resentment to British rule increased among students and the educated Sudanese in general for the blunt refusal of the Sudan Government [in response to] the Egyptian offer to reform al-Ma'had."[51] Furthermore, when the commercial journal *al-Jarida al-tijariya al-misriya* assessed nationalist efforts in the Sudan just prior to its decision for independence, the reckoning was generally one of economic failures, but schools, educational missions, and al-Azhar's religious efforts were the noted successes.[52]

One final religious issue normally linking the regions was Egypt's appointment of the grand qadi of the Sudan. After decades of permitting an Egyptian to occupy this top religious post in the Sudan, the British authorities in Khartoum announced in late 1946 their plan to appoint Sheikh Ahmad al-Tahir, a Sudanese, as grand qadi the following year. Although Ahmad al-Tahir was qualified, this breaking of a Sudanese–Egyptian religious bond created quite a stir. Muhammad Sabri Abu 'Alam Pasha asked his fellow senators,

> What remains for Egyptians in the way of rights in the Sudan when the governor-general of the Sudan announced today that he dismissed the Egyptian grand qadi of the Sudan? Then he will announce tomorrow the dismissal of Egyptian representation existing within irrigation departments in the Sudan, then, after all of that, the dispatch of the Egyptian army [in the Sudan] to Cairo?[53]

This dispute blew up right in the middle of diplomacy Egyptians hoped might end the British occupation. Therefore, when the Egyptian prime minister Mahmud Fahmi al-Nuqrashi addressed the grand qadi controversy, he demonstrated a willingness to compromise and a concern for Sudanese sentiments, but also clearly considered Egypt's retaining this position a vital religious connection. On 31 December 1946 he responded to British correspondence received about appointing a Sudanese qadi:

> When I received this message I spoke with the British embassy on the importance of this position and that it is a strong spiritual and religious bond between Egypt and the Sudan whose destruction is not permissible. It pertains to the application of Islamic sharia in the Sudan, and it is beneficial to continue the cooperation between Egypt and the Sudan in this manner. So that it is not thought that we are refusing to recognize the Sudanese right to higher positions, I recommend that the Egyptian government pays the salary of the Egyptian grand qadi and the government of the Sudan establishes a top position among the sharia judges in the Sudan, and, thereby, facilitating the increase of the number of high Sudanese officials. I promised to research this subject, just as the British foreign minister promised the Egyptian embassy to study this subject also.[54]

Despite Egyptian concerns, when the prospects of an agreement on ending the British occupation disappeared, London officials gave approval to the Sudanese government's appointment of Sheikh Ahmad al-Tahir as the country's first Sudanese grand qadi. Losing their monopoly over this position was clearly not a positive development for Egyptian interests in the Sudan, but they still believed that Islam was an advantageous, centuries-old bond uniting the Nile Valley.

Historically United?

Finally, and incorporating many of the cultural connections described above, Egyptians maintained the valley had a history of unity—a history useful in their contemporary claim of sovereignty over the Sudan. However, this historical narrative of a valley perpetually united is not universally accepted. Our discussion of early Arab conquests or the spread of Islam and various Sufi orders includes no mention of specific states ruling all the Nile Valley. Pharaonic Egypt controlled some northerly Sudanese regions and conducted trade/military missions against Ethiopian rulers, but governance south of Aswan was infrequent and minimalist—confined to the rule of stronger, more imperially minded pharaohs. The Arab/Islamic conquests of Egypt did not include regions south of Aswan. Instead, the newly installed Arabs ruling Egypt established tributary relationships with independent leaders of southern Nubia. In subsequent centuries, Arab settlers and their language, religion, customs, and so forth slowly spread into the Sudan, but the states that emerged, like the Funj sultanate, were not valley-wide regimes. Still, Egyptian leaders maintained Egypt and the Sudan had been united historically. Egyptian senator Muhammad 'Alawi al-Jazzar Bey stated in 1924, "We are brought together by nature, joined by customs, linked by language, united by religion, and the Nile joins us together in a single realm. In the Sudan, there are antiquities from the pharaohs to the Arabs, to the Turks, to the Mamluks, to the current age."[55] Before the nineteenth century there may have been evidence of cultural unity, but there was little indicative of a shared history for a territorially defined entity ruling the entire Nile Valley—despite the hopes of Egyptian nationalists.

Egypt's modernizing leader of the early nineteenth century, Muhammad Ali, conquered much of the Sudan, providing Egyptian politicians with much stronger claims of a shared history.[56] Muhammad 'Alawi al-Jazzar Bey's comments on Nile Valley historical unity above followed his brief description of this nineteenth-century conquest. He stated, "We did not forcibly enter the country because it is our country and we are a part of it."[57] In fact, Egyptian military forces did move into the northern Sudan in 1820, dispersing Mamluk power around Dongola, conquering southward into Kordofan, and accepting the submission of the last Funj sultan. Egyptian rule of the Sudan would last officially from 1821 to 1885 and eventually extend to the Red Sea, the African Great Lakes, and the borders of Darfur. The inclusion of the Sudan within Egypt, all of which was nominally under the suzerainty of the Ottoman Empire, began a new era in Nile Valley history. The administrative purview of Cairene authorities extended to all of the Sudan, but differing assessments of this 'unity' exist. British officials or scholars produced most of the initial histories of Egyptian rule, and they uniformly described this era as one of Egyptian corruption, mismanagement, slave raiding/trade, and general oppression of the Sudanese. Since the same British officials dominated the Sudan subsequently, the Sudanese were influenced by this rendering of Egyptian rule. Influencing Sudanese opinion was critical, since it would eventually determine the Sudan's fate. Gabriel Warburg, who has written extensively on the history and historians of the Nile Valley, wrote of the Egyptian regime and the later British-dominated Condominium that "the fact that both of them are regarded by Sudanese as 'Turkiyya' is no coincidence. They were both colonial regimes seeking to control foreign people and territories with the pretext of a civilizing mission."[58] John Voll's study of unity of the

Nile Valley reaches similar conclusions on the importance of local opinion, noting that "developing Sudanese attitudes were crucial in either opening or closing the door to unity."[59]

Despite the subsequent assessments of Voll, Warburg, and others, Egyptians stressed different aspects of their rule in the Sudan. Actually, Warburg had noted that nineteenth-century Egyptian rule was not as totally negative as foreign historians asserted. He wrote that the later British officials followed policies similar to the Egyptians—devolution of the administration, undermining traditional local leadership, reliance on agricultural taxation, and even similar policies toward slavery.[60] Warburg summarizes the opinions of Egyptian historians on Egyptian–Sudanese union thus: "Almost all of them agree that there cannot be an 'objective' interpretation of the Nile Valley's history which does not accept its unity as axiomatic and as stemming from natural geographical, cultural and historical roots."[61] Most Egyptian nationalists did not bother to address at length what they considered to be an obviously modernizing, progressive, beneficial transformation of the Sudan under Egyptian governance in the nineteenth century. For instance, after apologizing for taking the time to even mention this history, when Egyptians were busy debating the merits of a proposed treaty with the British in 1936, 'Abd al-'Aziz al-Sufani stated, "I hope only that you will not forget that we had a fantastic position in the Sudan before the occupation, considering it was a part of Egypt. In fact, we had our whole army there, just as there were a great number of officials, exceeding 30,000. Likewise, there was a great number of Egyptians living and working in the Sudan, and our commerce there enjoyed lucrative returns."

This deputy continued the short, "unnecessary" history lesson for his parliamentary colleagues, emphasizing the tremendously negative subsequent developments in the Sudan: "That was the situation before the occupation [of Egypt by Britain]. As for after it, the situation was transformed. The English worked to weaken our influence and our position until it arrived at its current state, and you know this ended with the catastrophe which occurred in 1924."[62] Whether or not 'Abd al-'Aziz al-Sufani's assessment is correct, he is omitting a key part of Egyptian–Sudanese history. At virtually the same time that British forces were occupying Egypt, Muhammad Ahmad, a Sudanese Sufi leader, proclaimed himself the Islamic faith's messianic 'Mahdi' and led a rebellion against Egyptian rule that captured Khartoum by early 1885. Muhammad Ahmad al-Mahdi would die in June, but his eventual successor, 'Abdallah ibn Muhammad, headed an independent 'Mahdist' Sudanese state until 1898, an era often labeled the Mahdiya.

Egyptian scholars writing about the Mahdiya typically did not use the adjective 'independent' in their works. Gabriel Warburg's survey of Nile Valley scholars notes that Egyptian historians universally claimed both that the prior Egyptian rule had not been exploitative and that the Mahdiya was merely an "internal revolt"—possibly even anti-European, and certainly not anti-Egyptian.[63] Those Egyptian leaders who bothered to mention the Mahdist period in their speeches or writings most frequently emphasized that British officials occupying Egypt forced the evacuation of Sudanese regions. For instance, during the heightened nationalist activity of 1924, Sa'd Zaghlul briefly recounted Egypt's withdrawal from the Sudan by stating, "We were informed forcibly that we would give up part of it and that we would evacuate in defeat against our will."[64] Obviously, a speaker's or writer's perspective is critical, as the Mahdiya could be labeled an internal revolt, an Islamic reformist movement, or the start of Sudanese independence efforts. However one chooses to characterize the Mahdiya, it clearly must be considered a break in the history of Nile Valley unity.

A combination of improved financial stability in Egypt and British concern about French imperial objectives in the Upper Nile provinces of the Sudan led to Anglo–Egyptian military forces reconquering the Sudan in 1898. The following year, British officials in Egypt created a unique administrative arrangement for the Sudanese regions. The 1899 Condominium Agreement did not address sovereignty questions, instead delineating administrative responsibilities for the new regime. Lord Cromer, governing Egypt at that point, argued that an autonomous administration for the Sudan was a means of limiting or preventing the interference of other foreign powers in the region. However, the Condominium was also a means of extending British imperial reach over the region, since the British controlling Egypt at the time would hold all top positions in the Condominium administration and govern by martial law during the first decades of the new regime. Egypt financed the reconquest and provided the bulk of forces for the campaigns, but Egyptians occupied only lower-level positions in the Condominium and were often involved in activities not likely to improve their standing among the Sudanese. Heather Sharkey notes that one cause of growing Sudanese animosity toward Egyptians was the latter's involvement in tax collection, prison discipline, and other "oppressive" administrative tasks.[65] Despite the lack of influential policy-making positions, until the events of 1924 there were significant numbers of Egyptians working in the Condominium administration, and Egyptian leaders maintained that the reconquest had reestablished the unity of the Nile Valley.

They asserted that the Mahdiya had been a temporary disruption, and that the Condominium was a temporary administrative arrangement.

In fact, although British officials did not make public statements to this effect, they acted as if the 1899 agreement had established a new, independent state—being properly 'guided' by British leadership. In the early years of the Condominium they worked toward its separation from Egypt. For instance, British officials portrayed 'Mahdist' revolts as residual religious fanaticism—linked to Egyptian intrigue—thankfully suppressed by British-led and trained military forces, when actually the Sudanese population in these years was relatively conservative, complacent, and peace-seeking.[66] A Condominium memorandum of the early 1920s, advocating the need for a medical school in Khartoum, clearly portrays British opinions concerning an independent Sudan:

> In any consideration of Sudan questions a few main facts should be borne in mind.
>
> i. That Khartoum is over 1,000 miles from Cairo, four days by train and boat, and that it is the capital of *an entirely separate country*, differing from the Egyptians in physical characteristics, and in ideals, history, and origin.
>
> ii. That *between Egypt and the Sudan there is a physical barrier* of nearly 300 miles of arid waterless desert, bridged only by a single river fringed by a few yards of very sparsely populated cultivation, and that the natural outlet of the Sudan is by Port Sudan and the Red Sea.
>
> iii. That with the exception of the extreme south, the Sudan is occupied by an Arab race crossed to a varying degree with pre-Arab and Negroid races, and that this race is quick, intelligent, and eager for education. *It is intensely loyal to the British connection.*[67]

British control was significantly strengthened in 1924 after the British governor-general of the Sudan, Sir Lee Stack, was murdered in Cairo. British officials blamed Egypt's political leadership for failing to quiet nationalist agitation that led to this assassination, and they proceeded to threaten vital Egyptian water supplies and force the expulsion of virtually all Egyptians employed in the Sudan.

The 1936 Anglo–Egyptian treaty permitted the return of some Egyptian military and civil personnel to the Sudan, but British officials continued to rule largely unchecked until Sudanese independence in

1956. Most observers would conclude that during the Anglo–Egyptian Condominium era the Sudan was governed as an independent entity, yet Egyptians continued to believe that as soon as the British evacuated the Nile Valley, the historical unity, strengthened since the time of Muhammad Ali, would resume. In the early 1950s, Egyptian nationalists finally negotiated an end to British occupation, but the claimed historical unity was not reestablished. Ultimately, the Sudanese population chose independence, and accounting for Sudanese popular opinion may have been the key Egyptian shortcoming in the last decades of Condominium rule. John Voll argues convincingly that the unity of the Nile Valley was a "persuasive myth" of utility to the emerging Sudanese educated elite's effort to carve out a leading position in their country. He claims that this "myth was as useful as a more concrete set of elements. As long as the unity ideal fulfilled its identity function, it was a powerful force in Sudanese society. However, when that function was gradually lost, the ideal itself declined, even though the concrete conditions leading to unity may have been strengthening."[68]

From an Egyptian perspective, a shared history and various long-established cultural bonds were so manifest that the strengthening of them was hardly needed. The valley's inhabitants might have disagreed about a shared, 'celebratory' history of unity, but cultural connections were difficult to dispute. Heather Sharkey notes that all scholars, even Sudanese, have acknowledged the extensive cultural influence of Egypt in the Sudan, adding that "in the twentieth century, the colonial arrangement of the Anglo–Egyptian Condominium intensified this long-standing contact."[69] As diplomatic developments moved toward permitting a Sudanese decision on sovereignty, Egypt's leaders continued to proclaim the multifaceted and long-established connections of the entire Nile Valley. Prime Minister Mahmud Fahmi al-Nuqrashi described these bonds while recounting United Nations investigations of the dispute over the Sudan:

> The leader of my government presented to the Security Council the reasons which make necessary honoring the unity of the Nile Valley. Similarly he explained to them that there is no life for Egypt without the Sudan, and there is no life for the Sudan without Egypt. The life-bestowing Nile alone determines our brothers. There are customs that go back hundreds of years, and these customs have formed the Nile Valley, on whose generosity and blessings the entire people of the valley live. There is a shared language and a shared culture. All of this strengthens the bonds between us.[70]

Egyptian nationalists had been claiming the same since the nineteenth century. While Nuqrashi and others emphasized the historical, brotherly union of Egypt and the Sudan, Egyptians railed against British imperial interference among these 'brothers' of the Nile Valley. For instance, on 6 August 1951, Egyptian Minister of Foreign Affairs Muhammad Salah al-Din questioned Britain's changing justifications for its control of Sudanese affairs:

> Who has conceded that they speak in the name of the Sudanese? And who charged them with these responsibilities, which they claim to bear today in the Sudan? By what historical, legal, or moral right do they intrude in this sphere between Egyptians and their Sudanese countrymen who have been bound together since the earliest times by the bond of the Nile, the geographic unity, the economic unity, and likeness of race, language and religion?[71]

Conclusion

Many Egyptians agreed with Muhammad Salah al-Din and his listing of long-established and unquestioned bonds between Egypt and the Sudan. The brief survey in this chapter of these bonds has not refuted Egyptian claims but attempted to illustrate that there were some weaknesses or caveats necessary in respect to assertions of Nile Valley unity. The Nile River clearly connected northern and southern halves of the valley, but there were also topographical features that tended to divide these halves. A valley-wide ethnic or racial homogeneity might have distinguished Egyptians and (northern/central) Sudanese from their neighbors, but there was also certainly a great deal of diversity within the claimed 'nation.' Linguistic, educational, and religious norms were among the strongest cultural bonds between peoples of the Nile Valley. Yet even here there were problems. The overwhelming majority of Egyptians and Sudanese were Muslims, but the dominance of Sufi orders differentiated southern regions and became the focus of Sudanese independence efforts. Egyptian initiatives to strengthen educational or orthodox Islamic bonds with the Sudan were late and ineffective. Finally, Egyptian claims of a shared history would be more accurately summarized as "whenever a dynasty ruled Egypt, its political, cultural, religious, economic and racial influence extended into the Sudan."[72] As Baddour correctly notes, Egyptian "influence extended" to the south—clearly different from a historically united nation.

Despite the difficulties in claiming the absolute historical, cultural, or geographic unity of the Nile Valley, Egyptians and Sudanese had much in common. Considering there was plenty of diversity among Egyptian peoples, the commonalities of religion, language, ethnic background, and recent history between Egyptian and Sudanese regions at least made union a realistic possibility. At times, Egyptians included economic unity among the factors leading inevitably to a single Nile Valley nation. Normally, Egyptian nationalists raised economic bonds not as something well established and clearly evident, but rather as something to be created and strengthened. Furthermore, this urgency to create economic unity was a late development in the history of the Condominium era. Uppermost on Egyptians' minds as they achieved greater freedom of action in the immediate post–First World War period was ending the British occupation. Admittedly, much of the rhetoric on lifting the British occupation emphasized the whole valley, including the Sudan, but Egyptian leaders' overriding concern regarding the Sudan was guaranteeing their Nile water rights.

2 'Successful' Division of Water Resources

> If the reader will look at a map of the Nile system, he cannot fail to be struck by its resemblance to a palm-tree. At the top the green and fertile area of the Delta spreads like the graceful leaves and foliage. The stem is perhaps a little twisted, for the Nile makes a vast bend in flowing through the desert. South of Khartoum the likeness is again perfect, and the roots of the tree begin to stretch deeply into the Soudan. I can imagine no better illustration of the intimate and sympathetic connection between Egypt and the southern provinces. The water—the life of the Delta—is drawn from the Soudan, and passes along the channel of the Nile, as the sap passes up the stem of the tree, to produce a fine crop of fruit above. The benefit to Egypt is obvious; but Egypt does not benefit alone. The advantages of the connection are mutual; for if the Soudan is thus naturally and geographically an integral part of Egypt, Egypt is no less essential to the development of the Soudan. Of what use would the roots and the rich soil be, if the stem were severed, by which alone their vital essence may find expression in the upper air?
>
> —Winston Churchill, *The River War*, 363

Of all the potential bonds that united Egypt and the Sudan, the Nile River was unquestionably the most enduring, important, and universally accepted connection between the regions. It was the slogan and symbol of Egyptian nationalist intentions in the Sudan—the "Unity of the Nile Valley." Virtually every speech, editorial, or article from the nationalist leadership made reference to the central role this river had played in binding the regions since pharaonic times. Even British officials trying to forestall Egyptian dreams of governing the Sudan recognized that the Nile River united the northern and southern regions of the valley. Egyptians had manipulated the waters of the Nile to produce Churchill's "fine crop of fruit" since the dawn of history, but dependence on the waters had been increasing ever since Muhammad Ali's initiation of large-scale perennial irrigation in Egypt. Although scholars have offered various reasons for the reconquest of the Sudan by Anglo–Egyptian forces in 1898–99, one commonly accepted explanation for this undertaking is to ensure regularity in the Nile floods reaching Egypt. After his tree metaphor for the Nile River, Churchill wrote that the "honest reason" for the reconquest had been "to unite territories that could not indefinitely have continued divided; to combine peoples whose future welfare is inseparably intermingled; to collect energies which, concentrated, may promote a common interest; to join together what could not improve apart."[1] The Egyptian elite were always concerned about sufficient water supplies—even if their insistence on Egyptian priority undermined the development of "common interests" with their Sudanese compatriots.

Egypt's elite idealized the Sudan as an integral part of their nation, as an important trading partner, as a logical destination for the emigration of excess population, as a field for profitable investment, and so forth—but most Egyptians simply viewed the Sudan as the source of the all-important Nile River. Jacques Berque notes the historic importance of the Nile and the Sudan for Egyptians, stating that "the idea of the Sudan was linked in the mind of every fellah with that of the summer floods."[2] The editor of *al-Akhbar* wrote in 1922 that "the attachment of Egyptians to the Sudan derives from the sources of the Nile, which are 'the soul and life of Egypt,' being located in the Sudan."[3] Egyptians have consistently looked to the Nile, and hence the Sudan, as a means of developing their country's economic prosperity. Progress achieved during the nineteenth century revolved around more extensive and efficient utilization of the Nile. The limited nature of Egyptian industrial development, the importance of irrigated cotton production, and hopes for increased economic 'independence' through agricultural diversification all necessitated that Egypt's leaders pay special attention to Nile River planning.

However, when Egyptians planned measures for greater utilization of the Nile River, their concerns did not revolve solely around long-staple cotton or other irrigation-dependent crops destined for export. Egypt's growing population and local consumption needs only reinforced its reliance on Nile waters. In a 1921 report recommending various irrigation projects in Egypt and the Sudan, the Egyptian minister of public works,

Muhammad Shafiq Pasha, noted that "Egypt must import from abroad a portion of the foodstuffs which it needs, as the area of its cultivated lands has not increased in relation to the number of its inhabitants."[4] In 1932, Muhammad Salih Bey linked Nile water storage facilities in the Sudan to more land and work for Egyptians—again local needs exacerbated by population growth. He stated that the government sought these facilities because of "the fear of the continuously rising number of inhabitants and the necessity of finding the lands necessary for this steadily increasing number and raising their means of living."[5] As historians since the time of Herodotus have emphasized, Egyptian sustenance, work, culture, and so forth are all dependent on the Nile—and with the number of Egyptians rising, that dependence was only heightened.

Although officials at the time of the reconquest linked the reacquisition of Sudanese territories by Anglo-Egyptian forces in 1899 to Nile River concerns, little development of water resources in the Sudan had occurred by the end of the First World War. Work had begun on the penultimate project of British hydraulic engineers in Egypt—the Aswan dam—in 1898. This dam's completion in 1902 certainly added tremendously to irrigated agriculture possibilities in Egypt, but it did nothing for the Sudan and did not provide over-year security for Egyptian agriculturalists. Under the leadership of Sir William Garstin, British officials conducted two different surveys of the Nile Valley around the turn of the century, with reports issued in 1901 and 1904. In addition to Garstin, two other British engineers played a crucial role in project planning in Egypt, Sir William Willcocks and Sir Murdoch MacDonald. Ultimately the reports and proposals submitted prior to the First World War included similar plans, with few immediate projects in Egypt but provocative proposals for the Sudan. Specifically, the reports recommended a facility on the Blue Nile intended to irrigate the Gezira plain south of Khartoum and another on the White Nile to provide additional water for Egypt after the annual flood subsided. These were the Sennar and Jabal Awliya' dams. Although Egyptians would voice complaints about the Jabal Awliya' facility, the more troubling project initially was the Sennar dam and Gezira agricultural scheme.

From the time of Garstin's earliest surveys, reports singled out the Gezira plain as an ideal location for a major agricultural development, if officials could arrange the provision of water. The Sennar dam was intended to do precisely this. Agricultural development in the Gezira plain would provide both a livelihood for many Sudanese and significant revenues for the financially strapped Condominium administration. Unfortunately, harnessing the waters of the Blue Nile with this dam aroused Egyptian fears because it was precisely this tributary of the Nile that was responsible for the annual flood. Despite popular opposition, Lord Kitchener was able to cajole Egyptian leaders into approving MacDonald's plans for the Jabal Awliya' and Sennar dams by the summer of 1914, although the First World War delayed construction work. With the difficulties posed by the war receding and British financial assistance obtained to guarantee loans covering construction costs, British officials supervised the completion of the Sennar dam and the accompanying Gezira agricultural scheme by 1926.

Even though British officials had accepted the principle of Egyptian priority in Nile water distribution prior to the completion of the Sennar dam, the fact that a hydraulic work now existed with the potential to disrupt the annual flood was sufficient to enflame Egyptian fears. These fears were undoubtedly heightened by the fact that this structure and its accompanying agricultural scheme were seemingly in the hands of British imperial interests. In 1924, 'Abd al-Rahman al-Rafi'i stated in Egypt's Chamber of Deputies that projects proposed for the Sudan would not benefit either Egypt or Sudan but rather foreigners, capitalists, and British companies.[6] Although Egyptians most heatedly criticized foreign interests, especially British, animosity over water usage in the Gezira and elsewhere was indirectly aimed at Sudanese peasants. Egyptians sought political union, yet attacking schemes that provided Sudanese with a livelihood seemingly undermined their political objective. Still, they were not about to relinquish Egyptian priority in water distribution. During a 1934 agricultural mission to the Sudan, Fu'ad Abaza recognized the need for water resource cooperation but also emphasized whose needs should be met first. He wrote that "complete attention is given to providing Egypt what it needs of irrigation water and the utilization of the *excess* of its requirements in the irrigation and cultivation of our Sudanese brothers' lands."[7]

As might be expected, Sudanese opinion was not always in complete accord with that of their northern neighbors. For instance, *al-Ahram* reprinted the editorial of the Sudanese newspaper *al-Nil*, which claimed, "With respect to Egypt's water rights the natural condition for the distribution of Nile waters between Egypt and the Sudan is that the Sudan possesses a first right, not a right to the surplus exceeding [Egypt's] need."[8] Amazingly, Sudanese sources rarely expressed such direct criticism of Egyptian priority in respect to water usage—even the generally anti-Egyptian Condominium officials accepted Egyptian water rights. Still, even a more equitable division of water was heretical talk to Egyptian ears. In 1930 the president of the Sudanese Chamber of Commerce stressed the importance of agriculture to Sudanese economic development, emphasizing the need for more irrigated agricultural schemes and a fairer share of waters. He stated during a meeting in Khartoum on 17 April that he had learned from informal communications with Condominium officials that

> the government is prepared to assist in these directions in every manner the current situation permits. Thus it is willing to extend the present [agricultural] projects if it is possible both to obtain laborers and water and to permit the use of irrigation pumps from 15 July to the end of March if circumstances permit. And we have unshakeable trust that the agreement currently being reviewed will be shortly completed by Great Britain and Egypt and that following its conclusion there will be other reservoirs not only to satisfy the irrigation needs of Egypt but also the needs of the Sudan.[9]

In spite of Sudanese desires for a greater share and Egyptian fears of such, officials were able to reach an agreement on water usage. Still, Nile water distribution was clearly an issue capable of dividing Egyptians and Sudanese, and even 'agreement' on this issue implied a divided, not united, valley.

Ignoring the political implications of dividing Nile waters, most Egyptians after the First World War spoke of cooperation and the water needs of the Sudanese. A willingness to recognize such needs did nothing to lessen underlying fears of increased Sudanese utilization of Nile waters. Writing for the newspaper *al-Akhbar* in 1930, Hassan Ramzi al-Arna'udi asked, "What will be the fate of Egyptian lands if the lands of the Sudan use up all the water which possesses the silt which is the vital material in the fertilization of Egyptian lands?"[10] In addition to the completion of the Sennar dam and Gezira scheme facilities, Lord Allenby's ultimatum following the murder of Sir Lee Stack in 1924 was certainly reason for heightened Egyptian fears of Sudanese water usage. Specifically, part six of Lord Allenby's ultimatum instructed the Egyptian government to "notify the Competent Department that the Sudan Government will increase the area to be irrigated at Gezira from 300,000 feddans to an unlimited figure as need may arise."[11] The British never carried out this threat, but they completed the Gezira project and began to withdraw the allotted portion of water from the Nile. With little Egyptian presence in the Sudan after 1924, what was to prevent unauthorized water usage? In 1931 an article in *al-Akhbar* noted that British administrators of both the Condominium and the "Sudan Plantations Syndicate," the British company administering the Gezira project, planned to increase water usage outside the Gezira, since the increased storage capacity of the Nile projects would lead to excess water flowing into the Mediterranean Sea.[12] There was no evidence of Sudanese water usage exceeding its designated share, but as long as the Sudan remained an administrative or political entity separate from Egypt the fear of Nile water shortages continued. Egyptians faced a dilemma. They hoped to strengthen economic bonds and claim political unity with their Sudanese brothers, yet they were most concerned with differentiating Egyptian and Sudanese water rights and complained of the deleterious effects of Sudanese agricultural expansion on their own—separate—economy.

The 1929 Agreement and Project Supervision

Anglo–Egyptian negotiations definitively separated Sudanese and Egyptian water rights with the conclusion of the Nile Waters Agreement of 1929. Notes exchanged on 7 May 1929 between Prime Minister Muhammad Mahmud and High Commissioner Lord Lloyd made references to the administration of hydraulic works along the Nile, but the most important aspect of the agreement for Egypt was the assurance of water supplies. The agreement established definite water allowances for the present and future needs of both countries, with a disproportionate amount reserved for Egypt. In analyzing this facet of the 1929 agreement, more important than the actual figures are the precedents set by this action. In 1932, one Egyptian representative emphasized that Egyptians sought a broad economic and political union but lamented that "the relation between us and the Sudan has become, after this agreement, confined to the water issue."[13]

Other Egyptians believed the 1929 agreement did not even strengthen water usage cooperation, but rather that the agreement had undone any semblance of Nile Valley unity. Years later, the Egyptian senator 'Abd al-Rahman al-Rafi'i concluded that the technical studies, proposed hydraulic projects, and eventual 1929 agreement all led to "the *separation* of Egypt from the Sudan in matters concerning water."[14] This senator's analysis was the more accurate assessment of the 1929 agreement because, despite recognizing the close relationship of Egypt and the Sudan in respect to Nile River development, the distribution of water resources clearly entailed treating the countries as independent entities. Decades of foreign-led economic development had created virtually autonomous Egyptian and Sudanese economies with firmer links to western powers than to each other. The division of Nile waters in the 1929 agreement reinforced this ongoing process.

The 1929 Nile Waters Agreement also addressed Egyptian concerns over actual hydraulic works constructed along the river and who administered such works. The agreement was based primarily on technical examinations of both Egyptian and foreign engineers in the early 1920s. Because of some discrepancies over the Nile water flow readings collected in the past, the Egyptian government appointed an international commission on 10 January 1920 to determine precise statistics and to recommend means of better utilizing the Nile. Although the Egyptian government insisted on personnel changes to this commission and formed additional investigative groups, all the experts involved endorsed roughly the same means of expanding irrigation capabilities in the valley.[15] The 1920 Nile Projects Commission's report concluded by stating, "We recommend that, considered from a strictly engineering point of view, the White Nile Dam [Jabal Awliya'], the Gezira Irrigation Scheme, and the Blue Nile [Sennar] Dam, and the Nag Hammadi Barrage should be carried out at once."[16] These commissions expected that Egypt would need to carry out canal and pump irrigation work internally and that water utilization improvements in the distant future would require a cut through the Sudd region of the Sudan, as well as additional projects beyond Sudanese borders.

In Egyptian eyes, the key issues of these commissions' reports were maintaining control of hydraulic works and guaranteeing that both present and future water needs would be met—even if potentially harming Sudanese development. Various stages of Nile River development included the involvement of foreign technical expertise, but Egypt hoped always to retain overall control. During the failed 1921 Anglo–Egyptian negotiations, Husayn Rushdi included in his draft proposal an article stating "the Egyptian Ministry of Public Works will have complete control of the Nile."[17] The formation of an independent Sudan Irrigation Service and the elimination of most Egyptian influence from the Sudan after 1924 heightened Egyptian fears over control.[18] In a telegraphic message from London during the Anglo–Egyptian negotiations of 1924, Egypt's representative 'Aziz 'Izzat Pasha sought to allay his compatriots' concerns by stating that the water policies of the two countries were interconnected and that "the system of irrigation in Egypt and the Sudan has in fact been established and carried out on a basis of Egyptian–Sudanese unity."[19]

'Aziz 'Izzat Pasha was more generous than others when mentioning Sudanese rights. Most Egyptians were fixated on maintaining control of the Nile River, since their general influence in the Sudan was rapidly diminishing. In January 1925, Amin al-Rafi'i decried the dominance of British and decline of Egyptian interests in the Sudan, but claimed continued Egyptian control over water issues.[20] Two years later, with the Sudan's Gezira project beginning operations and expenditures for irrigation service employees in the Sudan rising, Egypt's Ministry of Public Works reiterated that hydraulic activities there were ultimately under Egyptian control and would profit Egypt alone. The minister testified before parliament that "those employees are undertaking general works on the Nile, which are for the welfare of Egypt only and [these works] do not favor the government of the Sudan."[21]

Even after concluding the Nile River agreement Egyptians remained concerned for years about administrative control over Nile River developments generally. For instance, notes exchanged confirming the 1929 agreement referred to control arrangements, but not in a manner completely satisfactory to all Egyptians. In reference to Sudanese agricultural plans, Prime Minister Muhammad Mahmud wrote that his government "has always been anxious to encourage such development" but that "the construction, maintenance and administration of the . . . works should be under the direct control of the Egyptian Government."[22] In 1932 parliamentary debates over expenditures on the construction of the Jabal Awliya' reservoir, representatives leveled criticism at the 1929 agreement and, especially, at the perceived lack of Egyptian control. Hafiz Ramadan, leader of Egypt's Nationalist Party in the Chamber of Deputies, was among the most vehement critics. He claimed that because of the existence of a separate Sudan Irrigation Service since 1922 and the retention of only one Egyptian engineer at the Gezira scheme to report water usage figures, "we have lost all of our supervision over the Nile, its control, and irrigation projects in the Sudan."[23] Moreover, Hafiz Ramadan pointed out that the 1929 agreement did not actually award Egypt control over the Nile. High Commissioner Lord Lloyd's note had stated that "this agreement is not to be considered in any way applicable to the supervision and control of the river, and this is reserved for free discussions between the two governments upon negotiation of the Sudan issue."[24] Additionally, Lord Lloyd's letter went on to state that "when the Egyptian government decides to undertake works in the Sudan on the Nile or its tributaries, or to take any measure to increase the water of the Nile for Egypt's benefit, it will agree beforehand with local authorities on what measures must be taken for the protection of local interests."[25] The last part of the 1929 agreement that Hafiz Ramadan criticized was the clause requiring the establishment of an international technical commission if disagreements over water usage or storage facilities occurred. In reference to this clause, Ramadan stated, "We administer the dams and we send the engineers and employees, but the final word on supervision and control of the Nile is not in our hand."[26]

Hafiz Ramadan and others may have disagreed, but the Egyptian government claimed that it retained supervisory rights throughout the interwar years. In the 1932 debate over Jabal Awliya' financing, the minister of public works stated that "as for the Egyptian point of view, which has been held on to in all sessions of negotiation, it is, as it began, that the Nile is Egypt's life and that its administration must remain under the supervision of the Egyptian Ministry of Works."[27] Egypt certainly did retain the most influential voice concerning Nile River matters, but foreign technical involvement, expanding Sudanese needs, and the rights of other Nile water users all gradually undermined Egyptian control. Although protecting current and future water requirements remained Egyptians' primary concern, other facets of Nile River development in the Sudan were potentially both economically and politically troubling.

Sudanese Cotton Competition

Egyptian administrative control and greater water usage did little to lessen the potential of Sudanese cotton exports competing with Egyptian supplies in the international marketplace. Egyptians voiced concerns about Sudanese cotton cultivation early in the First World War, when Condominium officials were only arranging the financial backing required for the planned Gezira project. A report at the time stated, "If irrigation works of the Sudan permit the offering of high quality cotton, this stock will even be superior [to Egyptian supplies], and as a consequence a considerable drop in the price of cotton will be inevitable."[28] As the Gezira project drew closer to completion, Egyptian senator 'Abd al-Aziz Radwan also warned of potential competition from high-grade Sudanese cotton, stating that some varieties were of "better quality than Manufia cotton which is the best type of cotton we have."[29] However, it was not merely the quality of Sudanese cotton that was threatening to Egyptians, but also its promotion by British officials, its commercial links to their markets, and the general strengthening of Sudanese economic ties to entities other than Egypt.

Lord Allenby's threat of unlimited irrigation in the Sudan, coupled with successful testing of cotton cultivation and continuing work on the Gezira scheme, caused Egyptians to entertain the idea of their cotton exports to Britain being replaced by those of the Sudan. A 1925 article in *al-Jarida al-tijariya al-misriya* expressed concern over "the future of Egyptian cotton in light of the continuous spread of cultivation of this commodity in the Sudanese Gezira; ... [this] activity is being multiplied by the government of the Sudan with zeal."[30] Egyptian public opinion increasingly believed that Britain was creating a "cotton producing" imperial possession. *Al-Akhbar* noted in early 1925 that "if England is successful in the diffusion of canals in those regions [the Gezira primarily], the Sudan will become an independent colony with a railroad stretching to the Red Sea to be used in exporting."[31] If Sudanese cotton was comparable to Egyptian supplies and British officials encouraged its cultivation and export, it seemed inevitable that Sudanese cotton would at least partially replace Egyptian exports to Britain. In its annual report for 1925–26, the Alexandria Chamber of Commerce claimed that "Britain, which imports half our crop, will be able in the near future to completely dispense with it by buying what the Sudanese Gezira and others produce for her."[32]

Additionally, Gezira cotton production began precisely as the Egyptian government was limiting the area of its own cultivation, thereby enhancing the likelihood of Britain substituting Sudanese for Egyptian supplies. In the parliamentary debate over restricting cotton cultivation to bolster prices, Egyptian senator Alfred Shamas complained that officials in the Sudan were planning to surpass the limit of irrigating three hundred thousand feddans in the Gezira and that British "spinners are replacing Egyptian cotton with Sudanese cotton, and therefore they are desirous of reducing the area [cultivated] here, while increasing [acreage] there."[33] An editorial in *al-Jarida al-tijariya al-misriya* on 20 March 1929 theorized not only that Egyptians soon would be reliant on British textile imports but also that these imports would be woven from Sudanese, not Egyptian, cotton. The paper warned of

> England doing without a large part of what it customarily imports in the way of Egyptian cotton, which increases year after year, and replacing that with Sudanese cotton production. It is well known that England imports annually around a third of what [the Sudan] exports. If Egypt loses this customer it will not find one to take its place. There is the danger that Egypt will become awash with textiles, most of which are manufactured from Sudanese or other cottons, while Egyptian cotton stagnates and is ruined.[34]

With the onset of the Depression in the early 1930s, Egyptians were increasingly anxious about their economic well-being, and continued reports of growing competition from Sudanese cotton only exacerbated these fears. A May 1930 article in *al-Akhbar* noted the tremendous fertility of the Gezira lands, which were expected to "yield millions of qantars of cotton of the best quality and strongest varieties." The editors asked what would be "the situation of the Egyptian farmers in the near future when the cotton markets are crowded by millions of bales of Sudanese cotton?"[35]

Preference for cheaper varieties of cotton—some of which the Sudan produced—also harmed Egyptian interests. The 1932–33 report of Egypt's parliamentary financial committee noted a decrease in cotton exports to

Britain because of that country's preference for the cheaper and more abundant supplies of the Sudan, Uganda, and other countries.[36] In Egyptian eyes the imperial machinations of British officials in the Sudan were all too readily apparent. *Al-Akhbar*'s editors stated in January 1931, "England wants to make the Sudan into a country estate on which varieties of cotton and other crops are cultivated which their country and their factories need, and on account of that they have established numerous irrigation projects."[37]

To Egyptians the linkages were clear. The acceptance of Sudanese water rights led directly to cotton cultivation, which led to market competition with Egyptian producers. Isma'il Sirri Pasha, who was Egypt's minister of public works in 1926, alluded to these interconnections before the Egyptian senate. He warned against compensating Sudanese for their lands lost in Nile River hydraulic projects with increased irrigation allowances. He argued that such compensation could only lead to cotton export competition and set a precedent for future water rights claims.[38] Beyond the negative consequences of greater water usage and cotton cultivation, the development of Sudanese irrigated agriculture did very little to strengthen ties with Egypt. Furthermore, Egyptian opposition to such development could not have fostered popular support for Nile Valley unity from any Sudanese group.

Costs of Nile Development

Aggravating the problems associated with Nile River development was the financial commitment required for undertakings in Sudanese regions. Paying for technical studies or actual hydraulic facilities stimulated most discussion, but the Egyptian government even funded ordinary expenses associated with the personnel and supply needs of the Sudan Irrigation Service. Prior to the First World War, the estimated annual costs of dredging and other activities on the Upper Nile were LE40,000.[39] 'Ordinary' expenses of irrigation services in the Sudan were still an object of criticism in the 1930s. Mahmud 'Azma Pasha, a former employee of the service, complained of the enormous salaries in Egypt's budget for two employees in the Sudan. He stated, "I was in the Sudan a long period, and I know nothing about these activities and about what the irrigation employees there do." This individual went on to characterize other expenditures of the service as excessive. For instance, in 1934 the irrigation service used a fleet of seventy vessels for its activities, but Mahmud 'Azma Pasha stated that "the forty boats which I supervised were enough for water transport south of Khartoum to Abyssinia and Uganda, and they were used in the transport of the army, tourists, for trade and for the transport of people in all regions of the Sudan."[40] Officials charged the Sudan's irrigation service expenditures to Egypt's budget, but the costs of technical examinations and construction of storage projects were more burdensome, especially since much of this work occurred during the Depression.

The major Nile projects financed by Egypt during this period were the second heightening of the Aswan dam, construction of the Jabal Awliya' reservoir, and studies of a possible dam at Lake Tana in Ethiopia.[41] The Egyptian government approved the funding and supervised the completion of the Aswan dam improvements by the early 1930s, but this project was less controversial since it lay within Egyptian territories. There was much greater concern over expenditures on irrigation works located in the Sudan, like the Jabal Awliya' reservoir. Although there was plenty of debate about the necessity and costs of Jabal Awliya' construction, ultimately the Egyptian government did agree to finance the project. Prime Minister Isma'il Sidqi finished the parliamentary debate on the Jabal Awliya' reservoir in 1932 by stating, "I have repeatedly said to you, sirs, that our budget is capable of bearing this project without recourse to reserve funds."[42] Egypt's budget could afford these expenditures, but the costs of all anticipated hydraulic works along the course of the Nile were high. In the 1932 discussion of Jabal Awliya', the government released a report that estimated all projects in Egypt and the Sudan would necessitate a LE24,000,000 commitment.[43] The government expected a return on this investment eventually through increased revenues from land taxes, irrigation fees, customs duties, and railroad receipts, but there was still concern over such large expenditures. During the same 1932 debate, Hafiz Ramadan noted that post–First World War commissions had been charged with investigating "the necessary, equitable division" between Egypt and the Sudan of project construction expenses, but now officials had assented to solely Egyptian financing of the Jabal Awliya' reservoir since the increased water supplies were designated for its use only.[44] Plus, the Sudanese administration's financial position did not allow serious consideration of its sharing the expenses.

Most Egyptian critics of heavy financial outlays focused on the question of each project's utility for Egypt. For instance, in 1933 the Egyptian senate approved a LE50,000 credit for a feasibility study of constructing a reservoir at Lake Tana, but only after multiple senators emphasized the future benefits for Egyptian agriculturalists.[45] A common complaint about Nile River projects, especially those projects located in the Sudan or beyond, was that attention and money should first be centered on improving irrigation facilities in Egypt. By 1941, Ahmad al-Diwani, a senator and landowner from Mahmudiya Province, stated that Egypt's Ministry of Public Works should finance canal improvements and increased water-raising capabilities instead of throwing away millions of pounds on technical studies and projects in the Sudan.[46] Officials consistently mentioned the unity of the Nile Valley, but when discussing the actual costs of irrigation works—like water allocation earlier—they were again treating Egypt and the Sudan as separate entities. Additionally, the criticism of expenditures for projects in the Sudan was always coupled with concerns over reduced Egyptian administrative control, fears of increased water usage by the Sudanese, or complaints of Sudanese cotton competition. The 'costs' of hydraulic works were undoubtedly high, whether such costs were immediate budgetary or long-term economic and political. A more detailed picture of such costs is possible through closer examination of the two most hotly debated projects of the period.

Jabal Awliya'

The Jabal Awliya' storage facility on the White Nile south of Khartoum was one of the major works completed during the 1930s. Egypt's Council of Ministers had actually approved this project in May 1914, but the outbreak of the First World War delayed the start of construction. After the war, the Ministry of Public Works reported that "in December 1919 the Sudan Construction Company began operations at Gebel Aulia—it being at that time anticipated that the work would be pushed on at full speed. Leveling the site of the colony, opening of quarries, making of roads was begun and plant was ordered."[47] However, due primarily to disputes between engineers in the immediate postwar period, the Council of Ministers decided on 25 May 1921 to "stop the present works at Jabal Awliya', with the safeguarding of what had been completed on it until now."[48] Meanwhile the Sudanese government completed work on the Sennar dam and Gezira irrigation scheme, while the Jabal Awliya' construction activities remained suspended.

In the early 1930s the Egyptian government finally resumed construction of the Jabal Awliya' project. Isma'il Sidqi, prime minister at the time, stated in 1931 that "the Jabal Awliya' project has always been considered the scheme to follow the irrigation undertakings of the Gezira. Egypt authorized the establishment of the dams of Makwar [the name of the reservoir created by the Gezira's Sennar dam] only because it reserved for itself the right of constructing Jabal Awliya' dam."[49] Isma'il Sidqi's government justified the expenditure on this White Nile dam through reference to the expectation of extending Egyptian cultivation with increased water supplies and possible increased agricultural processing establishments. A 1932 parliamentary report recommended funding the Jabal Awliya' project "because Egypt will remain dependent always on utilization of land as the most important means for taking care of the needs of its population."[50] In respect to processing industries, this report stated, "We do not believe that the policy aiming at agricultural expansion in the country is incompatible in any way with the industrial programs which are being undertaken on this basis [food processing], indeed in fact [agricultural expansion] assists in their realization."[51] Nationalist-minded officials and entrepreneurs hoped products of Egyptian agricultural processing industries might find a market in the Sudan. However, there were only tenuous links between the purpose of the Jabal Awliya' project and strengthened Egyptian–Sudanese economic bonds.

Although the project and its agricultural beneficiaries were located along the same river, Jabal Awliya' sparked debate that highlighted the division of the valley. Frequently, Egyptians made statements reflective of a 'what's in it for us' attitude—and the implicit 'them' in such attitudes were their Sudanese brethren. For instance, many Egyptian leaders believed there were plenty of potential hydraulic improvements that should be studied or constructed domestically first. Hafiz Ramadan recommended rejection of proposed expenditures on Jabal Awliya' "not because the dam will be placed in [Britain's] hand, but because we . . . are not able to disburse an investment of millions of pounds in a project like this before we ascertain, at least, the benefit accruing to the country from the raising of the Aswan dam."[52] This individual and others criticized expenditures on this project because of British dominance in the Sudan and the subsequent 'pressures' that could be applied to Egypt. He reminded his fellow deputies that technical reports had admitted storage facilities in the Sudan could potentially be used to delay the arrival of water in Egypt, and he questioned whether "something like this project will be used as a means of political pressure."[53] Hafiz Ramadan warned, "As for our going to the Sudan and constructing our dams there, far from our supervision, there is every danger in that because England will demand of us the Sudan's right to the increased water [supplies]."[54] The potential of political pressure from British officials in the Sudan and the need to first examine irrigation improvements within Egypt were two key criticisms of the Jabal Awliya' project.

Additionally, Egyptians complained about the actual sum to be spent on Jabal Awliya', especially the compensation fund Egypt would establish for those Sudanese displaced by the reservoir. The Nile Projects Commission's report of 1920 estimated that between 17,000 and 107,000 feddans of land would be lost in the Sudan, depending on the flood's annual fluctuations, but by the 1930s the estimated quantity of land that would be lost had significantly increased.[55] In April 1925, Amin al-Rafi'i wrote in *al-Akhbar* about developments occurring on lands that the Jabal Awliya' reservoir would submerge and the financial ramifications of such:

> The government of the Sudan informed the Egyptian government that the Sudanese owning lands lying behind Jabal Awliya' have refrained for seven years from cultivating their lands, . . . but now, as the Egyptian government persists in suspending construction of this dam, the government of the Sudan will allow the owners of those lands to cultivate their lands. And if the Egyptian government resumes work on establishing this dam tomorrow, the compensations which the Egyptian government is obliged to pay the owners of those lands will be multiplied.[56]

By the time the Egyptian government approved the resumption of work on Jabal Awliya', the amount of land for which Egypt would provide compensation had reached three hundred thousand feddans, well above the 1920 estimates. Furthermore, during the economically difficult times of the early 1930s, Hafiz Ramadan noted that Egypt was agreeing to pay landowners a price per feddan more than ten times higher than the earlier accepted value of these lands.[57] In addition to monetary payments for lands submerged, Egyptians were aware that compensation would also involve increased water usage in the Sudan, always troublesome for Egypt. An Egyptian senator provided details, stating that

> the Sudan requests that the compensation be [in] water and money: water taken from the reservoir or from the waters of the natural river course, or from both of them, to irrigate land exchanged for what the water of the reservoir will flood; and money to undertake the necessary labors for this irrigation and for other activities resulting from the raising of waters because of this reservoir.[58]

The Egyptian government did ultimately agree to compensate the Sudanese for their losses resulting from this project, but Egyptian disgruntlement over having to provide such surely did not promote nationalist sentiment among their Sudanese brothers.

Despite the various complaints leveled at Jabal Awliya', Egypt's Chamber of Deputies agreed to resume financing the project on 23 May 1932. Actual construction activities commenced that December.[59] Technical reports of the previous decade had led to a significant rise in the total expenditure required for the compensation fund and all works connected to the reservoir. Egypt's parliament approved a LE4.5 million cost estimate.[60] In 1937, 'Abd al-Qawi Ahmad Bey, later the first Egyptian to head the Sudanese Irrigation Service, reported that construction was completed in April 1936 at a cost of LE200,000 less than expected and that "thereby it is the least expensive of the reservoirs [along the Nile], just as it is the longest reservoir in the world, with the possibility of raising it further."[61]

Although this reservoir was finished under cost estimates, the frequently acrimonious debate over shouldering expenses of the project accentuated how Nile waters tended to divide rather than unite the valley. Like other hydraulic projects or agreements, Jabal Awliya' had done little to foster Egyptian–Sudanese cooperation, plus it was slow to fulfill its purposes. For example, the completion of Jabal Awliya' did not immediately lead to the extension of Egyptian cultivated lands or the guaranteed supply of sufficient summer water for all regions of Egypt. In 1941 Egyptian officials were still complaining about the lack of enough water for irrigation and especially about Jabal Awliya's failure to provide such supplies. 'Abd al-Qawi Ahmad Bey, by then minister of public works, responded to critics by explaining that the "Jabal Awliya' reservoir was utilized in summer irrigation for the first time in 1938 and filling it [to maximum capacity] will be gradually completed in the following five years. Egypt will obtain complete use of it in the summer of 1943."[62] The reservoir would eventually meet its water provisioning expectations, but Egyptian needs continued to rise, and the long period between the construction costs incurred and the project's full utilization remained a target of critics.

In addition to delays in water supplies from Jabal Awliya', Egypt benefited little from the actual building of the dam and subsidiary facilities there. In fact, foreign firms carried out construction, and any economic 'stimulus' resulting from these activities seemed to benefit Sudanese interests alone or Sudanese ties to the international economy—certainly not ties to Egypt. First, two British firms handled construction of the dam and accompanying structures. A British entity, the Sudan Construction Company, supervised activities until the work stoppage in 1921, and the firm of Gibson & Pauling Ltd. completed the project during the 1930s.[63] Egyptian construction companies presumably did not possess the requisite technical expertise for such a project at the time. In addition, this situation highlights one of the central, vitally important obstacles facing Egyptian nationalists' efforts to foster economic unity. For the Sudanese, the question was simply why unite with Egypt if financial, technical, or managerial expertise are what you need and these can be best supplied by nations other than Egypt.

Egyptian construction firms may not have been capable of completing the Jabal Awliya' project, but Egypt failed to profit from other facets of this undertaking as well. For instance, instead of Egyptian companies providing cement for the construction, an industrial sphere in which Egyptian manufacturers had made substantial progress, Condominium officials encouraged the establishment of a local cement factory. The Ministry of Public Works reported in 1921 that "a cement factory has been built at Makwar for the purpose of supplying cement for the Jabal Awliya' and Sennar Dams and a payment on account, of £100,000, has to be paid to the Blue Nile Division for this factory in the next financial year."[64] Furthermore, the Egyptian government 'lost' the potential revenues from transporting cement to the Sudan. So, Egyptian cement suppliers failed to profit from the construction work, and the Egyptian government paid for the Sudanese factory that both eliminated potential rail revenues and created local competition for future Egyptian cement exports. In 1934 the Sudan Chamber of Commerce reported on Jabal Awliya' that "there is no doubt that these works have already contributed to augmenting the receipts of the railroads and other revenues of the [Sudanese] government as well as the volume of our import trade."[65] Overall, the Jabal Awliya' dam was a costly project without immediate positive results for either Egypt's agriculture or its economic bonds with the Sudan. In fact, the planning and construction of Jabal Awliya' and other facilities in Sudanese regions encouraged international, rather than solely Egyptian, connections. The Lake Tana project would accomplish the same.

Lake Tana Project

The Lake Tana reservoir project was unique among the interwar Nile River development plans in that it lay beyond both Egyptian and Sudanese borders. Financing the technical investigations for this proposed facility in Ethiopia was not as financially burdensome as in the case of the Jabal Awliya' reservoir, but Egyptians saw no immediate benefits from the project and claimed that it further divided Egypt and the Sudan. Lake Tana had been among the projects recommended by Nile River commissions after the First World War. The *New York Times* published a report in 1927 that noted "the reservoir there would form an integral part of the system the British have built below."[66] However, Egyptians sought the completion of their own examinations prior to the start of a project that potentially would impact their agricultural sector. In 1927, Egyptian deputy Muhammad Hafiz Ramadan praised the sending of diplomatic representatives to Ethiopia and stated that it was among his country's duties to "dispatch scientific missions and others to those lands which are firmly connected to our life in view of the fact that our lifeblood is in the water of the Nile."[67] The construction of the Gezira scheme, the heightening of the Aswan dam, and the planning of Jabal Awliya' all delayed further consideration of the Lake Tana project until the mid-1930s. Ethiopian planning of the facility at this time conflicted with past commissions' conclusions, which led the Egyptian government to appoint a new investigative group in 1935.[68]

The Egyptian government financed these investigations and was most concerned with the reservoir's immediate utility, especially considering the numerous and expensive Nile River improvement plans already underway. Although Egypt's primary interest was water supplies and irrigated agriculture ramifications, the investigators also studied the impact of a proposed road between the Sudan and Lake Tana. A 1929 report from Egypt's consulate in Addis Ababa had noted that this road would be politically and economically beneficial to the region.[69] Egypt's Ministry of Foreign Affairs received a similar appraisal in 1935, at which time the consulate in Addis Ababa wrote of this road that "an invigoration of the commercial situation in all regions neighboring the lake, indeed in every area of Ethiopia, will result from its presence."[70] Despite these seemingly positive opinions, the improvement in this region's transportation capabilities would not have strengthened Egyptian–Sudanese economic relations. If anything, approving this Ethiopian–Sudanese connection was detrimental to increasing Egyptian trade with the Sudan. During this same period no serviceable road directly connected Egypt and the Sudan.

However, most criticism of expenditures on the Lake Tana reservoir revolved around the absence of any direct benefits to Egypt from the increased water supplies. Sudanese historian Mekki Abbas noted that the Sudan's Gezira scheme would be the primary beneficiary, writing that according to the Nile projects commission of 1920 "any extension of this area [the Gezira scheme] was made contingent on the construction of the Lake Tana Dam."[71] Egyptians were not necessarily opposed to irrigation expansion in the Sudan, as long as it did not harm their own interests, but they equated improvements there with increased British exploitation. Dr. 'Abd al-Hamid Sa'id stated of Lake Tana that "no one will benefit from this reservoir except England, the English treasury and English companies first of all, and the Ethiopian government secondly."[72] He made these statements during the 1933 parliamentary debate over spending LE50,000 on the study of the project, which was necessitated by the Ethiopian government's plan to proceed with the reservoir, with or without Egyptian participation. Critics of this LE50,000 expenditure argued that there were more urgent fiscal demands within Egypt itself during the Depression and that any possible benefits would materialize only in the distant future. Wahib Doss Bey stated during the same discussion that technical experts had reported "we have no need of the water, not in the immediate future, and not after ten or twenty years."[73] Still, the Egyptian government approved this expenditure, and criticism continued throughout the decade. In 1936, *al-Siyasa*'s editors expressed the opinion that "if it is possible that Egypt can benefit from the waters of the reservoir, then this would not be before the next one hundred years, or fifty years at least."[74] Like the Jabal Awliya' project, when considering the Lake Tana reservoir Egyptians simply weighed the high costs of such works during the Depression against the limited and distant advantages for their country. There was little concern from Egyptian leaders regarding what the Lake Tana or Jabal Awliya' projects might portend for the welfare of their Sudanese 'brothers' or for the unity of the Nile Valley.

Egyptian Laborers at Hydraulic Projects

One aspect of Nile River development that appeared to be immediately beneficial to Egypt was the employment of manual laborers, commonly from Upper Egypt, on the proposed projects. Considering Egypt's increasing population and the growing scarcity of both cultivable land and water supplies, Egyptian officials hoped employing laborers on Nile projects might help partially solve these problems.[75] Reports from the governor-general on conditions in the Sudan consistently noted the utilization of Egyptian labor for irrigation service works. In 1938 the governor of Upper Nile Province reported that construction activities at Malakal had been undertaken almost solely by Saidi laborers.[76] The previous year Kassala Province in eastern Sudan had imported two hundred Saidi workers for repairs on the Gash river irrigation system.[77] In fact, use of Egyptian labor by the Sudan's irrigation service was not a new development in the 1930s; it had been practiced for years. Egyptians were responsible for over half of all excavations carried out in the *hafir* water collection schemes of Kassala Province by 1929 and involved in the Gezira scheme works of the early 1920s.[78]

Although some Egyptians found employment in such activities, officials questioned whether these workers were contributing to stronger Egyptian ties to the Sudan or were simply being exploited by British interests. In 1924, representative 'Abd al-Rahman al-Rafi'i stated of Egyptians at the Gezira scheme that "most of the activities of these employees are for the welfare of English imperial companies."[79] The same year *al-Akhbar* reported that there were some five thousand Saidi workers at irrigation projects throughout the Sudan, but that Egyptians were paid less than the

Sudanese and had to obtain their own food rations.[80] Later reports noted an improving economic position for Egyptian laborers in the Sudan. 'Abdallah Husayn, who visited the Jabal Awliya' site as part of an Egyptian delegation in 1935, wrote that "the Sudanese worker receives a daily wage estimated at four piasters and the Egyptian eight piasters—and the Egyptian workers are mostly from Aswan and Qena provinces."[81] Whether exploited or not, the large hydraulic projects in the Gezira and at Jabal Awliya' resulted in increased employment opportunities. In 1921, Minister of Public Works Muhammad Shafiq Pasha reported a significant number of Egyptian workers on major projects during his visit that year. He wrote that there were 2,700 Egyptians out of 4,000 total workers at Jabal Awliya', and that of the 19,074 workers in the Gezira, 10,625 came from Egypt.[82] With work on Jabal Awliya' suspended in the 1920s and a dramatically reduced Egyptian presence after the events of 1924, the number of Egyptians employed on hydraulic projects declined. However, work on Jabal Awliya' resumed by the end of 1932, and the governor-general noted significant increases in the number of Egyptian laborers passing through Sudanese quarantine stations the following year.[83] 'Abd al-Qawi Ahmad Bey was able to report of the completed Jabal Awliya' project that "around ten thousand workers, half of them Egyptians," had been employed during its construction.[84]

The employment of Egyptians by the Sudanese Irrigation Service and on storage projects was among the few benefits resulting from Egyptian activities in connection to the Nile River. Certainly, work on the Nile permitted the gradual expansion of agriculture within Egypt, but not without significant financial allocations for technical studies, compensation funds, and construction of facilities. Additionally, these developments fostered Sudanese cultivation of cotton and subsequently greater competition for Egyptians in international markets. Finally, agreements of the interwar years divided Nile water resources between Egypt and the Sudan—pretty strong implications of an 'independent' character for each region.

The Egyptian Annual Subvention

The Egyptian elite consistently referred to the historical bonds or cultural unity of the Nile Valley, but when it came to water-sharing agreements or hydraulic projects they were clearly most concerned about *their* budget, *their* agricultural lands, *their* population, and so forth. References to Nile Valley unity were camouflage for purely Egyptian priorities and could not stop the drift toward two separate nations. Similarly, the statements and actions of Egyptian officials in respect to financial assistance to the Sudan seemed to indicate a divided Nile Valley. Once again, Egyptians were in a difficult position. Helping the Condominium administration balance its budget or finance various infrastructure improvements were means of both assisting their southern 'brothers' and maintaining their political claims on the Sudan. Yet it was difficult to simply forgive Sudanese debt when much of the development financed had not fostered greater unity of the valley or directly benefited Egyptians. Demands for debt repayment in the mid-1930s did not take monies directly from Sudanese pocketbooks, but these actions could hardly be expected to convince the Sudanese of their brighter economic future lying within a united Nile Valley nation.

By the mid-1930s Egypt had provided the Sudanese administration with almost a decade's worth of financial assistance in the form of an annual subvention—originally to compensate for the withdrawal of military units. After the expulsion of the Egyptian army in 1924, the Egyptian government sought to maintain, at least symbolically, what was left of its diminished presence in the country by financing Sudanese defense capabilities. Ahmad Ziwar's ministry informed British officials that "the Egyptian government desires to indicate its inalienable interest in this task by continuing to contribute to the defense of the Sudanese territory." In this letter to High Commissioner Allenby the Egyptian prime minister wrote, "The Council of Ministers has decided to authorize for the military expenditures of the Sudan the entire balance of the budget of the [Ministry of] War after deduction of military expenditures carried out in Egypt."[85] For the 1925–26 fiscal year, it was determined that LE750,000 would be paid to the Sudan, an amount that became the normal annual subvention. However, criticism soon arose over the purpose and amount of this payment, and simply over whether it was required.

The official view of the subvention's purpose was that it was needed in order to counter Egypt's deteriorating position in the Sudan. The Egyptian parliament consistently recommended continuing this payment as a means of "sustaining the complete rights of Egypt in the Sudan."[86] However, the Egyptian government also maintained that the annual subvention should not be interpreted as their acceptance of British-imposed changes in the Sudan after the 1924 events. In a proviso attached to the parliamentary recommendation to pay the subvention in 1927, the financial committee noted that this payment was agreed to "temporarily," that it did not signify acceptance of the changes made in the Sudan, that it was not to be considered a mandatory obligation of Egypt, and that it in no way altered the issue of Sudanese debts to Egypt.[87] Despite such claims the subvention certainly appeared permanent and mandatory, as Egypt continued to pay LE750,000 year after year.

With the onset of depressed economic conditions in the early 1930s, Egyptian leaders increasingly emphasized the 'symbolic' nature of this contribution to Sudanese defense. During the budgetary debate of 1933, 'Abd al-'Aziz al-Sufani asked, "Why is the amount not fifty thousand or two hundred thousand only? Or is it not possible that the symbol of sustaining the rights of Egypt is [other] than this large fixed amount?"[88] The following year an Egyptian senator claimed that the subvention was only symbolic, like the practice of raising both the Egyptian and British flags in the Sudan, and asked therefore, "Why are they not content . . . with fifty thousand pounds?"[89] Some officials contrasted the actual pre-1924 military costs in the Sudan with the annual subvention amount. In the 1934 discussion of the Ministry of War's budget one deputy stated that "the Egyptian army which was stationed in the Sudan before 1924 had not cost the Egyptian treasury more than 400,000 pounds. And this amount is much less than what the Sudanese government demands from us at the present time in the name of 'expenses for the army in the Sudan.'" Furthermore, this representative argued for reducing the subvention by noting that "the English government [of the Sudan] spent no more than 350,000 pounds of the 750,000 which Egypt pays for the defense force in the Sudan."[90] Other representatives involved in this debate took the issue of decreasing the subvention one step further. For instance, since the British had not demanded LE750,000 initially, 'Abd al-'Aziz Nuzuma reasoned, "If it was the Egyptian government which proposed paying the amount in 1925, then what prevents it now from stopping the payment?"[91] Despite such arguments the government did not reduce the subvention until after the return of Egyptian army units in 1937.

As noted above, the cost of maintaining Sudanese military forces did not always equal the amount of the subvention. Egyptians feared that Condominium officials were using these funds for nonmilitary purposes, especially in a manner that benefited British interests while further weakening Egyptian–Sudanese unity. In the Chamber of Deputies in 1930, 'Abd al-'Aziz al-Sufani complained about the absence of Egyptian fiscal supervisory powers and concluded that this money "is disbursed contrary to our interests and contrary to the welfare of the Sudanese also."[92] Actually, the Egyptian government had included two special provisions in its approval of the original subvention, the second of which demanded complete reports on how the money was spent. In 1933, 'Abd al-Majid Mahmud Nafi' stated that for the previous six years this stipulation had required that Egypt be informed of "the purposes for which this sum of money will be spent exactly and precisely, [yet] has anything resulted from this? No."[93] Hafiz Ramadan raised the same issue the following year. He claimed that he had been a Chamber of Deputies member since 1926 and that no report had been forwarded to Egyptian authorities since that time. He ended his remarks by stating, "We spend, yet we do not know to what fate our monies go, moreover I say that we will lose both the money and the Sudan."[94]

Although Egyptians had no precise knowledge of Condominium officials using the subvention for nonmilitary purposes, speculation was rife. 'Abd al-'Aziz al-Sufani stated in 1937 that since the subvention was forwarded to a British-dominated Sudanese administration, "they pay from it the salaries of the English employees, from the governor of the Sudan to the minor employee."[95] Other Egyptians claimed that the money was being used for purposes more directly at odds with strengthening Egyptian–Sudanese bonds, such as financing Christian missionary organizations in the southern Sudan. In January 1937, the Egyptian paper *al-Balagh* noted, "The government of the Sudan assists [Christian missionary societies] from its budget, which includes the amounts paid annually by Egypt in the name of maintenance of defense forces, and the societies of missionaries obtain from this budget fifty percent of the expenses of establishing churches and institutes of evangelization."[96]

That same year Dr. 'Abd al-Hamid Mahmud provided a somewhat more balanced, yet still critical, appraisal of how British officials used this payment. After noting that no more than LE200,000 of the subvention had been designated for defense the previous year, he stated that the remainder "is spent on the general administration and the English employees, [and] indeed a large portion of it is spent, with the governor-general's consent, on the missionaries."[97] For whatever reasons, by the mid-1930s general opposition to the payment had increased. In the 1937 parliamentary debate, Isma'il Sidqi, whose government had continued the payment during the early years of the Depression, said that "the presence of this subvention in the Egyptian budget is becoming a burden that does not make sense."[98]

By the end of 1937 the first Egyptian army units were returning to the Sudan, but the subvention was not immediately discontinued. During parliamentary discussion of the 1936 treaty, Egypt's minister of finance stated, "We have obtained an unequivocal declaration from the other party [British negotiators] stipulating that Egypt has complete freedom in refusing to pay this sum of money upon the return of the Egyptian army to the Sudan."[99] However, Egypt continued to pay a reduced subvention for the next three years. An agreement reached between the British and Egyptian financial ministries on 3 November 1936 confirmed Egypt's right to discontinue payment but also noted that "if the Egyptian Government decides on any such action, it will give fair notice to the Sudan Government in order that it may recast its programme of expenditure to meet the position thereby created."[100] In correspondence between the Sudanese and Egyptian governments the following year, Governor-General Miles Lampson informed the Egyptian government that his administration believed a five-year period necessary to make arrangements for the end of the subvention.[101] However, considering the extensive criticism of this payment in the past, there was little chance Egyptian politicians would agree to a five-year transitional period. Consequently in July 1938 the Egyptian parliament approved a subvention of LE500,000 for the 1938–39 fiscal year, and the financial committee's report concluded by noting its hope that the government would take the necessary measures as fast as possible to relieve the budget of this burden.[102]

With the final subvention payment in 1940 and earlier return of military units to the Sudan, a bothersome issue was finally resolved, but at a considerable cost. Even this resolution came with a price tag for the Egyptian government, as the military clauses of the 1936 treaty necessitated additional expenditures.[103] Besides the expenses, Egyptians complained of British control of forces returning to the Sudan. During the debate over the 1936 treaty, 'Abd al-Hamid Sa'id complained that "the governor-general is in charge of determining the number of Egyptian soldiers, their barracks, and the regions in which they are stationed."[104] Despite many similar complaints the treaty was ratified and the Egyptian forces' return to the Sudan was certainly an improvement upon the situation that prevailed for over a decade. Still, the combination of years without a military presence, the financial burden of the subvention, and consistent Egyptian disgruntlement over such did not augur well for the claimed unity of the Nile Valley.

Resolution of Sudanese Debts to Egypt

Egyptians' dissatisfaction with granting the Sudanese financial assistance in the form of an annual subvention was matched by their attitude toward loans provided to their southern 'brothers.' Most importantly, like the subvention or the division of Nile waters, haggling over the amount owed and rapid repayment of Sudanese debts implied an independent nature for each region and did little to sway the Sudanese toward the unity of the Nile Valley. Egypt had provided funds for infrastructure, various development projects, and simply balancing the Sudanese budget at times. Britain and Egypt often disagreed over precisely how much the Sudanese administration had to repay. In response to a parliamentary inquiry on the status of Sudanese indebtedness, the Egyptian government reported in 1933 that

LE5.3 million had been allocated in the past to balance the Sudanese budget, in addition to LE5.5 million in development loans and LE3.4 million spent on the military.[105] British officials disagreed with both the figures and which debts had to be repaid. Still, if one considers the economic progress of the Sudan by the 1930s, the lack of Egyptian influence in the region, and the tightened financial situation of the times, it is logical that Egyptians would have become increasingly concerned with the repayment of these loans.

Although Egyptians complained increasingly about the repayment of loans and how foreign exploitation had accompanied the Sudanese development they financed, the British emphasized the benefits for Egypt. Kenneth Perkins, in his study of the evolution of Port Sudan, wrote that the British reasoning behind Egyptian loans to the Sudan was that "anything which tended to develop the resources of the Sudan would reduce the necessity for [Egypt's] government to contribute towards the Sudan."[106] Former Condominium official Sir John Carmichael also noted how paying for Sudanese development would lessen the need for continued assistance. He wrote that "Egypt had not only obligations but also definite interest in seeing that the Sudan should become stable and defensible so that its rights to Nile waters could be safeguarded and its irrigation stations along the Nile could operate without hindrance."[107] Possibly, but by the 1930s the Sudan had long since overcome its dependence on Egypt to balance the budget. Furthermore, the Sudanese administration had certainly established stability in the region, and the country's economy was beginning to compete with Egypt in international markets. Under such conditions, and with Egypt increasingly in need of funds, the repayment of the loans became a central issue.

The extent and resolution of Sudanese indebtedness was normally addressed during Anglo–Egyptian negotiations or when the Egyptian parliament discussed the annual subvention to the Sudan. For instance, the financial committee's report on the 1927–28 budget had recommended continuing the subvention, but only with the inclusion of "the precautionary measure, which the parliament adopted in 1926, of directing the government's attention to the necessity of determining the enormous debts which the country has upon the Sudan and of knowing the proper method of their repayment."[108] That same year in the senate Egypt's minister of finance responded to a query concerning these debts by stating merely, "This issue is still under investigation."[109] Less than two years later, Egyptian and British negotiators came to an agreement on the debt question. Mekki Abbas wrote that during the Mahmud–Henderson talks of 1929 officials reached an understanding on the debt issue, but this resolution never came into being because of the general failure of the negotiations.[110] Although other topics, particularly Egyptian emigration to the Sudan, foiled the 1929 negotiating efforts, in discussions leading to the 1936 treaty the debt question remained among the most potentially disruptive issues.

As the 1936 treaty negotiations were in progress there were generally positive reports in the local press about Sudanese issues, including the debt question. Reflective of such was a July 1936 *al-Siyasa* article that stated in respect to the debts, "Here, as in the discussion of the military issues of Egypt, the good progress of the Cairo negotiations is being aided by the capability of the two governments to inspect the facts face to face."[111] Despite such encouraging reports, the British and Egyptian officials only reached agreement on the treaty through the addition of a last-minute note that left the debt question to future discussions between financial representatives of their governments. A key underlying aspect of the difficulty in concluding an agreement was the true objective of British officials engaged in these discussions. M.W. Daly, a British scholar who has written extensively on the Condominium era, notes that for British officials at these negotiations "the overriding goal was to write off the Sudan's debt to Egypt while re-insuring its debt to Britain."[112] The British government had consented prior to the First World War to guarantee the LE13 million loan the Sudanese government raised for the construction of the Gezira agricultural scheme. Egyptians viewed British merchants and textile manufacturers as the direct beneficiaries of investments in the Gezira scheme and Sudanese development generally. The British countered that Egypt profited most from Sudanese development and stability. Essentially, the conflict revolved around who benefited least from Sudanese progress and should, therefore, be repaid first.

The memorandum attached to the 1936 treaty and signed on 3 November by Egyptian Minister of Finance Makram 'Ubayd and H.E. Fass on behalf of the British Treasury pointed to other aspects of the debt controversy. In the letter attached to this memorandum, Mr. Fass stated that

> It is understood between us that though not actually recorded in the text, no claims for repayment other than of advances for development purposes—whether recorded in the books of the two governments as such or included in the Sudan deficits covered by the Egyptian Government—will be made against the Sudan by either the Egyptian or British Government, and that interest will not run on the debt before that date when it is agreed that the Sudan can commence repayment by installments.[113]

The actual memorandum also emphasized that the Sudan would only have to repay development loans. Egyptian military expenditures or funds advanced to balance the Sudanese budget were excluded. After noting the differences in debt estimates, the memorandum stated that "such additional claims as may be put forward by the Egyptian Government as being in the same 'development' category will be examined by the two treasuries on the basis of the records and accounts."[114] The last-minute addition of this correspondence and the inconclusive nature of the debt agreement reached were necessary to complete the 1936 treaty, but the treaty did not silence Egyptian critics of this debt.

The criticism in Egypt's parliament centered on three main issues: the disparity between the debt estimates, the larger amounts owed to Egypt reported by previous ministries, and the exclusion of nondevelopmental loans from the agreement. Avoiding these specific grievances, Egypt's minister of finance explained in 1936,

> We agreed that the Sudan is indebted to Egypt by the amount of 5.5 million pounds which we have called 'Development Debts' which are debts Egypt loaned to the Sudan for the advancement of its resources. We calculated these debts at the amount of 5.5 million pounds and the English representative calculated them at the amount of 5,100,000 and some. But these debts only are those which we agreed upon.[115]

Such bland explanations of debt agreements did not appease Egyptian representatives, who were also dissatisfied with the lack of specified processes for repayment. During the 1936 treaty ratification debates, 'Abd al-'Aziz al-Sufani complained that "as for the installment amount, the interest and the number of years in which this debt will be repaid, all of that is postponed."[116] These were certainly legitimate concerns for the Egyptian government. The memorandum of November 1936 stated, "The Sudan Government will use its best endeavour to commence payment as soon as possible," and "The period of years over which the installments will be spread, the rate of interest and the date from which interest will be paid, will be a matter for agreement between the Egyptian and Sudan Government."[117]

Agreement on developmental loans did eventually take place. On 24 November 1939, *al-Ahram* reported of meetings between Governor-General Stewart Symes and Egyptian Minister of Finance Husayn Sirry Pasha that an "agreement was concluded yesterday . . . conforming to the standpoint of the Egyptian government on this matter [of developmental loans]. Also, agreement was reached on the rules according to which payment would take place."[118] Even with these agreements Egyptian anxieties over debt repayment turned out to be well founded, as the Sudanese government was slow to make payments.[119]

During the 1936 treaty debate some officials realized the potential political impact of insistence on debt payments, countering critics with reference to the hope of Nile Valley unity. In response to accusations that the Sudan owed much larger amounts than the paltry sums to be repaid, Makram 'Ubayd said, "We have not spent 45 million only on the Sudan but [rather] we spent hundreds of millions. And what we spent in this manner are not debts because the Sudan is a part which is inseparable from Egypt."[120] Senator Louis Agnus Fanus expressed similar sentiments, stating, "Egypt does not have debts upon the Sudan, just as the Egyptian government does not have debts owed by Asyut or Buheira."[121]

Although the government accepted the 1936 debt arrangements, these comments hinted at the implications of this settlement. In a manner similar to the agreements on Nile River usage, the debt settlement that Egyptian nationalists ratified clearly treated Egypt and the Sudan as separate political entities. The financial contributions of Egypt to the Sudan, whether in the form of development loans or an annual subvention for Sudanese defense, did not significantly enhance the prospects of Nile Valley unity. Instead, these payments were a burden upon the Egyptian treasury, especially during the Depression, with few immediate or long-term benefits accruing to Egypt. Egyptians hoped that financial assistance would lead to expanded commercial activities or increased investment opportunities for their entrepreneurs, but instead developmental loans helped erect an economy tied to international markets and foreign investors. To reiterate, nationalist leaders were in a difficult situation. Denying financial assistance or demanding repayment of loans would not win Sudanese support for uniting the Nile Valley. Yet providing aid to the Sudan certainly came with no guarantee that British officials would be concerned about economic development also strengthening Nile Valley bonds.

Ultimately, Egyptian officials needed to convince the Sudanese population of the benefits of Nile Valley unity. Debt resolution and Nile water distribution could not have endeared the Sudanese to the Egyptian nationalists' objective. Gauging Sudanese public opinion is a difficult undertaking, but local newspapers provide some hints. In 1939, *al-Ahram* summarized a recently published article by the Khartoum newspaper *al-Nil* detailing the Sudan's debt history and how Egyptians were undermining support for Nile Valley unity. This article stated

> that it did not know the details [of Sudanese debts owed to Egypt] but it knew of the importance of the Sudan to Egypt and that the monies were spent to guarantee the security of Egyptian lands and to prevent foreign control of the Nile waters. And it stated that the agreement of 1926 [sic] concerning the distribution of waters benefited Egypt tremendously. Then the newspaper mentioned that the demand for [repayment of] these debts does not accord with the unity of the Nile Valley and that this demand oppresses the Sudan and hinders the spread of education. And it stated that the government of the Sudan recognized that this business does not please the Sudanese people.[122]

This quotation enumerates most of the issues raised in this chapter, all of which were detrimental to forming one nation. When it came to the issues of Nile waters or financial assistance/repayment, Egypt and the Sudan were two separate entities. Despite the damage done to nationalist aspirations from this 'successful' resolution of debt and water issues, important institutional and administrative changes were taking place in the mid-1930s that raised hopes of strengthened economic—and political—bonds in the future.

3 Agreement, Institutions, and Opportunities, 1936–39

> I do not demand that the expert carry out any political activity, indeed I am saying that it is incumbent that he work on economic and financial issues, for it is well known that the natural outlet for the Sudan is Egypt.
>
> The [1936] treaty did not set up this position for the appointment of employees to be given a salary from the nation's wealth and the blood of the fellah. Therefore we are reiterating that we must have an economic expert in the Sudan with attachés and offices, which have been established to work on the development of economic relations and the strengthening of such between Egypt and the Sudan.
>
> Therefore, I hope that the minister will work on remedying this situation.[1]
>
> —'Abd al-Halim Mahmud 'Ali, Egyptian Chamber of Deputies, 1946

Parliamentary representatives such as 'Abd al-Halim Mahmud 'Ali had raised concerns for years about the activities of the Egyptian economic expert in the Sudan. Egyptian leaders had emphasized the importance of this position as a conduit for economic projects that would strengthen bonds with the Sudan, clearly perceiving a diplomatic utility in such bonds—despite claims that the expert should not engage in political activities. Egyptians believed their economic specialist could raise awareness of Nile Valley potentials, lobby for policies preferring local goods in government purchases, facilitate communication between local entrepreneurs, or simply represent Egyptian interests before Condominium officials. Despite the claimed shortcomings in 1946, the appointment of the expert had been one part of nationalist efforts since the mid-1930s to establish institutional arrangements supportive of the economic union of the Nile Valley. Additionally, the expert's appointment signaled the return of Egyptian administrative personnel to the Sudan.

The assassination of Sir Lee Stack and High Commissioner Allenby's subsequent ultimatum to the Egyptian government on 22 November 1924 resulted in the expulsion of most Egyptian civil servants from the Sudan—a grave blow to Egypt's sovereignty aspirations. The Egyptian government wrote to the high commissioner on 25 January 1925, expressing its hope that the recent changes in the Sudan would "neither prejudice the solution of the question of the definite status of the Sudan, reserved for future negotiations, nor lessen the indissoluble bonds uniting the Sudan and Egypt."[2] Despite these hopes, the absence of Egyptian administrative and military officials after 1924 certainly did not strengthen those bonds. For over a decade the generally anti-Egyptian Sudan Political Service would make policies and take actions opposed to Nile Valley unity. British officials there did not have to work consciously to undermine Egyptian objectives. The now overwhelmingly British administration maintained order, defended borders, developed infrastructure, established agricultural schemes, and so forth, and while such accomplishments necessitated agreement and financial assistance from Cairo, the Sudanese credited Condominium officials. Basically, every successful year of Condominium government harmed Egyptian nationalists' hopes.

Financial Consequences of the Expulsion of Egyptian Personnel

In addition to the political 'damage' resulting from the forced expulsion of military units and civilian officials, there were also related economic 'costs' for Egypt. Egypt lacked an administrative presence that might have facilitated future investment, commerce, or service activities in the Sudan. There was no major public or private Egyptian institutional presence in Sudanese economic centers. Eventually, Egyptian nationalists would take measures to counter the long-term economic consequences of their post-1924 administrative absence, but the financial ramifications for Egypt were more immediate. British officials forcing Egyptian military units out of the Sudan did not eliminate Egyptian annual financial commitments to Sudanese defense. The last chapter analyzed Egypt's continued financial assistance to Sudanese defense, but there were also expenditures associated with integrating expelled personnel into Egyptian military units at home, paying retirement benefits to those ceasing their service, and the expenses of transferring Sudanese troops to the newly created Sudanese Defense Forces. Shortly after the 1924 events, a memorandum from C.W. Spinks, inspector general of Egypt's Ministry of War, stated that "Egypt will accept all liabilities as regards pensions and gratuities for past services up to the date of transfer."[3] In addition to funds for Sudanese formerly employed by the Egyptian military directly, the Egyptian government had to find employment for hundreds of returning military officials. L.A. Fabunmi notes that "two new battalions and a new squadron of cavalry were raised in 1925 to provide employment at home for most of the Egyptian men who had lost their positions in the military units and civil administration in the Sudan."[4] Creating a few new military units or finding positions within the bureaucracy for returning officials did not conclude Egypt's financial woes resulting from the 1924 events. The government addressed the financial complaints of dismissed officers for years.

Egyptian civil servants expelled from the Sudan in 1924 caused as many financial difficulties as their military brethren. Military personnel in the Sudan prior to 1924 were paid by the Egyptian government, but Egyptian civil servants at that time were the financial responsibility of the Condominium administration. Most of these officials were absorbed by the Egyptian administration, but their years of Sudanese service presented compensation difficulties long after 1924. For example, a group of such officials forwarded a memorandum to the government in 1939 in which they were still demanding "the adjustment of their ranks and salaries on a basis of including the periods of their service in the government of the Sudan" and "the addition of the actual period of inactivity between their dismissal from the government of the Sudan and their appointment in the Egyptian government to the period of their service calculated in pensions."[5]

The government's difficulties in reassigning civil servants dismissed following the 1924 incidents were exacerbated by additional dismissals during the early 1930s. Because of the Depression, the Condominium administration implemented a number of 'cost-cutting' measures, including reducing the salaries of civil servants, relying on 'traditional' leaders for the execution of certain administrative functions, and dismissing non-essential staff.[6] On 6 April 1932, Egypt's minister of interior reported in the Chamber of Deputies that since January 1931 Condominium officials had dismissed 340 Egyptians, a 27 percent reduction of the total Egyptian administrative presence and more than double the combined number of British and Sudanese officials dismissed.[7] Once again, as occurred after 1924, the Egyptian government had to reassign, pay, and assume responsibility for pensions and other financial commitments for these civil servants.

During the negotiations leading to the 1936 treaty, a committee of these dismissed officials sent a telegram to the British and Egyptian negotiators that stated, "The Egyptian employees, whom the government of the Sudan has dismissed since 1931, implore you to restore to them their stolen rights and to compensate them for what has afflicted them because of their dismissal for no other reason than the lack of political stability in the Sudan."[8] The Egyptian government's official report on the status of these officials implied that their situation was being successfully handled and that politics had not been a factor in their dismissal. The report stated that "most of those employees were dismissed for purely economic reasons. And they had in fact been granted what they are entitled to in the way of pensions and rewards."[9] The report also seemed to direct attention away from financial compensation by enumerating the problems, from poor health, deficient education, or technical qualifications to previously inflated ranks or salaries, preventing their employment in Egypt.[10] In 1936 the Council of Ministers finally decided to accept these officials' periods of service in the Sudan when calculating pensions, but had to authorize the use of reserve funds to pay the revised totals.[11] In response to a later parliamentary inquiry concerning the status of these civil servants, Prime Minister Mustafa Nahhas specified what measures were being taken to find government employment for them but concluded that "their appointment to positions, authorized by a ministerial committee, is a problem due to the pressure of expenses."[12] The expenditures necessitated by the expulsion of Egyptian civil and military officials did not reach the levels of Nile River projects or development loans to the Sudan, but these expenses were still burdensome during some of the most difficult interwar years.

In addition, the 'costs' of their physical absence were potentially more damaging to Egypt's long-term economic, and nationalist, objectives in the Sudan. The physical presence of greater numbers of Egyptians in the Sudan was no guarantee of better Nile Valley relations, but one could speculate on lost potential benefits. A sustained Egyptian official presence might have constituted a larger market in Sudanese urban centers, potentially encouraging the Sudanese economic elite to strengthen ties with Egyptian elements.[13] Undoubtedly, the absence of Egyptian personnel could be responsible for the scanty information on Sudanese economic conditions available to Egyptian entrepreneurs, agriculturalists, or merchants. Reporting on Sudanese economic conditions was not a task assigned to Egyptian personnel working for the Condominium administration, but knowledge of the local economic, social, or political situation would have found its way to Egyptian ears through informal channels of communication—or at least the lack of a presence prevented this possibility. Countering this deficiency in information on Sudanese conditions, the Egyptian elite established a number of new institutional avenues for the collection and dissemination of data on the Sudan. These institutions of the latter 1930s would play a key role in all facets of strengthening economic bonds of the Nile Valley.

The 1936 Treaty and Egypt's Economic Expert

Among the most important developments of this period for strengthening Egyptian–Sudanese economic ties was the conclusion of the 1936 treaty. The Anglo–Egyptian Treaty of Friendship and Alliance, ratified by the Egyptian government on 22 December, was largely a result of the changed domestic and international circumstances of the mid-1930s. Previously, there had been little headway in solving Egypt's paramount nationalist dilemma—the evacuation of British forces. Region-wide concerns became increasingly important to British interests, and Egypt profited from British measures to protect these interests. British leaders were apprehensive about Adolf Hitler's saber-rattling in Europe in the mid-1930s, but Benito Mussolini's military conquests in North Africa and the Mediterranean were direct threats to their access through the Middle East. The Italian conquest of Ethiopia placed the growing Italian North African 'empire' directly on the Sudanese borders. Furthermore, the same year that the Anglo–Egyptian treaty was concluded, a new, serious revolt erupted in the nearby Palestine mandate. From the British point of view, there were multiple advantages from a peaceful, content, stable Egypt. The country was the most important link in their transportation or communication with India and the East. Egypt was the obvious choice for a regional command center for the British dominions and its allies if there were a European conflict—and Egypt had served such a function in the First World War. A supportive, or at least quiescent, Egypt would be useful as British leaders pursued their foreign policy objectives in the Arab world. A stable Middle East, with Egypt being an essential part of this, would allow the British government to allocate more of its resources to other troublesome regions of the world. For years, British officials had been lukewarm on the urgency of reaching agreement with Egypt, but conditions had changed by 1936.

The Egyptian domestic situation had changed by this time as well. King Fu'ad passed away in 1936, and his son Faruq authorized new elections that resulted in the formation of a new Wafdist government that would successfully negotiate with the British. Egyptian officials were able to gain a greater degree of independence, but the complete evacuation of British forces did not occur and British interference with the Egyptian government continued. Although the military occupation clauses of the 1936 treaty were more important to the majority of the public, the treaty also offered significant possibilities for Egyptian economic interests in the Sudan.

For the first time in negotiations, and formally in the treaty, the co-domini clearly stated that the primary concern of the Condominium administration was the welfare of the Sudanese population. Virtually every speech or article from Egyptians on the Sudan had made reference to the heartfelt kinship and camaraderie of the people of the Nile Valley, but this was the first time that Egyptians had explicitly agreed that the objective of their interactions with the Sudan should be the latter's development. From their reading of other clauses of the 1936 treaty Egyptian leaders expected an expanded role in the Condominium administration. Although Egyptians hoped truly to participate in that administration after 1936, the Sudanese bureaucracy remained overwhelmingly British, with gradually increasing numbers of Sudanese employed. Almost a decade later, Isma'il Sidqi complained that the administrative clause of the treaty "requires the equality of Egyptians and British in the appointment to positions for which there were not sufficient Sudanese," but that little increase in Egypt's share of the administration had occurred.[14] Sudanese scholar Fadwa Abd al-Rahman Ali Taha, who studies specifically this post-treaty era, argues that Egypt's failure to expand its bureaucratic presence in the Condominium was a result of frequent government turnover in Cairo.[15] When the question of Sudanese sovereignty was finally taken before the United Nations Security Council, Egyptians held twelve 'high' positions in the administration, compared to 586 and 105 for the British and Sudanese, respectively.[16] Condominium officials explained that this situation was due to the "fact . . . that service in the Sudan is still regarded by most Egyptians as exile."[17] Although the overall number of Egyptians serving in the Sudan did not rise significantly, one administrative innovation of the treaty gave particular hope to Egyptian economic/nationalist interests.

Egypt's Economic Expert to the Sudan

In a letter to Prime Minister Mustafa Nahhas on 12 August 1936, High Commissioner Sir Miles Lampson acknowledged that "the suggestion for the secondment of an Egyptian economic expert for service at Khartoum . . . [was] noted and considered acceptable in principle."[18] This note was included in the 1936 treaty, and both public and private institutions involved in the Egyptian economy expressed their pleasure over the possibilities for Egypt in the Sudan through the offices of the expert. Hoping to avoid antagonizing a traditionally hostile British administration in the Sudan with grandiose expectations for this new position, Egyptian government bodies typically announced their hope that the expert would strengthen, improve, or mend Egyptian–Sudanese economic relations.[19] The Cairo Chamber of Commerce was brief and explicit in its expectations of this official: "His mission is to travel among [the Sudan's] markets in order to know what those markets need and what Egypt can export to them from its products."[20] The expert was a critical administrative position capable of expanding Nile Valley economic relations, but there were limitations on his powers and recurrent problems which hindered his effectiveness.

Before Egypt ratified the 1936 treaty some Egyptian representatives were already expressing their misgivings about the treaty and the new economic position in the Sudan. During the extraordinary session held to debate the treaty, Muhammad Hafiz Ramadan Bey emphasized the lack of influence the economic expert would have. He stated that the expert (and the military advisor to be sent) would have only advisory functions, would have no power in the administration of the region, would not participate in the governor-general's council, and along with the Egyptian army units would be under the governor-general's command.[21] Although the expert was to be only an advisory position in the Sudan and hence could only suggest reforms there, he was essential in the communication of interests and information between the private sectors of Egypt and the Sudan. As would be expected, considering the importance and possibilities of this new position in the Sudan, the Egyptian government took great care in selecting qualified candidates. The economic experts all had qualifications similar to those of 'Abdallah Fakri Abaza Bey, the first official dispatched to Khartoum in early 1939. He had completed advanced studies in commerce and served a number of years in the Egyptian Chamber of Deputies. He was also on a number of companies' boards of directors, notably for various components of the avowedly nationalist Misr group of companies, and had been the president of the Commerce Graduates Club.[22] In addition to government experience and ample connections within Egypt's private economic sector—prerequisites of all subsequent experts—'Abdallah Abaza Bey had experience in Egyptian–Sudanese affairs prior to his appointment. Despite such qualifications and experience, without any official role or responsibilities within the Sudanese administration, the possibility of strengthening commercial relations in the valley was much reduced.

Another early and consistent problem was the absenteeism of the Egyptian experts and the subsequent less frequent and direct contacts with Sudanese merchants. Without counting the two years that passed before

Egypt finally sent an official in January 1939, the first three experts spent roughly nine and a half months in the Sudan between 1939 and 1944.[23] In 1945, after years of difficulties with this position, 'Ata 'Afifi Bey of the Chamber of Deputies requested a number of reforms for supporting the expert's activities but stipulated that this person must also be "keen on actually residing in the Sudan."[24] This deputy noted the great expectations Egyptians associated with this position, yet he felt that nothing had been accomplished. Egyptians did not suddenly realize after the Second World War that the expert's absence from the Sudan was undermining successful completion of his objectives. Within a year of 'Abdallah Abaza Bey's arrival in Khartoum the local press was reporting bitter criticism from firm supporters of improved Egyptian–Sudanese relations.[25] With the onset of the Second World War, and raised expectations of even greater economic interdependence, the problems associated with the expert's absence from the Sudan became more apparent. When questioned about this official's "nonresidency" in 1942, the Ministry of Commerce and Industry stated that this was due to health reasons, which it hoped to solve soon.[26] By September of that year, 'Amr Tussun, the president of the Royal Agricultural Society, was urging Prime Minister Mustafa Nahhas to take whatever steps were necessary for the return of the expert to Khartoum because Egyptian–Sudanese trade had been "stopped since the outbreak of the war."[27] Despite such urgings the government never really solved this problem. For instance, the following year, Mahmud Zaki, the economic expert at the time, explained that he had been in Egypt since 27 April and was supposed to return in early July, but that completing various tasks in Cairo had necessitated the delay of his planned return until 12 October.[28] Certainly, strengthening Nile Valley trade or resolving provisioning issues during the Second World War called for activity in both Egypt and the Sudan. But Egyptian nationalists believed having an expert actually in the Sudan, whatever the international situation, was critical to both improved commerce and claims of Nile Valley unity. The fact that he spent the period from April to October in Egypt did little to solidify economic bonds.

Part of the difficulty with a consistently resident expert was the lack of enthusiasm for this official (if not outright opposition) on behalf of British officials of the Sudan. This was certainly the case when "the removal of Mahmoud Bey Zaki from this post came from His Britannic Majesty's Ambassador in Cairo" in early 1944.[29] Prime Minister Nahhas had earlier sent a memorandum to Governor-General Huddleston requesting information on the actions of the expert that would allow him to investigate complaints, since he felt this position was an absolute right of Egypt in the

Sudan.[30] The expert's removal was carried out "on account of the unfortunate anti-British speeches made in Cairo at a tea party organized for a party of Sudanese students by Mahmoud Bey Zaki."[31] Clearly, the British considered political questions regarding the Sudan to be outside of this official's sphere of responsibilities. Another factor in the expert's frequent absence from Khartoum was the lack of residential facilities. In 1939, the year in which the first expert left for the Sudan, the Egyptian government agreed to dedicate LE500 toward the purchase of land on which the expert's office would eventually be constructed.[32] However, with wartime financial restrictions, the government did not continue plans to construct facilities for the expert alone. Not until 1945 did the Egyptian government finally earmark funds for the construction of a new office and residence for the expert specifically.[33] Overall, improved commercial relations and the establishment of direct contacts with Sudanese merchants could not be accomplished by the Egyptian expert if he was not able to reside in Khartoum on a more permanent basis.

Another explanation for the experts' poor record of residence in the Sudan may be a general reluctance to serve in this region. Early histories of the Condominium, relying heavily on British officials' accounts, were quick to identify this antipathy toward the region as the cause of Egyptians not working—hence not residing—in the Sudan. However, Egyptian sources claim this was not the cause, yet their words allude discreetly to this problem. In a radio broadcast on 14 August 1939, 'Abdallah Abaza Bey stated in regard to Egyptian officials and service in the Sudan that misperceptions of realities there "make the majority of us refuse work in the Sudan, or accept it under compulsion, proceeding as if [we] were going to the unknown and furthermost regions of the world. So, we leave this field of employment to other peoples." 'Abdallah Abaza Bey was even more explicit when describing his own initial reaction to service in the Sudan:

> I cannot conceal from you that when the decree was promulgated appointing me economic expert for Egypt in the Sudan I greeted the news at first with fear and a bit of indignation, and I demanded time to think, and I reflected during this period on those frightening stories that I had heard from some people, in fact I heard from the mouths of many about the weather and heat of the Sudan, the difficulties of living there, the paucity of life's pleasures, the plethora of pests, and that wild animals roam freely in the cities just as they wander the jungles.[34]

Hearing these stories from the "mouths of many" did not promote Egyptian service in the Sudan, and stories of wild animals roaming city streets indicated the absence of reliable information on the conditions of their southern 'brothers.' The first expert was explicit in drawing attention to why Egyptians were less than enthusiastic about working in the Sudan. Most descriptions of Egyptians taking posts in the Sudan employed words such as "duties," "service," "honor," and so forth—implying that this was not work that highly qualified applicants were anxious to undertake. An *al-Ahram* article that summarized Egyptian opportunities in the Sudan obtained through the 1936 treaty described work there as more than mere employment, as service to a loftier nationalist cause:

> The observers of Sudanese affairs see that it is not enough that Egyptian officeholders in the Sudan take up their official duties, delineated in the text of treaties or found in laws and decrees, but they must work to raise the name of Egypt and preserve its honor, while respecting the traditions and customs of our Sudanese brothers. . . .
>
> Perhaps among the causes for joy is that many of the sons of Egypt and the Sudan have demonstrated excellent insight into matters and a grasp of the varying circumstances, and this is what heralds good news for the strengthening of ties between the halves of the valley, especially once the filling of the higher positions referred to in the Anglo–Egyptian treaty is accomplished.[35]

Unlike 'Abdallah Abaza Bey's radio broadcast, most reports about the appointment of Egyptians to positions in the Sudan made few references to reluctance to work there. Instead, most reports spoke of national service, of elevating Egypt's image in the Sudan, of the need to closely scrutinize who is selected, and of "the opportunity to truly share in the administration of the Sudan through being represented among its officials."[36] Other than the first economic expert, none of the subsequent Egyptian experts mentioned any reluctance to work and reside in the Sudan.

Even if economic experts resided in Khartoum for rather brief periods, there were still Egyptian staff in the Sudan and institutional supports assisting in the successful completion of their tasks. The 'Sudan Department' of Egypt's Ministry of Commerce and Industry was allowed to have an office in the Sudan according to the 1936 treaty.[37] Additionally, the expert was to have support personnel in the Sudan. Before the Egyptian government sent the first expert, the Ministry of Commerce and Industry dispatched a trade delegate who served as "a commercial attaché for the supervision of current operations in the Sudan."[38] The Egyptian government provided further assistance to the expert in 1939, when he initially arrived in Khartoum. That summer the Ministry of Agriculture emphasized the need to send scientific delegations to research agricultural potentials of the Sudan and recommended the dispatch of "a delegate from among the technical staff of the Ministry of Agriculture to Khartoum, in order that he be attached to the office of the economic expert and he cooperate in the study of agricultural issues there and the work of developing agricultural bonds between the two countries." This official and the expert's office generally would serve ideally as a conduit for agricultural cooperation between the regions. For instance, the director of publications within the Ministry of Agriculture recommended

> sending three complete collections of the printed materials of the Ministry to the expert's office and a large number of the publications that the Ministry distributes free of charge, and have the director of the information and publications department of the Ministry contact the economic expert in the selection of cinematic films suitable for the Sudan and aimed toward the spread of general agricultural education.[39]

Besides attached specialists in certain economic fields, the expert also benefited from a more permanent Khartoum staff that maintained activities during his absence. During the summer of 1939, the government assigned accountants and secretarial staff to the expert's office.[40] Among the most important staff members of the expert's office was its director—again a person more permanently resident in Khartoum. *Al-Ahram* correspondents reported that

> Mr. William Farid, director of the economic expert's office, zealously continues his activities in propagandizing for Egypt and studying the economic matters which connect the interests of the two countries. He has distributed to [Sudanese] associations and organizations publications that include reports on Egypt's progress in various facets of life.[41]

This article also noted that the director was investigating the poor condition of Egyptian fruit and vegetable shipments and would send the expert a report with suggested remedies.[42] Despite reports of such appropriate and potentially beneficial work by personnel of the expert's office, Egyptian officials had hoped for more progress. In late 1948, 'Abd al-Majid al-Rimali questioned the minister of commerce and industry about the decision to establish branch offices in al-'Ubayd, Wad Midani, and Kassala.[43] The establishment of these branch offices would have facilitated the process of establishing closer contacts with the Sudanese, but the proposal was rather belated. In the same debate the minister announced that the government was elevating the rank of the expert's position to 'general director' and had included funds for new offices, residences, and furnishings in the upcoming budget. Officials discussed the expert's salary in 1946, when the ministry suggested the substantial salary of LE6,000 per year for the position.[44] This concern over salary figures indicated either the need to attract an extremely experienced individual for the position or the need to overcome some resistance of the most highly qualified experts to being assigned to the Sudan. Despite various difficulties that inhibited the expert's effectiveness, his 'potential' contributions were consistently believed to be critical in the strengthening of Egyptian–Sudanese economic bonds after 1936.

Egyptian Economic Missions

Many Egyptians anticipated greater involvement with the Sudan because of activities of officials such as the economic expert, but private economic interests had already initiated 'institutional' undertakings to promote Nile Valley economic cooperation. The Egyptian entrepreneurial elements involved in an economic mission sent to the Sudan in January 1935 and subsequent expeditions were well aware not only of the economic benefits of this activity but also of the political importance of these undertakings. An official report on the first economic missions to the Sudan stated that the 1935 delegation "removed from Egypt the accusation, justly attached to it, that Egyptians have limited interest in the business of the Sudan and visiting it, and are satisfied by rhetoric without action."[45] The political utility of increased economic activities was apparent to private elements engaged in these efforts, but the initial absence of a coherent government strategy for organizing such missions or for strengthening Nile Valley economic relations generally undermined the effectiveness of actions taken.

The seemingly piecemeal or ad hoc nature of Egyptian efforts, and the mixture of both private and public entities involved, is reflective of broader explanations for the failure to unify the economies of the Nile Valley. Not only was the government late in initiating efforts but it also lacked any comprehensive plan. M.W. Daly, a historian of the Sudan, characterizes the pre–Second World War period as one of "increasing but poorly coordinated Egyptian official interest in the Sudan."[46] The lack of well-organized efforts was partly due to the wide variety of interest groups involved in these initial efforts. The first mission was composed of "32 members representing the [Royal] Agricultural Society, the Society of Graduates of Agricultural Schools, the General Agriculture Syndicate, the Cairo and Alexandria Chambers of Commerce and important agriculturalists, merchants and notables."[47] Many of the consistently influential figures in developing Egyptian–Sudanese relations were involved in this first mission, but the paramount role played by Fu'ad Abaza in urging the dispatch of this mission and the general rekindling of economic interest in the Sudan cannot be too strongly emphasized.

Fu'ad Abaza Bey and his extended family had long-established agricultural interests and political clout in Egypt.[48] Tracing their origins back to Yemenese contingents of the initial Islamic conquerors of Egypt, the family had solidified their economic, particularly agricultural, base in Sharqiya province during the reign of Muhammad Ali Pasha. In addition to their agricultural holdings, the family had become prominent players in the centers of Egyptian power, with representation on parliamentary bodies since the latter nineteenth century, editorial positions in the emerging Egyptian print media, and participation in some of the most important diplomatic/political undertakings of this era. Fu'ad Abaza was born in 1890 and obtained his BA in 1906 and an agricultural diploma in 1909, beginning his rise within the Royal Agricultural Society that same year. He held numerous positions with the society, garnering honors and titles from the Egyptian crown and from foreign countries specifically for his work in organizing agricultural and industrial exhibitions in Cairo during the interwar period. His interest and expertise in Sudanese affairs had begun to develop with his inclusion in earlier missions to the south. Fu'ad Abaza was a member of a 1911 investigative agricultural mission sent to Italian Somalia, returning to Egypt through the major centers of the Sudan. In January 1934 he set out on a trip to regions neighboring Lake Victoria and the countries of the Horn of Africa to collect information on cotton cultivation practices, in preparation for an international cotton conference that was held the following month. This mission, and particularly his study of the Gezira scheme and Jabal Awliya', would provide the groundwork for subsequent undertakings—ranging beyond cotton cultivation.

In the summer of 1934 plans for a major economic mission directed toward promoting specifically Egyptian relations with the Sudan began to take shape. The main supporter of a proposed new exploratory mission to the Sudan was the Royal Agricultural Society. During a meeting on 9 August 1934, the society's administrative council, under the leadership of

Prince 'Amr Tussun, agreed to organize a trip to the Sudan the following January.[49] This mission left Cairo on 25 January 1935 and spent roughly a month studying all aspects of the Sudanese economy.[50] Based on the mission's origins, one would assume an inclination toward agricultural interests, and there was much eventual investigation of agricultural potentials in the Sudan, but in fact during this trip and in subsequent meetings trade issues often dominated. In a speech before the Royal Geographical Society, Fu'ad Abaza noted that

> the group of merchants of the mission found a favorable opportunity supplied, as the traders of the Sudan became acquainted with their colleagues on the first day we arrived there, and they began to discuss, debate, and investigate the markets; and the deliberations brought to light proposals and recommendations which we submitted to the relevant departments in Egypt and the Sudan for the benefit of the brotherly countries.[51]

Most Egyptian sources greeted the mission's return with general enthusiasm and increased hopes for the future. However, from the beginning there were some portents of a troubled future. The Egyptian mission was noted with a rather noncommittal tone by Governor-General Symes of the Sudan.[52] In addition, based on a 1935 speech by the Sudanese Chamber of Commerce president, it was clear that the Egyptians hoping to achieve 'national' economic progress would have to work with non–Nile Valley entrepreneurial groups.[53] By this time in Egypt's economic history, cooperation with foreign businessmen and their capital was increasingly inevitable for Egypt's 'nationalist' merchants. Still, the dominance of foreign interests would undermine Egyptian economic and political designs on the Sudan, and their presence was noticeable from the first mission onward. During the following three years smaller groups of individuals held meetings to discuss ways of improving Egyptian–Sudanese economic relations. However, these unofficial discussions of mission members and Sudanese representatives achieved only minimal progress.

In November 1937, the Royal Agricultural Society proposed to the Ministry of Commerce and Industry the formation of a committee of experts that would assume the functions of the prior ad hoc meetings and discussion groups.[54] Requesting, and expecting, Egyptian government backing for and supervision of economic initiatives was not unusual during the interwar years.[55] There had simply not been sufficient local Egyptian interest in Sudanese economic affairs to provoke a state reaction until this time. By January 1938 the Egyptian government was sufficiently concerned about the development of economic ties with the Sudan to give the private sector's desires official sanction.

The Permanent Committee of the Sudan

On 24 January 1938, the Egyptian Council of Ministers agreed to the establishment and funding of a 'permanent committee of the Sudan' to be under the authority of the Ministry of Commerce and Industry.[56] This committee pursued the same basic objectives of the previous, more informal gatherings of interested individuals. The permanent committee chairman, 'Abd al-Rahman Fakri, claimed in a January 1939 speech, "We are at the gates of a new dawn of economic relations between the two countries, and the efforts which have been exerted in recent years have borne their blessed fruit."[57] Some "fruits" of their efforts may have been apparent, but most hope still rested on the future. Egyptian investment in Sudanese agricultural or industrial endeavors was years away, as the initial missions and meetings had barely begun investigating entrepreneurial opportunities. Egyptian nationalists believed that increased trade was a more attractive short-term objective to be pursued by the permanent committee. The committee chair prognosticated on Nile Valley commerce in 1939 by stating he believed "the future of commerce between Egypt and the Sudan will be brilliant when the opening of Sudanese markets has been extended to Egyptian trade to a farther degree than it is now."[58]

The permanent committee sought the establishment of an exhibition for Egyptian products in Khartoum, cheaper and more direct means of transport, tariff reforms, the founding of Egyptian financial facilities in the Sudan, granting priority to local commodities in government purchases, and so forth, all of which had been objectives since the 1935 mission and subsequent discussions. In fact, similar methods for stimulating commerce had earlier precedents in Egypt itself. The Fédération des Industries had advocated government preference of local products, protective tariffs, and lowered transport rates in the 1920s to gain a greater share of Egypt's domestic market.[59] It is also possible to make comparisons between policies of the permanent committee and the initiatives of other countries during the same period. Hiroshi Shimizu notes in his study of Japanese efforts to break into Middle Eastern markets the primary methods employed by this government. These included exhibitions of commodities, government-subsidized transport rates, and the establishment of financial institutions.[60] Basically, in their endeavors in the Sudan, the Egyptians had been following since the 1935 mission well-established means of encouraging exports.

Encouraging exports to the Sudan may have furthered the Egyptian nationalists' cause, but might other interested parties have viewed this as imperialistic, not nationalistic? The permanent committee held that promoting Egyptian–Sudanese trade generally would further nationalist objectives, but favoring only the Egyptian side of commercial relations would appear exploitative and be detrimental to the nationalist cause.

Egypt's leaders refrained from statements that might be construed as reflecting imperialist motives, instead consistently referring to their united, cooperative economic future with the Sudan—a future whose realization new official institutions might facilitate. However, the transformation of earlier informal, private gatherings of individuals concerned with Sudanese–Egyptian economic relations into a permanently established government committee was not without difficulties. In early 1939, reorganization of the committee's membership, its relationship with the newly appointed economic expert, and the committee's financial freedom all contributed to a momentary disruption of activities. Clearly a reorganization of committee membership, with an influx of government representatives, created problems. A February 1939 report described the composition and immediate intentions of the new committee in the following manner:

> The Ministry [of Commerce and Industry] began to study the organization on which basis the committee would be composed and it is expected that the new committee will include among its members representatives from several other ministries, such as the Ministries of Transportation and Works, and some senators and chamber deputies, also it will include some of those active in trade and industrial matters from the members of the previous committee.
>
> The authorities believe that the committee in its new form will be more capable than the previous committee of performing its mission in working to strengthen economic and social relations between Egypt and the Sudan.
>
> We have been informed that the committee is inclined to undertake annual trips to the Sudan of a restricted number of selected members assigned issues which they will investigate in the Sudan.[61]

When internal regulatory documents for the committee were composed the following month, the extent of official involvement was even greater. On 25 March 1939, the committee agreed to a new constitution that included membership from the Ministries of Transportation, Education, Agriculture, and Trade and Industry, in addition to parliamentary representatives, the economic expert, and the Egyptian head of irrigation in the Sudan.[62] Despite increased official participation in the committee, private interests were still well represented, including delegates from the Egyptian Federation of Industries and the Bank Misr group—though not from the Royal Agricultural Society that had been critical in all initial Egyptian–Sudanese efforts.

At the same time that this reorganization was taking place, a crisis arose. In February 1939, most members of the permanent committee resigned, allegedly because of disputes with the government over the appointment of the economic expert and insufficient financial support for the mission to the Sudan planned for that month.[63] Since its establishment the committee had been attached to the Ministry of Trade and Industry, and the government had agreed to provide LE1,000 for its trips and other activities, granting the committee "complete freedom in the disbursement of this credit."[64] Apparently, financial support had limits because the Ministry of Finance rejected a request for additional funds for the mission to the Sudan, claiming that the dispatch of the economic expert was sufficient at the time. Financial issues appear at least partially responsible for the resignations and disruptions. The committee was "unrestrictedly free in the disbursement of its *designated* funds," but when in need of additional assistance, possibly for a mission to the Sudan, then requests had to be forwarded to the Ministry of Finance.[65] In reports on their resignation, former committee members indicated that the new 'official' nature of the committee and the role to be assumed by the government's economic expert may have been more influential in their decisions. During a committee meeting in the first week of February, the members "tendered their resignation to the chair, hoping to provide the Ministry of Commerce and Industry freedom to compose the committee anew in the form of a government committee, establishing an organization whose objectives and activities take into account the new situation, so that it will work to strengthen relations between the regions."[66] A copy of the actual resignation letter published two days later seems to indicate that there was disagreement with the government's policies—especially concerning appointments and spheres of responsibility. The resignation letter stated, "We tender our resignation from membership in the committee to provide the government complete freedom in the establishment of its policy *in light of what happened recently with the appointment of the economic expert*."[67] Official sources and local publications were mute on precisely what "happened" in respect to the expert—but it can be surmised that there must have been some disagreement over the selection process or his responsibilities, possibly linked to the increased government representation on the committee. Reports concerning the newly composed committee and its internal regulations indicated a primary role for the economic expert, with other committee members assuming secondary roles. One account in local newspapers stated,

> As for issues related to Sudanese affairs in the Ministry of Trade and Industry the study of these should be *first entrusted to Egypt's economic expert* in the Sudan, and when he finishes that, present his findings to the ministry.
>
> Also the bylaws [of the permanent committee] stipulated that the committee choose seven of its members as a preparatory committee under the leadership of the deputy chair of the permanent committee, and include the Egyptian economic expert in the Sudan when present in Egypt, officials of the commerce and industry departments, and four members representing civilian agencies affiliated with the committee.[68]

When the new permanent committee met for the first time on 11 May, the economic expert seemed to be initiating all government activities directed toward the Sudan. The summary of this committee meeting stated:

> 'Abdallah Fakri Abaza Bey, the Egyptian economic expert in the Sudan, spoke of the results of his investigations during his recent trip to the Sudan.
>
> And among that which Abaza Bey proposed was that every ministry or organization represented in the committee prepare a list of issues considered important to study, then forward these to the committee, so that they can be investigated and an initial opinion on these can be produced.[69]

Undoubtedly, the expert was now playing the critical role in Egyptian–Sudanese affairs, even supplanting the previous collective leadership of the permanent committee in this activity. The expert reported directly to the ministries, he participated in investigative committees whenever possible, and he steered the permanent committee's own activities. The minister of commerce and industry singled out this official when praising permanent committee members' efforts, "which have been raised to a higher level of authority after the appointment of the Egyptian economic expert in the Sudan." In the same interview the minister also declared that the delay of the 1939 mission to the Sudan, which had led to the resignation of committee members, was not because of financial disputes, "but rather it was merely the [government's] intention to complete discussions with the recently appointed economic expert."[70] Whatever may have been the cause of the 1939 resignations and reconstitution of the permanent committee, this institution continued to be a critical forum for discussing means of developing Egyptian–Sudanese economic relations.

In order for it to function successfully as such a forum, the government assisted the permanent committee in a variety of ways. Inclusion of the formerly 'private' permanent committee in the Ministry of Commerce and Industry was a clear indication of the state's concern for the 'nationalist' issue of Egyptian–Sudanese economic relations. Besides the financial and personnel support provided as a part of this government ministry, the state also assisted the permanent committee through investigative committees and support staff, all included within a new section of the ministry that addressed Sudanese issues only. A report of the Ministry of Commerce and Industry dated 25 January 1938 noted the formation of the Sudan Department within its commerce division.[71] 'Abd al-Rahman Fakri stated in October 1938 that this department would receive the assistance of the Egyptian government and cooperation of the Sudan's and that it "is devoted to commercial issues peculiar to the Sudan, and is in contact with the permanent committee of the Sudan, and will undertake the preparation of what it [the committee] needs in the way of studies and information."[72] Supporting agencies were also established in the Sudan, as early as the first mission to the Sudan in 1935. In recounting his earlier work on Egyptian–Sudanese relations, the minister of commerce and industry during the Second World War, Rashwan Mahfuz Pasha, stated, "Among the most important results of this [1935] trip was the establishment of a permanent committee in Cairo and *another in Khartoum* for the exchange of opinions and the investigation of commercial and social issues and the liaison between the two governments and the agencies concerned with this matter."[73] The objectives of the permanent committee necessitated a presence in the Sudan. After the reorganization of the committee and its inclusion in the ministry, *al-Ahram* described its mission as

> organizing the display and sale of Egyptian manufactures in the Sudan by means of the permanent office for the Egyptian exhibition in Khartoum, organizing the means of distributing in the Sudan some samples for presentation to Sudanese traders, establishing direct relations between the Sudanese trader and the Egyptian manufacturer, and supplying the former with all specialized information on the type of products and their prices.[74]

In September 1939, the permanent committee agreed to form an official subcommittee to exhibit Egyptian goods in Khartoum, promote Egyptian products in all regions of the Sudan, and establish direct contacts with local traders.[75] Also, the Condominium government had decided by this time to delegate a group of officials to represent its various departments in discussions with Egyptian representatives sent to the Sudan.[76] Affiliated agencies of the permanent committee in Khartoum and other centers of the Sudan would be essential in strengthening Nile Valley relations. Like the need for the economic expert residing in the Sudan, some means of the committee having an actual presence in the country would facilitate the development of relations with Sudanese businessmen, landowners, and other economic leaders.

The Khartoum Exhibition

Both the permanent committee's establishment and the economic expert's appointment facilitated efforts to strengthen all aspects of the Egyptian–Sudanese economic relationship, but officials organizing an exhibition of Egyptian goods in Khartoum clearly intended to stimulate commerce. Egyptian interests were most concerned with developing a market in the Sudan for Egypt's products—with less attention for Sudanese exports to the north. The exhibition was to work toward marketing Egyptian goods in a number of ways. During a meeting of the permanent committee on 4 June 1938, 'Ali Shukri Khamis, secretary of the Alexandria Chamber of Commerce, noted the necessity of assisting the Khartoum exhibit in "continuous, organized shipments of fruit for disposal and the marketing of Egyptian imports, looking to acquire the Sudanese market."[77] In addition to the shipment and marketing of goods, the Khartoum exhibition also had an important role in advertising or making the Sudanese aware of Egyptian manufactures, especially considering the sharp foreign competition locally. In March 1938, the Cairo Chamber of Commerce noted the importance of the exhibit in relation to foreign competition and stated it hoped that "when the Sudanese consumer saw the quality of the Egyptian goods represented before him, he would take an interest in them based on personal motivation and incentives of nationalism and patriotism."[78] Even before the establishment of the exhibit some organizations had begun to promote Egyptian goods in the Sudan. For instance, in February 1935 the Royal Agricultural Society reported that "the Egyptian mission is asking Bank Misr and its companies to send samples of its [cotton] goods to the Sudanese Chamber of Commerce."[79]

The permanent committee of the Sudan slowly gained control over the various organizations anxious to participate with the Khartoum exhibit.

The Misr group, the Sudanese Chamber of Commerce, and the Egyptian Chambers of Commerce were all involved with the exposition. From the minutes of a meeting of the permanent committee with representatives of the Sudanese Chamber of Commerce on 21 February 1936, it is apparent that this Sudanese entity could not initiate the exhibition by itself. At the same meeting Talaat Harb indicated his willingness to "send [Bank Misr companies'] products to the Sudan accompanied by a representative and a car to enable this representative to travel in the regions of the Sudan in order to display these samples and publicize them."[80] The Egyptian state needed to organize effectively these initial isolated efforts of the Sudanese Chamber and Misr group. In January 1938 the permanent committee decided that the Egyptian Chambers of Commerce, the Royal Agricultural Society, and the Ministry of Commerce and Industry would all contribute specific amounts to lease a building for the exhibit and hire staff.[81] However, the Egyptians also claimed that purchasing land to construct a permanent exhibit, instead of displaying goods in a leased building, would demonstrate a greater commitment to Egyptian–Sudanese commerce. In the 1939–40 budget the state allocated funds for the purchase of land on which to build such a structure, but the outbreak of war necessitated the withdrawal of these funds.[82]

In addition to concerns about the exhibition building, there were misgivings over the type of 'sales' that took place in this structure. In a 1938 letter George Tutunji, the head of a Sudan import and export company registered in Egypt, cited the retail sale of products as one cause in the failure to achieve the exhibition's goals. He complained that the sales of the Khartoum office were directly to the consumer and that little contact with Sudanese traders had occurred. Furthermore, it was through such traders that it was hoped large orders for Egyptian goods would be requested. Tutunji wrote, "Certainly it was not the goal of the founding of the office that it be a shop for the sale of drinks and olives and similar commodities, the sale of which in the Sudan does not result in any benefit to Egypt."[83] The retail-sales aspect of the exposition was apparent from the beginning. In May 1937 the Cairo Chamber of Commerce reported that 'Ali Barir Effendi, a trader active in Egyptian–Sudanese commerce, had purchased "Egyptian commodities of 400 £E in value to send to the office in order to start its work."[84] Goods valued at LE400 were certainly a meager beginning for an office designed to stimulate wholesale trade.

Another basic goal of the office, according to Tutunji, was to enlighten Egyptian industries about the state of the Sudanese market. Egyptians believed that information on the Sudanese market, and the transmission of such knowledge to Egypt's industrial sector, was a primary responsibility of the office director. Tutunji noted some progress in this sphere by the director, but also stated that persistence in such work was necessary. He wrote, "The Khartoum office director is beginning to contact import merchants of the Khartoum and Omdurman markets in order to study the possibilities of the Sudanese markets and what the Sudan could purchase from Egypt. This requires unceasing daily research with each merchant individually."[85] 'Ali Shukri Khamis of the Alexandria Chamber of Commerce stated in response to Tutunji's comments that another representative was needed at the office but that the budget of the permanent committee at the time was not sufficient.[86] Increasing the personnel associated with the office in Khartoum did not occur immediately, but the committee gradually filled positions affiliated with the Khartoum exhibition. In a meeting on 3 December 1938, committee members "agreed on the appointment of an employee of the Cairo Chamber of Commerce, his mission being the establishment of direct contact with Egyptian manufacturers to work toward supplying the permanent office in Khartoum with their manufactured products, to speed up the dispatch of these goods, and to complete the execution of contracts."[87] Whether insufficient personnel, lack of clear objectives, or meager support for the physical establishment of the exhibition, there were plenty of opportunities for criticism. The local newspaper, *al-Balagh*, reported in 1939 that there was tremendous general support for the exhibition, but that the Egyptian government had been the least helpful, despite the clear nationalist/economic utility of this institution. The paper's editorial staff commented,

> It is in this exhibition that we hope our commerce and industry will find a favorable opportunity for the presentation of the distinguishing features of Egyptian manufactures in order to increase economic bonds between the two brotherly regions. We also hope that this will be a golden opportunity to increase knowledge between the two regions by increasing the number of visitors. The government of the Sudan has promised to offer assistance in the undertaking of the exhibition and we believe that traders and industrialists would be within their rights in demanding from the Egyptian government similar assistance in the transport of exhibitors and their products, as well as visitors from Egypt.[88]

Egypt's first economic expert, 'Abdallah Fakri Abaza, noted other problems with the exhibition. In addition to reiterating the problems of personnel, information sharing, and inadequate facilities, he wrote that the limited scope of Egyptian industries represented, the lack of sales outside of Khartoum, and the high prices of commodities all undermined the Khartoum office's effectiveness. He suggested that "the two chambers [Alexandria and Cairo] renounce the 10 percent commission which they take from every exhibitor's sales."[89] Although not explicitly stated in the sources, this commission must have contributed to the 'higher than market' prices and the tendency to avoid wholesale trade at the exhibit, since 10 percent of the merchants' profit margin on any sales was deducted. By the summer of 1939, the permanent committee had

> examined the report forwarded from the subcommittee delegated to investigate the situation of the Khartoum exhibition. And [the permanent committee] agreed on what it included in the way of suggestions, such as the chair of the committee agreeing to increase support for the Cairo and Alexandria chambers of commerce by 100 £E from the exhibition's budget. However, they are relinquishing the 10 percent commission on exhibitors that had been levied.[90]

Some measures advocated by the Cairo Chamber of Commerce to address the failings of the exhibit specifically also shed light on problems characterizing Egyptian–Sudanese commerce overall. In May 1938 the chamber suggested keeping a greater quantity of items in inventory, urging the presence of commercial agents, and instituting a price discount for Sudanese buyers.[91] The larger inventory was evidence of a lack of Egyptian knowledge about the local market or, more specifically, an inability to determine when demand would change. Second, the need for commercial representatives indicated the absence of a sufficient 'distribution network' of local merchants handling Egyptian commodities. Finally, the need to discount prices was a consequence of the high prices of Egypt's 'tariff-protected' industrial products, which resulted in their inability to capture a significant share of the local market. Meanwhile, Egypt's foreign competitors enjoyed well-established distribution and informal information-gathering systems and were able to offer commodities at lower prices.

The Second World War seemingly offered Egyptian manufacturers and the presentation of their goods in the Khartoum exhibition some relief from this stiff foreign competition. However, the administration of the exhibition, entrusted to the Alexandria and Cairo chambers of commerce, encountered wartime difficulties. In July 1940 at the Ministry of Commerce and Industry, a committee of both Egyptian and Sudanese administrators and representatives of the two chambers "examined the budget of the Khartoum permanent exhibition for Egyptian manufactures, and among the opinions [expressed] was the necessity of supplying the exhibition with various Egyptian manufactures which the Sudan needs, especially in the current situation in which [the Sudan] looks to Egypt because of the absence of means of importation from abroad."[92] Despite being aware of the wartime opportunities and the deficiencies in supplying the exhibition, problems persisted as the war progressed. *Al-Ahram* reported in the summer of 1941 that "what is sent in the way of Egyptian manufactures for display in the permanent exhibition in Khartoum is small in quantities and . . . does not meet the needs of the Sudanese population."[93] This newspaper concluded by noting that both merchants and exhibition staff expected the Ministry of Commerce and Industry would assist in their taking advantage of the war. In 1942 the exhibition staff requested that the chambers send specific amounts of textiles, oils, soap, and other Egyptian manufactures, but due to the restricted wartime situation they had to refer this request to the Ministry of Commerce and Industry.[94] The following year the Alexandria chamber reported that although it and the Cairo chamber were supposed to provide the exhibit with Egyptian goods for sale or display, wartime restrictions had hampered efforts and had forced them to ask that the permanent committee reexamine exhibition supervision.[95] In the end, despite slight sales increases after the war's onset, all parties involved with the exhibition agreed to administrative changes in 1944.[96]

During that year the chambers of commerce relinquished their administrative role to a newly formed Egyptian company. This transfer of responsibility was directly related to the problems of supplying the exhibition. Egyptian entrepreneurs interested specifically in promoting textile exports to the Sudan had established the Egypt and Sudan Company, but this company was also entrusted with general provisioning of the exhibition. In 1944 the newly appointed economic expert, Ahmad 'Abd al-Khaliq Bey, reported:

> Transferring the permanent Egyptian exhibition in Khartoum to the Egypt and Sudan Company was completed. . . . The objective of establishing this exhibition was to make Egyptian manufactures available to Sudanese customers. The Cairo and Alexandria chambers of commerce had arranged to supply [the exhibition] with goods, however the circumstances of the war began to prevent this, which forced the Ministry of Commerce and Industry to consider another means of ensuring it was supplied with manufactures of Egypt without interruption, and [the ministry] resolved to establish

> the aforementioned company to undertake the activities of the two chambers, providing that its guiding principle is the achievement of economic foundations, for which the [exhibition] office was established under the direction and supervision of the economic expert.[97]

On 15 May 1944, representatives of the newly formed company and the two chambers of commerce reached an agreement on both the transfer of responsibility and the financial compensation of personnel associated with the exhibition.[98] Whichever organization administered the exhibition, provisioning problems certainly undermined the possibility of success. It is difficult to measure the overall effectiveness of the exhibition in Khartoum, but probably the best answer lies in the analysis of commercial statistics for specific commodities in later chapters. However, Egyptian interests viewed the office as another means of achieving their goals in the Sudan, "and the most important of them . . . [was] informing the population of the Sudan and its merchants about the Egyptian commodities and accustoming the people to the use of them instead of foreign commodities."[99]

The Khartoum exhibition, the permanent committee, the early economic missions sent to the Sudan, and the appointment of an Egyptian expert were the most important institutional arrangements adopted in the latter 1930s. These developments were late in emerging and would have to overcome years of seemingly reduced Egyptian concern for Sudanese economic conditions. Condominium administration actions subsequent to the events of 1924 had prevented vigorous Egyptian economic efforts. Still, many years passed before there emerged a strong current of Egyptian opinion advocating the utility of greater economic interactions in uniting the Nile Valley. With the new institutional arrangements of the latter 1930s, Egyptian nationalist entrepreneurs hoped to more effectively work toward the 'strengthening of economic relations.'

Preference for Local over Foreign Goods in Nile Valley Markets

The new institutional developments described above assisted all facets of economic relations with the Sudan, but the Egyptian entrepreneurs and organizations involved were especially dedicated to strengthening Nile Valley trade. Officials involved in the various initiatives of the latter 1930s pursued multiple specific means of increasing trade levels. Members of the missions, committees, and the economic experts paid particular attention to gaining acceptance of the principle that local suppliers should have priority over foreign competitors and counteracting the lack of knowledge about local supply and demand.

Egyptian nationalists believed a unified Egyptian–Sudanese commercial market could take advantage of the perceived traditional or historical ties of the two countries, simultaneously weakening the foreign domination of both regions. Egyptian leaders had emphasized the interdependence of the Egyptian and Sudanese economies at various points after the First World War. In his proposed treaty draft during the 1921 negotiations with Britain, Husayn Rushdi Pasha had included an article giving Egypt priority over certain Sudanese exports, such as livestock and cereals.[100] As the hopes for increased trade with the Sudan intensified in the latter 1930s, so too did the frequency of expressions of economic interdependence. Mirroring the earlier sentiments of Rushdi Pasha, Fu'ad Abaza wrote in October 1935 that "the Sudan is in great need of Egyptian produce and cannot manage without our silk industry and various cotton textiles. Also the Sudanese cannot do without the cereals which are grown in Egypt, just as Egypt in many cases needs Sudanese grains and the import of livestock from [the Sudan] in most seasons of the year."[101] The Egyptian government aimed to establish permanent markets for each other's commodities as a method of improving the general welfare of all inhabitants of the valley.[102] The claim of being able to supply each other's needs, essentially forming a unified economic territory, fit in well with the nationalist agenda of Egyptians at that time. The government's financial committee made exactly this claim in the budgetary report presented on 20 June 1938. This report stated in respect to Egyptian–Sudanese commerce that it was "hoped to extend the range of this trade in particular and that Egypt and the Sudan are in reality nothing short of a single economic unit and each region can offer to the other what is needed in the way of commodities."[103] This supposed natural dependence of the two countries was one justification for the efforts to establish an accepted principle of favoring local commodities in Egyptian–Sudanese commerce.

However, the other major impetus for these efforts was the desire to break the hold foreign competitors had on the region's commerce. From 1935 onward, Egyptians consistently advocated preference for local commodities over foreign products in the markets generally and, especially, in the filling of government tenders. In September 1936 the Cairo Chamber of Commerce wrote that in each country the principle of preference for each other's products over similar foreign products was being established.[104] The permanent committee was especially concerned about making "contact with the Sudanese government to work on the preference of Egyptian products in tenders of the Sudanese government."[105] A good example of these efforts was the attempt to gain the Sudanese administration's agreement to use

Egyptian cement instead of foreign imports. Alfonse Girgis complained at various permanent committee meetings that despite the availability and inexpensive price of Egyptian cement, the Sudan administration continued to import British supplies. In the 4 June 1938 meeting the Condominium's response to these accusations was presented, stating that "Egyptian cement is used in many situations, except for those dedicated to some special purposes which require the utilization of British portland cement only."[106] Interested Egyptian parties never obtained governmental acquiescence to their hope of complete reliance on local supplies when available. Still, by 1938 the two governments were close to agreement on basic principles of preferential treatment for local bids in official tenders. In July 1938 the minister of commerce and industry noted that Law 8 of 1937 had laid a foundation for giving priority to Sudanese suppliers over those of other countries in Egyptian government tenders and hoped that the Sudanese administration would follow suit. The minister went on to outline the 'concrete' steps being taken by his ministry.

> The Sudanese articles in Egyptian government tenders are treated preferentially if the quality was similar and the increase in price [over other bidders] did not exceed 10%, and we requested from the government of the Sudan that this practice be applied to our products. This request is [currently] the subject of research within the above mentioned government.[107]

Although slow progress was apparent in gaining priority for local goods in government tenders, the private sector's trade with the Sudan presented to Egyptians a much larger potential field for profits if preferential treatment could be attained. On 31 January 1938, the permanent committee's chair, 'Abd al-Wahhab Pasha, requested the preparation of a report on commerce between the two countries and "especially the articles which the Sudan imports from countries other than Egypt [which] are found in Egypt, because he believes there are many articles which the Sudan consumes from [abroad], whereas their importation from Egypt is possible."[108] With these reports assembled and assessed, the permanent committee noted that foreign suppliers of certain commodities dominated Sudanese markets. Furthermore, some of these commodities—cotton textiles, cigarettes, soap, cement, shoes, and confectioneries—were manufacturing spheres in which Egyptians had made great strides, just not in exporting to Sudanese markets.[109]

Much of the failure in achieving preferential treatment for local goods at this time was due to the Sudanese administration's continued adherence to 'free trade' doctrines. Condominium officials never seriously changed their commitment to free trade principles in Sudanese markets, although they also remained reluctant to award any preferential treatment to Egyptians in state purchases. On the bright side, in 1938 the Egyptian minister of commerce and industry reported that in recent communication the Sudanese government had reiterated the "esteem, distinction, and sympathy" given to bids from Egyptian traders. However, the minister wrote that such "sympathy" was not sufficient, and his ministry continued to press for the promulgation of a Sudanese decree guaranteeing the Condominium's adherence to a policy of priority for Egyptian products.[110] According to 'Abdallah Fakri Abaza, prior to the Second World War the most beneficial assurance the Sudan administration agreed to was "the equality in treatment between the Egyptian and English products in the tenders of the Sudanese government."[111]

With the outbreak of the Second World War the terminology employed by officials and interested parties changed. Discussions increasingly focused on 'provisions' or 'wartime supplies,' but *priority* for Nile Valley interdependence remained the objective of Egyptian nationalists. Even before the war, the Egyptian government claimed that in periods of restricted commerce it should have control over all aspects of Nile Valley trade.[112] When the conflict began in Europe, representatives from Middle Eastern countries attended a number of meetings in Cairo. Subsequently, conversations took place between Egyptian officials and British administrators of the Sudan. At this time the Sudanese government agreed "to give Egypt priority over other regions in regard to the importation of its needs first from the produce of the Sudan and requested notice of the amounts which Egypt needs."[113] In February 1940 the Cairo Chamber of Commerce reported on the success of these negotiations and especially Egypt's import of Sudanese livestock to replace quantities it could not obtain from other regions.[114] Egyptians reciprocated this priority in satisfying Nile Valley demands. In July 1942 the Egyptian Ministry of Supplies wrote that at the outbreak of war the Sudan agreed to supply Egypt's market "with what it needed of Sudanese products, especially livestock, dhurra, sesame, and oleaginous grains, in return for Egypt's undertaking to export what exceeds its needs in the way of products which are indispensable for the Sudan, like sugar, cotton seed oil, wheat flour, and others."[115]

The economic expert in the Sudan summarized in 1943 the Egyptian rationale for giving priority to local markets before engaging in commercial relations with other countries.[116] First, close relations with the Sudan were a "natural" phenomenon. Second, according to Egyptian–British agreements on the administration of the Sudan, there were to be no customs barriers between the two countries; therefore restrictions on exports to the Sudan lacked legality. Also, Egypt formed a natural market for Sudanese produce, so giving this market priority during the war would not be disruptive. Finally, foodstuffs the Sudan provided to Egypt would indirectly assist the war effort through easing the hardships of the population. Despite the arguments put forward, Egyptian–Sudanese commercial relations encountered difficulties because the foreign powers controlling the Middle East viewed stability of regional commerce as the dominant concern.

The Middle East Supply Center (MESC), based in Cairo, became the overriding economic authority in the region during the war—and beyond. The Egyptian government (and British military authorities) generally followed the center's dictates, and "in April 1941 the Sudan's trade was brought under the aegis of the Middle East Supply Centre which was responsible for co-ordinating the import requirements of the countries in its area of operation."[117] Supervision of the Nile Valley economy by external authorities continued beyond the conclusion of the Second World War. For instance, the MESC controlled the export of cattle and sheep from the Sudan, a critical issue for Egypt, until August 1946.[118] In addition, with the end of the war the British Supply Mission (Middle East) assumed functions previously held by the MESC.[119] In whatever guise, foreign authorities typically sought to ensure regional economic stability through the use of import and export controls. Obviously, such controls conflicted with the previously declared desire of Egyptians for an increasingly autonomous Egyptian–Sudanese economy.

During the war some officials voiced complaints over the failure of the Sudan to meet Egyptian needs. Egypt's dire need of Sudanese produce and the Condominium administration's laxity in satisfying this demand were apparent in official correspondence. The economic expert Mahmud Zaki reported sending

> a letter to the government of the Sudan dated 8 July 1943 in which I requested that the government of the Sudan allocate to Egypt all of the excess of its crops of oleaginous grains for the 1943 and 1944 seasons, in order to take preventive measures against the danger of an anticipated scarcity in oils needed as food and for the soap industry in the coming season. I have not received a response yet.[120]

Egypt's dependence on Sudanese livestock was also apparent but seemingly not given great importance by Sudanese officials. In a letter to the governor-general in 1943, it was noted that the failure to meet Egyptian needs was attributable to insufficiencies of transportation. Some evidence, however, points to the Sudan simply putting greater emphasis on satisfying military requirements. The economic expert reported that in 1942 it had been possible to increase the import of Sudanese livestock "allocated for British forces by nearly three times what it was in 1941," but that imports during the first eight months of 1943 had fallen below normal levels.[121] It seems clear that the Sudanese administration (under MESC supervision) restricted exports to Egypt when necessary. The Egyptian Ministry of Supplies proposed in 1942 removing "the prohibition on the export of resources needed by Egypt from the Sudan (in the forefront of which were dhurra, sesame, peanuts and livestock), just as is actually occurring in respect to the exports of Egypt to the Sudan."[122]

Sudanese exports to Egypt were restricted because of MESC authorities giving regional needs the utmost attention. Wartime meetings in Cairo and Khartoum frequently addressed regional economic issues—not those of the Nile Valley alone.[123] Egyptians complained bitterly of what they felt were misplaced priorities. The 1943 report of Egypt's expert in the Sudan emphasized Egypt's claimed priority over other markets in obtaining excess Sudanese produce:

> Concerning the export of Sudanese crops to Egypt, I have had every interest in [obtaining] confirmation of Egypt's right to have priority over other foreign countries in the acquisition of excess Sudanese crops which Egypt continues to need. In reality it is absolutely not permissible that Egypt is placed on equal footing with Palestine, Syria, or other foreign countries.[124]

Yet the evidence leads to the conclusion that Egypt was indeed, at best, on an equal footing with the others. Muhammad Fakri Abaza, a vehement critic of Egypt's wartime supply policies, told his parliamentary colleagues in 1942 that

> the Egyptian government has not succeeded throughout the period of the war in importing a thing for us from the Sudan, . . . and there are resources and food supplies in the Sudan with which Eritrea, Abyssinia and Congo are aided. [The supplies] even pass by you here in Egypt on their way to Palestine. This is an exceptionally strange situation.[125]

The directing of Sudanese supplies to other countries was primarily due to MESC instructions, yet 'free market' forces were involved to some extent. For instance, the Egyptian expert in the Sudan noted that there was little chance of importing *masli* (clarified butter) because Darfur province, the largest producer of this product in the Sudan, exported a large portion through French Sudan (Chad) to Palestine, where it was sold for a significantly higher price.[126] Guaranteeing Egyptian priority in obtaining Sudanese produce obviously entailed denying the primacy of free market forces, and doing so required the participation or acquiescence of both Egyptian and Sudanese administrations. Clearly it would be easier for a single unified administration to 'combat' free market forces in its commercial policies. Unfortunately for Egyptians, there was no unified national administration of the Nile Valley and, therefore, little chance of Egyptian precedence over Sudanese produce.

Wartime obstacles encountered by Egyptian nationalists seeking priority for their country over Sudanese excess produce were mirrored by similar difficulties in Egypt claiming a position of primary supplier of Sudanese needs. At the outbreak of the war Egypt's prospects in the Sudan appeared rather bright. Egypt's continued industrial development since the First World War and post-1935 emphasis on developing ties with the Sudan were coupled with the latter's "loss of long-established sources of supply of some primary imports."[127] Administrative measures during the Second World War were again the main obstacle to the development of greater Egyptian–Sudanese dependency. In 1939 the Egyptian government issued a law that "forbade the export of some articles to foreign countries except by permission of the minister of finance."[128] The economic expert in the Sudan claimed in 1943 that this law did not apply to the Sudan, writing that "Egypt had [in the past] and still does export all commodities and goods to the Sudan without need of permission from the minister of finance."[129] Although Egyptians maintained that wartime commercial restrictions did not apply to the Sudan, Governor-General Huddleston felt it "necessary to insist upon the issue of import licenses for certain categories of imported goods."[130] These measures, like the Condominium's restrictions on Sudanese exports, were a consistent target of Egyptian critics. In a 1943 letter to the governor-general, after citing Egypt's continuing assistance to the Sudan, the economic expert claimed that no obstacles should be imposed on Egyptian products "for which a market continues to be found in the Sudan and which continue to be sent by non-sea routes."[131] By 1944 an Egyptian committee on exports to the Sudan was pressing Condominium officials to lift Sudanese import restrictions, claiming this was an unjust practice since the Sudan was a part of Egypt.[132]

Obviously, whether or not the Sudan was a part of Egypt would eventually have to be decided, but Egyptian nationalists worked to increase economic interdependence as a means of encouraging a favorable future decision. However, Egyptian efforts to gain recognition of the primacy of local markets remained elusive from the time of the first missions until the end of the Second World War and beyond. Both countries remained largely 'tied' to areas outside of the Nile Valley. The failure to develop an increasingly dependent relationship, one more independent of the international economy, was at least partially due to a lack of commitment from the administrations.

Ignorance of Market Conditions and Active Merchants

Egyptian nationalists' efforts to overcome the general ignorance of local market conditions in Egypt and the Sudan were less dependent on government support. During the interwar period Egyptians employed various means of raising awareness of current economic trends and future potentials. Egyptians worked toward the creation of a larger market for their products in the Sudan through improved advertising. As early as 1920, the high commissioner for Egypt had noted the failure of local merchants to effectively publicize their goods.[133] Despite early criticism of advertising practices among the local entrepreneurs, most serious efforts to promote their commodities in the Sudan did not commence until the post-1935 period. By that time Egyptians increasingly viewed advertising as a key means of combating foreign competition in various Sudanese markets. For instance, one reason for Japan's dominance in the Sudan's textile trade was the lower prices of its products, which Hasan Saqr, director of the Sudan Agency within the Ministry of Commerce and Industry, hoped to counter by emphasizing the equally low quality of Japanese goods through "effective superior publicity."[134] Khartoum exhibition director 'Ali Mawardi included among the factors in poor sales of Egyptian manufactures "their lack of adherence to modern methods of commercial publicity."[135] However, 'modern' advertising alone would not solve the limited commercial interaction between Egypt and the Sudan.

Egyptians needed comprehensive knowledge of Sudanese market conditions and effective transmission of supply and demand information between Egypt and the Sudan. Lack of familiarity with conditions in the Sudan was a serious problem for Egypt. Egyptian prime minister Muhammad Fahmi Nukrashi stated in 1947 that British officials had so isolated the Sudan for decades that "even the Government in Cairo finds difficulty in getting through official channels the information to which it is entitled."[136] The private sector had experienced similar difficulties getting information for years. As early as 1924 the editors of *al-Majalla al-tijariya al-nubiya* wrote that "many have requested that we set aside a section in the magazine for the publication of general and specialized news of the Sudan."[137] In a speech to members of Egypt's first mission to the Sudan eleven years later, Mr. Kontomichalos, president of the Sudanese Chamber of Commerce, expressed great hopes for the future but lamented Egyptians' continued ignorance of the Sudan: "The Egyptians speak a lot about the Sudan, but few of them are sufficiently familiar with our living conditions and the circumstances of life here. I am certain some of them do not have a correct notion of the progress which the country has achieved since the re-establishment of the occupation."[138]

A correct notion of the Sudanese economic situation was certainly still absent at that time. A June 1935 article in *al-Siyasa* stressed that local merchants needed to know specifically what produce of Egypt and the Sudan could be profitably traded and could replace foreign imports.[139] A critical institution in developing improved market awareness was the Khartoum exhibition and office. However, this office reported in 1940 a continuing inability to assess local market conditions.[140] The office director hinted that one obstacle to the development of greater familiarity with specific needs was the absence of commercial liaisons in Khartoum. He stated that Egyptian imports remained limited "and the precise determination of their prices is not possible, due to the absence of agents on whom reliance is possible in preparing reports. [This is] because the merchants here request what they need in the way of Egyptian commodities from the traders in Egypt directly."[141] Given that official bodies encountered such problems, some Egyptians advocated resorting to radio broadcasts, various publications, or specific individuals as avenues to improve awareness of market conditions.

Some journals, newspapers, and other publications attempted to inform local entrepreneurs of specific market demands and merchandise available. There was little administrative interference in this process, although at times postal rates on printed material were raised.[142] In 1921 *al-Majalla al-tijariya al-nubiya*, published in Cairo, produced a couple of articles on general economic conditions in the Sudan. These articles included details on agricultural production, currencies in circulation, weights and measures used, and the market situation (including where and how often major local markets were held).[143] In August 1936, *al-Siyasa* reported that "after Hasan Sabhi, the former director of the Sudanese newspaper *(The Nile)*, returned from the Sudan, he wanted to work on the strengthening of relations between Egypt and the Sudan. [Therefore,] he opened an office for the presentation of reports, which were requested of him, about all activities in the Sudan."[144] Information on the general situation in the Sudan was certainly an improvement, but the Egyptian entrepreneurs involved after 1935 wanted increased promotional, rather than merely informational, efforts to strengthen Nile Valley commerce.

According to Fu'ad Abaza, the publication of the letters and telegraphs of the 1935 mission had "the greatest influence in notifying the Egyptian and Sudanese people of the activities of the mission and its deliberations."[145] The Royal Agricultural Society believed the information gathered on Sudanese economic conditions during the 1935 mission was so beneficial to Egyptians that it decided to allocate "an amount of LE250 in advance to Mr. 'Abdallah Husayn the lawyer who wrote a book about the Sudan on the occasion of his accompanying the Egyptian mission to the Sudan."[146] Of this amount LE150 was to go directly to the author, while the remainder was used for copies of the book to be distributed to society members and interested individuals. In April 1938 an announcement for another book on the Sudan appeared. This book covered the activities of the permanent committee of the Sudan, included "administrative and commercial information and a comprehensive description of the conditions of the population . . . and complete customs information and commercial statistics," and recorded the names and addresses of many merchants and businesses of the Sudan.[147] During the permanent committee's March 1938 meeting in Khartoum, the Sudanese Chamber of Commerce encouraged Egyptian members to take greater notice of its monthly magazine, which included "regular reports on the state of the market with detailed statistics."[148]

Not only did the chambers of commerce, permanent committee, and other groups hope to raise awareness of general market conditions, they also employed various media specifically to sell Egyptian goods in the Sudan. Egypt's economic leaders utilized radio broadcasts, but this method had limited utility in promoting local commodities. 'Abdallah Fakri Abaza wrote that Egyptian broadcasts to the Sudan spanned only two hours every night, due to the lack of powerful transmitters. At the same time he noted that the Sudanese listen to news and specialized information on prices of various products night and day, but "they receive news of Egypt and its conditions by way of foreign broadcast stations."[149] Foreign sources of information could not be expected to promote Egypt's products, but Egyptians had a newly established presence in the Sudan capable of doing just that—the economic expert and the Khartoum exhibition office.

Coupled with the permanent committee and other initiatives from Cairo, this presence in Khartoum had the potential to increase publicity for Egyptian goods. In 1939 the committee proposed that Bank Misr and its companies send the economic expert all publications on their products.[150] Actually, local merchants placed greater stock in the abilities of the Khartoum exhibition office director because he resided in the Sudan more continuously and, consequently, had closer contacts with local traders. In addition to his other duties, Egyptians expected the director physically to visit local markets in order to ascertain their needs and to determine what Egyptian products could be exported to them.[151] Based on his familiarity with their Sudanese counterparts, Egyptian merchants hoped that he would become a facilitator of exports to the Sudan. For instance, the editors of *al-Jarida al-tijariya al-misriya* thought that the Khartoum office could supervise and encourage advertisements for Egyptian agricultural and industrial produce, especially during periods of lessened foreign competition.[152] The Cairo Chamber of Commerce described its relations to the director and his duties in this manner:

> The director of the office undertakes to tour the regions of the Sudan in order to become familiar with its needs. He sends the reports about it one after another, and the Cairo Chamber undertakes to print these reports and distribute them to those who are interested in the matter. And the result of this is that the Egyptian manufactures find a good market in Sudanese quarters.[153]

The chambers of commerce, the permanent committee, and others envisioned the Khartoum office director as a liaison of sorts—promoting Egyptian products, but also assisting in the transmission of market demands and the development of commercial contacts.

More comprehensive market knowledge without the development of real, active contacts between entrepreneurs would not improve Nile Valley trade. One method of establishing such contacts was simply the exchange of names of merchants, industrialists, and so forth. Egyptians expected that the Khartoum office director would not only furnish reports on market conditions but also provide interested Sudanese with "the names of Egyptian traders and industrialists."[154] The process of developing direct contacts between merchants and manufacturers had begun with the 1935 economic mission. In a meeting of mission members and Sudanese representatives on 13 February 1935, the three chambers of commerce agreed to exchange "lists of the names of traders of Khartoum, Cairo, and Alexandria."[155] Direct contacts with their counterparts in the Sudan would assist Egyptian merchants in identifying and satisfying the variable market demands.

In addition to exchanging lists of merchants, Egyptians realized that direct, personal, and consistent contacts linking local industrialists and Sudanese markets were needed. In 1939 the permanent committee decided that officials dispatched to tour Sudanese markets should carry product samples for local traders and should strive both "to establish direct relations between the Sudanese merchant and the Egyptian producer and to supply the former with all information about the kinds of commodities and their prices."[156] In June 1938, 'Abd al-Majid al-Rimali of the Cairo Chamber of Commerce noted the "necessity of appointing an employee in Egypt to facilitate the establishment of contacts with Egyptian factories and to concern himself with the reports arriving from Khartoum, and their transmission to manufacturers."[157] In fact by December 1939 the Cairo chamber decided that one of its employees would assume this duty of transmitting pertinent information to Egyptian industrialists. Also, this official worked on "supplying the permanent office in Khartoum with [the Egyptian industrialists'] products, more rapidity in the sending of these products, and the successful fulfillment of contracts."[158]

The development of active contacts and transmission of market information between regions was especially important for greater commercial autonomy in the Nile Valley. It was essential that interested parties were aware of the specific merchandise desired, the potential sources of supply, and especially government announcements for the submission of bids. Fu'ad Abaza stated on 25 April 1935 that during the economic mission members of the Sudanese Chamber of Commerce identified two methods by which Egyptians could obtain information on government invitations for bids. Egyptians could subscribe to Sudanese newspapers directly, or the Sudanese Chamber of Commerce could forward copies of the announcements to its Egyptian counterparts.[159] The permanent committee noted later that information on Sudanese government tenders could also be transmitted "by means of agents residing in the Sudan."[160] Besides information on government tenders, the "presence of local agents for Egyptian manufactures in Khartoum" would also insure the timely submission of the contracted merchandise.[161]

These local agents or Egyptian merchants actually in the Sudan were potentially the best means of gathering information on market conditions and reacting to it advantageously. However, these individuals could also be detrimental to efforts to increase trade with the Sudan. In 1937 an article in a Sudanese newspaper, *Hadarat al-Sudan*, included complaints about agreements made with Egyptian commercial agents who demanded 40 percent of a shipment's costs in advance but who then would ultimately send nothing, less than the agreed amount, or goods of inferior quality.[162] The Cairo Chamber of Commerce took some measures to remedy this problem, such as having the Sudan government refrain from granting visas to merchants until after checking on their reputation through the Egyptian chambers. Apparently the remedies had little lasting effect, because in 1940 Sudanese merchants were still complaining "that some traders in Egypt send to the Sudan the worst of what they have in the way of products" and that after signing agreements the Egyptians would raise the prices of goods, which led some Sudanese to use other sources of supply.[163]

The negative ramifications of some Egyptians' trading practices continued to bedevil efforts to strengthen Nile Valley economic unity. In 1947 and 1950 the Cairo chamber was still printing reports of unscrupulous Egyptian trading agents, and the economic expert warned of the "tremendous influence in weakening the marketability of Egyptian products and in the reluctance of [Sudanese] traders to import them" because of the continued illegal practices of some Egyptian traders.[164] 'Ali al-Barir, a member of the 1935 mission to the Sudan and a merchant active there for years, disagreed with the expert's assessment of this problem. He stated that "the subject [of Sudanese being taken advantage of by Egyptian merchants] is trivial, is of limited scope, and is composed of small-time [Sudanese] traders doing business with any Egyptian agent who travels to the Sudan for a short period without any previous experience; and [the subject] does not deserve investigation nor spending of time."[165] Whether or not 'Ali al-Barir was correct, the Cairo chamber and government agencies continued to view the issue as important enough to warrant offering certificates to reputable Egyptian merchants.[166] Furthermore, if the practices described above were true, this would nullify the anticipated increased exports and improved Sudanese market knowledge derived from more Egyptian commercial agents residing in the Sudan.

This assessment of efforts to improve awareness of local economic conditions has not focused on increasing Sudanese exports to Egypt for a couple of reasons. First, direct contact between merchants (or industrialists) would have been just as potentially beneficial to the Sudan's exports as to Egypt's exports. Likewise, the various publications describing the Sudanese economy included the nature and quantity of supplies present, as well as specific market demands. Also, the Sudan's dominant export, cotton, was controlled by foreign interests and not directed toward Egyptian markets. Finally, Sudanese exports consisted mainly of agricultural goods and livestock—and trade levels were largely dependent on supplies of such commodities in each region and, therefore, were much more resistant to manipulation.

Still, there were some efforts to increase Sudanese exports through raising awareness of commodities potentially traded with Egypt. As early as 1920, Condominium officials reported Sudanese participation in commercial exhibits of the Egyptian government.[167] However, as in other matters, greater activity was apparent after 1935. In meetings before the first mission's departure, the Royal Agricultural Society decided that Sudanese involvement in a proposed exhibition of the society would be included in the array of forthcoming Sudan-directed efforts. To encourage Sudanese participation in this exhibition the society was able to obtain a 50 percent rate reduction for passengers and commodities on Egyptian and Sudanese railroads and Nile steamships.[168] This exposition of Sudanese goods did not take place until 1936. The governor-general reported that "an exhibition of Sudanese produce, most of which was arranged by the [Sudanese] Chamber, was shown at the exhibition of the Royal Agricultural Society of Egypt in Cairo in February and March."[169] Additional exhibitions in Egypt of Sudanese goods took place between this date and the start of the Second World War, but wartime conditions resulted in a suspension of these activities for almost a decade.

On 1 March 1949, a major economic exhibition began in Cairo. Based on local media coverage, the exhibition clearly was intended to highlight the progress achieved by the Egyptian economy. The Cairo Chamber of Commerce claimed that although major expositions of Egyptian manufactures had occurred in 1931 and 1936, this new undertaking was the most important since 1926. Detailed descriptions of the goods to be displayed in the 1949 exhibition highlight the expected dominance of Egyptian products, but organizers attempted at least to include the Sudan in this 'national' event. The Alexandria Chamber of Commerce described the intentions behind the 1949 exhibition as

> the deep widespread desire within society and the government to give the exhibition a purely nationalist hue, not fanatical and not hatred of cooperation with foreigners, but desirous that the exhibition be a clear representation of the nationalist effort and to facilitate . . . the representation of the southern part of the valley by allocating a worthy position for our Sudanese brothers in the "Wadi Nil" section, which depicts the north and south of the valley.[170]

Organizers designed the "Wadi Nil" section of the exhibition as a geographically determined arrangement of commodities produced in the Nile Valley, including products from the delta to the southernmost regions of the

Sudan. In describing expectations of this exhibition, the same Alexandria chamber article noted the satisfaction with which true nationalists would greet this physical representation of the economic unity of the valley.[171] However, reports of the Sudanese goods displayed in 1949 indicated less than sterling results in publicizing Sudanese economic potentials. Despite a prominent position at the end of "Wadi Nil" and a magnificent structure raised there by the Sudanese Chamber of Commerce, the goods displayed tended to be of an 'exotic' nature (not exportable to Egypt on a large scale) and relatively few in number. One report was rather pointedly critical of the organizers, stating that "it was possible *with a little effort* to give prominence to the wealth of the Sudan in the exhibit and to portray the special characteristics and lifestyle there."[172] The 1949 exhibition is representative of most efforts to establish institutional supports for furthering Egyptian–Sudanese economic bonds—late, limited, and ultimately ineffectual.

Organized economic missions after 1935 contributed to increased contacts between entrepreneurs of the regions but were a rather tardy development. The establishment of the permanent committee and the appointment of an economic expert in Khartoum just before the Second World War constituted the Egyptian government's institutional arrangements for strengthening Nile Valley economic connections. However, for a variety of reasons, which cannot be attributed to British Condominium officials, these new bureaucratic entities were also ineffective in unifying the economies. The Khartoum exhibition of Egyptian goods and its director were somewhat more successful than the other pre–Second World War institutions. However, even in this case there was little genuine success in developing economic interdependence, or even a more comprehensive understanding of regional conditions. The institutions established by the 1936 treaty or soon after had raised the hopes of Egyptian nationalists and certainly would serve as the primary forum for discussing relations with the Sudan. The actual progress in developing infrastructure, stimulating investments, or increasing commerce would be the true test of these institutions' effectiveness—and these results were crucial in determining not only the economic but also the political future of the Nile Valley.

4 A Valley Divided: Transportation Difficulties

Without a doubt among the foremost factors in unifying Egypt and the Sudan in every respect is the improvement of transportation, as the current means are slow moving and long, to say nothing of the excessive costs. . . .

The permanent committee of the Sudan has not allowed any opportunity to pass without emphasizing the great importance of linking Egypt with the Sudan by railroad because of the various economic, social, and national benefits of such—especially what this span offers in facilitating the movement of commercial goods between the two regions and easing the transport of travelers to a couple hours instead of two whole days.

—'Abdallah Fakri Abaza, former Egyptian economic expert in the Sudan, 1940[1]

With specific institutions finally established and personnel appointed for the improvement of relations with the Sudan by the mid-1930s, Egyptian nationalists were poised to begin remedying specific obstacles that undermined the economic unity of the Nile Valley. As 'Abdallah Fakri Abaza indicated in his 1940 study, Egyptians clearly understood that inexpensive and efficient transportation between Egyptian and Sudanese regions was essential. They knew that policies, procedures, and the actual facilities for transportation of produce, manufactures, workers, merchants, officials, and others had to be improved. The concerted Egyptian interest that emerged in the mid-1930s encountered transportation policies or procedures established decades earlier that continued to discourage travel or commercial exchange. Both Condominium and Egyptian officials had enacted policies to protect their people or their industries, not necessarily those of their northern or southern 'brothers.' Additionally, the Egyptian and Sudanese administrations consistently viewed transportation policies as means of producing revenues, rather than of improving economic relations with one another. The same assessment could be made of the actual infrastructure established by each administration. Railroad facilities, harbor construction, and the development of roads in each country were centered on the production and export of cotton and the import and distribution of manufactured goods. These economic activities dominated transportation and produced the greatest revenue for the state. Subsequently, from brief investigation of transportation facilities and policies an objective observer would have to conclude that Egypt and the Sudan were separate entities. This was a situation Egypt's economic elite hoped to rectify.

Egyptians were certainly well aware of the importance of transportation—for both their internal economic development and their hopes of improved relations with the Sudan. The commission studying trade and industry during the First World War had written that either the government or private interests should improve local rail, river, and motorized transportation capabilities "because the actual situation is not advantageous for our commerce."[2] Improving transportation capabilities would necessitate attention to rates, reliability, regulations, and so forth, but Egyptian businessmen were most concerned with the actual facilities available. And as this economic elite became more interested in developing ties with the Sudan specifically in the 1930s, shortcomings in facilities were blatantly apparent. A 1935 meeting of concerned individuals, which would later become the permanent committee, discussed a range of transportation issues central to improved commerce with the Sudan. This committee's report directed attention toward

> the facilitation of lines of communication, the necessity of connecting the Egyptian railways to the Sudanese railways between Shellal and Wadi Halfa, the extension of telephone lines between Egypt and the Sudan and the reduction of their fees and the fees for telegraphic communications, and road construction for the passage of cars. And in general, the facilitation of means of transport by land, sea, river, and air.[3]

Clearly, increasing trade with the Sudan required extensive improvements in various means of communication and transportation.

Travel Restrictions

The lack of a direct, efficient connection between Shellal and Wadi Halfa was the most glaring deficiency of Nile Valley transport in the mid-1930s, but many long-established policies and procedures were equally frustrating to Egyptian hopes of strengthened economic relations with the Sudan. For instance, the Condominium administration maintained firm control over the entry and movement of persons within the Sudan. The primary means of accomplishing this was through the Passports and Permits Ordinance of 1922. With the exception of military personnel, civil servants, and their families, this regulation mandated that "no person shall enter or re-enter the Sudan without permission, and such permission may be refused without reason assigned by the authority competent."[4] The authorities controlling permission to enter were the Sudan agent in Cairo and the governors of the Halfa and Red Sea provinces. Condominium officials completely barred Egyptians from entering the Sudan briefly in the aftermath of the 1924 unrest. Egyptian travel to the Sudan was generally permissible, but because Sudanese laws—especially travel regulations—were so "foreign," one local newspaper advised that prospective travelers become familiar with these rules before proceeding to the Sudan.[5] In addition to supervising entry procedures, the Condominium determined where people could travel within the Sudan. Section 22 of the Passports and Permits Ordinance authorized the governor-general to declare any part of the Sudan completely closed to non-native travelers and to restrict when and what "classes" of people could enter certain areas.[6] Clearly utilization of such powers would limit where Egyptians developed commercial relations.

Local commercial groups placed particular importance on eliminating procedural difficulties associated with travel to the Sudan. The 1934 annual report of the Sudanese Chamber of Commerce stated that barriers to the travel of Egyptians to the Sudan should be lifted, reasoning that "their presence here and their interests contribute greatly to the development and the prosperity of the Sudan."[7] Egyptians worked to abolish travel restrictions, but they also believed simplifying procedures could more quickly facilitate travel. Members of the 1935 mission to the Sudan lobbied for the Condominium administration's "acceptance of identification certificates from the Cairo and Alexandria Chambers of Commerce instead of passports, thereby facilitating travel by traders between the two countries."[8] Travel problems were a central concern of the 26 February 1938 meeting of the permanent committee. Although Condominium and Egyptian officials had permitted travel between the two regions generally, procedural difficulties remained. During the February 1938 meeting Fu'ad Abaza suggested that "all of those desiring to travel who were merchants should obtain a certificate from the Chamber of Commerce, whereas for others the certificate of the *'umdah* [village head] should be enough."[9] Besides the basic documentation required for travel, the acquisition of permits was also problematic. The chair of the committee reiterated the need to simplify the acquisition of permits for commercial travel specifically when he noted that "there are two types of travelers, one is he who travels for the establishment of residence and the other is he who travels for touring. . . . We must work toward the facilitation of travel for the second type."[10] The inconvenience of various documents and permits was not confined to Egyptians planning to visit the Sudan. In 1940 Condominium officials imposed seemingly minor procedures in the way of passenger traffic to Egypt. The passports office of the Sudanese government decreed that "it is not permissible for any individual to travel north of Halfa except with his possession of an Egyptian visa to enter or pass through the Kingdom of Egypt."[11] This measure may have been only a minor nuisance to travelers since these 'transit visas' were issued free of charge to Egyptians, Sudanese, and officials employed by the Sudanese government. Yet, when such 'visas' are added to customs inspections, physical hardships, and high costs, it becomes clear that travel between the regions was not an entirely painless process.[12]

The Second World War did little to ameliorate travel along the Nile Valley. In fact, during the conflict merchants were singled out in the process of defining restrictions on travel to the Sudan. A 1943 government memorandum noted that "there are no stipulations for granting visas to Egyptians, with the exception of traders who desire to go to the Sudan to carry out commerce there. Their requests are forwarded to the responsible authorities in Khartoum prior to granting permits for practicing the profession of trade."[13] The end of the conflict did not result in the immediate lifting of control over the movement of traders and others in the Sudan. An Egyptian Ministry of Finance parliamentary report in December 1948 stated that transit trade along the Nile Valley had increased during the past year because the licensing system imposed during the war had finally been repealed.[14] In a 1950 interview on improving economic relations between Egypt and the Sudan, Ahmad al-Tawil, one of the more active merchants in the Sudan, was still emphasizing the need for "freedom of travel between halves of the Nile Valley for all individuals without special visas, whether the travel is by sea, air, or railroad."[15] Members of a single, unified nation might expect to enjoy freedom of travel within the entirety of their country. However, Egyptians and Sudanese did not constitute such a nation, and their governments continued to treat their respective regions as separate entities. Condominium officials claimed Egyptians were treated fairly in Sudanese regions, permitting them just as wide a range of movement as any other 'foreigner' in the country. For instance, in response to merchants' requests to repeal restrictions, Governor-General Huddleston wrote in 1944 that "no difficulties are placed in the way of Egyptians travelling to the Sudan, and any control to which they are subject is imposed on all travelers alike—including British."[16]

Greater freedom of travel might have given Egyptians a slight advantage over foreign interests in the competition for Sudanese markets. Yet, despite Huddleston's claims, the evidence suggests that foreign residents of the Sudan enjoyed either equality with Egyptians or even greater ease of travel. Before the war, a 1938 report to the permanent committee from the foreigner-dominated Sudanese Chamber of Commerce recommended it "be permitted to foreign residents in the Sudan . . . that they need not obtain Egyptian permission when passing through Egypt on their return to the Sudan," as long as they paid entry duties.[17] In 1943, Mahmud Zaki reported that the Sudan's foreign community was seeking additional changes to travel regulations. Included in their desires were a special "business type" passport, permission for travel to Egypt more than once a year, and the granting of return visas by Egypt before their departure.[18] In the same report it was noted that the Egyptian government had accepted most of their requests in principle and that it was undertaking measures to facilitate travel by foreign residents of the Sudan to and through Egypt.[19] The issuance of Sudanese passports also facilitated foreigners' travel to and from the Sudan. Port officials in Alexandria reported a limited number of such passports in the possession of foreign merchants as early as 1927.[20] Almost twenty years later, the Sudanese administration was still issuing a significant number of such passports to "persons of foreign extraction permanently resident in the Sudan."[21] By the post–Second World War era, the Condominium's authority to issue a Sudanese passport—certainly detrimental to Egyptian sovereignty claims—was an increasingly contentious diplomatic topic. Still, passports and other measures simplifying travel procedures seemed to provide the foreign competitors of Egyptian merchants in the Sudan with a definite advantage.

Another obstacle that certainly did little to encourage Egyptian travel to the Sudan was the passenger rates on the railroad systems. Although fourth-class passenger rates are of relevance in assessing issues such as Egyptian fellaheen emigration to the Sudan, local merchants and other entrepreneurs were interested in lowering first- through third-class rates. 'Abdallah Fakri Abaza's report on the Sudan noted that its rates were generally 20 percent higher than those in Egypt.[22] He wrote that such high transport rates had far-reaching consequences for the public in a poor country with few means of transport and wide distances to cross.[23] He also stated that working for lowered rates would provide "important advantages for the commerce, agriculture, and related spheres of activity."[24] In addition to general rate reductions, advantageous to all Sudanese commercial activity, Egyptians sought reductions specifically between the Sudan and Egypt. The rates did not appear to be excessively high, but both Egyptians and Sudanese argued that lowering rates would stimulate commerce.[25] A March 1938 report indicated that the Sudanese Chamber of Commerce was seeking rate reductions for merchants traveling to Egypt during certain seasons of the year.[26] The Alexandria Chamber of Commerce proposed to both governments that they reduce the price of "tickets in the first class between Egypt and the Sudan by 15 to 25 percent."[27] By July 1939 the Egyptian government had agreed to a 50 percent reduction in the fares charged, and the Sudan had consented to a 40 percent reduction.[28] The lowering of passenger rates remained a concern of various interested groups, but commodity rates were even more important for commerce between Egypt and the Sudan.

Procedural requirements and passenger rates continued to be impediments to Nile Valley transport, but the movement of people was normally not prohibited. Still, Egyptian efforts to facilitate such movement failed miserably, especially considering the perceived importance of more frequent direct contact between entrepreneurs of the two regions. Placing the blame for this failure is difficult. Both administrations could be criticized for the 'red tape' involved in travel, the long, tiresome means of travel available to passengers, or the high price of travel between the regions. However, each administration can also be forgiven for these problems. Charges for travel, transport, and services were important revenue producers, and transportation policies purporting to protect the local population from exploitation, manipulation, or insecurity in times of conflict are certainly justifiable. Ultimately, despite Egyptian claims concerning the unity of the Nile Valley, when it came to the movement of passengers neither administration treated the two regions as a single entity. Instead, each viewed transportation as a sphere of revenue production and a public service for their inhabitants alone.

Commercial Restrictions

Travel restrictions between Egypt and the Sudan corresponded roughly with various administrative measures directly impacting commercial relations. In fact, the 1922 Passports and Permits Ordinance, mentioned above, contained clauses directed specifically at merchants. Section 23 of chapter 5 of the ordinance allowed the governor-general to "declare that in any part of Sudan trading other than by natives of such part shall be permitted only under permit. Such Order may exempt from its operation such persons or classes of persons as the Governor-General may think fit."[29] Although this ordinance applied to all of the Sudan, its most consistent purpose was to isolate the southern, largely non-Muslim and non-Arab regions of the Sudan (part of the Condominium's 'Southern Policy'). A key element of this policy was winning the confidence of southern Sudanese "by building up a protective barrier against northern merchants."[30] This regulation targeted 'northern merchants,' meaning primarily Sudanese Muslim merchants active in northern Sudan but also including Egyptians and other 'foreign' traders. In December 1936 the Egyptian government sent a note to the governor-general complaining of problems Egyptians encountered in the south. The Egyptian prime minister claimed that Christian missionaries enjoyed Sudanese administrative support, while Muslim traders and employees encountered numerous obstacles and were often deported on the basis of the missionaries' opinions of them.[31] The 1922 ordinance had allowed the governor-general to prohibit or restrict merchants' activities in any area of the Sudan. By 1925 the Sudanese government used these powers to restrict trade in all of southern Sudan and parts of the provinces bordering Abyssinia and French Sudan.[32] Egyptian merchants complained of exclusion from southern Sudan, but not vociferously because of the limited purchasing power of the people of the area and, therefore, the small demand for goods Egyptians were likely to offer. However, other restrictions were more potentially damaging. For instance, in September 1922 an order was issued by the Sudanese administration closing certain districts to trade, including Halfa and Dongola, the areas bordering Egypt.[33]

In addition to specific travel restrictions, there was a variety of other administrative processes or regulations that raised the costs for Egyptians or Sudanese desirous of engaging in trade. Although not excessive, there were financial outlays necessary for simply conducting business in the Sudan. For instance, the schedule of annual fees for commercial permits included in the 1922 Passports and Permits Ordinance did not appear to be particularly burdensome, but additional fees were applied to specific provinces.[34] Also, less consistently active merchants faced an additional LE50 deposit to ensure they observed the conditions of their permit.[35] Merchants who sought to export Sudanese goods had to have a certificate of export from the administration. Until 1938, such a document could only be procured from Khartoum, instead of the place of origin of the goods. This, therefore, required either increased travel within the Sudan or the added expense of stationing commercial agents in Khartoum.[36] Additionally, designated agents or employees were required to be at customs stations for the entry of goods into the Sudan. Without this representation the forwarding of goods to the Sudan's interior was prohibited, and 'abandoned' commodities could be sold by the administration after a specified period of time.[37] Even with the greater interdependence required during the Second World War because commercial contacts with foreign markets were less reliable, the Condominium administration did not relax such requirements. For instance, in late 1940 the Sudanese Railways Department announced that goods arriving from Egypt via the Nile Valley route would not be inspected, and hence not enter the country, without the exporter's presence or that of his agents at Wadi Halfa.[38]

Transportation and customs processes along the Nile Valley route were disruptive and detrimental to merchants and their goods, as well as the general traveler. The span between Wadi Halfa and Shellal, connecting Egypt and the Sudan, necessitated transferring from train to steamship service and back to train, customs inspections at one or both ends of this stretch, possible delays in connections, and other inconveniences—all in some of the least pleasant surroundings of the entire trip. Efforts to ensure rapid transport along this route and to protect goods transported from damage are examined in greater detail below. However, a cursory examination of sources indicates that transportation in this region was undoubtedly problematic for trade. Egyptian sources describing the transit of goods along the Nile Valley route consistently employed phrases such as the "*obligation* to unload property frequently," "the *necessity* of unloading manufactures and produce in Shellal and Halfa," or "*harm* from the *wear and tear* of repeatedly loading and unloading."[39] Both governments handled customs procedures to the best of their abilities, but there were difficulties that delayed merchants. In September 1933 *al-Ahram* noted that discrepancies between the two countries' veterinary departments over the inspection process had caused a three-week delay in the shipment of leather to Egypt.[40] Similar, seemingly minor or isolated, incidents led to the demand for a reexamination of the entire Halfa–Shellal customs process soon after the 1935 mission.[41]

The rigmarole of the Halfa–Shellal stretch was not only problematic for goods shipped. Passengers endured similar 'wear and tear,' unpacking bags, undergoing inspections, waiting for connections, and other inconveniences, often in less than pleasant weather. In August 1938, *al-Ahram* described some of the problems passengers encountered at one end of the Halfa–Shellal stretch:

> The office of the Egyptian economic expert in the Sudan was informed by some organizations and individuals of their complaints about difficulties encountered by travelers between Egypt and the Sudan, that was either due to the time waiting at the Shellal station or the slowness of the customs inspection process.
>
> The economic expert was very concerned with these complaints and notified the Railways Department in order that it might eliminate the causes [of the complaints].
>
> When the department investigated the subject it reported that the difficulties encountered and complained about by travelers are attributable to the processes of customs inspections taking place at Shellal station. And the reality is that the location is much higher than the anchorage of the ships, a level higher than the water level reached during the flood, and passengers encounter hardships in moving to the station, especially in the summer. Therefore, the Railways Department is working to eliminate the causes of the complaints by carrying out the inspection at a location opposite the [current] anchorage.[42]

Solving this particular problem may have been as simple as relocating a customs station but the broader inconvenience of travel in the region remained. Egypt's economic expert to the Sudan during the Second World War, Mahmud Zaki, reiterated that the basic problem was that "the traveler from Egypt to the Sudan is obliged to board the ships of the Sudanese government at the interval lying between Shellal and Halfa, and this stretch [of the trip] lasts two entire days."[43]

The inconveniences and obstacles to commercial exchange along the Nile Valley route are illustrated well by various proposals to resolve problems over the location of the Shellal customs station. The Egyptian Railways Department had investigated moving the Shellal station, but some Sudanese merchants called for its elimination altogether. The Egyptian government wanted to facilitate transport through the region, but it could not simply eliminate customs procedures. *Al-Ahram* reported in December 1939 that

> the Egyptian Customs Department has researched this issue [Sudanese calls to eliminate the Shellal station] and sees the necessity of retaining this branch. However, it is limiting its mission to general supervision.

> As for what pertains to travelers coming to Egypt from the Sudan, customs employees there will desist from opening their luggage, except one or two of the passengers in each ship arriving at Shellal, and through this [change] the less arduous passage of travelers will be accomplished in conformity with the request of the Sudanese government.
>
> And it should be mentioned on this occasion that travelers from Egypt to Shellal open their luggage at the Wadi Halfa customs station in an effort to prevent smuggling of goods prohibited from sale without authorization in the Sudan, especially those goods which the government monopolizes or that it controls the sale of, such as sugar, liquor, and the like.[44]

Procedures injurious to trade between Egypt and the Sudan did not lessen with the onset of the Second World War. For instance, in 1941 a decision of the Sudanese Railways Department required that the Khartoum Chamber of Commerce inform the director of this department of all shipments intended for export because of the genuine lack of means of transport within the country.[45] Such procedural requirements did not end with the conclusion of the war. The economic expert's office reported in 1946 that the Sudanese Railways Department was "requesting that all documentation pertaining to the shipment of goods from Egypt is sent to it, so that there are no hindrances at the Wadi Halfa customs because of a lack of providing these documents," noting particularly that failure to include payment in this correspondence was unjustifiable.[46] Various documents, payments, or the presence of representatives at customs stations are just a few examples of the procedural hurdles that discouraged the exchange of goods. Administrative measures undermined trade of all commodities to some extent, but one Sudanese export was closely linked to transport capabilities and controls.

Forces of supply and demand greatly influenced exports of Sudanese cattle to Egypt, but the Egyptian administration impacted this trade through transport restrictions. Egypt imposed various measures mainly because of veterinary fears over the spread of disease to local livestock. These controls limited the use of the Nile Valley route for cattle and imposed comprehensive restrictions on Sudanese livestock transportation within the Egyptian delta in the latter 1930s. Yet, when extraordinary conditions arose, such controls could be relaxed. During the First World War the Egyptian government had made special arrangements so that "cattle would go from Shellal direct to the Quarantine Park [in] Alexandria."[47]

Egyptian authorities would make similar arrangements for livestock transport by rail from the Sudan to Cairo and Alexandria in the early years of the Second World War, although not as rapidly as Sudanese exporters desired. Seeking to accommodate Egyptian desires for control, cattle exporters requested in 1934 the "establishment of a special train departing Shellal once a week for the transport of cattle from [Shellal] station to the main stockyards of the capital."[48] Egypt's Ministry of Commerce and Industry assigned this request to the Railways Department, but no opinion on the matter was quickly produced, nor did transport controls change. In 1939 the Sudanese government requested not only that Egyptian authorities open the Nile Valley route to Sudanese livestock but also that they lift restrictions on cattle transport generally. *Al-Ahram* reported that

> the Egyptian government received recently a memorandum from the government of the Sudan on the matter of the cattle trade in which it expressed its desire to adjust the specific systems of this commerce and to permit the transport of cattle from the Sudan to Egypt on the Wadi Halfa–Shellal route, instead of the Port Sudan route, and send [cattle] directly to Alexandria or to any other region of Egypt.
>
> This memorandum was turned over to the Ministry of Agriculture, and the Veterinary Section decided to compose a technical committee to study the submitted proposals from the Sudanese government.
>
> We note on this occasion that the regulations applicable now impose a quarantine on Sudanese cattle in order that diseases do not spread in the Egyptian interior. Local Egyptian authorities have and still fear the spread of cattle plague caused by the lack of regulations on cattle imported from abroad.[49]

The transportation arrangements eventually organized by Egypt facilitated the wartime cattle trade, and the continuation (or not) of such accommodations remained a key determinant of livestock export levels after the war. Ahmad al-Tawil, an active merchant in the Sudan and a member of an economic delegation sent there prior to the Second World War, was still advocating in 1950 for government efforts to "facilitate the shipment of cattle and sheep from the Sudan to Egypt and lower freight rates on these and the speed of their shipment—also improve the stockyards present at Suez to encourage shipment of these animals."[50] Government supervision of livestock transportation was a specific example of officials impacting Egyptian–Sudanese commerce.

Other administrative measures, in this case tax policy, were more broadly detrimental to commerce. Egyptian merchants had enjoyed relative freedom from taxation in Egypt throughout the interwar period. Only in 1939 did the Egyptian state introduce the first income tax measure, to be followed by an excessive profits tax in 1941.[51] However, such financial advantage had never been available to those Egyptians active in the Sudan. As early as 1913 the Sudan administration introduced the Traders' Tax Ordinance, which made all persons or companies engaged in trade, transport, hotels, restaurants, factories, and other such enterprises in the Sudan liable to certain duties. This measure made no distinction in regard to one's nationality, taxing "every person, firm or company carrying on [whether on behalf of himself or any other person] a trade within the Sudan."[52] In 1924 *al-Akhbar* reported dissatisfaction among Egyptians who came under the Traders' Tax Ordinance. It reported that merchants were complaining that no European country had such a law and that "many of [them] refused to pay the traders' tax," which ranged from 4 to 6 percent of the profits.[53] The Condominium administration also began to tax commercial undertakings specifically during the interwar period, beginning with a business profits tax ordinance in 1928.[54] Later, in 1944, "higher and more steeply progressive rates of Business Profits Tax were imposed as an alternative to an Excess Profits Tax."[55] Whether or not these tax rates were a discouragement to Egyptian traders' efforts in the Sudan is open to speculation, but they certainly did not provide Egyptians with any advantage over their foreign competitors.

Similarly, Egyptian commercial interests found little advantage through establishing their companies in the Sudan. The bureaucratic requirements of the Companies Ordinance of 1925 included registering with the government all pertinent information, establishing permanent offices, paying a number of required fees, and so forth. At the culmination of a long process, after the registrar submitted an application to the governor-general, the latter could "in his absolute discretion either authorize or refuse the incorporation of the company."[56] For some time, therefore, it may have been more advantageous for Egyptians to function as foreign businesses in the Sudan. However, in 1930 the ordinance was amended to require "compulsory registration in the Sudan of all foreign companies operating in the country."[57] Company registration ordinances, like the taxation measures, were not necessarily detrimental to Egyptian desires for increased commerce with the Sudan, but, again, such regulation provided Nile Valley interactions with no special status. Furthermore, just like the Egyptian merchants' 'expenses' from taxes, permits, licenses, required travel, or communication, the fees associated with registering one's company simply reduced profitability while adding to the Condominium's revenue stream. The hopes of Egyptian trade interests never superseded administrative concerns with revenue collection.[58]

Egyptian–Sudanese Customs Arrangements

In contrast to most other administrative policies or procedures, customs arrangements between Egypt and the Sudan were designed purposefully to give special consideration to Nile Valley trade. The Egyptian–Sudanese customs system was based on Article 7 of the 1899 agreement, which stated, "Import duties on entering the Soudan shall not be payable on goods coming from Egyptian territory."[59] Since the Egyptian government reciprocated for Sudanese-produced commodities, goods originating in either Egypt or the Sudan were exchanged without any duties levied. In a study of Anglo–Egyptian competition over the Sudan, L.A. Fabunmi considers Article 7 to have given Egypt a position "similar to the British imperial trade preference" and "could be stretched to imply that the Sudan is Egypt's domestic sphere of influence."[60] Although neither government imposed duties on local commodities sent between Egypt and the Sudan, intense opposition to the Sudan's customs system arose. Contrasting the British and Egyptian interpretations of Article 7 and their differing assessments of the 'proper' objectives underpinning the Sudanese customs regime explains this opposition.

The British attitude toward Egyptian–Sudanese commerce was that the 'traditional' trade along the Nile Valley was the proper pace of exchange. Subsequently, British Condominium officials showed little concern for improving Nile Valley transport capabilities, instead focusing on the Red Sea/Port Sudan facilities, which generated greater revenues. As with their handling of transportation, Condominium officials viewed their customs regime primarily as a revenue producer, and since no duties were collected on Egyptian goods, the rates imposed on foreign products were a key issue. In his 1920 report, the high commissioner for Egypt stated of Sudanese imports from foreign countries that "the same imports (whatever they may be) if diverted through Egypt are more expensive and bring in a reduced rate of duty under the terms of the existing arrangement with the Egyptian Government."[61] Because of this situation, he noted that "Egypt figures less prominently as the inter-medium between the Soudan and foreign markets."[62] If the Egyptian annual subvention to the Sudan is not considered, the combination of customs duties and revenue produced from the levy on imported sugar (which was basically a 'disguised' duty collected on an

Egyptian import) consistently amounted to over 30 percent of total government revenues.[63] Since customs revenues formed such an important part of the Sudanese government's budget, officials there placed greater emphasis on the collection of foreign import duties than on altering customs policies to encourage Egyptian–Sudanese commerce.

Egyptian officials' view of the Nile Valley customs regime and commerce differed. They claimed that the Condominium administration's concern for revenue production and its customs policies undermined Egypt's commercial position in the Sudan. Many years later, however, Sir Alexander Cadogan (before the United Nations Security Council in 1947) stated that this commercial decline was due to other reasons, such as the existence of better markets for Egyptian exports.[64] Egyptians maintained that the deterioration of their commercial position in the Sudan was largely a result of Condominium officials' 'interpretation' of the 1899 agreement. For instance, Article 5 of the agreement stated that "No Egyptian Law, Decree, Ministerial Arrêté, or other enactment hereafter to be made or promulgated shall apply to the Soudan," which presumably included commercial or tariff measures.[65] Thus, while Fabunmi argues that Article 7 of the 1899 agreement created a single domestic market, composed of Egypt and the Sudan, Mekki Abbas claims that Article 5 "gave the Sudan a separate commercial regime."[66] In fact, the Sudanese government did create a separate regime. The Customs Ordinance of 1913, actually put into effect on 1 July 1915, replaced "All Laws, Decrees and Regulations of the Egyptian Government relating to customs which have heretofore been in force or observed at Suakin or elsewhere in the Sudan."[67]

Egyptians continued to argue, however, that the intent of the 1899 agreement had been to create a unified customs regime for Egypt and the Sudan. In addition to the agreement's prohibition of duties on locally produced goods, Article 7 required that tariffs on foreign articles entering the Sudan "shall not exceed the corresponding duties for the time being leviable on goods entering Egypt from abroad."[68] When preparing documentation for Egypt's case before the United Nations years later, Taha al-Sa'id Nasr wrote that this section of Article 7 implied a unity of customs between the two countries and even "the subordination of the Sudan to Egypt."[69] During the interwar years, Egyptians felt that Article 7 mandated identical duties on imports to Egypt and the Sudan. They complained consistently that the Sudan did not adhere to the intent of the 1899 agreement. As the years passed and hopes for increased exports to the Sudan remained unfulfilled while the separate customs administrations became more firmly entrenched, Egyptian frustrations increased. After enumerating multiple

Nile Valley trade and tariff problems, the 1936 parliamentary financial committee noted its "hope that the time in which the customs barriers between Egypt and the Sudan disappear is drawing near, and there will be no need for discussions of this sort."[70] Still, the barriers remained in place, and Egyptians continued to rail against the lack of adherence to even the most basic principles thought to have been applicable to the customs situation. There were allegations of duties being collected on Egyptian-manufactured goods—a category clearly exempt from duties. On 10 July 1924, 'Abd al-Rahman al-Rafi'i stated in the Chamber of Deputies that Egyptian goods sent to the Sudan were exempt from customs, "but in reality duties have been paid on them."[71]

The problems Egyptians had with separate customs administrations and the supposedly 'unlawful' policies followed by the Sudanese officials were further aggravated at times by the process of customs revenue sharing between the two governments. Since no duties were imposed on local goods exchanged between the two countries, the problems in the apportionment of customs revenues concerned foreign goods passing through each country to the other. Commodities designated as 'transit' goods had duties imposed on them by the country of final destination, which in itself caused no difficulties. The small quantities of foreign goods arriving in Egypt through the Sudan had a supplementary duty (the difference between tariffs of the countries) imposed, which also caused little difficulty in accounting.[72] The major problems occurred primarily on the greater quantities of foreign goods destined for the Sudan but arriving via Egypt. In these cases, more of the revenue collected in Egypt was to be credited to the Sudan. Based on the 1921 agreement, a fixed percentage of the total value of goods sent to the Sudan (both Egyptian and foreign) was to be payable to the Sudanese government.[73] However, dissatisfaction with this process heightened as the economic situation in the area changed toward the end of the Depression years. By 1938 the financial committee's report in the Egyptian parliament stated that "in view of the change of economic conditions the committee thought proper the reexamination of this percentage."[74]

The determination of fixed rates based on statistics collected independently in each country had inevitably led to disputes. In 1925 *al-Jarida al-tijariya al-misriya* reported a typical case: "The dispute still exists between these two [customs] departments about the matter of the amount of LE11,000, and the government of the Sudan is still vehement in its refusal to pay, demanding [instead] the adjustment of the proportion of regular duties."[75] The Egyptians had their complaints as well. One deputy in the parliament in 1924 proposed lessening the amount paid to the Sudan because the payment included duties on supplies sent to Egypt's army in the Sudan.[76] This particular grievance was especially galling to Egyptians because at the same time "the commodities which are sent to the British army in Egypt are free from the payment of duties."[77] Ultimately, all the grievances over customs adjustments were grounded in the Egyptian nationalists' belief that the two regions formed one country. 'Abd al-Rahman al-Rafi'i outlined this belief in a speech on the method of paying the Sudan the customs adjustment. He stated, "This method is incompatible with the right of Egypt in the Sudan. It does not agree with the principle that the Sudan is an inseparable part of Egypt because it is unreasonable that Egypt should pay duties on commodities which are transported from one province to another."[78]

While government officials raised political issues such as this, the Egyptian private sector was influenced more by the actual tariff rates. Sudanese tariffs on foreign imports would have had an important impact on the ability of Egyptian merchants to obtain a larger share of the local market. The Sudan's Customs Ordinance of 1913 called for a levy of 8 percent ad valorem "on all goods save otherwise provided in this schedule."[79] The commodities of importance on the attached schedule included tobacco products and alcohol. The latter was not a major export of Egypt, but higher rates on tobacco products assisted Egyptian exports, which remained free from tariffs. The 1913 ordinance also applied a 5 percent duty on imports from Abyssinia, the Belgian and French Congos, and Uganda.[80] In 1938 the Condominium administration amended the customs ordinance by adding a list of imports that would have no duty imposed on them. These items included aircraft and parts for such, educational/instructional films, antiquities, fertilizers, live animals, and seeds/bulbs.[81] Other than tobacco, none of the listed commodities in these schedules was a major Egyptian export to the Sudan. Abyssinia, the Congo, or Uganda was little competition in Sudanese markets. Egyptian merchants needed Sudanese tariffs on targeted commodities, and high enough to undermine their foreign commercial competitors.

Prior to 1930, duties on foreign imports into Egypt and the Sudan were fairly similar. Internal Egyptian government correspondence in 1919 described the duties applied to imports at the time. Because of capitulatory conventions with foreign countries, Egypt imposed no higher than an 8 percent ad valorem duty on imports, with the following exceptions: "Alcohol, refined sugar, building wood, petroleum and animals which may be taxed, the three first up to 10% ad valorem and the two last, as well as alcohol having over 50% alcohol content, up to 15%."[82] Egypt's 'regular' duties and the exceptions were virtually the same as those of the Sudan. Significant changes in these rates began to occur, however, with Egypt's customs reforms of 1930 and afterward.

An initial reform measure was instituted on 17 February 1930. The leading formulator of the changes adopted was I.G. Levi, a foreign resident in Egypt who served as the secretary general of the Egyptian Federation of Industries.[83] This initial measure came in reaction to something the high commissioner had noted some ten years earlier: the affinity of smaller Cairo merchants for ad valorem duties, which allowed them to pay their fees in kind when the precise monetary value of goods fluctuated.[84] In contrast to the standard 8 percent rate of the past, the reform established "a more intricate system combining specific and ad valorem duties," which amounted overall to roughly a 13 percent levy on imported goods.[85] One of the primary goals of the 1930 reform was to protect fledgling Egyptian industries. In his study of the development of Bank Misr, Eric Davis writes that the protective tariffs were, "without doubt, the single most important factor" in the expansion of the Misr companies after 1930.[86] The new tariffs in Egypt did not have an immediate or direct impact on trade with the Sudan.

In fact, the reforms seem to have had less than satisfying consequences for Egyptian–Sudanese commerce. The governor-general reported that the "new Egyptian customs tariff, which came into force in Egypt in February 1930, raised questions which were unsettling to trade for a short time."[87] The reform may have been temporarily "unsettling" to merchants, but by 31 March 1930 it was reported that the two countries had arrived at an agreement that essentially maintained the customs practices begun by the 1899 agreement.[88] Although Egyptian manufactures gained a larger share of the local Egyptian market, no similar improvement occurred for commerce with the Sudan. The Condominium administration did not match Egypt's raised tariffs on foreign imports. Therefore, after 1930 higher-priced Egyptian manufactures may have begun to prosper in the 'protected' local economy, but they faced stiff competition from relatively inexpensive foreign products in the 'open' Sudanese market. Since Egyptian commercial interests struggled to increase exports in such circumstances, they sought special assistance in order to succeed in the Sudan.

Transportation Facilities

Success in boosting trade or other economic endeavors between Egypt and the Sudan also required significant government assistance in upgrading transportation facilities. Nile Valley entrepreneurs needed fast, efficient, and cost-effective means of moving goods and people between the two regions. Without such means of transportation, improved economic relations were unlikely to develop, a further blow to claims of a politically united Nile Valley. Unfortunately for the hopes of nationalists, since the time of Muhammad Ali Egypt's economic development had been tightly linked to the west. The transportation facilities established throughout the Nile Valley mirrored this strong propensity for domestic–international linkages.

The railroad was the dominant means of transportation in the valley throughout the period under study, and there was no direct rail connection between Egypt and the Sudan. Prior to the First World War both countries had established rail lines leading to modern port facilities in order to encourage foreign trade. The building of Egypt's railroad network through Upper Egypt had accompanied Anglo–Egyptian military forces in the late nineteenth-century campaign that would overthrow the Mahdist regime in the Sudan. However, after extending the railroad to Shellal in 1898 officials decided to stop construction because of engineering difficulties and the expenses that would have been required.[89] The Shellal station remained the southern terminus of Egypt's system from that time onward.

After the Condominium government was established, its administrators immediately began the planning and construction of a railroad network in the Sudan. On 10 June 1900, Egypt's Council of Ministers agreed to finance the construction of railroad tracks that would reach Wadi Halfa, the northern terminus of the Sudanese system.[90] The following year Governor-General Reginald Wingate justified his request for additional funds to upgrade rail and telegraph facilities along this route by stating that "if one wishes to maintain communication between Egypt and the Sudan, and this is a question which affects the commercial interests of the two countries at the same time, it is indispensable that the expenditures in question be carried out without delay."[91] In spite of his apparent understanding of the commercial advantages for the countries of improved communications along the Nile Valley, his administration did little to directly connect the two systems.

Instead, during the following years the Condominium government established a railroad from the Nile Valley 'core' of the country to Port Sudan on the Red Sea. In his description of early Sudanese transport construction, Mekki Abbas wrote of the railroad reaching toward Wadi Halfa that "the construction of the railway brought the two countries nearer to each other but Sudanese economic development and trade could never have flourished had it not been for the construction of a railway line across the eastern desert to Port Sudan."[92] Early technical reports had explained that

Sudanese economic development would require a direct link to the Red Sea because of the costs of constructing a Nile Valley railroad to Egypt and the high rates that would have to be charged for goods being transported on such a line.[93] K.M. Barbour notes in a 1972 study of Egyptian industrial development that "none of the successive rulers of Egypt over the last century and more have thought it worthwhile to link the Egyptian and Sudanese railway systems."[94] However, Egyptians consistently called for a direct railroad connection, despite the engineering and financial obstacles involved. L.A. Fabunmi notes that Egyptians considered the Nile Valley to Port Sudan railroad "one of the British policies directed towards severing the Sudan from Egypt, economically."[95]

Although Egyptians often claimed British imperialist designs were behind the Sudanese railway link to the Red Sea, some of their own actions confirmed the economic prudence of such a route. For instance, during the interwar period the Egyptian government investigated a possible railroad running directly from Qena Province in Upper Egypt to al-Qusayr on the Red Sea. Responding to a question about this rail line in 1936, the minister of transportation noted that eighteen kilometers of this route had been constructed between 1929 and 1931 and that his ministry hoped to resume work when financial circumstances permitted.[96] During the Second World War the Egyptian government again considered this project, primarily to relieve pressure on Egypt's ports. *Al-Jarida al-tijariya al-misriya* reported in October 1941 that a group of engineers studying this project recommended its establishment and the enlargement of al-Qusayr's harbor.[97] Constructing this railroad would have undermined the argument that the Halfa–Shellal link was absolutely necessary for the strengthening of Egyptian–Sudanese economic relations.

Egyptians also argued that the Halfa–Shellal railroad would foster agricultural development in Upper Egypt, especially Nubian regions. Improving transportation facilities in order to encourage economic development in various areas of the country was a central facet of the Egyptian Department of Railways' planning during these years. This department consistently faced the dilemma of providing services to remote areas of the country while remaining a financially profitable entity. A 1928 parliamentary report on the Ministry of Transportation explained the dual role Egypt's railroads were required to assume. It stated that "the Department of Railways is a commercial department that seeks a profit but at the same time it is a governmental department which is discharging a service, and it must concern itself with the ease of the public without their exploitation."[98] In 1933 a government report on possibly separating the department's budget from that of the state's noted that the government had determined transport rates and where new services should be extended, "paying no attention to the effect of that on revenues."[99] This service–profit dilemma was certainly a critical issue for officials considering the establishment of a railroad connection between Egypt and the Sudan.

Although officials would consider a Halfa–Shellal link, the railroad networks created in Egypt and the Sudan were completely independent of each other. The administrations of each country had designed rail construction to correspond with economic development plans. Since such planning had focused on cotton exports and the import of manufactured goods, the two regions had established systems that provided efficient transport to international markets—not each other. In his economic analysis of Egypt, Charles Issawi writes that "the main defect of the Egyptian railways was their isolation from the adjacent countries," mentioning specifically Palestine, Libya, and the Sudan.[100] However, if the government's intent was to establish transportation networks that produced revenue and linked the local economies to global markets, then the absence of connections to neighboring countries was a minor blemish on its record.

Halfa–Shellal Steamship Service

Although a direct Egyptian–Sudanese railroad connection was absent, there were means of transport that permitted the exchange of goods along the Nile Valley route. The Sudan's Department of Railways operated a steamship transport service, normally running twice a week between the termini of the two railroad systems. Although this allowed the transport of commodities, the limited frequency of service, the necessity of transferring goods between rail and river facilities, and a host of other minor problems led to high costs and frequent delays when sending goods via the Nile Valley route. The editors of *al-Ahram* described the problematic riverain connection between the two countries in 1939:

> The Egyptian railways terminate at Shellal, then the Sudanese railways begin at Wadi Halfa, and it is incumbent upon the traveler from Egypt to the Sudan to traverse this distance, and it amounts to about 200 kilometers, by means of the river while enduring much in the way of physical hardships and expenses, aside from the loss of time.[101]

Since the mid-1930s Egyptian nationalists had been especially concerned with resolving these problems in order to strengthen commercial possibilities with the Sudan.

However, another reason for Egyptian interest in the Halfa–Shellal connections was to challenge the Sudanese government's monopoly of this transport business. Potentially there was a twofold economic benefit from Egyptian involvement in steamship service, both expanded transport capabilities for commerce and profitable investment opportunities. In his analysis of transport between Halfa and Shellal, Mahmud Zaki, Egypt's economic expert in the Sudan during the Second World War, noted that "this region is Egyptian land, nevertheless the travelers (and goods) traverse it in Sudanese government ships."[102] Therefore, he proposed that the government encourage Egyptian participation in the transport business, side by side with the Sudan's steamships. The Condominium administration dominated this shipping, but no legal restrictions specifically prevented Egyptian entrepreneurs from engaging in this business. A Sudanese ordinance on river navigation stated that "boats whose owners are resident in Egypt and which do not ply above Wadi Halfa Cataract need not be registered" in the Sudan.[103] The First World War commission studying Egyptian commerce and industry recommended greater utilization of the Nile in transportation planning, including shipping along the Halfa–Shellal stretch.[104] Still, there was little Egyptian involvement in this river transport business, and mainly from the latter 1930s onward.

Some Egyptians had expressed interest in the river transport business of the Halfa–Shellal reach much earlier. One of the earliest proposals for such involvement came from within the Halfa–Shellal region itself. Responding to a request from *al-Majalla al-tijariya al-nubiya* for suggestions on methods to promote the development of the Nubian region, a number of individuals cited the need for a local Nile River transport company. The most specific proposal came from Mahmud 'Uthman al-Sukuti, a Bank Misr employee in Alexandria, who suggested "forming a Nubian joint-stock company for the purchase of a number of Nile steamships in order to relieve the people from the troubles of foreign steamship owners."[105] Apparently, no lasting ventures emerged from these suggestions, as the same journal reported in 1929 that the governor of Aswan had promised to contact representatives of Misr Navigation Company for assistance in founding a locally owned transport company.[106] Still, steamer transport remained largely a preserve of the Sudanese government. When Egyptians raised the possibility of investing in the steamer transport business, frequently they referred to a Condominium monopoly. In fact there had been a private presence in this activity for years. The governor-general's report in 1934 stated that his administration controlled 63 percent of the Halfa–Shellal traffic but that the remaining business was handled by privately owned vessels.[107] One foreign firm involved in this business for years was Thomas Cook & Son. Hassan Dafalla, a former administrator of Sudanese Nubian areas who wrote about the difficulties encountered later with the construction of the Aswan High Dam, mentioned in his study's introduction that this company had provided steamer service as far back as the nineteenth century.[108] References to this company's continued activities in the Halfa–Shellal reach were made throughout the Condominium era.[109]

Although there seem to have been opportunities in this transport business, actual Egyptian involvement appeared only late in the period under review. On 11 April 1938, the permanent committee decided to assign the job of promoting Egyptian activity to 'Abd al-Hamid Abaza, "a member of one of the navigation companies involved in transport between Shellal and Halfa."[110] Only when dependence on the Nile transport route increased markedly during the Second World War did Egyptians begin serious engagement in this activity. 'Abdallah Fakri Abaza wrote that the outbreak of war induced some Egyptian river companies to establish shipping lines between Halfa and Shellal.[111] The Sudan's civil secretary mentioned in a letter to the provincial governors on 18 September 1940 that "three Egyptian inland water transport companies are running self-propelled barges" along the Nile route.[112] Although some interest in riverain transport business had emerged with the extraordinary wartime conditions, profits from Halfa–Shellal traffic remained overwhelmingly in the hands of the Sudanese government. Egyptian entrepreneurs would look to other spheres of activity for investment opportunities, while criticizing the negative consequences for Egyptian–Sudanese relations of the problematic Halfa–Shellal connection.

Among the negative consequences of the Halfa–Shellal steamship connection were transport delays, disruptions of service, and higher costs, but steamships were not the only vessels plying between Shellal and Halfa. Sailing ships were also active in the transport of some goods in the region, especially the export of Sudanese dates. 'Abdallah Fakri Abaza wrote that all Sudanese date exports to Egypt arrived via Wadi Halfa, and that "most are transported by means of sailing boats, some of which are often completely engaged in either coming or going depending on the situation of the Nile cataracts."[113] Ensuring the safe transport of goods by these boats or by steamers was a concern of both administrations. In 1932 the governor-general's annual report noted that the last of the rocks in the cataracts had been removed, an essential improvement for sailing ships transporting dates along this route.[114] Egyptians had an eye to shipping more than dates along the Nile Valley, making reliable steamship service essential.

Therefore, the Egyptian government was most concerned about issues that impacted the regularity and reliability of steamship service. The 1936 report of a joint Egyptian–Sudanese committee studying transport facilities noted that "the navigable channel in the Aswan region is in need of widening and deepening."[115] Egyptian and Sudanese authorities met again in 1941 to investigate methods of improving transport in this region, especially possibilities of increased steamship usage during the war.[116]

Despite the official attention, river transport was disrupted at times. For instance, the Sudanese government reported "the closure of the Shellal–Halfa reach of the Nile to navigation for one month both in 1943 and 1944 as a result of the opening of the Assuan Dam."[117] The normal seasonal Nile floods also impacted the movement of Sudanese exports to Egypt. For instance, in 1946 the Cairo Chamber of Commerce reported that "the Sudan agent [in Cairo] notified the Egyptian government that there are 10,000 head of calves and large numbers of sheep prepared for export from the Sudan to Egypt, and their dispatch was scheduled for the first of September if transportation is not suspended because of the Nile flood."[118] More frequent than flooding difficulties, river transport in the region was discontinued when the Nile reached its lowest levels. Muhammad Shahin Hamza referred to the usual time period when steamship service was halted when complaining of the difficulties Nubian peoples were encountering in the final years of the Second World War. He asked, "What are the measures which the ministry has taken to ensure the provisioning of the Nubian lands whenever navigation of the Nile's river course in the Halfa–Shellal region is suspended, from the end of May to next August approximately."[119] Egypt's economic expert in Khartoum during the war, Mahmud Zaki, also mentioned the stoppage of service every summer.[120] A complete suspension of service, albeit for limited periods, was obviously not conducive to strengthening economic bonds between Egypt and the Sudan.

However, since transportation between Egypt and the Sudan along the Nile Valley required use of both rail and river facilities, there were inherently delays for goods and passengers choosing this route. Although not all sources singled out the Halfa–Shellal connection as the cause for the arduous, lengthy trip, this region was undoubtedly the problem. It was in this inhospitable, often extremely hot, stretch of land that goods had to be unloaded and loaded twice, and had to undergo customs inspections from both administrations—all of which both slowed transport and tested the durability of the packaging of potentially perishable goods. Jean Schatz, director of the statistical section of Egypt's Ministry of Commerce and Industry in the latter 1930s, emphasized that creating new means of transport in order to cut the duration of shipment times was essential for increased trade.[121] Shortening the time of transportation necessitated not merely better means, but also a coordinated or 'united' system. For instance, there were problems in coordinating arrival times of trains at Shellal with the departure schedule of Sudanese government steamships leaving for Wadi Halfa. Muhammad Shahin Hamza requested that the government take measures to ensure the timely arrival of trains in Aswan daily, and "on the days when the Sudanese steamships depart from Shellal especially."[122] A 1939 editorial on the permanent committee's transport deliberations, which focused on proposals to replace steamship service between Halfa and Shellal, concluded that "the activities of this committee will be of no use for the advantages sought, except if the connections between the countries are completed with railroad or they utilize some other speedy means of transport." After clearly favoring a railroad connection because of the elimination of consequent loading/unloading delays, the editorial stated that "the direction in the countries today is toward strengthening connections by all means possible. And it is certain that facilitation of transport and travel, speeding up and lowering rates for both, is among the most important means of success."[123] Replacing steamer service with rail or road service would accelerate transport, and for certain perishable goods the trip's duration was especially critical. In a July 1939 meeting, the economic expert and officials of the Ministry of Agriculture agreed that the government should be "working to establish all possible aids in accelerating the transport to the Sudan of fresh agricultural produce, and its preservation, and in encouraging its sale, especially during the seasons in which it does not encounter much competition."[124] Steamship service between Halfa and Shellal continually undermined Nile Valley transportation. For instance, after having traveled to the Sudan in the winter of 1945, Muhammad Zaki 'Abd al-Qadir noted that traversing the Halfa–Shellal stretch in steamers took two days, while passage via car only required five to six hours. He concluded that "the passenger traffic and the transport of goods between the two countries have become deficient and tiresome from that delay."[125]

Just as they sought to improve the speed of travel between Egypt and the Sudan, Egyptians were concerned about the wear and tear to goods sent via a system necessitating multiple loadings of cargo. They hoped goods could arrive both more quickly and in satisfactory condition through the improvement of packaging methods. The latter issue was especially critical for Egyptians seeking to export citrus fruit to the Sudan. Due to problems encountered, the permanent committee decided on 26 February 1938 to send two test shipments to Khartoum, one along the Nile Valley route and the other via the Red Sea.[126] Apparently exporters had improved packaging, because neither route caused extensive damage to the products and the Ministry of Commerce and Industry reported that "all of them arrived in good condition at the Khartoum Chamber of Commerce."[127] Egyptian authorities may have improved the packaging of certain exports to the Sudan, but the general multiple-leg process of transporting goods had not improved.

A Halfa–Shellal Railroad Connection

Eliminating a multiple-leg trip could be truly accomplished only through establishing a direct railroad connection between Wadi Halfa and Shellal. Fu'ad Abaza, at the head of renewed economic interest in the Sudan after 1935, wrote that in all meetings of the permanent committee, members had agreed that both governments needed to be convinced of "the necessity of binding the Egyptian railroads with the Sudanese railroads in the section lying between Shellal and Wadi Halfa."[128] Egyptian scholar Tamam Hamam Tamam expressed similar sentiments on this subject and laid much blame on the Sudanese government's reluctance to establish the connection. He stated that the Sudanese government "did not encourage the building of a railroad line between Aswan and Halfa ... [which would] protect the Nubian lands from demise, so that [Nubia] does not become a truly natural division between the Sudan and Egypt in which no people live."[129] Although costs and engineering difficulties reinforced Condominium officials' unwillingness to establish this connection, the idea that this area formed a genuine division of the Nile Valley still had serious implications for both increased economic activity and sovereignty claims.

Other sources also emphasized Britain's role in the ultimate failure to establish the railroad connection. When Issawi describes the absence of Egyptian railway links to adjacent countries, he writes that "it may be suspected that the failure to connect Aswan and Wadi Halfa . . . was due to the desire of the British to isolate the Sudan strategically and to divert its trade from Alexandria."[130] Egyptian politicians certainly heaped the blame on Britain at times. After the conclusion of the 1936 treaty, Muhammad 'Ali 'Aluba complained in a speech that although Egypt would be paying enormous sums for infrastructure related to the redeployment of British troops within Egypt, no funds were earmarked for linking Egypt and the Sudan by either rail or road.[131] Criticism of British disinterest in a Halfa–Shellal connection was to be expected, but this Egyptian attitude should not have prevented local officials from independently pursuing the project.

Yet neither administration—cooperatively or independently—built a rail connection during the Condominium era. During the same decades Egyptians budgeted huge sums for hydraulic works, while maintaining that a railroad was essential for strengthening economic relations with the Sudan. Egypt's first economic expert in the Sudan noted in his study of economic relations with the Sudan that "the permanent committee of the Sudan has not allowed any opportunity to pass without emphasizing the great importance of linking Egypt with the Sudan by railroad."[132] Although Egyptians stressed constantly the need for a Halfa–Shellal rail connection in the mid-1930s, officials had been aware of this transport deficiency years earlier. The Ministry of Communications reported during the Second World War that officials raised the issue of this rail link in 1926, and again in 1929.[133] No documentation from either government, scholarly works, or the local press of that time indicated that a rail connection was ever built, but an Egyptian newspaper referred to some type of former link between the countries. *Al-Siyasa* reported in 1937 that "Fu'ad Abaza mentioned to His Excellency the minister [of transportation] that there is an old path for the railroad between Shellal and Halfa still existing and that its renovation is easily done."[134] Apparently a route along the Nile existed for some type of transport (camel, cart, or motorized lorry), but its condition was insufficient to coax the government into action.

Prior to the Second World War, Egypt's commercial community was anxious for just such action, because it believed that its inability to capture a greater share of the Sudanese market was due in part to the lack of a railroad link. For instance, Hasan Saqr of the Ministry of Commerce and Industry wrote in June 1939 that a leading cause of Egypt's failure to replace Japanese textiles in Sudanese markets was inadequate transport between the two countries, citing specifically the Halfa–Shellal section.[135] With the outbreak of the Second World War later that year, this connection became critical not only for Egyptians' commercial success in the Sudan but also for trading interests throughout the Nile Valley. The governor-general's report for the first years of the war noted that since Red Sea shipping was limited and the trade routes through East Africa threatened, "it was imperative to find alternative routes for Sudan trade and the obvious solution lay in the encouragement of trade via the Nile Valley."[136] Finally, under such conditions both governments began seriously to consider a direct railroad connection. In May 1939 select members of the permanent committee met to discuss commercial exchange in the event of a conflict. On 25 May, *al-Ahram* summarized their conclusions on railroad transport between Halfa and Shellal:

> Then the committee turned to the issue of linking the two countries by a rail line connecting Halfa with Shellal . . . crossed by car in six hours at most, while Nile steamer crosses it currently in two days.

The result of this project would be a savings of time when it is possible for the traveler to go from Cairo to Khartoum in two days rather than four days. And this would yield comfort and savings of money for the traveler, because of this speed. It would be among the most important factors facilitating the transport of various fruits and vegetables, which Egypt exports to the Sudan, without exposing them to spoilage.

It has been mentioned previously that the permanent committee studied this subject before and proposed establishing the railroad, and exchanging it for motor vehicles if [the railroad's] construction was infeasible currently.

It has come to our knowledge that the inclination is toward the idea of establishing the railroad because it possesses many advantages that have been previously mentioned. It will have the greatest influence in the organization of provisioning matters between the countries if war breaks out.

The expenses of this project were estimated at more than one million pounds.[137]

The Cairo Chamber of Commerce also reported as early as December 1939 that "the Ministry of Commerce and Industry had begun to reconsider a project of extending a rail line between Shellal and Wadi Halfa, due to the potential results through facilitating commercial activity between Egypt and the Sudan."[138]

Although Egypt's commercial interest in this project was readily apparent, the Sudanese government cited wartime provisioning needs as its primary motivation. The Condominium's civil secretary, Douglas Newbold, stated in a September 1941 letter that because of heavy traffic of supplies from Port Sudan to Cairo via the Nile route, "a proposal for extending the Sudan railway to Shellal is afoot and a first instalment of 60 miles to Tushka has been approved."[139] Egyptian officials recognized the wartime supply functions this connection would have assumed, but continued to stress its importance for commerce generally. *Al-Ahram* reported on transport discussions of a permanent committee meeting in early November 1939 and described current Egyptian inclinations regarding a rail connection:

> We have pointed out what has been going on in respect to discussion of establishing a railroad line between Shellal and Wadi Halfa, and we stated that plans are currently leaning toward delaying construction of this line in view of the excessive expenses.

> And today we note that the Ministry of Commerce and Industry decided to reexamine this project. It is anticipated that the speeding up of commercial exchanges between Egypt and the Sudan will result from [a rail connection's] completion, especially in wartime when [fast transport] is needed for provisioning.
>
> And Mr. 'Abdallah Fakri Abaza Bey, the economic expert of Egypt in the Sudan, and Mr. Kamal al-Khashn Bey, the general secretary of the Railways Department, have been charged with studying this project and presenting their report on it to the committee.[140]

The same 'Abdallah Fakri Abaza would write in his 1940 study of economic relations with the Sudan that the volume of goods shipped via the Nile Valley route increased roughly 55 percent after the start of the Second World War and that the Halfa–Shellal railroad was necessary "not from a commercial standpoint solely, but indeed in regard to the exchange of provisions and defensive needs."[141] In the Chamber of Deputies on 1 April 1940, Muhammad Shahin Hamza stated of the proposed railroad line, "I am aware that the expenses of this project are enormous, but I am also certain of the economic and military benefits that our countries will derive by means of this project."[142]

The enormous costs of constructing the Halfa–Shellal railroad were certainly a key factor in the failure to establish this line. In his 1940 statements, Muhammad Shahin Hamza proposed that the two administrations split the costs, as had been done in the work to connect Cairo and Khartoum with telephone facilities. During the war officials completed studies of the railroad route, with an estimated LE1.25 million being required for the project.[143] In 1945 an article on wartime Egyptian railroad projects noted of the Halfa–Shellal proposal that the financial "assessment was performed on the basis that the line between Shellal and Wadi Halfa is [to be] a wide track, like the main Egyptian railroads, and that making it a narrow track, like the railroads of the Sudan, will lead to a savings of around two thirds of a million pounds."[144] Irrespective of what width of track was to be laid, the expenses were consistently prohibitive. In 1949 the Alexandria Chamber of Commerce reported that the government had approved budgetary adjustments to permit beginning a railroad connection, the completion of which would ultimately require LE4.5 million.[145]

Although the costs involved were certainly detrimental to ever establishing a railroad connection between the countries, Egyptians continued to investigate the possibilities. Members of the first Egyptian missions sent to the Sudan in the mid-1930s studied and strenuously urged construction of a rail link, but efforts remained stalled throughout the Second World War. In June 1943 *al-Ahram* reported that "the studying of the special project to establish a railroad between Shellal and Wadi Halfa in order to facilitate transport between Egypt and the Sudan is being renewed."[146] Although officials in the Nile Valley often referred to the wartime dependence of the two countries, this situation had not pushed a railroad connection beyond the research stage. By 1946 a much more extensive study of this transport dilemma had been completed.

> The Railroad Department had formed a mission of five engineers under the leadership of Hasan al-Nasr and fifty technicians for surveying all of the route to Halfa from Nag Hamadi on the west bank of the Nile, a length of 610 kilometers, and the route to [Halfa], via Shellal on the east bank, a length of around 500 kilometers, in preparation for the establishment of a rail line to Halfa, bringing together the two tracks [of Egypt and the Sudan].
>
> The head of the mission prepared a report on its work, to be presented to His Excellency 'Abd al-Majid Badr Pasha, director of the department, that included its nine-month-long survey of the first route and the three-month-long survey of the second route, which were finished at the end of last January.
>
> It is worthy of mention that this work the mission completed is the first of its kind undertaken by Egyptian engineers, and its significance is increased in that the mission completed [its work] successfully in spite of various difficulties which befell it, and among these was the unevenness of the terrain, the remoteness from areas of supplies, and the lack of ample detailed maps.[147]

Undoubtedly, these investigations, which included vast swaths of Upper Egyptian rail lines, were much more wide-ranging than earlier studies. Still, 1946 was more than a decade after the Anglo–Egyptian treaty and the concomitant interest in improved economic ties with the Sudan. On 12 November 1947, Prime Minister Mahmud Fahmi al-Nuqrashi in his speech opening a new session of the Chamber of Deputies would state that the government had "*started* study of a project for extending the railroad from Shellal to the city of Halfa, easing transportation between Egypt and the Sudan, and joining the halves of the valley."[148]

Any railroad connection would assist commerce generally, but the precise location of the proposed line was critical in determining construction costs and the region's economic growth. Initial studies in the latter 1930s focused on the east bank of the Nile, primarily due to the ease of connecting to the current termini of the two rail systems. However, it appears that the eastern bank itself was a factor in the high costs of the project. In December 1939 *al-Ahram* relayed information from a local notable of Edfu, who was very familiar with the Halfa–Shellal stretch. This individual stated "that the railroad line project from Shellal to Halfa on the east bank of the Nile costs the state Treasury enormous expenditures in view of the roughness of the path and the lack of level ground, and he was certain that the rail line on the west bank is less expensive and easier to construct because it is a simple flat surface and it requires only some leveling and laying the rail."[149] As noted earlier, officials were still debating the issue of which river bank to employ during the major Upper Egyptian rail capacity study of 1946. Despite months of study and an extensive report, the director of Egypt's railroad department and two assistants later went personally to inspect and "report which of the two areas is more suitable for the execution of this project."[150] Most commentaries on the rail link's location focused on costs and technical difficulties involved, but Muhammad Shahin Hamza focused on the railroad's local economic development possibilities in his parliamentary comments. Despite his claims of having no "personal interest" in the railroad's location, being from the region he was clearly concerned that costs or technical difficulties might force the railroad far from the local population that could benefit from it. He stated on 30 December 1947 that engineers studying the project were saying

> that its close proximity to the Nile costs more than its extension through the deserts, but I hope—in view of the moral and spiritual benefits obtained from it—the competent authorities do not scrutinize long this matter because the rail line begins close to the Nile at Shellal and ends near it also at Halfa and it is most important that all the line extends close to the Nile because that contributes to the prosperity of the region.[151]

Whatever factor was most influential—determining the best location, the prohibitive costs of the project, technical problems, or something else—the result was still that neither greater local interest after 1935 nor wartime provisioning needs led to the establishment of this connection. In a letter to Egypt's prime minister on 18 May 1944, the governor-general wrote that despite shortages of railroad stock at times the current "transport on the Nile Valley route should suffice for normal further increase."[152] Although an additional survey by Egypt's railway department would be conducted in 1949, by the end of the Second World War the likelihood of a Halfa–Shellal railroad had diminished greatly.[153] Also by this time Egyptians were increasingly utilizing other means of transporting goods between the countries. Issawi, in his 1947 study, refers to the presence of a desert road in the region, stating that "it is probable that this road, together with the development of air transport, will obviate the necessity for a railway between Aswan and Wadi Halfa."[154] Other means of transportation, some of which will be addressed directly, may have assisted in the movement of goods and people between Egypt and the Sudan, but the symbolic—political—importance of a railroad connection was not lost on Egyptian leaders. Even the post-1952 Egyptian leadership recognized the importance of a railroad link, although they were *still* advocating examining the project. The Cairo Chamber of Commerce published the new government's transportation policy report in November 1953. This report concluded by stating, "We should not forget this research is necessary to further the connecting of the Sudan and Egypt by railroad which would be among the wisest expressions of nationalism."[155] Like the division of the Nile waters, the failure to establish a direct railroad connection was an obvious symbol of the independent nature of each region and a major blow to the hopes of Egyptian nationalists.

Motor Vehicle Transport in the Halfa–Shellal Reach

Despite the railroad failures, the establishment of roads and employment of motor vehicles in the region became an increasingly attractive option from the mid-1930s forward. Such capabilities might have lowered costs in the shipment of goods and certainly would have solved the problems of river transport delays, disruptions, and the length of time required to traverse this region. In 1932 the Halfa Province governor noted the potential of improving transportation through motor vehicle usage when he reported that "there are now 300 miles of motorable road between the Egyptian boundary and Dongola Province, so that six days' journey by steamer and train between Dongola and Wadi Halfa has been reduced to two days by car."[156] Despite such encouraging prospects, there were some factors that hindered large-scale adoption of motor transport within both countries, especially in the Halfa–Shellal region.

First of all, during this period the potentials of vehicular transport in the Sudan were only just beginning to be realized. In 1928 the governor-general reported that "costs are too high to permit motor transport of more than a few high-priced articles, and the camel is still a strong competitor with the lorry."[157] Still, the following year's report did note that road traffic in the Sudan had seen a significant increase.[158] The introduction of motor vehicle transport in Egypt had progressed further. In the Chamber of Deputies on 18 April 1934 Ahmad Wali al-Jundi noted that the latest statistics reported that fifty thousand people were employed by the motor transport sector.[159] The movement of people and commodities by motor vehicle was certainly not the dominant means of transport in the region, but by the 1930s this option was increasingly a threat to the existing rail and river system.

Increased use of motor vehicles was problematic for both administrations because revenues from their respective railroad networks were an important financial resource. In response, the governments began to enact legislation designed to limit competition with railroads by requiring licensing, setting fees, and prohibiting usage of motor vehicles in some areas. In 1932 Egypt's Ministry of Transportation reported its complete concurrence with the Council of Ministers' decision to "place strict supervision upon the activity of these cars."[160] The primary method of such "supervision" in Egypt was through the government's passage of Law No. 44 in 1934, which established registration procedures and annual fees for all types of motor vehicles.[161] The Condominium administration enacted similar legislation to control motor vehicle traffic and limit competition with the railways. The Public Order Ordinance of 1921 allowed each provincial governor to "provide for the regulation of road traffic in any town or on any public road within his province."[162] Subsequent decrees in 1929, 1930, 1932, and 1938 reaffirmed governors' powers over motor traffic in their provinces, through control of registration procedures and licensing fees.[163] In 1934 the Sudanese government issued a new ordinance that appeared designed to discourage the use of vehicular transport between the two countries. The annual report for that year stated that "the 'Carriage of Goods by Motor (Control) Ordinance, 1934' was enacted in August to prohibit competition with the railways in the northern districts of the Sudan."[164] Clearly, this ordinance's objective was to discourage entrepreneurs from establishing motor transport enterprises, undertakings that could have facilitated Egyptian–Sudanese exchange.

Although the governments tried to control motor traffic and limit competition with the railroad systems, vehicular transport capabilities still expanded. With the renewed efforts to encourage Egyptian–Sudanese commerce after 1935, interested Egyptian parties increasingly viewed motor vehicles as a means of ameliorating the transport difficulties in the Halfa–Shellal region. Members of the 1935 economic mission consistently discussed transportation with their Sudanese counterparts and

Condominium officials, but the first proposal for a road would not emerge for a year. In a 1936 meeting of the Chamber of Deputies, 'Abd al-Sadiq 'Abd al-Hamid proposed the "establishment of a land route on the west bank of the Nile River linking Shellal with Halfa so that the movement of cars transporting passengers, commodities and produce is possible, and in order to facilitate the governance of these regions."[165] However, the following year Ministry of Transportation officials recommended rejecting this idea, stating of the proposed road that "cars are not found in this region, and it is not anticipated that cars from another area will use it, and therefore the ministry sees no reason to construct it, being content with the means of water transport between Shellal and Halfa."[166] 'Abd al-Sadiq 'Abd al-Hamid brought the issue up again during the chamber's debate of the Ministry of Transportation's budget for that year. This deputy mentioned that transport facilities between Halfa and Shellal were essential for the success of agricultural projects being established there, and that since prisoners could be used for the construction work, the costs should not exceed LE35,000.[167] Still, the ministry opposed this project because, according to its investigation, road construction would have to cross deserts and cut through mountains, leading to expenses more than ten times the estimates of this representative.[168] 'Abd al-Sadiq 'Abd al-Hamid had advocated the establishment of a road in this region for a variety of reasons, but when the permanent committee, the Egyptian economic experts in the Sudan, and other government officials debated the merits of the project, they singled out the road's utility for the exchange of goods between Egypt and the Sudan.

Just prior to the Second World War there were increased efforts from these and other sources to establish a road or, more precisely, to repair routes whose condition had deteriorated. On 26 February 1938, the permanent committee agreed that among the measures needed to promote Egyptian exports to the Sudan was the establishment of a Halfa–Shellal land route more conducive to motor transport. The committee had received reports indicating that this project could be easily carried out.[169] Subsequently, the permanent committee decided to forward "an extensive memorandum in respect to constructing a road" to Egypt's Ministry of Transportation.[170] In addition to gaining administrative support for the project, 'Abdallah Fakri Abaza noted that the committee and other interested parties sought the opinions of the Royal Car Club of Egypt on the commercial viability of such a road.[171] Although private-sector interest in a motorable road had increased steadily, the growing likelihood of conflict in the latter 1930s and subsequent wartime provisioning requirements of the region resulted in greater government involvement.

A road between Halfa and Shellal offered not only another means of Nile Valley transport but also faster transit of the region at a time when Red Sea shipping was seriously hindered. On 11 May 1939, Egypt's Ministry of National Defense decided

> to reexamine the road between Wadi Halfa and Shellal and its improvement so that it is possible to use it in the movement of military forces and the demands of wartime transport on the southern borders. To achieve this objective the ministry dispatched yesterday a number of members of the frontiers department to study the region which the current road traverses and to come to an agreement with the supervisory board for roadways in Upper Egypt of the Ministry of Transportation on means of preparing a new road.[172]

Furthermore, it appeared that the prospect of war and transport problems led to an urgency among government agencies to upgrade road facilities in the region. *Al-Ahram* reported later in May that a committee reviewing provisioning needs in the Nile Valley in case of war had recommended to the Egyptian government that it

> pursue the improvement of the road between Shellal and Halfa, in view of its military importance and the necessity of using it in addition to the waterway in emergencies.
>
> The Ministries of Defense and Transportation had in fact agreed on expediting the execution of this project, and instructions had been sent to the inspector of roads in Upper Egypt to travel to Shellal and arrange with personnel of the frontiers department for the exploration of the road to estimate improvements and the required costs for this.[173]

Improving means of transportation, capable of handling wartime traffic, was not an objective of the Egyptian government alone. British officials of the Condominium, who had done little to encourage rail or any means of linking the two regions earlier, were now equally involved in exploring vehicular possibilities in the region. Actually, British administrators of Wadi Halfa compiled the initial reports on road prospects. A Halfa–Aswan road would traverse some 350 kilometers and require ten hours of travel time rather than two days via steamship. The road was readily motorable for all but a twenty-seven-kilometer span that had heavy sand, requiring vehicles to travel at a speed of thirty-five kilometers per hour to pass safely.[174] 'Abdallah Fakri Abaza, the economic expert at the time, noted that an official from Wadi Halfa Province had made experimental trips along the east bank of the Nile and that "it was clear from reports that the route is appropriate for use and that it is possible to traverse the distance . . . in cars intended for travel in the desert."[175] The requirement that vehicles using this route be capable of desert travel was obviously not conducive to increased motorized transport in the region. In April 1939 Muhammad Shahin Hamza attempted to interest his government in an easily improved route on the west bank "because it is a sandy route whose paving can be readily accomplished. Moreover, there are some motor vehicles passing between various regions in this area."[176] Unfortunately, similar to the multiple proposed railroad connections, the Egyptian government seemed to spend more time studying the prospect of a new or improved road rather than actually constructing it.

The existing Halfa–Shellal motor transport facilities were improved sufficiently to meet Britain's regional military needs during the Second World War. Reports indicated that British interest in the road was simply part of their responsibility for the defense of Egypt and the Sudan. For instance, in October 1940 *al-Ahram* reported that "the correspondent of the 'News Chronicle' in Cairo has learned that the primary result of British commitments to spend on defensive preparations in Egypt will be the construction of a paved road between Wadi Halfa and Aswan."[177] In August 1942 the Ministry of Transportation stated that the road's "preparation was completed and it had become suitable for traffic, and that the British authorities are undertaking from time to time the placement of a layer of asphalt in the sandy places."[178] Repair of a road for traffic other than that absolutely necessary during wartime seems an unlikely Condominium concern, especially since this administration had done so little to facilitate transport along the Nile route for decades. Egyptian officials were not oblivious to the wartime utility of a serviceable road, but they still had broader objectives in mind. The economic expert, when summarizing the 1939 report from Wadi Halfa officials, stated, "The Ministry of Trade was interested in this subject, and that was because of the economic benefits to be derived from the improvement of this road [and its] facilitation of the transportation of goods between the two countries."[179] However, the main factor undermining the actual establishment of a motorable road was not the multiple purposes for which it might be used but rather the continuing debate over whether road or rail better served Egyptian–Sudanese interests.

Egyptians generally favored a railroad over a road connection between Halfa and Shellal. However, financial constraints and the desire for the rapid establishment of some type of more efficient transport led to much debate, which may have undermined both plans. In early 1939, as war loomed and the need for a shorter route to the Sudan increased, the Egyptian government proposed "the establishment of a road for motor vehicles, if the budgetary situation and lack of time do not allow the construction of a rail line between Halfa and Shellal."[180] Clearly, the road option was not the first choice. By the summer of 1939 the permanent committee members had spent years examining transportation with the Sudan and were intrigued by reports of much shorter trips utilizing a road, but this did not lessen the importance of a railroad connection. In June *al-Ahram*'s editorial staff wrote,

> Previously we have alluded to the permanent committee's studying of the project of joining the Egyptian railways to the Sudan railroad to facilitate communications between the countries. We have noted the importance given to this matter, whose implementation is currently difficult because of weighty expenses, and that the car road may be a substitute for it temporarily.
>
> However, among the truths which cannot be ignored is that the car road cannot be traversed except in the winter. As for the summer, the trip would be impracticable, unless stations for rest and supplying cars with fuel and water were established.[181]

Despite both such shortcomings and the Egyptians' preference for a railroad, a serviceable road existed during the Second World War, largely because of British insistence. The conflict eventually ground to a halt, but the road versus rail debate among Egyptians did not. On 11 December 1945, in the Chamber of Deputies, Muhammad Shahin Hamza objected to the Ministry of Transportation's statements that the road between Aswan and Wadi Halfa was sufficient for current needs. Although this deputy had supported establishing the road earlier because of the expenses of railroad construction and the dire needs of the war years, he now stated of the supposedly "satisfactory" road,

> As for what the committee stated, it is only half correct in that there is an existing road there [between Aswan and Halfa], and the incorrect part is that the road is sufficient for the intended objectives. Because the British military authorities constructed a road between Aswan and Halfa that parallels the Nile in some regions of Nubia and then penetrates deeply into the deserts for 150 or 200 kilometers and then returns to run along the Nile again. And in this shape it does not pass

> through the country and it does not assist in the transport of produce or people in the region. Therefore, I hope for a reexamination of this proposal and that the committee will form an opinion of greater depth than that produced, and my intention is no mere desire to facilitate transportation in Nubian lands, indeed the most important objective is working to bind the regions of Egypt and the Sudan.[182]

Although Muhammad Shahin Hamza clearly had a special interest in the Halfa–Shellal region, like other Egyptian nationalists he stressed the diplomatic importance of any Sudanese connection. However, the road needed during the Second World War was unsatisfactory for normal transport traffic, and Egyptians were 'back to square one,' relying primarily on steamship service for the Halfa–Shellal stretch.[183] Muhammad Shahin Hamza, always the most vocal proponent of transport improvements in this region, favored establishing both rail and road services. On 10 February 1947, he stated that "among the means which would assist in bringing together the halves of the valley is a railroad extension between Shellal and Halfa and establishment of a road for cars." Additionally, he claimed the railroad should be less costly and difficult since he heard the British had proposed selling Egyptian authorities rail line that had been laid during the war.[184] Yet a year later he was raising the same 'possibilities' in parliamentary debates, stating,

> The Ministry of Transportation is now *interested* in a project of extending railroad between Shellal and Halfa to tie Egypt to the Sudan. There is another project I think would be considered helpful to this project, and it is building a road for cars between Aswan and Halfa or Shellal and Halfa, and the Roads and Bridges Department had already made great *progress in studying* it. Therefore, I hope that His Excellency the Minister of Transportation will work to finish this research and be concerned with it so that it comes to a conclusion, especially in that the [car] project does not cost much in the way of funds in proportion to the railroad project which requires heavy expenditures and a long time.[185]

Evidently, the need to conduct studies, the concern over expenses or construction time frames, and the debates over rail or road connections that Egyptians had faced in the 1930s were still facing them a decade later.

Interest in establishing a road to link Egypt and the Sudan emerged late, and may have been symbolically less useful than a rail connection, but a road would have aided commercial exchange and other economic activities. However, increased efforts and activities after the 1936 Anglo–Egyptian treaty, and even wartime restrictions on traditional Red Sea traffic, did not result in the construction of a Halfa–Shellal road. In his examination of the Nile Valley's transportation system at the time of Sudanese independence, Fabunmi notes that "there is no motorable road between Egypt and the Sudan."[186] Overall, the desire of local entrepreneurs to establish improved transportation along the Nile route, whether via railroad, steamship, or motor vehicle, remained unfulfilled. To a great extent transport to and from the Sudan along the Nile had changed little since the founding of the Condominium administration. Travel or transport of goods from Cairo to Khartoum required a twenty-hour trip by rail to Shellal, followed by two nights spent on steamships operating twice a week to reach Halfa, and a final forty-hour journey via train to the destination.[187] Such difficulties were certainly a hindrance to the development of an Egyptian–Sudanese commercial relationship, and therefore local interests hoped to improve transportation via the Red Sea.

Egyptian–Sudanese Transportation via the Red Sea

Well before the Condominium era, the two primary routes for Egyptian–Sudanese commercial exchange were either along the Nile River valley or by sailing ships in the Red Sea.[188] Early Sudanese government studies of transport options suitable for economic development recognized the necessity of a direct railroad link to the Red Sea. Furthermore, increasing the Sudan's foreign trade had required the construction of a modern port capable of handling larger commercial vessels at the terminus of the railway. Although these facilities were necessary for economic development, Egyptian interests believed that this system was also a deliberate British method of separating the Sudan from Egypt. In his study of Port Sudan, Kenneth Perkins notes that most Egyptians felt the new harbor was designed to deflect trade from Egypt, whereas "others believed that the establishment of a new port was a plot to undermine Suakin, the one Sudanese city in which Egypt had maintained a modicum of influence throughout the Mahdia and whose continued prosperity would clearly have benefited Egypt."[189] Reflective of Egyptian opinion on British transportation planning is *al-Jarida al-tijariya al-misriya*'s 1939 statement that "the Sudanese government has not worked to facilitate this transport on the Wadi Halfa route, instead favoring the Port Sudan harbor route."[190] The absence of a railroad connection between Wadi Halfa and Shellal may have symbolized the 'independent' economic nature of the two countries, but the construction of Port Sudan and a railroad linking it to the Sudanese Nile Valley created the reality of two independent economies. The combination of no Halfa–Shellal link and the new Sudanese link to the Red Sea transformed Egypt into merely one of the many commercial 'partners' of the Sudan in the global economy.

In addition to providing the Sudanese with access to international markets through Port Sudan, the transport of goods to and from this harbor was mainly a preserve of foreign shipping firms. Foreign shipping companies not only dominated Sudanese commercial exchange with international markets but also were a strong presence in shipping to Egypt. Increased foreign shipping directly to Alexandria cut into the revenues of local maritime companies Misr and Khedival lines and that of the Egyptian railways, which relied on receipts from Suez-to-Alexandria traffic. By November 1938 the Ministry of Transportation awarded these two local shipping lines a 25 percent rate reduction if they sent all their consignments from the Sudan via the Suez–Alexandria rail.[191] Clearly, Egyptian–Sudanese trade carried out via Port Sudan, the Red Sea, and foreign shipping firms had multiple negative consequences. If Sudanese transport plans were funneling its trade along this route, one method of mitigating the negative impact of these circumstances was to encourage Egyptian involvement in Red Sea transportation. Although the Khedival shipping company had been engaged in this traffic, most nationalists' hopes rested on increased participation from Misr Navigation Company.[192]

One member of the initial economic mission in 1935 was a Misr Group representative whose reports contributed to the expansion of Misr Navigation Company activities in the Red Sea. Eric Davis notes that Isma'il Gad Baraka Bey's reports were "instrumental in the creation of a committee of Misr Group directors and managers which flew to the Sudan later that year to finalize plans to open offices of the Misr Navigation Company."[193] Prior to the actual establishment of Misr Group offices in the Sudan, its shipping company had already begun service in the area. On 26 March 1935, *al-Siyasa* reported that Misr Navigation "began an organized line of communication for trade on small ships in the Red Sea between Suez and Port Sudan and ports in between."[194] In November of that year, speaking to the Khartoum Chamber of Commerce, Talaat Harb delivered a wide-ranging speech on the recent efforts of the Misr Group and stated "we have established a shipping route between the ports of Suez and Port Sudan and operating between these ports are ships of Misr Maritime Navigation Company, which has representatives in your beautiful capital."[195] During the first mission, Fu'ad Abaza sent a telegram to Talaat Harb noting how the arrival of another Misr Group ship to Port Sudan for the first time had pleased Sudanese traders.[196] Davis' study mentions Misr Group activities in Port Sudan and explains that "Bank Misr sought to make profits on its transport of goods between Egypt and the Sudan and through selling products of the Misr companies" there.[197] Prior to the Second World War this company's business steadily improved, but it never seriously threatened foreign shipping companies' dominance of Sudanese cotton exports and imports of manufactures. The 1938 annual report on Misr Navigation noted of the Red Sea service that "this line had become regular, so that a boat departs Suez every week."[198] The apparent profitability of these activities was alluded to as well. The 1938 report also hinted at the profitability of the activities, noting that due to increased business the company had acquired an eighty-year, 4,500-square-meter lease on a good location in Port Sudan to construct a warehouse and branch office.[199]

Misr Group involvement in Red Sea transport was a positive development, though service once per week was not overly encouraging. Additionally, there were clearly other problems for this transport route. For instance, transport from Suez to Port Sudan was not more rapid than the Nile Valley route. Egypt's first mission to the Sudan traveled by steamship in the Red Sea and spent four whole days going from Suez to Port Sudan alone.[200] Most Egyptians hoping to utilize this route for increasing commerce with the Sudan focused on lowering the costs of transport. The rates charged by shipping companies were a critical component of the high costs of Red Sea transport. In 1936 the Cairo Chamber of Commerce reported that during discussions of obstacles to increasing rice exports to the Sudan, members decided that the Egyptian government should "work to reduce the rates of transporting it by means of an agreement with the companies that carry out sea transport between Egypt and the Sudan."[201] Although this initiative was designed for one specific product, Fu'ad Abaza recorded that the permanent committee had sought general rate reductions. He stated that among the committee's primary objectives was

> the lowering of rates of transporting Egyptian goods between Egypt and the Sudan—the committee endeavored before the Misr Navigation Company for the reduction of transport rates on its ships between Suez and Port Sudan because these rates are oppressive. And the said company promised to study this plan, while the committee contacted the remaining navigation companies about this objective.[202]

The costs of transport via the Red Sea were problematic for Sudanese exports, too. For example, normally exporters moved Sudanese livestock along the Nile Valley route, but veterinary restrictions in Lower Egypt just prior to the Second World War compelled exporters to use Red Sea transport in order to reach the Alexandria market. These circumstances led to complaints regarding oppressive rates charged by shipping companies and excessively high harbor dues collected on vessels entering Alexandria's harbor.[203]

Although the permanent committee and other concerned parties achieved no success in reducing shipping rates, harbor duties were eventually modified. The permanent committee postponed taking any action on this issue initially, but during its meeting on 8 March 1938, representatives of the Khartoum Chamber of Commerce "clearly stated the desire of the Sudan for lowering the Alexandria harbor fees on ships carrying Sudanese cattle."[204] Consistent protests and Egypt's increasing need for meat supplies with the outbreak of war finally led to major reductions. 'Abdallah Fakri Abaza wrote that harbor duties at Alexandria were lowered from LE32 to LE13 on ships transporting Sudanese livestock or produce, on condition that the vessels were 'coastal' ships plying between Egypt and the Sudan only, and with a maximum carriage of 1,000 tons.[205] Although the government had to implement special veterinary measures to protect Egyptian livestock, it is noteworthy that the development of exceptional circumstances during the war was a prerequisite for lowering port fees.

The improvement of the port fee situation was an exception in respect to the impact the Second World War had on Red Sea transportation. Assessments of this impact varied considerably. Egyptian and private-sector Sudanese interests noted difficulties with the war's outbreak, while Condominium officials claimed wartime transport concerns caused little trade disruption. Mahmud Zaki, Egypt's economic expert during the war, wrote of maritime transport restrictions impacting trade, but also noted that "Sudanese imports from Egypt are not limited if they arrive by a non-sea route."[206] Controls on maritime traffic imposed with the outbreak of war were causing inflationary trends in Sudanese markets. In the annual meeting of the Khartoum Chamber of Commerce, its president stated of inflated prices that "the reality is that the basic cause is the destruction of the system of maritime shipping," but the government's provisions committee was seeking a solution to the problems.[207] This same Condominium government committee had claimed in January 1940 "that developments had not occurred in the naval war to cause interruption in shipping for the Mediterranean Sea and eastern routes. And it is probable that there will be sufficient space on board ships for the transport of Sudanese exports, except cotton which sometimes encountered difficulties in its transport to western markets."[208] Obviously this committee was concerned with all Sudanese foreign trade, but the director of the Sudan's Department of Economics and Trade dismissed the idea that maritime transport restrictions might impact trade with Egypt. After noting maritime restrictions, he stated, "As for commodities which are exported by rail or parcel post, they are unrestricted . . . which has had the greatest influence on the continuation of commodity export from Egypt to the Sudan."[209] Although this Condominium official dismissively implied that Egyptian–Sudanese trade proceeded along the Nile route, in fact some vital commodities were shipped via the Red Sea and such transport was certainly restricted.

Maritime transport during the war was limited because of allied shipping demands. The customs departments of the two countries instituted a special measure to ensure that shipments of essential items, the transport of which was permitted, were not directed to other, more profitable markets. The Cairo Chamber of Commerce reported that customs departments had not forbidden the shipment of such goods to the Sudan, "except that in order to guarantee the arrival of commodities exported by sea to Sudanese ports they have decided to obtain financial sureties in relation to the value of the commodities, and to return these sureties after the assurance of their arrival in the Sudan."[210] The imposition of this procedure was an inconvenience for Egyptian exporters, but simply the shipping space requisitioned for the war effort had a greater impact on trade via the Red Sea. A good example of this problem occurred in 1943, in regard to Sudanese cotton seed exports to Egypt. The Egyptian government had taken special measures to lift the ban on cotton seed imports in response to extraordinary local demand for edible oils, but the Ministry of Commerce and Industry claimed the allied war effort dictated whether or not a sufficient number of vessels for transport could be found.[211]

Obviously, the war presented Egyptians who sought to facilitate Red Sea transportation with temporary difficulties, but the earlier efforts of the interwar period had achieved mixed results at best. Short-lived or narrowly targeted rate reductions occurred, but no mention of broad, permanent lowered rates from shipping companies was evident. Additionally, despite the efforts of Misr Group, Port Sudan's maritime transport remained predominantly a preserve of foreign firms. Throughout the Condominium era Port Sudan remained the primary outlet for Sudanese trade with the world, including Egypt. However, Egyptian officials knew very well that Sudanese trade through Port Sudan did little to bind the Sudan to

Egypt—dependence on the Nile Valley route did. Essentially, officials of the two regions worked at cross purposes. For instance, in response to claims that Egyptian regulations harmed Red Sea traffic, Prime Minister Mustafa Nahhas advised the Sudanese governor-general that "the protests about the lack of easing transport by the Red Sea route are not correct because transport by railroad is easily done."[212] In the end, maritime transport via the Red Sea was one of many options for moving goods between Egypt and the Sudan, none of which were tremendously advantageous to the development of economic bonds between the regions.

A further, and fundamental, blow to encouraging closer Egyptian–Sudanese relations was the fact that *both* countries' transportation systems were oriented primarily toward international, nonregional markets. Egyptian nationalists complained of Condominium railroad orientation and Port Sudan construction, but their own infrastructure was also designed to export cotton and import foreign manufactures. Altering the destination of exports or the source of imports would have given the Egyptian and Sudanese governments greater impetus to change transport facilities and policies. Egyptian nationalists' efforts to change trade patterns are explored below, but for the period under study the transport infrastructure matched economic trends. Simply stated, both administrations gave priority to transport facilities and policies that encouraged trade with the developed world. Neither wholeheartedly discouraged transportation along the Nile Valley; rather, they were most concerned over the budgetary implications of such development. Transport restrictions, freight or passenger rates, customs procedures, and even the existing physical facilities all gave the impression that transport between Egypt and the Sudan was 'foreign' trade or travel, rather than simply moving from region to region within a single nation.

5 Disguised Exploitation: Agricultural and Industrial Designs on the Sudan

> We encourage all people and the government to strive for the perfection of our economic and financial position in the Sudan. And I appeal to the capitalists among Egyptians to employ their money in various economic spheres in the Sudan. The projects in need of money there are numerous . . . [and] the mission of the [Egyptian] economic expert is the guidance of money to these projects, whether they are agricultural, industrial, or commercial, and by this method we may serve our nation and fulfill our duty in respect to our Sudanese brothers.[1]
>
> —Muhammad Tawfiq Khashba,
> Egyptian Chamber of Deputies, 1945

Were Egyptians, such as Muhammad Tawfiq Khashba, proposing investment in Sudanese development for their own financial benefit or for the betterment of the entire Nile Valley, with potentially no return on their investments? The latter altruistic explanation seems rather doubtful. Still, Egyptians did consistently disguise personal or national expectations of financial gain behind a façade of concern for their 'brothers' in the Sudan. Egypt's Minister of Finance Makram 'Ubayd stated after the signing of the 1936 treaty that Egyptian entrepreneurs should recognize their responsibilities in the Sudan and that he hoped to encourage "their participation in the *activities of rebuilding* in the Sudan, through their money and efforts."[2] Makram 'Ubayd's comments do not imply any exploitative motive behind Egyptian involvement in the Sudan, but some private individuals rather explicitly acknowledged such motivations. For instance, local merchant/entrepreneur Salvatore Cicurel wrote in 1937 that the Egyptian and British governments must cooperate on specific measures to facilitate "the exploitation of the natural treasures of the Sudan."[3] Whether exploitative or not, Egyptians cloaked any true motives behind their investment initiatives in a guise of promoting the nationalist cause.

The analysis above of both transportation and Nile water usage indicates less than satisfactory results in promoting this nationalist cause. However, a critical concern of the new institutional and administrative bodies established in the mid-1930s was assisting Egyptian investment in the Sudan. Besides determining what fields of investment drew the most interest and activity from Egyptians, a central question in this analysis is which Sudanese or Egyptian groups expected to benefit from such investments (or actually did benefit). Furthermore, how might Egyptian investment have strengthened the economic unity of the Nile Valley and supported claims of sovereignty over the Sudan? The potential loyalty of the general population of the Sudan, resulting from Egyptian-backed development, could be considered a successful result of efforts. Popular support for the Egyptian cause within the Sudan is difficult to determine generally, and directly attributing such support to Egyptian investment is even more problematic. Did the Sudanese find employment in new Egyptian manufacturing plants? Did Egyptian land management result in a higher standard of living? Egyptians hoped that their entrepreneurial and general economic activities would promote popular support, but scholars of nationalist movements have been unable accurately to gauge such sentiments. Eric Hobsbawm writes about the degree to which popular support was measurable in established states: "We know too little about what went on, or for that matter what still goes on, in the minds of most relatively inarticulate men and women, to speak with any confidence about their thoughts and feelings towards the nationalities and nation-states which claim their loyalties."[4] Another scholar notes that "until quite recent times it is doubtful whether ostensibly nationalistic elites even considered the masses to be a part of their nation."[5] Although Egyptians presented their investment efforts as beneficial to the general population, winning the support of the Sudanese elite would have been more immediately useful to the nationalist cause.

If Egyptians could convince the Sudanese elite—a multifaceted but increasingly visible and influential group—that its economic future coincided with increased Egyptian entrepreneurial activity, then the investment initiatives would pay political dividends for Egypt. A truly united Egyptian–Sudanese elite, sharing a common view of their economic future, would have been a powerful impetus toward the single independent state Egyptians sought. However, in the colonial era, local elites—the Sudanese, in this case—could "create a magnificent monopoly for themselves" in economic, political, and other affairs by excluding those deemed to be foreigners—Egyptians, in this case—through the establishment of national frontiers.[6] In short, why share the Sudan's 'natural treasures'? Although written decades ago, Rupert Emerson's study of nation formation still accurately depicts the problem faced in unifying the economic interests of Nile Valley elites. He wrote that economic interests and national considerations do not necessarily coincide. "Deep cleavages of economic interest divide the bourgeoisie of any one country," Emerson explained, "and economic dealings with non-nationals across the frontiers may be far more advantageous than business conducted at home."[7] In the Nile Valley context, this meant that Egyptians had to convince their Sudanese counterparts that increased locally confined investment, development, and interactions were more advantageous than continued dealings with British and other "non-nationals" of the international economy.[8]

Egyptian efforts to overcome commercial ties to the international economy are the subject of the coming chapters. Although new commercial establishments founded to lessen these global market connections could be viewed as an investment activity, Egyptians also explored possibilities in industrial and agricultural fields. Furthermore, investing in agriculture or industry had greater potential of garnering the popular support needed politically to unify the valley. However, neither of these fields was free of difficulties. The founding of industrial establishments in the Sudan encountered the least administrative resistance from local British authorities. Unfortunately, although Egyptians expressed interest in Sudanese industrial potentials, frequently mentioning raw materials that could be utilized, western entrepreneurs were better positioned to provide the required financial, technical, and managerial resources and expertise. On the other hand, if Egyptians could overcome Sudanese administrative opposition, they had the experience and skills needed for agricultural investment in the Sudan—and a much greater desire to put forward their capital. Throughout the Condominium era Egyptians petitioned unsuccessfully for land ownership rights, lease of agricultural concessions, or simply a managerial role in agricultural schemes. Condominium officials maintained that any Egyptian control of Sudanese land would inevitably harm the interests of the local population.[9]

Egyptian nationalists claimed that investments in the Sudan would improve the lot of their Sudanese brothers. Successful industrial undertakings would translate into job creation, increase government revenue from fees and taxes, and lessen dependence on foreign imports. Egyptians conceived of such investments as part of efforts to achieve economic and political independence for Sudanese regions—ideally in a union with Egypt. Similar reasoning lay behind Egyptians' interest in agricultural ventures. Potentially, more land cultivated, increased agricultural production, and subsequently a raised standard of living for the average Sudanese peasant would translate into popular support for Nile Valley unity. Even if the benefits of investments did not 'trickle down' to the average peasant, profitable agricultural undertakings with the Sudanese elite might result in this group supporting Egyptian hopes of union. Obviously, Egyptian nationalists were hoping for many political 'potentials' and 'possibilities' from investing in the Sudan. Before assessing how diplomatically effective investment results might be, Egyptians had to achieve them.

Investment in Sudanese Agriculture

Egypt's large landholders were potentially the most active investors in the Sudan for a number of reasons. This group had the most extensive capital, already having become substantial investors in local trade and industry. It was also the politically dominant group in Egypt, potentially currying the greatest government assistance for its Sudanese initiatives. Finally, land ownership had been the most prevalent, or desired, investment option among Egyptian capitalists for decades. In his comprehensive history of land ownership in Egypt, Gabriel Baer writes that "land was considered a sign of social status, a secure investment, and, in periods of prosperity and high rents, a profitable one; and it was therefore greatly sought after by the very rich elements in the cities, such as members of the Muhammad 'Ali family, merchants and contractors, members of minority groups (who acquired land partly through land companies), and foreigners."[10]

Consequently, considering both the increasingly reduced scope for such activities in Egypt and the political motives behind closer bonds with the Sudan, the eyes of wealthy Egyptian landholders naturally turned southward. Egypt's first economic expert in Khartoum wrote, "There is no doubt that the Sudan [has] ample acreage suitable for agriculture and most of it is fertile, virginal land, which yields good amounts of crops without fertilizers."[11] Despite awareness of Sudanese agricultural potentials prior to the First World War, there were few expressions of interest and no specific actions until the latter interwar years.

During the earlier interwar years, most Egyptian concern about Sudanese agriculture was manifest in criticism of the British-dominated Gezira agricultural scheme. In addition to expressing fears about water usage and cotton production there, Egyptians criticized the overall results of the scheme and how British officials handled land ownership claims in the area. In June 1922 *al-Akhbar* printed claims by Sudanese agriculturalists that "ownership of the Gezira lands has been taken away, so that the landowner has become a poor laborer on his land."[12] Later that year the same newspaper published its letter to the governor-general, criticizing the chaotic ownership situation in the Gezira and the administration's unwillingness to permit land sales—to Egyptians or even to fellow Sudanese. This letter concluded by requesting from the governor-general "a detailed announcement on the methods by which these lands will be distributed, and the manner of their possession, their utilization and the prerogatives of the peasants."[13] Although British officials did not entirely disregard Sudanese ownership claims in the Gezira, the free disposal of one's property was subordinated to the government's desire to establish a technically sound and well-managed scheme, capable of benefiting owners, renters, and laborers.[14] Despite claims that land policies were largely dictated by scheme engineering requirements or concern for peasant welfare, Steven Serels has demonstrated that British imperial interests actually lay behind the policies. He argues that "in the first decades of the twentieth century the colonial government always constructed the definition of indigenous land ownership, and the rights and responsibilities that this signified, to suit its specific needs"—specifically, the need of raw cotton supplies, increasingly expressed by the British Cotton Growers Association.[15]

When the bountiful harvests of the Gezira scheme's initial years began to decline, Egyptians questioned the overall success of the project. For instance, during the Egyptian senate's debate on the 1936 treaty, Wahib Doss Bey stated, "It is known that the cotton growing project in the Gezira has in fact failed completely."[16] Some Egyptians attributed the lack of success to the British companies and Condominium officials involved in managing the Gezira scheme. After highlighting the shortcomings of the companies administering the scheme, *al-Akhbar*'s editors wrote, "If Egyptians undertook the administration of these companies, and the effective Egyptian labor force which is accustomed to working in weather like that of these regions was employed on them, then the harvests of these lands which have not been previously cultivated would be very abundant."[17] Egyptian government reports on agricultural conditions also noted production difficulties in the Gezira, implying again that increased Egyptian involvement would achieve better results. The 1938 report on the economic missions and permanent committee painted a dismal picture of the Gezira's future because of the anticipated increase in salinization and pest control problems. This report also stated of the Condominium's Gash River Valley scheme that the harvests there "are small in relation to the excellence of the soil cultivated."[18]

The validity of Egypt's criticism of British agricultural management in the Sudan is certainly open to questioning.[19] Furthermore, British-led agricultural development, various irrigation schemes primarily, generally improved the economic situation of peasants, at least those peasants on such schemes. Egyptian criticism of Condominium agricultural initiatives may have resonated with those Sudanese not linked to the Gezira and other schemes, but it was unlikely to win broad popular support for union with Egypt. Ultimately, Egyptians wanted to replace foreign control with their own 'brotherly' supervision of Sudanese lands. Some indications of Egyptian desire to acquire land usage rights were apparent in the early interwar period.

After visiting the Sudan in the First World War, Isma'il Sidqi commended the Condominium administration's concern for local peasants through its supervision of property transactions but felt that the extensive control would actually diminish the value of land and paralyze development. He alluded to the desire for possession of Sudanese lands by highlighting the critical role entrepreneurs had played in the success of Egyptian agricultural development. Sidqi asked, "The small Egyptian peasant, in spite of all his efforts, has he been capable with his means alone of succeeding in a similar enterprise?"[20] The statements of other Egyptians mirrored Sidqi's paternalistic or imperialistic tone. In 1924, Muhammad 'Alawi al-Jazzar Bey stated in Egypt's senate that his country did not demand colonization or possessions in the Sudan as payment for the Egyptian blood and money spent there, but that "sources of livelihood" were expected.[21] Egyptians would have to counter criticism of their exploitative motives eventually, but in the early interwar years interest in Sudanese lands was not widespread. "It was not until 1935," notes Eric Davis, "when the severity of the Depression began to make itself felt, that there was increased talk of investing in Sudanese agriculture."[22]

Nile Valley irrigation capabilities restricted the extent of agriculture in Egypt, but there was a greater variety of cultivable lands in the Sudan that could be profitably developed. The most extensive Sudanese agricultural areas were the rain lands of the central region of the country (generally south of the Gezira scheme), which required neither irrigation nor fertilizers. Some Sudanese residents noted the potential of these areas. In 1939 the Alexandria Chamber of Commerce reported that two Sudanese families with strong ties to Egypt had established farms there: "They have grown grains of various types, berseem, and fruits, and have produced good crops."[23] However, at the time these families were the exception because extensive development of agriculture in this region would have to wait for mechanized cultivation practices in the 1950s. Still, critics pointed to the Condominium's reluctance even to explore development of these lands. Dr. Rashed el-Barawy wrote in

1952 that Sudanese groups favoring union with Egypt had complained of their administration's focus on the riverain cotton-producing areas of the country, while only 1 percent of the estimated 2.9 million acres of grassland in the central region was being cultivated.[24] In an April 1947 lecture before the Royal Society of Engineers in Cairo, Dr. Husayn Kamil Salim stated that the Sudanese had been unable to benefit from these fertile lands because the region remained cut off from external markets. He added that "improved communications, organized production, and marketing facilities would work wonders in such a region."[25] Because the Condominium administration had not made marketing or infrastructure improvements, Egyptians interested in agricultural investment looked to other regions of the Sudan.

The primary areas of interest to Egyptians were the northern regions of the Sudan, where the establishment of pump irrigation schemes within the range of Sudanese infrastructure facilities was potentially profitable. From the early Condominium years Egyptians had been involved in this region, with British officials even encouraging an Egyptian presence. El-Haj Bilal Omer, in his study of Dongola Province merchants, writes that "it was a major policy of the early administration to encourage foreigners, especially Egyptian pensioners, to come and invest in the province's agriculture." This author also notes that two Egyptian Copts, previously associated with the forces that reconquered the Sudan, were the first to start pump schemes in the area during the First World War.[26] The Egyptian government had also been involved in northern Sudanese agriculture during this period. Prior to the establishment of the Sudan Irrigation Department in 1921, basin irrigation development had been supervised by Egyptian officials.[27] Reliance on basin irrigation methods and the limited acreage available did little to encourage early Egyptian investment, but still there were indications of entrepreneurial interests. The governor-general's report of 1929 stated that "in the northern riverain provinces, applications continue to be received for pumping licenses in spite of the low cotton prices prevailing."[28] With the requisite marketing facilities and similar agricultural techniques employed, increased involvement was almost completely dependent on Egyptians' ability to acquire land from private owners or the Sudanese government.

Efforts to purchase Sudanese land or acquire concessions to utilize it came mainly from private interests, with the Egyptian government assuming an advisory role at most. Even this limited governmental assistance did not begin until the Second World War. In December 1939 *al-Jarida al-tijariya al-misriya* noted that among the decisions of the permanent committee was the assignment of an agricultural specialist to study Sudanese conditions, to inform Egyptians of opportunities there, and to strengthen the agricultural ties between the countries.[29] Earlier that year Egypt's Ministry of Agriculture had enumerated its anticipated activities in respect to Sudanese agriculture: "This program includes sending of agricultural missions to the Sudan, selling implements of the Gardens Department, distributing the ministry's publications and technical circulars in the Sudanese regions, and showing agricultural films in the Sudan."[30] It is difficult to assess the impact such programs had, if any, on enhancing Egyptian–Sudanese agricultural cooperation, and the dispatch of an agricultural expert to the Sudan had still not been accomplished by the latter years of the war.[31] Fabunmi writes of these efforts that "Egypt sees economic linkage in the technical and financial assistance she can give to Sudanese agricultural development," but also notes that Britain had been providing the same.[32] However, British assistance included its direct involvement in, and profiting from, the management of agricultural schemes. Egyptian government technical or educational assistance may have been less 'exploitative,' but these activities were also a less effective means of immediately promoting Sudanese farmers' interests—and potentially winning Sudanese farmers' support for a united Nile Valley.

Although the Egyptian state left most of the actual investment in and management of Sudanese lands to private entities, one British official did suggest direct government involvement. Sir Murdoch MacDonald, an expert involved in the technical examinations of Nile River development, suggested placing regions west of the Nile in the northern Sudan under Egypt's control to facilitate communication with the staff at Jabal Awliya' reservoir. After noting that a private company could potentially utilize these lands, he stated that "from another perspective the expansion of [these lands'] resources and their improvement is possible by means of the government with its financial capabilities."[33] The Sudanese administration would never have considered relinquishing such a sizable portion of land, and although the Egyptian government had more extensive financial resources, acquiring Sudanese land remained primarily an endeavor of private interests.

During a meeting on 9 August 1934, the Royal Agricultural Society decided "to study a project of forming a company from notables of Egypt and the Sudan in order to purchase agricultural lands and utilize them."[34] Participants in this meeting also planned what would be the first economic mission to the Sudan, during which the process of examining lands that might be acquired began. It became quickly clear which regions most interested Egyptians. Fu'ad Abaza noted in a speech delivered in the Sudan on 19 February 1935 that the fertility of northern lands and the better possibilities of acquiring them made them the primary target.[35] Although the mission of 1935 was concerned with a variety of economic issues, especially strengthening commercial ties, the Royal Agricultural Society sent delegates to investigate land acquisitions. On 8 August 1935 the society decided on "the appointment of Husayn Farid Bey, deputy general director, and Mahmud Mustafa 'Ali Effendi, chief of the inspection department, to travel to the Sudan and examine some of its lands for the purpose of the society's purchasing a portion of them."[36] In November *al-Siyasa* reported that these individuals had successfully completed their work and that possibilities were being analyzed by the society.[37]

During the first economic mission an important meeting was held with members of the Khartoum Chamber of Commerce, at which time discussion touched upon the details involved in acquiring land. Although numerous individuals attended, the main spokesmen at the time were Fu'ad Abaza, the leading official of the Royal Agricultural Society and the primary initiator of Egypt's renewed economic interest in the Sudan, and Mr. Kontomichalos, the president of Khartoum's Chamber of Commerce, who was heavily involved in a variety of Sudanese agricultural, commercial, and transportation undertakings. At the beginning of this meeting on 18 February 1935, Kontomichalos noted that in spite of earlier successful discussions Egyptians had not moved any closer to establishing an agricultural company.[38] In response to Egyptian inquiries about how much he and other Sudanese would be able to contribute financially to a company, Kontomichalos indicated that "if it is possible to reach an agreement to include the plantation of his company in the new company, . . . he is prepared to contribute an amount equivalent to fifty thousand pounds of shares."[39] Kontomichalos went on to state that for the company to succeed it probably needed to acquire between forty thousand and fifty thousand feddans of land, necessitating an initial capitalization of at least LE500,000, and Egyptians could expect one-third of this amount from the Sudanese.

A critical subject addressed briefly during this meeting, which would constantly bedevil Egyptian efforts, was the question of actually acquiring land. Fu'ad Abaza hinted at a long, politicized process when explaining why no movement had occurred in forming the agricultural company: "The obtainment of reports, which we have not yet received, is naturally necessary, and it is understood that meetings . . . with the [Sudanese] financial and civil secretaries perhaps will assist in the gathering of information concerning the purchase of lands."[40] At this meeting Kontomichalos indicated that the two land acquisition options were obtaining a concession to use government land and forming an agricultural scheme in cooperation with current Sudanese landowners. At a party honoring a delegation from the Khartoum

Chamber of Commerce visiting Cairo in March 1935, 'Ali Barir, a Sudanese entrepreneur, stated that "we, as Sudanese, hope that this purchase will be from the nationalist landowners," rather than acquiring Sudanese government land, which would not benefit the local population as much.[41] This individual also noted that small plots of land were plentiful in the Sudan, while larger areas were most readily acquired through arrangements with influential Sudanese landholders, such as Sayyid 'Ali al-Mirghani or Sayyid 'Abd al-Rahman al-Mahdi (the main sectarian leaders of the country).

Despite the intense interest in forming an agricultural company in 1935, over the following decade Egyptians accomplished little other than continued studies or repeated expressions of interest. For instance, the economic mission of 1937 dispatched two individuals *to study* the Gezira region while Fu'ad Abaza *inspected* pump- and basin-irrigated lands in the northern provinces.[42] A 1939 report from the first economic specialist in the Sudan *hoped to spur interest* in Sudanese agriculture by describing the similarity of conditions there to those of Egypt and noting the tremendous yields from cotton, wheat, and dhurra cultivation.[43] The economic expert during the Second World War, Mahmud Zaki, included in his 1943 report specific plans for Egyptian involvement in Sudanese agriculture. He wrote that agreement was needed between the Royal Agricultural Society and Egypt's Ministry of Agriculture to

> establish a test field in the Sudan, whose area would amount to about 500 feddans, in which specialists from the society and the ministry would work under the direction of the economic expert, and from which sections would be formed for the cultivation of fruit, vegetables, grains and cotton, the raising of poultry, the production of dairy products, and the production of preserved foodstuffs. And whenever this project has succeeded, its transformation into a company for agricultural development is possible afterward.[44]

By the end of the Second World War, without any concrete results from purely private ventures, the Egyptian government became more involved in organizing agricultural investments, albeit with plans less grandiose than those of 1935.

The Condominium Administration's Control of Sudanese Lands

The failure of Egyptians to acquire lands capable of being profitably utilized was almost solely due to the strict Sudanese government oversight of land transactions. The Condominium did not oppose the development of agricultural potential, but worked constantly to protect the interests of local peasants. British officials were well aware of the central role agriculture played in the economy and were anxious to develop cultivable land across the Sudan. With the onset of the Second World War and the rising need for cereal cultivation in particular, Sudanese government encouragement of land use increased. In October 1939 *al-Ahram* reported of Condominium efforts that

> one of the official reports mentioned the persistent effort of the Sudanese government for the diffusion of utilizing pumps to exploit fallow lands, and the report indicated that people are beginning to investigate on their own the utilization of these pumps. And it stated that this development is cause for great satisfaction and its influence will be great in increasing the general prosperity.[45]

This 1939 report addressed potential pump irrigation throughout the Sudan, but some documents indicate Condominium hopes of developing agriculture in precisely the regions of interest to Egyptians. For instance, in 1940 the Sudanese Ministry of Commerce and Industry linked "improving the agricultural system by making use of basin irrigation in the northern provinces" to onion, tomato, bean, and other agricultural processing industries as means of solving wartime provisioning needs.[46] Still, wartime needs and supposed Condominium acquiescence usually did not result in permission for Egyptian entrepreneurs or companies to control Sudanese lands.

Despite a history of preventing foreign control of Sudanese lands, Condominium officials had given tentative assurances to the first Egyptian economic mission that acquiring land was permissible. *al-Jarida al-tijariya al-misriya* reported in February 1935,

> In respect to agricultural concerns, the two delegations [Sudanese and Egyptian delegates] were pleased by encountering the government of the Sudan's willingness to accept in principle the sale of agricultural lands for development, and this will result in support for the current idea of establishing a company with capital from Egypt and the Sudan to initiate this utilization [of land] for the advantage of both countries.[47]

The Ministry of Commerce and Industry's official report on post-1935 Egyptian activities confirmed that "the government of the Sudan sanctioned the possibility of Egyptians possessing lands in the Sudan, and their purchase from the Sudanese government itself or from owners in the Sudan after [gaining] the consent of the Sudanese government."[48] Obviously, the critical point here was that Egyptian acquisition of land would only occur with the consent of and under conditions imposed by the Sudanese administration.

Lands of the Gezira region were not transferable to Egyptians because a 1921 law required that these pass only to the government or residents of the region. Regulations governing property elsewhere were also problematic for Egyptians interested in agricultural investment. In his 1940 study, 'Abdallah Fakri Abaza complained that "as for land ownership transactions in other areas of the Sudan, it is permissible on condition of registration which cannot be accomplished other than through the consent of the provincial governor; and without his consent it is not possible to transfer ownership under any circumstances."[49] British officials maintained that difficulties Egyptians faced in purchasing land were not a result of discrimination against them specifically but rather of general landholding policies. The Sudanese civil secretary explained to Egyptians in 1946 that sales of land

> were not permitted, except with the agreement of the provincial governor, and the objective of this was to intercede between the Sudanese and the loss of their means of livelihood through the sale of their lands to wealthy foreigners, and these restrictions are applicable to the Egyptian, the Englishman, and all foreigners equally. The [Condominium] government has projects permitting the long-term lease of lands in cities to Sudanese and foreigners equally.[50]

Egyptian investors were not interested in leasing urban property. Additionally, Condominium concern for the welfare of Sudanese farmers essentially precluded the likelihood of purchasing tracts of private property sufficiently large to be profitably cultivated.

Still, the Condominium government controlled extensive areas that could be leased to individuals or companies. Egypt's first economic expert reported that in such concessions the Sudanese government retained control over the purposes for which the land would be used, the duration of the concession, and whether or not it would be renewed. All these conditions caused a great deal of anxiety among concessionaires about their future prospects and discouraged them from making permanent improvements to the property.[51] In a 1943 letter to the governor-general, Egypt's president of the Council of Ministers, Hasan Sabri, raised other objections to the Condominium's land policies. He urged the governor-general to alter regulations limiting a concession holder's ability to profit from increases in the value of the land, resulting from improvements made. The problem was that the existing procedures

> required that if the Egyptian government is given a piece of land in the Sudan according to these conditions, and [Egypt] comes to the point of not needing to use those lands, . . . then the possession of those lands or the portion of them not needed returns to the government of the Sudan upon repayment of the purchase price which the Egyptian government paid or upon repayment of its value according to the prevailing market price at that time, if this price was less than the purchase price. The government of the Sudan has, in addition to that, the right of purchasing the buildings then existing at the nominal price after the deduction of an appropriate value in consideration of wear and tear.[52]

Officials purportedly designed such policies to protect Sudanese farmers and prevent land speculation, but the policies also dampened Egyptian interest in land concessions.

Regulations that discouraged agricultural investment just when Egyptian interest rose in the 1930s were actually part of the Sudanese government's long-established administrative supervision of land ownership. In fact, within three months of the Condominium's establishment, British officials there issued a decree stating that "no person could deal with land or pass a valid title to such land" before a comprehensive land policy was promulgated.[53] In addition, the Land Settlement Ordinance of 1905 sought to prevent the activities of speculators by requiring government approval for the sale of land, the first manifestation of a guiding principle that would frustrate Egyptians in the 1930s and beyond.[54] Besides imposing administrative control over future land transactions, the Sudanese government also limited the ability of non-Sudanese, including Egyptians, to claim ownership of land. Few Egyptians successfully registered ownership claims, and those who did encountered various difficulties in retaining their property during the early Condominium years. The ordinances of 1903 and 1918 allowed government acquisition of land for public purposes. Most important for Egyptians, these laws required that documents contesting such acquisitions be presented in person to officials in the Sudan within a certain time limit, which was more problematic for absentee Egyptian landowners than for the Sudanese.[55] In 1925, the Sudanese administration issued an updated land law that firmly adhered to the same guiding principles of earlier legislation, namely, protection of local ownership and maintenance of the government's supreme authority over all land matters.[56] Any objective assessment of Condominium landholding policies would have to conclude that a general protectionist policy remained unchanged for the duration of this administration.

Likewise, the level of Egyptian interest and activity in agricultural pursuits in the Sudan remained unchanged—and unsuccessful. Egyptian entrepreneurs advocated the establishment of an agricultural company after the Second World War, just as they had in 1935. Yusuf Nahhas Bey, a member of a delegation sent to the Sudan in January 1946, stated that this economic mission "requested the establishment of a company with initial capital of LE50,000 with Egyptians and Sudanese participating in the undertaking of an agricultural project in the Sudan. The mission proposed to the government of the Sudan granting [the company] a concession to one of its projects in the south where the soil was excellent and workers were available."[57] By 1946 Egyptian interests may have changed to include Condominium-held lands and a more southerly location, but the financial scale, type of agricultural scheme, and Sudanese participation were no different than initiatives proposed over a decade before. Also in 1946, Egyptians attending an economic conference in Cairo drew up a list of proposals to improve links with the Sudan. This list included the "establishment of Egyptian–Sudanese agricultural companies to be entrusted with the development of lands and their preparation for cultivation and their sale to small property owners under easy conditions, with the utilization of a portion of [these lands] as model farms."[58] Apparently, having experienced years of obstruction from the Sudanese government, Egyptians had learned to employ phrases like "small property owners" and "easy conditions" in the hope of finally obtaining landholding rights.

Other Egyptian voices of the post–Second World War era were less concerned about directly linking Egyptian entrepreneurial and Sudanese peasant interests. A June 1946 article in *Majallat Ghurfat al-Iskandariya* on Egyptian unemployment and the potential of emigration to the Sudan concluded that "Egyptian entrepreneurs will be presented with an opportunity for investing their funds in agricultural projects capable of tremendous success. Profiting from the resources of the Sudan necessitates that it is shared work since Sudanese, Egyptians, and their representatives are inhabitants of a single valley, with a unified customs [system] and a common land."[59]

Whatever Egyptians claimed motivated their interest in agricultural investment, the actual project that was desired remained unchanged throughout the Condominium era. Egyptians sought a concession or ownership rights to sufficient land for the development of an agricultural scheme, similar to the Gezira, though not on that scale. Equally apparent from the continued expressions of the same objectives year after year is that Egyptians never gained a foothold in Sudanese agriculture. To a great degree, the conclusions of *al-Akhbar*'s editors in the early 1920s—that "the Egyptian is forbidden from purchasing [land] and from becoming an owner of anything in the Sudan"—retained their validity throughout this period.[60]

Condominium administration policies were the primary reason for the failure of agricultural investment plans, but by briefly reconsidering those plans it is clear that such investments were generally exploitative in nature. A large irrigated agricultural scheme could have benefited the common Sudanese farmer, but criticism of the exploitative nature of such systems would be equally applicable to either British or Egyptian managers. Increased productivity and revenues in such schemes were typically counterbalanced with a rise in the financial outlay required of individual farmers. Additionally, in these agricultural projects the 'external' management often increased regimentation of peasant work routines. Sudanese peasants would not have universally welcomed such changes—again, irrespective of whether those scheme managers were British or Egyptian. Furthermore, the Sudanese desire that Egyptian investors focus on privately owned land in their planning seems to imply that local Sudanese capitalists wanted a larger share of the anticipated profits gained through the peasants' labor. Even if exploitative of local peasants, shared entrepreneurial interests in agriculture might have aided the growth of Egyptian–Sudanese elite unity—potentially useful in Nile Valley union claims. However, there is no record of a cooperative Egyptian–Sudanese agricultural venture prior to independence. Finally, Egyptian objections to Sudanese government control over land transactions reveal the true nature of investment interests. Egyptian concerns about being allowed to profit from increases in land value indicate that their investment intentions were as much speculative as developmental.

Egyptian Emigration to the Sudan

Less speculative or exploitative of the Sudanese, but equally unimpressive in the development of economic ties between regions, was the encouragement of fellaheen emigration to the Sudan. Egyptian emigration is obviously not an 'investment,' but Egyptians frequently linked interest in Sudanese lands with potential employment of an increasingly numerous and land-hungry Egyptian peasantry. Matching the Egyptian fellaheen's need of agricultural work opportunities was the persistent absence of sufficient laborers in the Sudan. Sudanese participants in discussions concerning the establishment of an agricultural company in the 1930s mentioned the general need of agricultural laborers. At the meeting on 18 February 1935 that addressed this project in detail, Mr. Kontomichalos emphasized the necessity of acquiring land near Khartoum's larger labor pool if the company was to succeed.[61] In addition to the general lack of manpower, both Egyptian and Sudanese sources made reference to the potential benefits that could be reaped when the 'expertise' of Egyptian fellaheen was applied to the vast, fertile lands of the Sudan. Whether or not Egyptian fellaheen were truly experts capable of making Sudanese agriculture flourish is open to question. However, if their presence facilitated the establishment of agricultural projects capable of raising the standard of living or increasing profits for the Sudanese entrepreneurs involved, such developments might garner support for Egyptian hopes of economic and political unity.

A Sudanese 'solution' for Egypt's growing population problem was an additional benefit. Because of topographic and technical limits to increasing the area of cultivable land in Egypt, the population problem was becoming more of a concern to Egyptians. A 1946 article in the Alexandria Chamber of Commerce journal explored overpopulation and rising unemployment problems. The editors claimed that extending cultivable lands or expanding industrial development were insufficient remedies, and that "the only remaining solution is emigration to the Sudan."[62] High levels of emigration and more extensive intermixing of the Egyptian and Sudanese populations would have strengthened Egypt's claim of cultural and social unity in the Nile Valley. Because of such reasoning Egyptian officials consistently raised the emigration issue during talks with British representatives about the Sudan's future.

Anglo–Egyptian negotiations immediately after the First World War addressed Egypt's desire for complete independence, so extensive discussion of emigration to the Sudan was infrequent.[63] With a seriously diminished presence in the Sudan after 1924, emigration became a more critical issue for Egypt's negotiators. A 1936 parliamentary report recounting the history of past negotiating efforts noted that "Egypt demanded in 1930 the return of one army battalion to the Sudan and permission to emigrate to it."[64] Mekki Abbas noted that emigration was probably the chief cause of failure to reach a settlement in 1930: "The point on which the negotiations seem to have broken down was the introduction of a totally new issue in the dispute. The increase in Egyptian population became alarming by 1930, and the Egyptian delegation insisted on unrestricted emigration to the Sudan as a possible solution of this problem."[65] Egypt eventually obtained British recognition of its citizens' right to emigrate to the Sudan. The 1936 treaty specified that "Egyptian immigration into the Sudan shall be unrestricted except for reasons of public order and health."[66] However, obstacles to increased emigration remained in place, and the 1939 economic mission to the Sudan included the elimination of these obstacles among its primary objectives.[67] Like Egyptian property rights in the Sudan, emigration to the Sudan was permissible—except in certain conditions the Condominium administration determined.

Although emigration had not been a central Egyptian concern in negotiations until the 1930s, Egyptians had long considered the Sudan a natural destination for their excess population. For instance, after visiting the Sudan in 1918, Isma'il Sidqi concluded that with growing population and land problems in Egypt the government should consider the eventual need to colonize the Sudan, which he claimed would benefit the people of both regions.[68] Egyptian papers in the 1920s also emphasized the need for emigration to the Sudan and the prosperity it would elicit. In a 1922 article on Egypt's economic development and concern over Sudanese irrigation plans, Taraf 'Ali, a European-trained Egyptian engineer, wrote that "the continuous growth of the number of inhabitants in Egypt will make our resources inadequate for our numbers someday, and then we will find in the Sudan a spacious, fertile place."[69] *Al-Akhbar* noted in 1927 that increasing emigration to the Sudan to alleviate population pressures was a responsibility of Egyptian officials that required the cooperation of entrepreneurs, landowners, and even the common people. Moreover, the editors claimed that "the Sudan is the natural place of emigration. And we have emigrated to it in the past, we have made it a home, we have brought it culture, and we have developed its resources and made it a prosperous country."[70]

When the economic difficulties of the early 1930s were added to the existing population and land problems, emigration concerns became even more acute. On 4 January 1933, in the Chamber of Deputies, 'Abd al-Majid Mahmud Nafi' complained that the Sudan was the natural destination of Egyptian emigrants but that "the English policy is beginning gradually to deny Egypt's right in the Sudan."[71] In a 1936 article concerned primarily with Sudanese irrigation projects, *al-Siyasa*'s editors wrote that the Egyptian government should focus on its two uncontested interests in the Sudan, namely priority in Nile water distribution and "the organization of emigration to the Sudan as a precaution for the growth of Egypt's population in the future."[72] Actually, British and Condominium officials had contested Egyptian emigration rights, and therefore the 1936 treaty included firmer commitments on this issue. However, the treaty did not result in a surge of emigrants, and Egyptian officials continued strongly to urge movement to the Sudan. Prince 'Amr Tussun, the most active member of the royal family in Sudanese affairs through his leadership of the Royal

Agricultural Society, noted that because of land scarcity in Egypt and the limits on industrial employment Egyptians must look to the Sudan as a remedy.[73] He stated, "The one outlet open before us is the southern area where [one] finds extensive country with a small population and land of the nature of Egypt's land, which is irrigated by the same Nile."[74] After visiting the Sudan in 1935 a delegation of top Misr Group officials connected emigration and employment to increased investment, trade, and general prosperity. These officials highlighted

> the interest of Egypt and the Sudan in strengthening economic bonds between the two, and opening doors for work to many of the unemployed of the two countries when financial and industrial projects are established and when commerce of the countries finds good markets, not to speak of the upsurge of activity in the factories and subsequently the upsurge in transport activity and what follows that in increasing prosperity.[75]

Egyptians had initially advocated fellaheen emigration as a solution to growing land scarcity at home, but by the latter 1930s Misr officials and others included emigration as simply one facet of their nationalist economic development plans.

With the onset of the Second World War Egyptians continued to advocate emigration as a solution to both immediate domestic problems and future nationalist objectives, while simultaneously complaining of British officials imposing restrictions. For instance, on 28 November 1939, 'Abd al-Majid Mahmud Nafi' stated that the Condominium should end emigration restrictions and establish complete equality among Egyptians and Sudanese. He claimed that Egypt was the most heavily populated country in the world: "Indeed it is more crowded than Belgium and China—and there is no natural place of emigration for her other than in the Sudan."[76] The statements of some Egyptian politicians seemed to confirm Condominium officials' suspicions of Egyptian imperialist, exploitative designs upon the Sudan. Muhammad Fakri Abaza claimed that population growth and land scarcity were not problems because "we have the Sudan," and that "there are extensive areas of land which have not been utilized yet, and it is necessary that these be our home and that we cultivate them. We give the people of the Sudan from Egypt that which they are lacking, and take from them what exceeds their needs."[77] Most Egyptians were less cavalier concerning the Sudan and emigration. For instance, a December 1939 editorial in *al-Ahram* on emigration referred to Egyptian employees as "ambassadors" and the expectation that Egyptians working there would "encounter youths eager for connections to Egypt."[78] On the occasion of Prime Minister Ali Maher's visit to the Sudan that winter, one Egyptian business student noted,

> He hopes that [the prime minister's visit] opens paths before the youth of Egypt in emigrating to that brotherly region, and that they invest their energy and expertise in the development of idle resources there, and likewise he hopes that trade between the two countries progresses and induces large capitalists to invest in the Sudan, and build for Egypt its rightful position in this field of great abundance.[79]

Egyptians hoped that the involvement of landowners, industrialists, and other entrepreneurial elements in the Sudan would aid development and create jobs, but Egypt's population and land problems made the emigration of fellaheen the most important objective.

The Condominium administration did not strenuously oppose the emigration of Egyptian peasants, in contrast to other potentially troublesome groups. Because British officials were convinced that Egyptian 'intriguers' had been behind the 1924 disturbances, the Condominium government's general policy discouraged an Egyptian presence in the Sudan. Egyptian nationalists hoped to overcome this opposition to their presence by stressing the Sudanese need for skilled, educated Egyptian employees. A February 1935 article noted that because of the economic stagnation in the Sudan "the country is in need of the efforts of workers and experts who are capable of serving their country and protecting its interests and rights."[80] *Al-Jarida al-tijariya al-misriya* reported in 1938 that "in regard to the issue of Egyptian employees in the Sudan, the [permanent] committee studied it and contacted the Sudanese authorities about facilitating the employment of Egypt's educated youth in the Sudanese companies."[81] In another article, Fu'ad Abaza noted the importance of emigration as a means of quelling growing unrest within Egypt. He wrote, "It is necessary that the Sudanese region forms a wide sphere for the activity of the Egyptian youth who are on the point of unemployment, which carries their life away and increases their agitation and unrest."[82] Although Egyptians viewed emigration as a method of both mitigating the population problem and lessening political turmoil at home, Condominium officials were not likely to allow politically restive elements into the Sudan.[83]

However, the Sudan's chronic need for agricultural laborers and the similarity of agricultural practices were factors that would seem to have encouraged the fellaheen's emigration. Sudanese labor needs were such that the governor-general even approved Egyptian fellaheen employment on the Gezira scheme. 'Abd al-Halim Ilyas Nasir reported in 1922 that the governor-general had said he would "welcome the Egyptian fellaheen and he prefers them over the fellaheen of other lands for cultivating the land of the Gezira. It is understood by this that the governor-general means a special class of Egyptians, those who till the soil."[84] Egyptian sources consistently linked Sudanese labor needs to supposed Gezira failures and the fellaheen's farming expertise. For instance, a 1931 article in *al-Akhbar*, highlighting the difficulties the Gezira scheme was experiencing, stated that "the English have realized that it is not possible to make the Sudan prosperous with the Sudanese government's prohibiting Egyptian laborers from emigrating to these regions."[85] This article concluded by noting that "perhaps the secret to the failure of the Gezira irrigation plans is attributable to the lack of allowing Egyptians to work in these regions out of fear of political propaganda."[86] In the Egyptian senate, Wahib Doss Bey also argued that the absence of Egyptian fellaheen had exacerbated agricultural difficulties in the Sudan: "The English have found that the Sudanese are not suitable for development, and they have perceived the great need of Egyptian labor."[87] Not only were the Egyptian fellaheen most inherently appropriate for the farming of Sudanese lands, they were also the most practical remedy to persistent labor shortages.

Those entrepreneurs planning to establish an Egyptian–Sudanese agricultural company after 1935 were well aware that the lack of farmers posed a serious obstacle to their objectives. Fu'ad Abaza noted that even though Condominium officials had acknowledged Egyptian rights to possess land, investors would have to overcome the scarcity of Sudanese peasants.[88] The two experts sent by the Royal Agricultural Society in the summer of 1935 to study agricultural possibilities in the Sudan reported favorably on the fertility of the land but noted "there are problems surrounding its utilization, the most important of which is the obvious scarcity of manpower."[89] Besides remedying the limited labor force, potential investors also mentioned Egyptian agricultural knowledge as an essential ingredient to successful cultivation in the Sudan. During a speech in Omdurman at a party honoring members of the first economic mission, Mustafa Abu al-'Ala, a local entrepreneur, stated that "many of our lands are in need of expertise from you."[90]

Mustafa Abu al-'Ala was referring to all Egyptian social classes—from laborers to owners—involved in agricultural projects, but others specifically mentioned the knowledge and characteristics of the Egyptian fellaheen. 'Abdallah Husayn's account of the first economic mission recorded that

Sayyid 'Abd al-Rahman al-Mahdi's plantations employed a less intensive crop rotation because "the Sudanese fellah does not have the expertise of the Egyptian fellah in regard to fertilization, and because the lands are so abundant."[91] This author also claimed that the Sudanese were not as "attached" to agriculture as the Egyptian fellaheen, preferring such activities as livestock raising or gum Arabic collection at times.[92] It was not only Egyptians who claimed the Egyptian fellaheen were critical for Sudanese agricultural development. In 1937 Sudanese merchant 'Ali al-Barir wrote that "the Sudan is in the greatest need of the Egyptian farmer, famous for his vigor and well-known for his steadfastness, in order to utilize the extensive, fertile lands."[93] Egypt's first economic expert in Khartoum recommended countering insufficient Sudanese agricultural knowledge through the establishment of a test field with Egyptian specialists and fellaheen to instruct the Sudanese in person. He also wrote of labor shortages that "there is no remedy to this situation except the use of modern machinery in many agricultural processes and the utilization of some Egyptian fellaheen as a nucleus in the work to attract the greatest number possible of the [Sudanese] people to cultivate the land."[94] Whether as a means of improving Sudanese agricultural practices and participation or as a portion of the total labor force, the emigration of Egyptian farmers was an integral component of post-1935 agricultural initiatives in the Sudan.

Despite Egyptian nationalists' efforts to increase emigration, there was little evidence of fellaheen or others actually moving to the Sudan. References to Sudanese population statistics in Egyptian sources indicate that roughly four thousand Egyptians may have emigrated to the Sudan between 1935 and 1945.[95] When assessing this increase, one should remember that the 1936 treaty called for the return of military units and administrative personnel, some of whom would have been accompanied by relatives. In addition, four thousand individuals was not a truly significant level of emigration for an Egyptian population well in excess of fifteen million by 1930. Also, neither scholars of Egyptian–Sudanese relations nor Egyptian officials of the time period referred to large-scale emigration to the Sudan. For instance, a 1941 report from Egypt's Ministry of Foreign Affairs stated "that the emigration of Egyptians to the Sudan is still weak."[96] In 1952 Mekki Abbas wrote that despite the 1936 treaty's emigration provisions and the Condominium's preference for Egyptian immigrants over West African laborers, "no emigration in any appreciable quantity has taken place into the Sudan since the signing of the 1936 Treaty."[97]

Egyptian officials attributed the lack of significant emigration to obstacles the Condominium administration had placed before Egyptians wishing to travel to the Sudan. The 1936 Anglo–Egyptian treaty specified that "Egyptian immigration into the Sudan shall be unrestricted except for reasons of public order and health."[98] Mahmud Zaki pointed out that "the government of the Sudan imposes as a condition upon those Egyptians desiring to travel to it, the obtaining of a visa from the Sudan Government Agent in Cairo upon payment of a fixed sum of money."[99] He expressed his pleasure that Egypt's prime minister was planning personally to discuss this problem with the governor-general. However, Governor-General Huddleston's eventual response indicated no planned changes. He wrote that "entry into the Sudan is at present governed by the 1922 Passports and Permits Ordinance which requires permits to be obtained by all (including Sudanese) wishing to enter the Sudan" and that the cost of this travel was only a ten-piaster fee for border-control expenses.[100] Certainly this fee was not a huge expense, but it was a further discouragement to Egyptian fellaheen with few financial resources.[101]

Although Egyptian officials most often singled out Sudanese administrative measures as the cause of limited emigration, there were other factors involved. In analyzing which Sudanese regions piqued the most Egyptian interest, this study has argued that the northern Sudanese provinces were the primary target of preliminary examinations. Yet some of these areas were precisely those in which there was an abundance of laborers. The governor-general's report for 1933 noted that 80 percent of the male population of Halfa Province (the northernmost province) emigrated each year to Egypt and other parts of the Sudan in search of a livelihood.[102] There were labor shortages in Dongola Province and regions south of it, but even here certain characteristics of the Sudanese labor market inhibited increased Egyptian emigration. Most studies of Sudanese agricultural development have noted that the Sudan needed seasonal workers to meet the demands of peak labor periods on the irrigation schemes along the Nile River.[103] Seasonal work was clearly not sufficient impetus for increasing the number of Egyptians permanently resident in the Sudan. Also, the level of Egyptian emigration may have been indirectly curtailed by Sudanese water usage restrictions imposed through earlier Nile development agreements.

Finally, although difficult to determine precisely, the reluctance of fellaheen to leave Egypt must be considered. When addressing the movement of Egyptian laborers in his economic study, Issawi notes that "there is practically no emigration from Egypt."[104] This same general lack of enthusiasm for emigration was also apparent in respect to the Sudan. Fu'ad Abaza noted in 1935 that "we perceive some of the Egyptian youth do not take an interest in emigrating to the Sudan and do not care to reside there."[105] However, it was not merely younger Egyptians who were reluctant to move to the Sudan. In a radio address on 14 August 1939 promoting stronger ties to the Sudan, Egypt's first economic expert, 'Abdallah Fakri Abaza, described his own initial negative reaction to being recommended for the position. He said he was saddened, distressed, and fearful because he had heard of the terrible weather, poverty, and general lack of life's pleasures in the Sudan.[106] Egyptian officials or young graduates with higher socioeconomic aspirations would logically be somewhat averse to appointment in the Sudan, but this reluctance to emigrate was just as readily apparent among Egypt's land-hungry fellaheen. For instance, in 1946 the Alexandria Chamber of Commerce's journal alluded to peasant hesitancy to emigrate when assessing the potential results from combining Sudanese agricultural resources with Egyptian fellaheen expertise—a perfect economic, and nationalist, union. The editors wrote of the Sudan:

> There are extensive, extremely fertile lands and abundant water, while the small number of laborers is insufficient. And if the Egyptian fellah went to the Sudan he would produce miracles through employment of his capabilities of toiling, patience, expertise in agricultural matters, and love of the soil. We know that the Egyptian fellah loves his land and does not like to leave his country, or even his region. However, if some encouragements were arranged for him he would not hesitate to go to a country actually considered to be his country and would find himself among his family there.[107]

The same journal reported a year later that the only solution for Egypt's growing population and unemployment problems was creating jobs in commerce and industry, since "convincing the fellah of the necessity of emigration to [the Sudan] will take a long time, especially since we know the extent to which he clings to the piece of land that he farms and his aversion to leaving his country for another. If we do not presume that we can overcome this difficulty, emigration will remain limited to a small number of people."[108]

This antipathy toward working in the Sudan was not a new development. From the time of Muhammad 'Ali's first venture into the Sudan, Egyptian governments had used appointments in the region as a type of 'punishment,' and military service there, and elsewhere, was something fellaheen sought to avoid. Additionally, when confronted with Egyptian protests about their exclusion from the Condominium administration, British officials frequently claimed that Egyptians viewed Sudanese service as 'exile.' It is doubtful that any single factor was the primary cause of low emigration levels, but Egyptians claimed greater emigration would facilitate economic development in both regions.

Egyptian nationalists expected that the combination of emigration, agricultural investment, and subsequent economic development would convince the British, Sudanese, and Egyptians of the need for Nile Valley unity. Emigration that solved the strains of population growth and rising unemployment would solidify Egyptian public opinion behind unification. Increased emigration that blurred any lines between Egyptian and Sudanese identities would buttress traditional claims of Nile Valley unity. If the Egyptian fellaheen's presence accompanied new, profitable agricultural schemes, or their expertise raised productivity and the standard of living, potentially more Sudanese farmers and local entrepreneurs would be favorably inclined to a union with Egypt. Egyptians hoped coupling agricultural investments with Egyptian emigration to the Sudan might become politically advantageous in the end.

Investment in Sudanese Industry

Egyptians also hoped that political advantage might arise from investment in the industrial development of the Sudan. Such endeavors would ideally have the same sort of results as efforts related to agricultural projects, namely increasing entrepreneurial opportunities for the elite of the valley, providing new employment opportunities for both Sudanese and Egyptians, and raising the standard of living generally. Even though Egyptians were most interested and capable of investing in agricultural projects, the Sudanese economy needed entrepreneurial assistance in a variety of fields. Officials were well aware of the Sudan's dependence on outside sources of capital from the moment the country was reconquered by Anglo–Egyptian forces. In fact, a key reason behind the unique Condominium arrangement had been to facilitate foreign investment, without permitting the problems associated with capitulatory privileges to enter the Sudan. When requesting support for the new administrative arrangement, Sir Evelyn Baring (later Lord Cromer) wrote that "numerous demands had been received from Europeans who wished to reside, to invest capital, and to acquire real property in the country. They could not be refused access, and the introduction of their capital was considered necessary for future development."[109] British officials knew European capital would be critical to Sudanese progress, but some individuals had argued for Egyptians having a role in such activities. When later presenting the United Nations Security Council with Egypt's case for sovereignty over the Sudan, spokesmen referred to Winston Churchill's statements on the interdependence of the two countries. Churchill had said that Egyptian development depended on the Sudan to ensure its water supplies but also that "Egypt is no less essential to the development of the Sudan."[110] Churchill was among the very few British officials willing to consider Egyptian commercial or industrial investment in the Sudan, but the country's need of capital was apparent from the start.

In the immediate post–First World War years, most prominent Egyptians were occupied with gaining political independence and liberating their own economy from foreign control, but some leaders referred to investment possibilities in the Sudan. In a 1918 report Isma'il Sidqi wrote that with increased emigration, greater Egyptian involvement in utilizing Sudanese wood supplies and other raw materials might result.[111] A 1922 article in *al-Akhbar* also referred to forestry resources, as well as entrepreneurial activities in Sudanese livestock or agricultural produce processing. This article stated that "if interest in the refrigeration industry was shown, then it would be possible to export frozen meat to Europe and elsewhere from the country, just as Australia is now doing." The article concluded that if sufficient investment interest was forthcoming, "there will be a great industrial future for the Sudan."[112] However, like other aspects of Egyptian–Sudanese economic relations, concerted efforts to stimulate industrial investment were not consistently apparent until the mid-1930s.

By this later date Egyptians conceived of the industrial development of the Sudan as more than simply investing capital. Instead, officials hoped Egyptians would invest in industry, manage such undertakings, market industrial goods, foster nonagricultural employment, and undertake other such activities in the Sudan. Local officials and media encouraged all Egyptians to participate in Sudanese development, from peasants and manual laborers to capitalists. For instance, a 1935 article worded its appeal to Egyptians in the following manner:

> The powers which were able to empty the Sudan of Egyptians have not been able to safeguard prosperity and happiness for the Sudan. They have not been able to tolerate economic and financial difficulties, and the condition of the inhabitants has deteriorated. Stagnation and underdevelopment have befallen them. Despite the concern for agriculture and for ending [its stagnation] and the establishment of economic and financial institutions, the country is in need of active and intelligent men who can serve their country and protect its welfare and rights.[113]

In the years following the conclusion of the 1936 treaty, there would be growing expectations of profitable investments for Egyptians in the Sudan. 'Abd al-Majid al-Rimali, editor of the Cairo Chamber of Commerce journal, considered the key elements of the 1936 treaty to be its facilitating an end to capitulatory privileges in Egypt and its permitting Egyptians to emigrate to and work and own property in the Sudan.[114] The same article included statements from Egyptian minister of finance Makram 'Ubayd about the employment of Egyptian graduates in the Condominium administration and the "responsibilities" of local entrepreneurs in the Sudan. The minister hoped to encourage "their participation in the activities of rebuilding in the Sudan, through both their money and their efforts," and believed that with time Egypt and the Sudan could form "an economic bloc and a commercial whole."[115] Egyptian entrepreneur and 1935 mission member Salvatore Cicurel saw investment potential in the exploitation of Sudanese agricultural and mineral resources. He wrote of these possibilities, "I believe it is a duty of the Egyptian government's administration to undertake [this] work by itself or designate a mixed committee."[116] Additionally, he stated that "the Egyptian government must cooperate with the English government in taking steps to restore and simplify the avenues allowing the exploitation of the natural treasures of the Sudan."[117]

As Egyptians became more aware of the Sudan's overall industrial and commercial potential, investment initiatives concentrated on specific fields, although not on the most developed and lucrative field—cotton production. Cotton-related activities remained a tightly controlled economic sector in which government or foreign entities dominated. Still, by the Second World War Egyptians had acquired a better understanding of 'other' investment possibilities in the Sudan. When 'Abdallah Fakri Abaza described Sudanese industrial development in his 1940 study, he indirectly identified the fields in which Egyptian investment would be feasible. Among the most promising were the dairy industry, processed fruit and vegetables, the production of sweets and edible oils, which was "in need of much improvement," and the leather tanning industry, "in view of the abundance of [both] various types of leather and the materials needed for tanning."[118] In his analysis of manufacturing buttons from Sudanese doum palm supplies, Egypt's economic expert indicated that the possibilities depended on limiting Japanese competition. He wrote that promotion of this industry within the Nile Valley required administrative measures to discourage exporters from sending doum palm supplies to Japanese manufacturers.[119]

Investment interest in doum palm processing did not entail establishing factories in the Sudan itself, but rather gaining control of the raw material for Egyptian industries. Nationalists faced a troubling dilemma in situations like doum palm processing, namely the balancing of investment profitability with the political utility of activities in a particular field. Should Egyptians view Sudanese regions as a source of supply for Egyptian industries, with more immediate profits realized? Or should the Sudanese raw materials draw Egyptian capital and expertise to Sudanese locations, with financial returns in the more distant future? Clearly the latter view would be more politically useful to those desiring the unity of the Nile Valley, because Condominium officials could characterize the former view as imperialistic and exploitative—and therefore unlikely to win British, Sudanese, or international support for political union with Egypt.

Still, some Egyptians viewed the Sudan as a means of furthering Egyptian industrial production of certain commodities, such as processing foodstuffs in the Asyut region. A 1941 Ministry of Commerce and Industry report to parliament included proposals to expand this industry in Upper Egypt and increase the number of workers, "especially in Asyut, which was intended to become a supplying station for the Sudan."[120] In January 1940, *al-Ahram* published an article on Egypt's industrial resurgence based on a speech delivered by Isma'il Sidqi. Sidqi stressed the Sudan's role in development but not as a location of industries. Instead, he viewed the Sudan as a source of raw materials and a market for Egyptian industrial production. In addition to increasing manufactures exported abroad, Sidqi stated that Egyptian industrialists must be "concerned about taking advantage of Sudanese markets and their exploitable natural resources, [as] pursuing this is the reasonable and correct path and these markets and resources are of the utmost importance."[121] Some Sudanese commodities were not raw materials Egyptian industries needed, but rather products Egypt currently imported from abroad. For instance, in 1935

> Mr. Mahmud al-Jamal, one of the members of the Egyptian mission to the Sudan, examined a variety of compressed charcoal produced from the wood of Sudanese jungles. Nobody expected to find this industry in the Sudan, and it is a type [of compressed charcoal] called briquettes, and large quantities of this are exported to Egypt from England. . . . Mr. Mahmud al-Jamal took some samples of this charcoal for testing in order to investigate possibilities of its diffusion throughout Egypt.[122]

Acquiring raw materials for Egyptian industry was definitely more exploitative than investment in Sudanese production of charcoal briquettes, but still such import substitution hopes were more beneficial to Egyptians than to their Sudanese 'brothers.'

Egyptians were clearly aware of the potential benefits to their industries of greater reliance on Sudanese raw materials or markets, but they also expressed a desire for industrial investment in the Sudan itself. The fields commanding the most interest changed little over time. From the initial Egyptian mission in 1935 forward, both public and private sources consistently cited meat/dairy, fruit and vegetable processing, edible oils, leather, and a few other agricultural processing industries as the most enticing to Egyptian investors.[123] However, as early as mid–Second World War it was apparent that potential entrepreneurs had accomplished little. The economic expert's report of 1943 advocated increased Egyptian activity in the same fields singled out eight years earlier. He stated, "As for industrial development, interest is needed in the establishment of some industries in the Sudan, especially those for which the necessary raw materials are abundant in the Sudan, such as the various agricultural industries, dairy products, the tanning of leather, oil pressing, and the soap industry."[124]

Egyptian leaders were still pressing for greater industrial involvement as the Second World War ended. Muhammad Tawfiq Khashba stated in parliament that Egypt's economic expert in Khartoum had been unsuccessful in his mission and that Egyptian capitalists needed to become more active there: "I request that we direct all people and the government toward working on the perfection of our economic and financial position in the Sudan. And I appeal to the capitalists among Egyptians to employ their money in various economic spheres in the Sudan. The projects in need of money there are numerous."[125] Additionally, this deputy highlighted the nationalist 'angle' of investing in the Sudan, when he argued that one facet of "the mission of the economic expert is the guidance of money to these projects, whether they are agricultural, industrial, or commercial, and by this method we may serve our nation and fulfill our duty in respect to our Sudanese brothers."[126] The end of the Second World War and the gradual normalization of economic conditions led to no dramatic change in industrial projects in the Sudan. Officials still sought local entrepreneurs targeting the same fields. During an April 1946 conference on economic development in Cairo, among the means of strengthening bonds with the Sudan were the following suggestions:

> 8—Encouragement of agricultural industries in the Sudan, in the forefront of these is the preservation and dehydration of vegetables and fruits, milk products, and freezing and preserving meats.

> 9—Establishment of new industries in the Sudan, by either Sudanese or Egyptian–Sudanese companies, in order to raise the standard of living of its inhabitants.
> 10—Cooperation of the halves of the valley in the exploitation of mineral resources that [Sudanese] lands contain through establishing joint companies for this purpose.[127]

Members of the first Egyptian mission in 1935, the economic experts, the staff of Egypt's office in Khartoum, and multiple Egyptian officials all noted both the potential nationalist and economic rewards of industrial investment in the Sudan. Yet in 1946 officials were still suggesting, encouraging, or hoping for industrial initiatives. Finally, the following year the Cairo Chamber of Commerce reported,

> The Ministry of Commerce and Industry had decided to appoint an industrial attaché to the office of the economic expert for Egypt in the Sudan in order to strengthen industrial relations between the halves of the Nile Valley, but then it concluded after study that this objective necessitated more than an industrial attaché, and this because of the number of industries in Egypt. It resolved to dispatch one industrial specialist for a period of two months, after which he will return and then the next specialist will be sent, and so forth until the ministry is successful in spreading and strengthening Egyptian industry in the Sudan.[128]

Dispatch of an industrial expert finally in 1947 seems more than the proverbial "a day late and a dollar short," especially since the Condominium needed developmental initiatives from 'day one' and the post-1935 period of intensified Egyptian economic interest was over a decade old.

The tardiness and limited Egyptian government support may help explain the lackluster performance of investing in Sudanese industry. However, there are multiple potential explanations, and neither Egyptian nor Condominium sources attributed the lack of Egyptian industrial investment to any single cause. Entrepreneurs may have found the Sudan less attractive because similar investment possibilities existed at home—only landholding and commerce were congested or foreign-dominated in Egypt. Potentially, narrower profit margins or a lack of needed labor might have discouraged Egyptian industrialists. Despite some economic progress in the interwar period, Egyptians were unlikely to have been as capable as foreign entities of providing the expertise and capital Sudanese industrial development demanded. Egyptians needed the Condominium government to provide extraordinary advantages in order to overcome foreign competitors.

The most prominent and potentially active Egyptian 'investor' prior to Sudanese independence was the Misr Group, but this conglomerate confined its activities in the Sudan primarily to transport services. In his study of Misr Group development, Eric Davis states that "through its airline and shipping company, the Bank Misr established commercial ties throughout the eastern Mediterranean and the Sudan."[129] This connection to the Sudan was a positive step, but when Talaat Harb and associates traveled to the Sudan in 1935, Egyptians hoped they would establish both branch offices and new firms.[130] During their visit these directors finalized the establishment of the shipping company office in Port Sudan, but other Misr Group undertakings in the Sudan were small in scope and achieved mediocre results. For instance, the 1935 economic mission visited the Misr Group representative in the Sudan, 'Abd al-Latif Abu Rajilih, who was involved in export and insurance on a limited scale with the aid of some Sudanese merchants.[131] The mission reported of this agent that "he will establish a branch of the Misr Fishing Company," which was going to necessitate the development of refrigerated transport and storage capacities for export to Egypt.[132] Although this might qualify as 'industrial' investment, there was no further reference to this undertaking and this commodity never became a major item of trade. The Misr Group mainly sought markets for its Egyptian manufactures through the addition of branch offices in the Sudan. It established offices in Port Sudan and Khartoum, but Davis notes that sales of textiles, buttons, and other products were "hampered somewhat by customs tariffs between the two countries."[133] The Misr Group's preference for commercial ventures rather than industrial undertakings was characteristic of most Egyptian entrepreneurs, who were reluctant to engage in regional investments. Davis points to this tendency, writing, "Investing in economic projects in other Arab countries entailed considerable risk, and not even financial tycoons such as Isma'il Sidqi and Ahmad Abbud tapped these external markets."[134]

Conclusion

Egyptians maintained that the Sudan was not a neighboring Arab country, but their record of investment prior to 1953 demonstrates little concern for the Sudanese regions of their purported nation. In the end, analysis of investment interests and activities depends largely on one's perspective. From a Sudanese point of view, lessening reliance on western assistance could be accomplished by solidifying ties with Egypt. Some Sudanese groups consistently advocated strengthening investment and other economic bonds between the peoples of the Nile Valley. For instance, "the sedentary agricultural and commercial communities along the river Nile in the Northern Sudan" and merchants of the larger Sudanese cities who had connections to Cairo were favorably disposed to Egyptian claims of economic, cultural, and even political unity.[135] Some Sudanese may have viewed the replacement of British with Egyptian industrial or agricultural investment as a step forward—despite both being potentially equally exploitative. However, the abilities of Egypt and Britain to offer the necessary capital and expertise differed greatly. Therefore, successful Egyptian efforts would have entailed replacing a distant, 'foreign,' but capable ruler with a closer, more familiar, yet 'less qualified' imperial power. This supposition portrays the Egyptian elite as desirous of what could be labeled an 'internal colony,' but one can hardly avoid this conclusion when examining the documents. For instance, just prior to Sudanese independence, an article in *al-Jarida al-tijariya al-misriya* described the activities of a recent American economic mission in the Sudan, comparing its objectives with those of Egypt. The American delegation came to the Sudan with "an economic goal that aims to exploit the Sudan by various means and methods and to employ its money in a broad scope, whether it be virgin lands or its various resources." The article continued with a description of benefits for the Sudanese from foreign investments, enumerating for its audience once again possibilities in the Sudan:

> The Sudan should still be considered especially fertile ground and a wide field for the employment of vast financial capital and the creation of a number of various specialized industries, and what we state about gum Arabic can be reiterated, without any changes or alterations, for the cultivation of cotton, . . . the raising of cattle, the meat industry, the production of cereals, and other crops and manufactures, which are actually in urgent need of sharp minds and money invested.[136]

This article urged both the solidification of 'brotherly' Egyptian–Sudanese economic bonds and "cooperation in thwarting that which the usurping imperialists are planning, which will weaken the economic essence of this [southern] part of our dear valley."[137]

Obviously, this article was alleging a sharp contrast between 'brotherly' Egyptian assistance and 'exploitative' and 'imperialistic' western investment. Egyptians maintained that their investments in the Sudan were inherently less sinister than those of 'foreign' westerners. Developing investment or other economic ties to the Sudan was a means of both promoting economic independence and loosening the global economy's grip on the entire Nile Valley. Egyptians claimed they were merely seeking to reconstitute a 'historical' Nile Valley system that European intruders in the late nineteenth century had dismantled temporarily, and unjustifiably. They believed in the historical unity of the valley, sought sovereignty over this territory, and argued that investments were merely another 'benign' strand of a broad spectrum of bonds with the Sudan. The success of investments in the Sudan might have benefited the Egyptian capitalist more than the common Sudanese peasant or laborer, but such success would have assisted all desirous of a united Nile Valley.

However, speculation on what might have developed in the Nile Valley if Egypt's economic elite had achieved some success cannot overshadow the fact that virtually all investment initiatives came to naught. Reference to a number of issues readily explains the failure of Egyptian agricultural or industrial investment in the Sudan. For instance, how capable of investing abroad were Egyptian entrepreneurs? Did they truly view Sudanese regions as an attractive target for their capital? What level of government support would be provided to Egyptian investors in the Sudan? Egyptian entrepreneurs raised these and other specific issues, but the underlying, and ultimately fatal, cause of their failure was that the Condominium economy was 'open' to all entrepreneurial aspirants, with no preferential treatment for Egyptians. The only participant in the economy with a distinct advantage was the Sudanese government. As Mansour Khalid notes in his study of the Sudanese elite, "The fundamental fact about the economy throughout the Condominium was that the Government possessed what was for all intents and purposes a monopoly on many areas of activity; private foreign investment and entrepreneurship in general were discouraged, resulting in a total lack of investment in development excepting the Gezira scheme."[138] Treated as "private *foreign* investment and entrepreneurship," the hopes, plans, and limited activities of Egypt's economic elite in the Sudan from the 1920s through the 1940s were destined to fail, as was its claim of sovereignty in the following decade.

6 An Expanded Sudanese Market? Egyptian Exports to the Sudan

> Some men have said that the [current diplomatic] proposals are limited to permitting the English a presence in the Suez Canal zone only with the outbreak of war. Others have said that they can only extend their presence for three years, but everyone agrees that these proposals pay no attention to the matter of the Sudan. We have not heard anything on this subject from the government or from any official announcement, but the people feel, and for the most part what the people feel is reality itself, that the Sudan issue is in fact being ignored or it is an issue forgotten.
>
> And this [feeling] is indicative of the attachment embedded deep in our souls for the brotherly country, the country in which we have sacrificed much of our money, our blood, and our history in order to preserve—us and them—our united nation.[1]
>
> —Dr. Muhammad Bilal, Egyptian Chamber of Deputies, 1951

Dr. Muhammad Bilal's claims in 1951 that Egypt had "sacrificed" its blood and money in the Sudan were not unique to this era, nor to this deputy. Whatever their specific grievances against the Condominium or their frustration with the Egyptian state's response, deputies often began their speeches to the chamber with a recitation of the innumerable, selfless actions of the Egyptian people on behalf of their Sudanese 'brothers.' Egyptians had helped administer the Condominium during the early years. They had provided developmental loans, balanced the Sudanese budget, assisted physically and financially in the defense of the Sudan, and come to agreement over Nile water usage. By these and other means, Egyptians had 'invested' in the Sudan, but with very little apparent return. Egyptians had achieved virtually no success investing in agricultural or industrial projects in the Sudan—a 'double' blow to both their financial interests and their hopes of sovereignty over the Sudan. Hope remained that increased commercial relations might bolster their pocketbooks and their diplomatic position regarding the Sudan.

Furthermore, in contrast to agricultural or industrial investment there were fewer obstacles to Egyptian efforts to increase commerce. Agricultural investment consistently aroused Condominium opposition in defense of local inhabitants' well-being. Industrial investment opportunities in the Sudan were limited and likely to require a longer time horizon before entrepreneurs could expect a return. On the other hand, commercial opportunities attracted Egyptian and Sudanese interest without encountering administrative obstructionism. After the 1935 mission, the appointment of an economic expert, and the establishment of both a Khartoum exhibition and a permanent Sudan committee within the Egyptian government, the institutional structure to facilitate increased commerce was in place. Also, by this period Egypt's internal economic development had progressed to the point where excess manufacturing or agricultural production might find a market in the Sudan. Supply and demand factors within the Sudanese economy would play a key role in commercial levels as well. By the mid-1930s general economic development, local interest in greater trade, and limited direct opposition appeared to offer great possibilities for Nile Valley merchants. Plus, there were international developments, specifically the Depression and the Second World War, which seemingly lessened the competition with Egyptian goods in the Sudanese market and weakened the latter's links to the global economy.

Since at least the First World War, the primary thrust of Egyptian development had been to lessen its dependence on cotton exports to global markets, largely through agricultural diversification and industrialization. With the growth of a nationalist 'bourgeoisie' seeking to lessen this international dependence, the Sudan naturally became a potential solution to Egypt's "needs for external markets and capital investments."[2] These needs could be characterized as 'imperialist,' but Egyptians stressed the benign or beneficial nature of their commercial interests in the Sudan. They were only developing trade within their 'nation,' not exploiting a 'colony.' Of course, local merchants would profit in the process of strengthening commerce with the Sudan, just as they could expect to profit from trade in any single, united state. Increased Egyptian–Sudanese commerce was simply one facet of economic interdependence, which would reinforce claims of sovereignty over the valley. Dr. Abbas Ammar, a leading proponent of union working at what was then Fuad I University, stated that a "study of various natural factors, particularly those of agriculture, industry and commerce, river communications and transport, shows that both countries are closely interdependent."[3]

Claims of interdependence are difficult to substantiate with available statistics, certainly in respect to commercial bonds. Between the First World War and the declaration of Sudanese independence in 1956, both the Egyptian and the Sudanese economy remained solidly reliant on exporting raw materials to and importing manufactured goods from foreign countries. The table below illustrates Egypt's insignificance as a supplier of commodities to the Sudan—especially when contrasted with foreign suppliers. Only when the Second World War severely restricted foreign imports was Egypt capable of regaining the share of Sudanese imports it held prior to the Depression.[4] The wartime recovery was short-lived and allowed 'new' foreign entities to gain a greater share of Sudanese imports, with Egypt's portion falling precipitously. Diminishing interdependence certainly damaged nationalists' hopes of sovereignty over the Sudan. Furthermore, if commercial relations with other states were more important and profitable, would that encourage the elite in either Egypt or the Sudan to advocate union? Were their interests best served by maintaining strong bonds with international markets, or was the development of Egyptian–Sudanese commercial interdependence more beneficial? Did the development of such interdependence improve the lot of the bulk of the population in the Nile Valley? Egyptian nationalists had questioned the utility of Nile Valley water usage, transport, investment, and other issues. Now, Egyptian officials raised these sorts of questions as they considered how beneficial increased commerce would truly be for their political objectives.

Table 1. Egypt's share of Sudanese imports[5]

Year	Egypt (%)	Britain (%)	Japan (%)
1919–29	35.9	28.9	3.9
1930–34	22.0	27.6	13.1
1935–39	22.8	27.0	17.7
1940–45	30.8	11.9	3.7
	Egypt (%)	Britain (%)	India/Pakistan (%)
1951	9.1	34.8	16.5

The apparent deterioration of commercial interdependence by the 1950s resulted from events and decisions beyond Egyptians' control. Still, they are not entirely blameless for the decline. For instance, there was no significant organized trading interest or activity in the Sudan from Egyptians prior to 1935. Certainly there were occasional references to commercial possibilities before that date, but most Egyptian concern focused on Nile water priority or the political rights of Egypt in the Sudan. Egypt's leading advocate of 'nationalist' industrialization and the head of Misr Goup, Talaat Harb, wrote in *al-Akhbar* on 3 December 1935,

> Our trip to the Sudan was a good opportunity to *become acquainted* with officials and people, and also to gather memories and desired information that will be useful and beneficial in *helping to form an idea* from which it will be possible to study and research what can be undertaken in [the Sudan] for the benefit of the brotherly countries, and to what extent it is possible to establish economic cooperation between them.[6]

Talaat Harb and other leading entrepreneurs were still gathering information or studying the possibility of marketing goods in the Sudan at this rather late date. The Egyptian government was even more sluggish in attending to commerce with the Sudan. Officials normally limited themselves to a simple reiteration of the need to protect "the rights of Egypt and the Sudan, which is an inseparable part of Egypt."[7] In May 1938, Ahmad Abu al-Futuh raised the issue of trade with the Sudan, complaining that the government had not informed parliament of "what it was doing in the interest of strengthening the economic relations and commercial exchange between Egypt and the Sudan."[8] As concerted interest in augmenting trade with the Sudan emerged in the latter 1930s, Egyptians often linked this to developing the local manufacturing sector—viewing industrialization and greater Nile Valley trade as interrelated aspects of the single objective of economic independence. In 1939, 'Abdallah Fakri Abaza, the first economic expert sent to Khartoum, noted that the Sudan would be "the natural outlet for the increase of Egyptian industrial production in the near future."[9] Ultimately, whether local industrial products or noncotton agricultural commodities, the expert and others sought increased exports to the Sudan. A vibrant, interdependent, and mutually beneficial commercial exchange was a central element of the broader economic and political objectives of Egyptian nationalists.

Egyptian Agricultural Exports to the Sudan

Egyptians were most anxious to increase the export of manufactures or processed agricultural goods, such as refined sugar, but some effort went into stimulating the trade of agricultural produce. The unquestioned premier cash crop of both countries, cotton, was exported to foreign markets, but a local market for foodstuffs remained. Generally, the movement of agricultural produce was from the Sudan to Egypt, but there was a market in the Sudan for some specific commodities.

By the mid-1930s the cultivation of citrus fruit in Egypt had become among the more potentially viable agricultural commodities. The Egyptian government encouraged the growth of this agricultural crop as part of its desire to lessen dependence on cotton exports. From 1933 to 1937 exporters of citrus fruits actually received on average LE40,000 yearly in government subsidies.[10] Early encouragement of fruit export was not specifically directed at the Sudan, but this market seems to have been the implied target in various measures. In 1931 the Ministry of Agriculture suggested establishing special gardens in the Upper Egyptian provinces of Qena and Aswan for the cultivation of citrus fruits for export "to other countries in which the harvest of these kinds [of fruit] appears late."[11] In 1939 the Ministry of Commerce and Industry founded a fruit processing plant in Asyut.[12] Neither of these reports singled out the Sudan, but Qena and Aswan were the closest Upper Egyptian provinces, and processed fruits from Asyut with cheaper transport could have found a ready market in the Sudan. Actually, with the first economic mission in 1935, the government had clearly identified the Sudan as an attractive market for citrus fruit. That year,

> the Ministry of Agriculture announced that the marketability of Egyptian fruits and vegetables in the Sudan had become evident and that it intended to contact producers of these crops and turn their attention to exporting such to Sudanese markets, advising them on procedures in respect to their exports being accompanied by quality certificates declaring the Egyptian regions free of plant diseases.[13]

Egypt's permanent committee of the Sudan reported on 26 February 1938 that artificial silks, sugar, and oranges could be the most successful commodities in the Sudan.[14] With the onset of the Second World War and restricted access to other markets, relief for local fruit producers and merchants came directly through "the encouragement of exporting citrus fruit to the Sudan."[15]

The war resulted in more than restricted access to international markets, as both Nile Valley administrations closely regulated the local trafficking of virtually all commodities. In December 1939 the Cairo Chamber of Commerce published an article that illustrated the multiple concerns of wartime citrus fruit exporters, describing train schedules, types of train cars used, proper packing methods, needs for representatives at specific points, names of the leading citrus importers in the Sudan, and so forth.[16] The administrative processes of wartime commerce were problematic, but the biggest obstacle facing Egyptian citrus fruit exports was simply their high market price in the Sudan. In 1938 the Cairo Chamber of Commerce stated that sales prices expected of fruits and vegetables at the Khartoum exhibit were problematic. It reported, for example, that "the produce of the gardens department, which achieved great success and for which there is great demand, has been accompanied by a price increase of 100 percent . . . for the public."[17] After conducting shipment tests, the Ministry of Commerce and Industry reported later in 1938 that the high prices of most fruit prevented marketing success in Khartoum, but a couple of varieties from Upper Egypt remained popular.[18]

However, just days after highlighting the poor market for fruit in the Sudan, *al-Ahram* reported, "Citrus fruit there had been considered luxuries because of their high price. However, among the results of reducing the transport costs has been that Egyptian citrus fruit have flooded the Sudanese market and have become marketable to various social classes."[19] The critical phrase in this rosier portrait of citrus fruit sales was "reducing the transport costs." Although other factors contributed to the pricing, and marketability, of citrus fruit, Egyptians had concentrated on lowering transport costs since the initial economic missions in 1935. Fu'ad Abaza reported that participants in those missions and subsequent meetings had concluded that "the Sudan is a substantial market for the retail of Egyptian fruit if the obstacles preventing such are eliminated, especially the freight rates, which have increased greatly."[20] He further noted that committees in Cairo and Khartoum were working on rate reductions from their respective governments. While the Sudanese administration did agree to lower its rate to 50 millièmes on every 10 kilograms of produce by 1937, the Egyptian government refused a reduction to 13.2 millièmes on the same quantity.[21] Both merchants and fruit producers were displeased with these measures, and by early 1938 the Sudanese Chamber of Commerce had begun lobbying the Condominium administration to further lower the rate of transport "between Shellal and any Sudanese region" to 13 millièmes.[22] The Sudanese government continued to resist rate reductions. *Al-Ahram* reported in October 1939 that Egypt's Ministry of Commerce and Industry "observed that among the obstacles lying in the way of marketing Egyptian citrus fruit in the Sudan is the elevated costs of shipping on the Sudanese Railways, and therefore the Ministry of Commerce has directed its efforts toward reducing these rates."[23] As the Second World War's impact on commerce intensified, the Condominium government would eventually relent on lowering transport rates.

The Egyptian government also finally acquiesced to demands for transport rate reductions. Actually, a year before the war's outbreak Egypt had agreed to lower the cost of shipments consisting entirely of fruit to 14.6 millièmes, and to 17 millièmes for shipments mixed with other products.[24] To facilitate export during the war the Egyptian government agreed to additional rate reductions for citrus fruit, and "in respect to shipments sent to the Sudan . . . the reduction in its rates will be 75 percent if exported from Lower Egypt and 50 percent if exported from Upper Egypt."[25] The importance of transport costs for citrus fruit exports is evident not only from the consistent references in ministerial reports, trade journals, and daily newspapers but also from the actual volume of this commerce. As noted above, rate reductions from the Condominium and Egyptian administrations began in 1937, and table 2 clearly indicates increased exports from those years forward. Moreover, and importantly for hopes of 'proving' Nile Valley commercial interdependence, Egyptian produce was replacing foreign imports. The Egyptian share of the Sudan's citrus market rose to 85.7 percent by 1939.[26] 'Abdallah Fakri Abaza confirmed the importance of transport costs, writing that "the reason for the increase of imports from Egypt is due to the lowering, which both the Egyptian and Sudanese railroads brought about, of the shipment rates for citrus fruits between Egypt and the Sudan."[27] Rate changes in the early 1940s may have contributed to the continued growth of the citrus trade with the Sudan, but the lack of access to foreign markets during the war also clearly influenced the increased exports of that period. Despite a decline immediately after the war, by the 1950s the level of Egyptian citrus exports had rebounded to the 'improved' pre–Second World War levels.[28]

Another factor in the pre–Second World War increase in citrus exports was a reduction of administrative 'red tape.' For instance, in March 1936 the Cairo Chamber of Commerce "requested that the Chamber of Commerce in Khartoum try to convince the government of the Sudan to lift the requirement of the accompaniment of [citrus] fruits by a quality certificate, in order to facilitate exportation; and members of the Chamber of Commerce in Khartoum promised to exert this effort."[29] The minutes

Table 2. Citrus fruit exported to the Sudan

Year	KG	Value (LE)	Year	KG	Value (LE)
1918-1929 (avg.)	89,622	664	1939	1,056,700	10,298
1931	105,412	643	1940	1,145,274	12,032
1932	168,008	999	1941	2,469,510	26,622
1933	180,010	1,313	1942	1,636,161	27,307
1934	175,219	1,138	1943	1,951,907	38,400
1935	229,153	1,638	1944	1,816,977	31,156
1936	296,987	3,068	1945	660,000	27,056
1937	631,481	6,562	1950-1955 (avg.)	802,029	22,685
1938	896,348	8,559			

of a meeting of the permanent committee on 31 January 1938 recorded the elimination of this requirement.[30] Considering the constant attention of officials regarding transport rates, it is difficult to maintain that eliminating one administrative regulation was vital to the citrus trade, but this change did correspond with the pre–Second World War increased volume. And the Egyptian government was actively working on all potential administrative impediments to the citrus fruit trade, which was not the case for many other critical exports to the Sudan. *Al-Ahram* included in its report on the 3 December 1938 meeting of the permanent committee the following illustration of the general encouragement of this trade:

> Among that which the permanent committee researched was the issue of exporting Egyptian citrus fruit to the Sudan and choosing the easiest means of encouraging this export. It decided that the markets administration would dispatch test shipments to the permanent office in Khartoum to determine the extent of their marketability, and transmit observations on this issue sent from the office to the Egyptian exporters.[31]

Test shipment results and reports from merchants in the Sudan highlighted another component of improved Egyptian fruit exports, namely proper packaging and subsequent preservation of the commodities in transport.[32]

Egyptian officials consistently, and unsuccessfully, raised the issue of ensuring the good condition of citrus fruit upon its arrival in the Sudan. In his 1940 study 'Abdallah Fakri Abaza noted that the handling of Egyptian exports "by the Sudanese and Egyptian railroads is rough; also crates are piled up, some on top of others, in the Nile steamships, and the load is heavy on the bottom crates, causing damage."[33] The Egyptian government hoped that merchants exporting fruit might assist in safeguarding commodities destined for the Sudan. For instance, "the Ministry of Commerce and Industry remarked that shipments of Egyptian citrus fruit exported to the Sudan run the risk of damage caused by loading it in baskets of weak construction" and provided specific guidelines for crate construction.[34] Although how crates were constructed or stacked may have been part of the problem, an inherent cause of greater damage was simply the loading and unloading caused by the multiple means of transportation required along the Nile Valley route. Egyptians could not eliminate the recurrence of fruit arriving in damaged condition at times. For instance, in 1943 the manager of the expert's office in Khartoum reported that "Egyptian fruit and vegetables, when they arrive in the Sudan, are in a damaged condition," which had seriously undermined the reputation of Egyptian fruit in local markets.[35] In spite of this concern over the potential harm to citrus fruit exports, the statistical record above indicates success in this field.

Egyptians also hoped for similar success in the export of rice to the Sudan, again possibly developing a politically useful dependent relationship. The government's report on the 1935–37 activities of the permanent committee and economic missions stated that "from the research it is evident that the sole rival to [Egyptian rice] is Rangoon rice."[36] In 1934 Egypt provided only just over 15 percent of all Sudanese rice imports, which officials attributed to the cheapness of its competitors' supplies.[37] Some thought that the best way to improve Egypt's position would be to lower transport costs and grant government subsidies to promote marketability. By 1936 a committee of Egyptians had contacted the Sudanese Chamber of Commerce and "beseeched it to get in touch with the Sudanese government in order to lower the rate of transport of rice by the Sudanese railroads," one part of the committee's determination to reduce the costs of Egyptian–Sudanese rice transport.[38] Transport rate reductions would certainly aid rice exports, but Egyptians also sought government financial assistance specifically for this commodity. A delegation of interested individuals met with the Egyptian minister of finance about granting Egyptian rice bound for the Sudan an export subsidy so that it could compete with Rangoon supplies.[39]

The Egyptian government consistently refused to permit an export subsidy, but some progress was achieved in other areas. In 1938 Egypt's railroad department announced a 10 percent reduction of the rates on rice transport in order to encourage the use of rail facilities.[40] 'Abdallah Fakri Abaza argued that Egypt's pre–Second World War share of Sudanese rice imports had increased because of the opening of railroad stations in the rice-producing areas of Egypt.[41] This official also reported that the proportion of Egyptian rice arriving in the Sudan via the Nile Valley route had doubled between 1937 and 1938.[42] Increased utilization of the Nile Valley route is noteworthy, but most exporters shipped rice to the Sudan via the Red Sea. Actually, the rate reductions and the railroad stations mentioned here helped rice exports to all destinations—not just the Sudan. Promoting rice exports was simply part of lessening Egyptian dependence on cotton. Rice was an important commodity traded with many countries, not something uniquely suited to strengthen Egyptian–Sudanese relations.

In fact, developments at the start of the Second World War indicated that administrative measures were required to ensure that attractive foreign markets for rice did not supersede local consumption needs. As provisioning difficulties mounted in 1940, a meeting of Egyptian and Sudanese officials determined that increased exports of sugar, wheat, and rice from Egypt to the Sudan were possible.[43] Throughout the war local provisioning needs forced greater commercial interdependence for rice and other foodstuffs. As the war wound down, more restrictive measures were necessary to ensure Sudanese and Egyptian needs were met before exports drifted to other countries. In 1944 *al-Ahram* reported,

> The customs administration received a message from the Ministry of Finance informing it that [the ministry] had decided to restrict the amount of rice authorized for export to the Sudan during the current year to 2,400 tons.
>
> In fact the Ministry of Provisions required that no quantity of rice could be shipped to those regions other than by those possessing special permits from it, so that the limited export amounts are not surpassed.[44]

Measures such as those in 1944 indicated that the two regions clearly relied on local supplies to meet popular needs, at least during the war.[45]

This wartime commercial interdependence was apparent from review of export statistics as well. Rice exports in excess of 1.5 million kilograms annually are apparent during most of the war in table 3 below.[46] Moreover, the table reflects the general success of Egyptian efforts to promote rice exports to the Sudan since the time of the first economic missions in 1935. Not only did rice exports recoup their pre-Depression volume by the start of the Second World War, but the new levels reached during the war were also maintained afterward. By 1948–49 Egyptian rice was meeting 100 percent of Sudanese needs, and the quantities sent to the Sudan in the 1950s were five times that of the pre-Depression years.[47] Seemingly, Egyptians had strengthened Nile Valley provisioning dependence, at least in respect to rice, but this development was not ideal for Egyptian hopes of sovereignty over the Sudan. Exports of rice to the Sudan had improved, but these quantities were virtually insignificant when compared to rice shipped elsewhere. The average value of rice exported to the Sudan during the Second World War was LE35,564, while Egypt exported LE2,474,443 annually to other countries over the same period. In the 1950–55 period, the figures were LE81,745 to the Sudan and LE5,483,415 annually to all other countries. So the Sudan's complete reliance on Egypt for its rice needs was promising for nationalist economic objectives. However, Egyptian farmers or merchants of rice had far greater financial interest in their connections to international markets.

Table 3. Rice exported to the Sudan

Year	Kilograms	Value (LE)	Year	Kilograms	Value (LE)
1918–29 (avg.)	589,249	11,205	1939	778,220	8,069
1931	186,790	1,993	1940	919,552	10,366
1932	152,379	1,447	1941	2,485,476	36,286
1933	172,300	1,648	1942	50,896	1,019
1934	164,041	1,809	1943	1,515,117	45,060
1935	726,450	8,078	1944	1,823,980	52,336
1936	375,831	3,710	1945	2,023,000	68,318
1937	344,337	3,309	1950–55 (avg.)	2,461,187[48]	81,745
1938	342,147	4,155			

Overall, then, Egyptians had varied success in the development of markets for agricultural goods in the Sudan. Admittedly, two commodities is not an extensive examination of agricultural exports, but an analysis of rice and citrus fruit exports highlights some of the obstacles—from transport and packaging to direct government assistance—to increasing trade. Additionally, the greater local dependence necessitated by the Second

World War was apparent for other commodities sent to the Sudan. In some cases, like the two examples here, commodities saw higher levels of export after the war. However, in respect to agricultural goods, Egypt most commonly relied on Sudanese imports and sent its own fruits and vegetables to more lucrative markets in Europe and beyond.

Ultimately, both Egypt and the Sudan were agricultural countries that depended heavily on cotton exports to international markets, not one another. Table 4 below provides some indication of how lucrative the cotton trade was for Egypt. This table, however, primarily illustrates the continued insignificance of Sudanese agricultural markets for Egyptian exporters. During the period under study, cotton was clearly the most valuable export, and it was destined for non-Sudanese markets. Export of rice to the Sudan and other countries certainly improved, but it still paled in comparison to cotton. Even if one ignores cotton export statistics, comparing only total rice exports with rice exported to the Sudan, the picture is not encouraging for Egyptian nationalist hopes. Rice exports to the Sudan were among the most successful agricultural commodities, but such paltry figures could hardly be expected to garner much interest from local entrepreneurs. Yes, Egyptians had increased exports of some agricultural goods to the Sudan, but it is difficult to maintain that such development bound the regions together.

Table 4. Selective comparison of Egyptian agricultural exports (by value)

Year	Cotton Exports (LE) (Excluding Sudan)	Rice Exports (LE) (Excluding Sudan)	Rice Exports to the Sudan (LE)
1930	24,000,000	600,000	2,500
1940	19,000,000	2,000,000	23,000
1950	164,000,000	14,000,000	150,000

The same conclusions are reached when the commercial relationship is examined from the Sudanese perspective. For instance, although total Sudanese imports ranged from LE3 million to LE5 million annually during the 1930s, Egyptian fruits, vegetables, cereals, and nuts imported added up to between LE20,000 and LE40,000 each year.[49] Furthermore, during that period Egypt supplied 22.4 percent of all Sudanese imports, but only 3.9 percent of this consisted of agricultural produce. Other statistics could be examined that lead to the same basic conclusion: Egyptian agricultural produce remained an insignificant sector in Sudanese commerce.

Egyptian Textile Exports

Since agricultural goods formed such a small portion of Egypt's trade with the Sudan, most exports were 'manufactured goods'—although many were produced in what observers would not consider industrial establishments. Textiles were the most valuable category of Sudanese imports and the key manufacture on which Egyptians pinned their hopes of economic diversification. Potentially, therefore, there was a congruence of Egyptian supplies and Sudanese needs. As with other economic initiatives in the Sudan, concerted interest in textile exports did not emerge until the mid-1930s. In August 1934, after emphasizing the need for strengthened commercial and financial relations generally, Muhammad Najib Wilaya wrote, "What could be especially easily accomplished is the promotion of products of the Misr companies, like silk, cotton, linen, and wool textiles."[50] The following year, after the first economic mission to the Sudan, the permanent committee requested that the Ministry of Commerce and Industry encourage "producers of tricot, handkerchiefs, and stockings made of cotton to send samples of their products to the Khartoum Chamber of Commerce in order to determine the extent of their marketability and the amount of competition from Japanese products."[51] In 1939, the Cairo Chamber of Commerce declared that Egyptian textile production "soon will be sufficient for the needs of the entire Egyptian country" and that the excess production would not find "a more natural market than the Sudan."[52] Similar sentiments were expressed by *al-Jarida al-tijariya al-misriya* later that year. It claimed the most prosperous local economic sector was "the spinning and weaving industry which meets a large portion of the domestic consumption needs . . . [while] working also toward exportation, especially to the Sudan."[53] These comments highlight Egyptian textile export hopes, but also include overly optimistic assessments of local production and allusions to some of the more pronounced obstacles facing this commerce.

A critical issue in assessing export results is drawing some distinctions between types of textiles. Egyptian manufacturers and merchants targeted specific textiles, especially natural and artificial silk fabrics, as the key commodities in finally breaking into the foreign-dominated Sudanese market.[54] However, the only non-cotton textile that had any success was a unique, handcrafted textile mix from a specific region of Egypt. This commodity was a cotton–silk/artificial silk mixture produced by Egyptian artisans of Naqqada in Upper Egypt that had a well-established, exclusive market in the Sudan.[55] In his 1972 history of Egypt, Jacques Berque writes of the Naqqada artisans' "flexibility," countering foreign competition through successfully incorporating artificial silk into their traditional "*qutniya*, a silk and cotton mixture."[56] By the middle of the 1930s this mixture of cotton and artificial silk was known locally as *firka*.[57] When listing the most promising potential Egyptian exports for the Sudan, the director of the permanent office in Khartoum wrote in 1939 that the "most important of these articles is the *firka*, produced in Naqqada; and the Sudan imports close to LE100,000 worth of it annually."[58] 'Abdallah Fakri Abaza's study that same year reported that Egypt had maintained a 93.2 percent share of the Sudanese market for this mixed textile over the previous six years.[59] Although some hoped to increase exports of this commodity, Egyptian producers appeared to have already reached the commercial limits.

In spite of Egyptian hopes and activities designed to increase export levels, table 5 below illustrates that cotton–artificial silk mixes provided little field for expansion. It is apparent from the table that there was a slight increase in the volume of the trade by the 1950s, and the value of exports clearly fluctuated, largely resulting from exceptional wartime conditions. However, with the gradual fading of depressed economic conditions after 1932, mixed textiles exported to the Sudan hovered around 300,000 kilograms per year—even through the Second World War. Therefore, the statistics reinforce the idea that mixed textiles had a static market in the Sudan, immune to Egyptian promotional efforts or exceptional conditions, including the restricted international exchange of goods during the war. Most important, this cotton–artificial silk mixture became *the* most valuable textile export to the Sudan from the 1930s forward.

Why was this commodity so successful? The success was largely a result of having a long-established market and virtually no foreign competition. The *firka*, earlier called *qutniya*, was handmade, had a very fine weave, and had a solid distribution network in the Sudan.[60] But the production of

Table 5. Mixed textiles (cotton–artificial silk) exported to the Sudan

Year	Kilograms	Value (LE)	Year	Kilograms	Value (LE)
1928–34 (avg.)[61]	168,149	47,304	1941	337,072	386,823
1935	317,003	153,957	1942	304,482	588,465
1936	312,690	130,583	1943	348,398	807,443
1937	361,441	139,317	1944	132,625	181,420
1938	363,012	215,570	1945	66,043	105,806
1939	292,308	192,011	1950–55 (avg.)	484,652	1,428,584
1940	311,418	247,750			

this commodity appeared to be peripheral employment for the Naqqada population, not an industrial or commercial sphere attracting significant investment and expansion. In 1952, a Misr company official briefly described this commodity's production:

> We observed the region called Naqqada, among the districts of the Qena governate and the interest of its people in the raising of cattle and poultry and the production of textiles . . . which are exported to the Sudan in large quantities. You will find in every house of this region a loom or two for this manufacturing, and all of the family, both young and old, are trained in this production, and they profit from this activity probably more than from agricultural activities.[62]

In addition to its artisanal nature and established market in the Sudan, this cotton-artificial silk textile was a rare beneficiary of the Condominium administration's customs regime. Between 1934 and 1938 the Sudan raised duties on foreign textile imports containing over 10 percent silk or artificial silk from 10 to 50 percent ad valorem. The Egyptian *firka* was composed of more than 10 percent artificial silk, but since the Condominium's establishment, locally produced goods traded between Egypt and the Sudan had been exempt from duties.[63] Despite this commodity's local reputation, reception, and price advantages, there was little to gain from an article produced only by artisans for a small, unchanging market in the Sudan. Yet there was little doubt as to the value of this export. For instance, a 1951 official report noted that Egypt sent cotton–artificial silk mixes worth LE1,090,000 to the Sudan, while purely cotton textiles were ten times less valuable—and the second most valuable export was actually confectioneries.[64]

Textile mixes were valuable, but most Egyptian interest centered on the cotton piece-goods market. This commercial field was the most expansive and lucrative in the Sudan, and this sphere of manufacturing was among the most developed and favored in Egypt. In spite of increasing interest, a lucrative market, and improved domestic production of cotton piece goods, the statistical results displayed in table 6 indicate a failure of efforts to strengthen this trade. The highest volume cotton textile trade occurred in the 1920s—before the organized efforts of nationalists. The most successful post-1920s period was during the Second World War, when conditions restricted competition in Sudanese markets. Furthermore, despite the greater interest in developing commercial ties after 1935, cotton textile exports actually declined steadily. Finally, although the value of Egyptian cotton piece goods sent to the Sudan after the war did rise to levels very similar to those maintained in the 1920s, the increase was largely due to inflation and the growth of the Sudan's total market for textiles. During Egypt's most profitable year, 1943, its share of all cotton piece goods imported by the Sudan was only 27 percent, and by 1949 this figure had dropped to 8.7 percent.[65]

Table 6. Cotton piece goods exported to the Sudan

Year	Kilograms	Value (LE)	Year	Kilograms	Value (LE)
1918–29 (avg.)[66]	1,376,329	476,588	1939	63,660	8,512
1931	324,540	47,206	1940	36,311	6,076
1932	556,377	76,763	1941	173,397	46,370
1933	386,160	52,096	1942	470,478	262,159
1934	438,990	63,502	1943	944,345	883,971
1935	286,434	43,887	1944	249,484	194,427
1936	149,244	23,257	1945	354,600	191,182
1937	165,603	19,980	1950–55 (avg.)	674,782	591,579
1938	127,618	17,126			

Egypt's inability to strengthen its position in the Sudan as a provider of cotton textiles was due mainly to two interrelated factors. Egypt was unable to overcome advantages held by both foreign textiles and their merchants in the Sudan. Being the first to industrialize manufacturing, Britain dominated global textile production for many years and was the foremost supplier of cotton textiles to the Nile Valley—a situation buoyed by its political supremacy in the region. Only after the First World War did the situation begin to change. Hiroshi Shimizu, in his study of Anglo–Japanese trade rivalries, noted that during the 1920s Italy became Britain's main rival in the Nile Valley.[67] By the Second World War, India was the primary foreign competitor that Egyptian interests encountered in the Sudan. In 1943, Egyptian textile exporters had their best showing of the war years, but even then India still provided 73 percent of all cotton piece goods to the area.[68] Indeed by 1943 Indian exporters had a well-established marketing and information-gathering system in the Sudan.[69]

When Egyptians first began serious work toward establishing their own textile market in the mid-1930s, the main foreign rival in the Sudan was Japan. In 1938, before a dramatic downturn corresponding with the outbreak of the Second World War, Japan's share of all textiles imported by the Sudan was 94.5 percent.[70] Commonly Egyptians explained this dominance through reference to the lower prices of Japanese textiles. 'Ali Mawardi, director of the permanent office in Khartoum and intimately familiar with local markets, reported in 1940 that a Japanese version of the basic cotton cloth, *damuriya*, was initially offered at Sudanese ports for 18.6 shillings (three shillings less than the same British-made cloth) and was successively lowered to a price of 4.9 shillings.[71] Egyptian textiles had already struggled to match the price and quality of British textiles, so the Japanese presented an even greater challenge. Egyptian newspapers reported widely on this commercial competition in the Sudan—placing blame domestically and abroad. *Al-Ahram* summarized and explained Japan's textile dominance thus:

> From these numbers it is evident that Japan alone accounts for 90 percent of the value of cotton import totals to the Sudan. The methods of Japan are well known. In fact, we have struggled against them in Egypt. The gist of [these methods] is that the Japanese purchase the cheapest varieties of cotton and manipulate workers' wages, exchange rates, and the cost of shipping so that the price of their products is reduced to prevent competition from any other country. The costs of shipment from Tokyo to Sudan are less than its costs from Cairo to Khartoum, first because the cost of maritime shipping is naturally cheaper and secondly because the government of Japan gives shipping companies huge subsidies, which are in reality subsidies to Japanese exporters.[72]

Clearly, government support, transport issues, manufacturing processes, and other factors contributed to the dominance of inexpensive Japanese cotton textiles. Knowing the strengths of their competition was a step in the right direction, but Egyptians needed a plan of action if they hoped to capture a significant share of the market. In a 1939 interview after returning from the Sudan, the Egyptian economic expert complained that "Japanese commodities flood the Sudanese markets and certainly stifle every other commodity" and that

> there is no doubt that this subject demands attention and induces serious consideration of the necessity of cooperative effort, and when I state cooperative effort, I mean by this the producers among Egyptians and the consumers of the Sudan who must understand that every piaster coming into the hands of the Egyptians returns to them again, since Egypt ranks second among nations that purchase Sudanese products.

> And we must not forget the Egyptian and Sudanese governments' responsibility of real, fruitful cooperation by various means to protect Egyptian industry and the interests of consumers. The Sudanese are our brothers and we must place their welfare in the forefront in every instance.[73]

The expert's comments included typical nationalist rhetoric, but also identified what most Egyptians viewed as the solution to foreign dominance, namely government assistance.

Government support for textile exports to the Sudan meant customs duties had to be altered. Policies, procedures, and rates applied by customs agencies of both regions impacted commerce in all goods, but Egyptians considered customs especially critical for textile success in the Sudan. Initial customs policies between the countries were based on specific articles of the 1899 Condominium agreement. The combination of this agreement and the Egyptian government's not imposing duties on Sudanese-produced commodities had produced a system with no tariffs on goods exchanged that originated in either Egypt or the Sudan. As explained in chapter 4, problems arose over how officials interpreted the initial customs policies. Egyptians claimed a unified customs administration existed since the reconquest, while British officials believed the Sudan enjoyed complete autonomy in respect to tariffs. Early British administrators could and did use policies, such as the Customs Ordinance of 1913, to protect Sudanese consumers or to produce needed revenues—with Egyptian commerce remaining a wholly secondary concern. In 1920 the British high commissioner stated of Sudanese imports from foreign countries that "the same imports (whatever they may be) if diverted through Egypt are more expensive and bring in a reduced rate of duty under the terms of the existing arrangement with the Egyptian Government."[74] With the prevailing customs system, greater trade with Egypt meant financial hardships for the Condominium government and the Sudanese people. British officials believed that raising tariffs on foreign imports would lead to lower revenues from fewer foreign commodities arriving, while also forcing the local population to purchase higher-priced local or Egyptian-produced commodities.

However, raising tariffs on foreign textiles, and manufactures generally, is exactly what Egyptians sought. They had interpreted the 1899 agreement to have established a commercial 'union' of the Nile Valley, a single entity that would not impose duties on commerce between regions and that would impose the *same* duties on foreign imports. Article 7 stated that tariffs on foreign articles entering the Sudan via Suakin or any other Red Sea port "shall not exceed the corresponding duties for the time being leviable on goods entering Egypt from abroad."[75] The tariffs remained the same until 17 February 1930, when the Egyptian government initiated the first of several measures to raise duties on foreign imports, hoping to encourage local industrial development.[76] In contrast to the past 8 percent rate, the reform established "a more intricate system combining specific and ad valorem duties," which amounted to roughly a 13 percent levy on imported goods.[77] Eventually, the Egyptian government would raise tariffs on foreign textile imports in 1930, 1935, and 1938, providing local producers with less competition in Egypt. However, Egyptian protectionist policies were not applicable in Sudanese regions and resulted in significant commercial ramifications. In 1940, Muhammad Shahin Hamza described what many of his parliamentary colleagues viewed as "a big obstacle in encouraging the marketability of Egyptian commodities in the Sudan" by explaining that "the customs tariff was 8 percent in the two countries, then after Egypt became independent . . . it raised the duty to 40 percent on foreign imports. Yet the tariff applied to [foreign imports] in the Sudan remained 8 percent."[78]

Officials lamented the impact of tariff differences for all trade, but for merchants with great hopes of marketing cotton textiles the lower Sudanese tariffs meant Egyptian commodities were simply too expensive. In March 1937, Hasan Saqr, a permanent committee member from the Ministry of Commerce and Industry, stated that raising Sudanese tariffs on textiles was an "urgent need."[79] Salvatore Cicurel, an Egyptian entrepreneur and member of the 1937 mission to the Sudan, wrote that the Sudanese government was unwilling to raise tariffs on foreign textiles and increase Egyptian imports "due to the fact that every increase of articles imported from Egypt . . . leads to a decrease in customs revenues and a deficit in the budget of the Sudan."[80] Cicurel correctly noted Condominium officials' reluctance to change duties, but a 1938 government report suggested that both British and Egyptian traders faced stiff foreign competition in the Sudan and had common cause in tariff changes. This report stated that both countries' textiles were too expensive and the natural solution was an "agreement with the government of the Sudan to set the customs tariffs for the Sudan at the same rates as those applied in Egypt."[81] As the Second World War approached, and after four years of intensified efforts to improve trade with the Sudan, Egyptian dismay over tariff problems continued. In June 1939, the Cairo Chamber of Commerce stated of Sudanese tariffs that "these duties are in great need of immediate modification which will ensure for Egyptian cotton textiles the holding of the position which they have the right to assume in the Sudanese market."[82] In November of that year, the British governor-general of the Sudan held meetings with top officials in Egypt. *Al-Ahram* reported of his meeting with Egypt's Minister of Commerce and Industry that

> foremost among topics that the discussion addressed is the customs administration issue. This system had operated in the past on a unified basis, and when the Egyptian customs duties were adjusted necessarily for the welfare of local production, the [Sudan's] system of customs remained as it was, and that led to the continuation of duties on foreign imports being lower. This situation allowed Japanese imports to flood and dominate Sudanese markets.
>
> The minister of commerce believes that Egypt and the Sudan are a combined unit that, therefore, requires the reexamination of the customs system in Sudanese regions in order to match the Egyptian customs system.[83]

From Egypt's point of view, increasing its textile exports to the Sudan was simple and the poor showing was a direct result of foreign competition that clearly arose from insufficient tariffs, which the Condominium administration had failed to rectify for years.

After some instability during the first months of the Second World War, market conditions in the Sudan began to improve. The president of the Khartoum Chamber of Commerce stated in January 1940 that Sudanese exports and local purchasing power had risen dramatically and that "importers of textiles consider themselves lucky if they are granted the opportunity to garner the profits realized from the improvement of the prices of cotton [textiles] and the paucity of stockpiles."[84] Sudanese market conditions may have improved, but Egyptian producers and traders still had to take advantage of the opportunity. 'Ali Mawardi, director of the permanent office in Khartoum, reported in February 1940 that Egyptian importers had no presence in the Sudan. He explained what foreign importers had done to capture the local market while urging Egyptians to take advantage of wartime conditions:

> The reality is that Japanese factories know how to reconcile their requirements and the needs of the [Sudanese] people. They export to the Sudan commodities produced in accord with local needs. And after study of these needs in detail, and if some effort was exerted in the production of Egyptian manufactures to correspond with Sudanese incomes, their situation and their customs, there would be great

> sales. I believe the current circumstances are auspicious for Egyptian industry, [since] the prices of Japanese commodities are beginning to increase because of rising costs of raw materials, rising insurance rates, and difficulty of shipment. And if the people of Egyptian industry considered making some sacrifice to conquer the Sudanese markets, flooding them with Egyptian manufactures matching the needs of the people currently, there would be great gains.[85]

The statistics in table 6 above do indicate an increase in Egyptian exports during the war, but the improvement was a transitory phenomenon and foreign dominance remained firmly in place—even during the war. A commercial official of the Condominium administration reported in 1941 that there had been no drop-off in textile import levels since the start of the war, partially because of the continued import of "Japanese textiles to the Sudan via Bombay," where there remained a "plethora of stockpiles."[86] Later in the war, "Mr. Cauldry, supervisor of wartime provisions in the Sudan left Khartoum on his way to India to participate in a conference to be held in New Delhi. Among the issues to be discussed at this conference will be the provision of India with Sudanese cotton and supplying Sudanese needs of Indian textiles."[87] Ultimately, the Second World War facilitated the rise of new foreign suppliers of textiles to the Sudan but did little to improve Egypt's position.

Although the lower Sudanese tariffs and the subsequent foreign competition were critical, they were not the only explanations for Egyptian textiles encountering little success. Another consistent factor was Egyptian manufacturers' inability to meet the needs of their own population. A 1929 report of the Misr Group research staff, looking at the textile industry specifically, stated that "Egypt should produce at this stage only what it could consume."[88] By the mid-1930s Egyptian officials had discussed with British authorities the possibility of establishing a quota system to curtail foreign textile imports to Egypt, illustrating the difficulties Egyptians had in capturing their own market.[89] At times difficulties meeting local Egyptian needs precluded any possibility of an improved showing in the Sudan. According to the Ministry of Commerce and Industry, the initial sharp drop in textile exports to the Sudan at the start of the Second World War was because of "the insufficient production of Egypt's factories to meet the need of the country in the present circumstances."[90]

Both the Egyptian and Sudanese administrations made decisions with the welfare of local consumers in mind, and some of these decisions certainly negatively impacted Egyptian textile exports to the Sudan. The

Condominium government reasoned that higher-priced foreign imports would unnecessarily burden the Sudanese, so it refused to raise tariffs to help Egyptian exports. During the Second World War and beyond, Egypt's government restricted the export of cotton textiles to the Sudan—again, to ensure local needs were met first. Various Egyptian ministries and committee reports in the immediate postwar years consistently referred to the welfare of local inhabitants when defending continued textile export regulation. In 1947, the minister of finance decided to permit export of a million meters of textiles, allotting

> the largest amount of the surplus production of textiles from hand looms and small mechanical looms remaining at the sales office of al-Ghazal al-Misri on the government account to the Sudan, provided that they are sold at the same prices that they are sold to Egyptian traders, following the conditions and rules which the ministry will impose after sufficient assurances are received concerning the traders that will be entrusted with the export of those textiles, *guaranteeing their arrival in the hands of Sudanese at reasonable prices.*[91]

The following year, the Cairo Chamber of Commerce reported that "the Ministry of Commerce and Industry authorized wholesale traders of textiles, who have rights to deliver an allotment from the sales office of al-Ghazal al-Misri to retail traders in the Sudan, to send such to them. The share of each wholesale trader will be limited according to estimates of local committees in the Sudan."[92] Earlier that year the chamber reported that the Egyptian government had authorized the shipment of 4 million meters of textiles to the Sudan, utilizing specific regulations and procedures to ensure equal opportunity for "all Sudanese traders who have previously exchanged textiles between Egypt and the Sudan."[93] Although the government maintained export restrictions to protect the welfare of consumers and commercial classes, merchants were increasingly anxious for free rein in the markets. In August 1948, "a group of retail traders of the Sudan requested of the Egyptian Minister of Commerce and Industry permission for them to purchase Egyptian textiles on the free market without being restricted to the concession of the Ghazal al-Misri sales office as is [currently] followed."[94] The Egyptian government lifted all textile export restrictions by the end of that year, citing its "desire to encourage commercial activity between sections of the valley to the farthest extent possible."[95] Even with restrictions lifted in the last years before Sudanese independence, Egyptian cotton textile exports made little headway.

The figures in table 6 demonstrate that the volume of cotton textile exports in the 1950s was still half that of the 1920s. As with other commodities, a variety of factors influenced textile trade, but the combination of tariffs and foreign competition was unquestionably most critical. Without significant government assistance Egyptian exporters had little chance. One Egyptian manufacturer, the owner of Harun & Sons Weaving, described in 1951 the extent of assistance needed to solve the problem of meager textile exports:

> The only solution to this problem is that the government work to encourage the export of Egyptian textiles by various means and I believe that the Arab markets and the Sudan are the closest markets to which these textiles could be exported, [facilitated] through the establishment of a very simple supervisory body that would have as its duty assuring the quality of goods exported to these markets so that they could overpower the competition and have staying power against other foreign goods that might undermine them. Also it must be seen to that [the textiles'] prices are moderate.[96]

Such textile owners could request government supervision, could target specific markets, and ensure high quality exports, but "moderate" prices were essential for success in the Sudan—and apparently Egyptian prices were not "moderate" enough when compared to those of foreign competitors. The economically and politically influential Sudanese sectarian leader 'Abd al-Rahman al-Mahdi indirectly referred to this problem when visiting an Egyptian textile establishment in 1952. He commented more than once that the factory's textile production "is superior in its workmanship to the foreign commodity that arrives in the Sudan. And he asked about the reasons that prevent manufactures like this from entering the Sudan instead of the foreign manufactures within our countries."[97] Certainly, there are various responses to 'Abd al-Rahman al-Mahdi's question, but all documentation points to higher-priced Egyptian textiles being unable to compete in the Sudan's 'open' market.

All the factors that affected Egyptian textile export levels were closely interrelated. Foreign competition had led to protective tariffs in Egypt and demands that the same be imposed in the Sudan. Because of the protected local market in which the Egyptian textile manufacturers operated, there was less pressure on them to produce inexpensive, quality items, which led to difficulties competing in the Sudan's 'open' market. Customs rates and regulations, foreign competition, and the inability to satisfy domestic needs were all factors affecting Egypt's inability to increase its exports significantly.[98] Only in the previously established, and relatively static, market of cotton–artificial silk mixes did Egypt encounter any success. In sum, Egyptian efforts to make a mark in the Sudanese textile market, the most potentially profitable sphere of activity in the Sudan, must be considered a failed endeavor. Furthermore, like other commercial fields, the failure to make gains in the textile market represented both an economic and political 'missed opportunity.' The director of economic research for Egypt's customs department published a detailed report on Egyptian–Sudanese commerce in which he defended post–Second World War textile restrictions by stating that "naturally these textiles were not exported, as how could citizens be deprived of goods produced in their country, to be bestowed upon others, unless there was a greater benefit in this for the country."[99] The logic of this statement is sound if Egypt and the Sudan are separate nations, yet Egyptians hoped that improved trade might confirm the unity of the Nile Valley.

Exports of Sugar

Egyptian commercial efforts after 1935 included multiple possible exports to the Sudan, but most fields were of minor importance and value to both Egyptians and Sudanese. Officials and private entrepreneurs discussed cement, soap, cigarettes, matches, leather shoes, and other manufactures in meeting after meeting in the latter 1930s. All such manufactures encountered the same basic problem of needing to overcome foreign competition in the Sudan, normally through one or both administrations providing some sort of financial, transportation, or marketing advantage.[100] Also, for virtually all these commodities, local supply and demand or changes in the international economy (the Depression or the Second World War) had the greatest impact on Egypt's export results. In none of these commercial spheres did Egyptians make significant and permanent progress in strengthening relations with the Sudan.

However, there was one Egyptian commodity that had strong ties to the Sudanese economy and was remarkably consistent in its development through the 1920s and 1930s. Other than a Depression-era decline, refined sugar exports to the Sudan progressed steadily—gradually increasing as Egyptian production capacity and Sudanese consumption needs grew. By the latter 1930s not only was the total volume of sugar exported increasing but Egypt was also providing over 95 percent of all Sudanese sugar imports. Egypt's economic expert at the time attributed this development "to progress in the economic situation of the country . . . [and] to the lowering of sales prices which was carried out in November 1935 and in January 1937. It is also possible to attribute [the increase in total sugar exports from Egypt] to the spread of tea drinking among all the inhabitants of the Sudan and the consequent rise of sugar consumption."[101] Whatever the claimed causes, export levels remained steady through 1942. The amounts exported in 1937 and 1938 compare favorably with those of the first three years of the war (see table 7). Export levels were a reflection of Sudanese demand or purchasing power, relatively immune to transport rates, excise duties, or international economic conditions.[102]

Table 7. Refined sugar exported to the Sudan

Year	Kilograms	Value (LE)	Year	Kilograms	Value (LE)
1918–29 (avg.)	8,861,948	343,461	1939	37,653,210	421,604
1931	3,706,060	39,729	1940	27,532,191	461,660
1932	502,100	7,273	1941	28,415,980	669,022
1933	9,909,038	133,367	1942	16,810,575	408,972
1934	16,153,948	222,805	1943	4,244,824	115,806
1935	21,731,121	238,993	1944	6,664,201	239,095
1936	21,032,659	190,490	1945	3,150,000	103,963
1937	32,950,000	314,674	1950–55 (avg.)	3,711,056[103]	144,859
1938	31,886,020	342,113			

There was a simple reason for this 'successfully' interdependent commercial relationship. From the First World War on, the Sudanese government had contracts with the Société des Sucreries et Raffinerie in Egypt to fulfill all the Sudan's sugar requirements. A 1919 agreement between the company and the Sudanese government was adhered to until just prior to the Second World War. During the First World War, the Supplies Commission of the Egyptian Government mentioned the official arrangement with this company, "which guarantees the meeting of all demands made in Egypt and in the Sudan for the need of general consumption and of the British army."[104] The contract to supply sugar also prohibited its export to the Sudan without a delivery certificate from the Condominium administration.[105] Therefore, from the start of the interwar period Egypt was the primary provider of sugar to the Sudan, but the Condominium government monopolized this commerce in the country.

The Condominium's monopoly of the sugar trade provided Egyptians with little opportunity to profit financially—or politically. Instead, the Sudanese government was able to procure sugar at fixed prices, distribute it through traders it chose, and profit tremendously in the process. M.W. Daly states of this monopoly during the post-Depression period that "the mark-up was about 100 per cent, and profits never accounted for less than 11.7 per cent of government revenue."[106] As early as 1922, an *al-Akhbar* editorial complained of British officials' manipulative and exploitative practices in respect to sugar:

> When [Sudanese officials] have seen the possibility of obtaining sugar from Egypt at less than half its price in foreign countries, they have said "Egypt and the Sudan are one" and have purchased sugar for 60 pounds or less and have sold it to the people of the Sudan for 120 pounds. But when they perceived the possibility of obtaining sugar abroad more cheaply than in Egypt they have said "the Sudan is separate from Egypt."[107]

Besides reaping huge profits, the editors of this article stressed that the Sudanese sugar monopoly also undermined the interests of Egyptian farm and factory workers, as well as Egyptian transport revenues when the Condominium imported foreign sugar via Port Sudan. In a meeting on 14 February 1935 of the first Egyptian economic mission with members of the Khartoum Chamber of Commerce there was discussion of ending the monopoly, but the Sudanese claimed that their government's revenues had to be preserved and that it would be difficult to establish taxes on other imports from Egypt.[108] Clearly the sugar monopoly was an indirect method of imposing duties on Egyptian–Sudanese commerce.

In addition to deriving tremendous profits from the sugar monopoly, the Sudanese government determined who would handle distribution within the country. The Berber Province report of 1931 noted the presence of "sugar middle-men" who wanted to "reduce their allotments substantially in 1932" due to hardships during the Depression.[109] Considering the Condominium administration's generally anti-Egyptian orientation from 1924 or earlier, there was little chance of Egyptian involvement in the Sudanese sugar market. 'Abdallah Fakri Abaza described a situation less than conducive to Egyptian activity: "Not all merchants have the right to purchase from the government directly, indeed, that was confined to a small number of wholesale traders distributing it in their turn to small traders on specific conditions and prices which the government determines."[110]

British officials modified the system in 1939 to allow most traders of moderate means to purchase directly from the government, but this did little to improve Egyptian prospects in a commercial field where the Condominium still handled all import and wholesale trading activity.

The Condominium's monopoly of sugar was not opposed by Egyptian interests alone. Some Sudanese were angered by both their lack of involvement and the economic harm caused by the government's monopoly. At the start of the Depression in 1930, the Khartoum Chamber of Commerce advocated ending the monopoly and allowing the profits from the sugar trade to enter and stimulate the economy.[111] Mr. Kontomichalos, president of the chamber at the time and later heavily involved in Egyptian–Sudanese economic relations, stated in 1934 that

> the sugar monopoly is one of the factors that arouses the most indignation among traders of the region. We cannot believe that, in the current circumstances, the government is incapable of renouncing the revenues produced from this monopoly, which is estimated to be around half a million pounds annually. We do not see the difficulty in finding another means for the government to obtain the same revenues, leaving then the trade of sugar to merchants.[112]

The sugar monopoly was essentially a hidden, and valuable, Condominium tax on trade, denying merchants potential profits while risking popular discontent when local prices were raised. The latter situation was precisely what *al-Ahram*'s correspondent in Khartoum reported in December 1939: "The government here raised the price of sugar tremendously, and the population is oppressed by this increase, especially since sugar is considered a staple in Sudanese life, with equal amounts consumed by the poor and the rich. Newspapers indicated that the cost of sugar in Khartoum, including shipping and duties, is only around 40 percent of the price at which the government sells it."[113] Ignoring Sudanese critics of the monopoly in the 1930s, Condominium officials maintained the arrangement of Egypt supplying Sudanese sugar requirements. They even negotiated a new agreement to ensure sugar provisions during the Second World War.

Discussions leading to this wartime agreement illustrated the significance of the sugar trade—significant to more than merely better commercial relations or the profits sought by a few merchants. Egyptian officials and the private interests involved in local production frequently linked the increasing demand for refined sugar to extending cane cultivation. During the First World War, Henri Naus, the director of Egypt's sugar refining company at the time, informed the government of the need to bring an additional twelve to fourteen thousand feddans under cultivation to meet Nile Valley needs.[114] In 1910, 1915, and again in 1928 the sugar company made arrangements with the Société Anonyme de Wadi Kom-Ombo for the cultivation of cane in Egypt.[115] Just before the Second World War, Egyptian officials began discussing a new agreement with the Sudanese government that tied increased cultivation to guaranteed exports to the Sudan. *Al-Ahram* described the meetings and basic agreement as follows:

> The director of Sudanese customs recently spent several days in Cairo, during which he had discussions with the competent authorities within the Ministry of Trade on the issue of providing the Sudan with its needs of Egyptian sugar during wartime, without [Egypt] having to resort to importing raw sugar from Java, refining such, and then exporting to the Sudan, as is now practiced, [and] which is impractical with the outbreak of war.
>
> The ministry studied this subject and it became clear that its implementation required increasing the area on which cane is grown in Egypt by around fifteen thousand feddans. Therefore, [the ministry] stipulated that the Sudanese government guarantee to import the quantities it needs of Egyptian sugar for a period of five years or it raise the customs duty on foreign sugar imported to the Sudan by 20 percent.[116]

By the fall of 1940, *al-Ahram* reported that "agreement was also reached that Egypt will undertake to supply the Sudan with sugar throughout the war."[117] The decades-long arrangement to supply the Sudan with sugar led to steady export results, avoided the problems posed by the Sudan's 'open' market, and lessened Egypt's dependence on cotton—thereby facilitating both Egyptian economic independence and the unity of the Nile Valley. Some of the most politically influential Egyptians, not only those desirous of union with the Sudan, supported the sugar provisioning arrangements. Agricultural interests dominated Egyptian politics and "sugar was cultivated on the Upper Egyptian estates of some of the largest and most powerful landowners, including the royal family."[118] Yet profitable and strong commercial relations along the Nile Valley would be most politically useful when the Sudanese benefited as well. Egypt's Second World War expert in the Sudan, Mahmud Zaki, concurred when he wrote that Egypt's continuing to meet Sudanese sugar demand would have "the greatest influence" on public opinion.[119]

Unfortunately, Egypt was unable or unwilling to export sufficient sugar over the course of the Second World War, and its standing in Sudanese eyes was affected accordingly. Based on the export figures in table 7 above, the Egyptian sugar trade maintained its prewar, and promised, levels through 1942, after which there is a noticeable decline.[120] Officials and scholars have provided different explanations for why Egypt apparently failed to provision the Sudan. Before the United Nations Security Council in 1947, Britain's representative stated that in 1942 the "Egyptian Sugar Combine defaulted on a long-established contract and refused to supply the Sudan in her need."[121] Mekki Abbas notes that "the sugar producers in Egypt disagreed over the prices and the Sudan Government began to import from somewhere else."[122] Egyptians countered charges of their greed or lack of concern for the Sudan, however, with claims of simply insufficient local production. The cultivation of sugar cane in Egypt alone had not been enough to satisfy the needs of the Nile Valley. In 1937 the governor-general's report stated that "imports of raw cane sugar into Egypt from the Dutch East Indies are about equal to the quantity of sugar supplied by Egypt to the Sudan."[123] Just as officials negotiating the sugar agreement before the war had feared, the outbreak of hostilities disrupted the regular arrival of raw cane from abroad. 'Abdallah Fakri Abaza confirmed that difficulties supplying the Sudan were mainly due to Egypt's reliance on "refining raw sugar imported from abroad."[124] Plus, parliamentary reports, local commercial journals, and official statistics on sugar exports all describe an Egyptian state struggling to satisfy its own population's needs, before delivery of the remainder to the Sudan.[125] From 1943 to 1945 Egypt exported between 3 and almost 7 million kilograms of sugar annually to the Sudan when 'defaulting' on its obligations, but shipped to all other countries during those same three years just over 40,000 kilograms total.[126] There may have been disagreement over the price of sugar exported, but it is difficult to attribute the failure to supply the Sudan to Egyptian greed or indifference.

In addition to the importance of sugar production and commerce for stronger Egyptian–Sudanese relations, this industry had played a critical role in Egypt's drive toward 'economic independence' for years. In 1914 a note from Henri Naus to Husayn Rushdi Pasha, president of the Council of Ministers at the time, stated that "the production of sugar constitutes actually the sole, large industry of Egypt consisting of the transformation of agricultural products, [and] the utilization of an enormous number of workers and artisans."[127] Naus was advocating the extension of sugar cane cultivation, but his remarks were not without foundation because sugar refining remained one of the larger domestic industries throughout the period of this study. The cultivation and processing of sugar cane contributed to Egypt's own economic development, while the provisioning links to the Sudan helped bind the two halves of the Nile Valley. Yet the dramatic decline in the volume of this trade after 1942 did not bode well for the diplomatic utility of this economic bond. Furthermore, considering that the trade was a closely guarded monopoly of the Sudanese government, there was little chance of developing common interests between Egyptians and Sudanese—whether they were farmers, factory workers, industrialists, merchants, or consumers of sugar. Despite being a valuable export of Egypt for much of the period, it is difficult to characterize the sugar trade as a 'success.'

Egyptian–Sudanese Commerce during the Second World War

Excluding refined sugar, the analysis of selected commodities above indicates a degree of success for each during the Second World War. However, the war deserves a brief examination on its own because it presented Egyptians with real commercial opportunities that were not truly seized since commerce with the Sudan after the war returned to normal or worse. The Depression had also restricted international trade and presented Egyptians with opportunities in the Sudan, but during those years tariff reforms and industrial beginnings had not yet transformed Egypt into a capable trading partner of their southern neighbor.[128] Now, Egypt was not an industrial power by the Second World War, but exporting certain manufactures to the Sudan was at least feasible. In 1941 the Alexandria Chamber of Commerce described wartime expectations, including improved manufacturing as one component of better commercial relations with the Sudan:

> It is expected that the exports of Egypt to the Sudan during this war will surpass [previously] evident increases, in view of the difficulties of transport which raises expenses [for foreign suppliers]. We hope that our efforts, which we exert in our permanent exhibition in Khartoum, will lead Sudanese traders to familiarize themselves with and take an interest in Egyptian products. The industrial rebirth in Egypt and the absence of tariffs on our [products] will inevitably lead to an increase of what we export to the Sudan.[129]

This linking of industrial development in Egypt with potential Sudanese markets during the war was echoed by other sources. The Cairo Chamber of Commerce singled out textile exports as a field for wartime expansion, especially if Egyptian raw cotton supplies, improved local manufacturing, and cooperation from Sudanese merchants could be successfully integrated.[130] In addition to manufactures, Egypt was increasingly diversifying agricultural production and seeking external markets for such. The Sudan was the logical market during the war since Egypt was "cut off from its traditional European trading and investment partners and was thrown back on its own resources."[131] Finally, wartime maritime transportation restrictions forced the increased use and development of facilities between Egypt and the Sudan. *Al-Jarida al-tijariya al-misriya* reported in 1941 that "the activity of transporting articles by railroad and the Nile grew energetically."[132] Officials in the region also took measures during the war to simplify the bureaucratic processes associated with the transit trade.[133] Obviously, improved transit trade is not successful development of Egyptian–Sudanese commerce, but Egyptians had consistently attributed their trade failures to inadequate transport facilities along the Nile, which the war might now rectify.

Improved transportation or greater economic 'independence' from industrial and agricultural diversification would be the natural result of increased exports to the Sudan. Therefore, Egyptian officials and entrepreneurs consistently emphasized the wartime commercial possibilities. 'Abdallah Fakri Abaza wrote that "most of the [Sudan's] traders who had done business with foreign countries were forced to resort to the Egyptian manufactures."[134] In 1941 *al-Jarida al-tijariya al-misriya* reported that "the financial and commercial departments in both countries are expressing satisfaction in the recent progress in the commercial relations of the countries, and they are putting forth cooperative efforts for the expansion of these relations and for their continuance after the end of the present world war."[135] All Egyptian sources echoed the sentiments of the expert in the Sudan, who reported in 1940 that restricting foreign commodities in local markets "will lead to the increase of Egyptian imports in the future to a great extent."[136]

Considering the decades spent developing Sudanese links to international markets, it is unsurprising that Condominium officials were less enthusiastic about wartime reliance on Egypt. In 1943 Governor-General Huddleston mentioned "the very strenuous efforts which have been and are being made by the Sudan government to *keep alive the natural trade* between Egypt and the Sudan."[137] Sudanese documentation indicated less concern for augmenting this "natural" trade. Instead, British officials focused on supervision of the expected greater volume of traffic. *Al-Ahram* summarized for its readers an October 1939 circular distributed by the Condominium administration thus:

> It is stated in it that foodstuffs in the Sudan are plentiful and sufficient for all classes of people on condition that every individual confines himself to buying what he needs normally and that every trader works for the benefit of society, as much as he works for his personal benefit.
>
> And it states also in the circular that the government is desirous of establishing the least possible restrictions on commerce, but it will not hesitate in being severe with traders who proceed to hoard large amounts of foodstuffs, and the traders who refuse to sell in normal quantities that for which there is demand, or those who are working to raise prices without justification.[138]

Although the Condominium administration's circular mentioned plentiful foodstuffs and its desire to increase commerce, the tone of the memorandum clearly indicated the likelihood of commercial restrictions.

Both the Egyptian and the Sudanese government imposed restrictions on commerce—whether foreign or local—to ensure economic stability, sufficient supplies for popular consumption, and provisions for the war effort. And administrative controls effectively negated any opportunities the war raised for Egyptian–Sudanese commerce. The Egyptian government restricted export activities with Law No. 98 of 1939, which prohibited the export of commodities to any country without authorization from the Ministry of Finance. By the middle of the war, with the direct military threat receding, local traders questioned whether or not this restriction should be applied to the Sudan. Egyptians were most interested in textile exports, which had increased tremendously in value. The editors of *al-Jarida al-tijariya al-misriya* claimed in 1943 that "Egypt's exports to the Sudan are not subject to . . . the jurisdiction of Ordinance Number 98 of 1939 concerning the prohibition of export of some articles to foreign countries."[139] Mahmud Zaki confirmed this view of Law No. 98, noting only that these exports must not undermine Egyptian consumption needs nor be reexported to foreign countries.[140]

Law No. 98 was only the opening salvo in a series of commercial restrictions the Egyptian government imposed during the war. In 1940 the Egyptian parliament passed legislation that restricted virtually all wholesale trade of agricultural produce to designated and closely monitored markets.[141] Rice, onions, and a few other agricultural commodities had been valuable exports to the Sudan before the war, but after 1935 Egyptian entrepreneurs concentrated on increased export of manufactures. As the war progressed both agricultural and industrial products became increasingly profitable items of trade, and by the later stages of the conflict, restrictions encompassed almost all major exports to the Sudan. In July 1943 a committee in the Ministry of Finance categorized exports to the Sudan, designating them as free from restrictions, restricted (permits required), or completely prohibited.[142] Commodities for which a permit was required included such traditionally important exports as rice, citrus fruits, soap, shoes, cigarettes, and cotton cloths (including artisan-produced mixes). Controls had lightened little a year later.

> The customs administration was informed of instructions from the Ministry of Finance laying down some rules to facilitate commercial activity and the transport of goods from Egypt to the Sudan, restricting some goods authorized for dispatch and the quantities which could be shipped, while differentiating between Egyptian commodities and foreign imports, on whose shipment special rules were imposed.
>
> It is evident from the details that the Egyptian commodities which have had conditions imposed upon their export to the Sudan are rice, oil, textiles, wheat, millet, barley, bread, varieties of flour, sugar, and kerosene, and the Sudan specified limited quantities of the first three items.
>
> The majority of commodities are not included in the previously mentioned restrictions, and especially shoes, tanned leather, sweets, fruit preserves, cigarettes, seed potatoes, and the like.[143]

The Egyptian government itself was clearly preventing increased export to the Sudan of some profitable, and previously promoted, commodities. In 1944 a committee of Egyptian officials investigated the implications of restricting trade with a region purported to be an integral part of their own nation, but no policy changes resulted.[144]

Although the Egyptian government controlled all commodities bound for the Sudan, there was more extensive regulation of textile exports. This concern is entirely justifiable, considering that the Sudanese textile market had been the most extensive and profitable, as well as the most alluring to Egyptians, and was now less dominated by foreign competitors. Not surprisingly, Mahmud Zaki reported in 1942 that the Egyptian textile market "has become in great need of organization because of speculators and hoarders of cotton textiles attempting to sell large quantities of them on the black market at high prices, especially to those who wish to export them to the Sudan because of the lack of any restriction on exportation to the Sudan."[145] Consequently, by the end of 1942 the government limited the amount and type of textile that could be sent to the Sudan.[146] Imposing restrictions on textile exports to the Sudan allowed the Egyptian government to prevent speculation and protect local distributors and producers of these commodities, but such wartime control clearly would not assist in 'capturing' the Sudanese textile market.[147]

During the war a group of Egyptian entrepreneurs, largely from the permanent committee and chambers of commerce, established a company specifically for the marketing of cotton textiles on a wider scale in the Sudan. At a meeting of the Cairo Chamber of Commerce on 22 June 1942,

> a group of the larger traders and owners of factories met under the leadership of Mr. Hafiz 'Afifi Pasha, president of the chamber, to look into forming a company for the trade of Egyptian manufactures in the Sudan. The group came to an agreement on this proposal and the [extent of their] participation in the formation of the company. And they assigned to a subcommittee the task of writing a charter for the company, determining the capital, and announcing its objectives.[148]

This new commercial firm, the Egypt and Sudan Company, was established by private Egyptian entrepreneurs interested in the textile trade especially, but its activities in the Sudan quickly took on a more 'official' character. The company would eventually take over the Khartoum permanent exhibition and office, and the latter's mission of promoting commerce generally. Back in July 1940 local entrepreneurs met with both Egyptian and British officials to look "into the budget of the permanent exhibition in Khartoum for Egyptian manufactures, and among that which was examined was the necessity of provisioning the exhibition with various Egyptian manufactures that the Sudan needed, especially in the current circumstances in which it looks to Egypt because the means of importing from abroad are becoming impossible."[149] In January 1944 the Cairo Chamber of Commerce reported that during the previous year

> a new company for the sale of Egyptian goods and manufactures in the Sudan, and likewise Sudanese produce in Egypt, was founded under the auspices of the chamber, with capital of approximately fifty thousand pounds.
>
> Whereas the permanent office of Khartoum had been established by the Cairo and Alexandria chambers for the promotion of Egyptian goods in the Sudan, the new company had been carrying out this task

on the widest scale, and the Alexandria and Cairo chambers have decided in principle to include that office in the new company.[150]

The Egypt and Sudan Company assumed responsibility for the Khartoum office and promoting Egyptian trade with the Sudan, working closely with the Egyptian economic expert in this undertaking.

Despite hopes that the company could better promote trade generally, it was most interested in the textile trade. On 16 August 1943, *al-Jarida al-tijariya al-misriya* reported that "this nationalist company will begin its operations this week," and that "the objectives of the company are *limited* to the export of textiles from Egypt to the Sudan."[151] Textile imports constituted the largest, most valuable market in the Sudan. The war presented clear opportunities for Egyptians to enter this market. So, as expected, the Sudanese government closely supervised commercial activities in this field. Just two weeks after reporting the company had commenced operations, *al-Jarida al-tijariya al-misriya* noted that the company would import Egyptian textiles and distribute them locally, "under the supervision of the Sudanese government."[152] The company hoped to avoid an adversarial relationship with the Condominium administration. *Al-Ahram* reported in early 1944 that "agents of the 'Egypt and Sudan' Company of Khartoum contacted the [Sudan's] provisions department to arrange the import of Egyptian textiles and their sale in the Sudan. The economic expert offered his assistance in this matter to protect the rights of importers and consumers."[153] In a 1943 interview, Mahmud Zaki explained that both governments would monitor the company's textile trade, imposing the following guidelines:

> On condition that the company undertakes to follow what the Egyptian government decides in respect to the limitation of quantities of each article, the times of their shipment, and the limitations on wholesale prices in the Sudan; and that [the company] implements what the Sudanese government decrees in the matter of distribution, whether in relation to the regions or the individual traders, and that it is confined to wholesale distribution.[154]

With prices, quantities, and distribution methods restricted in this fashion there was little chance of permanently replacing foreign competitors during the war.

The Egyptian government imposed restrictions on this company during the war, but most Egyptians directed their complaints about interference in trade at the Condominium administration. One method of controlling trade, and discouraging greater Egyptian involvement, was through fixing prices or establishing permissible profit margins—both ostensibly for the public's welfare.[155] The Khartoum Chamber of Commerce reported in late 1939 that "the maximum prices for goods will be fixed in the future according to the average prices in Port Sudan."[156] By May 1941 the Sudanese Department of Economics and Trade announced that the government was changing its price control method. Imports would now be subject to fixed profit percentages, and it sent lists of the rates on certain commodities to Egyptians via the Sudanese Chamber of Commerce.[157] The Cairo Chamber recognized the Condominium's need to protect local consumers while granting merchants a reasonable profit margin, but complained bitterly that the change from maximum prices to specific profit percentages was the wrong method of achieving these goals.[158]

Price and profit controls indirectly discouraged Egyptian commercial involvement in the Sudan. The Condominium administration buttressed these measures with strict limits on the quantities of Egyptian imports. The problems posed by Sudanese import restrictions were most apparent in the records of meetings and correspondence from late 1943 to early 1944. In a 1943 letter to the Sudan's governor-general, Mahmud Zaki complained "that the government of the Sudan had forbidden the importation of many Egyptian products unless they obtain permits it issues."[159] A report on a meeting between Egyptian and Sudanese officials on 11 November 1943 concluded that "there is no doubt that the presence of restrictions on the exportation of Egyptian products to the Sudan is a matter that is unjustifiable."[160] In January 1944 Prime Minister Nahhas sent a memorandum to Governor-General Huddleston requesting "that hindrances should not be placed on the export of Egyptian products to the Sudan, just as it is necessary to ease the importation of Sudanese produce and avoid placing impediments in its path."[161] The governor-general explained away these complaints by writing that it was "necessary to insist upon the issue of import licenses for certain categories of imported goods," but stated that such restrictions had been required by the Middle East Supply Center (MESC).[162] Whether the impetus for commercial controls came from the Condominium administration or the MESC, the restrictions were certainly detrimental to Egyptian aspirations in the Sudan.

Actually, Sudanese supervision of commercial relations with Egypt and others during the war was based on the 1935 Defense of the Sudan Ordinances. At the outbreak of the Second World War, the Condominium's director of the Department of Economics and Trade implemented the Defense of the Sudan Ordinances by ordering local traders to prepare schedules with detailed information on the type, quantity, and record of sales or acquisitions of all commodities—in order to ease inspection.[163] This initial decree from the Sudanese administration was the first step in instituting comprehensive wartime control of trade. The Condominium's own celebratory account of its history, *The Sudan: A Record of Progress*, describes the extent of wartime control imposed through the Defense of the Sudan Ordinances: "These regulations made all imports and exports subject to licence and gave the Controller-General [of Supplies] complete powers (subject to veto on appeal) to control movement, storage, shipment, sale, purchase, distribution, use and all other dealings with any kind of goods, to requisition, to fix prices and to regulate the carrying on of any undertaking."[164] Considering the extensive commercial control, which was reciprocated by the Egyptian government, the inability to take advantage of 'opportunities' during the Second World War is readily understood. Egypt had enjoyed equal footing with its commercial competitors in the Sudan before the war, and government supervision during the conflict ensured this was maintained. 'Abd al-'Aziz al-Sufani of the Nationalist Party seemed justified when asking his parliamentary colleagues in 1942 about the failure to insist upon stronger ties to the Sudan: "Is the Sudan regarded as a distinct kingdom, far from us, with which we are not connected except by what connects us to eastern kingdoms like Syria, for example?"[165] Egyptian officials rarely even voiced this possibility of a divided valley, but the war years did not lessen the autonomous economic development of Egypt and the Sudan. In fact, the governor-general's report for 1942–44 stated that the war had forced the Sudanese administration "to endeavour to secure an *increasingly independent* economy."[166]

Conclusion: "Sealing the 'Commercial' Deal"

During the decade following the war, there was little disruption to the Sudan's separate commercial path or the Condominium's control of trade with Egyptians and other 'foreign' entities. When examining postwar commercial restrictions, it appears that officials did not specifically work to undermine Egyptian bonds, but they also had no intention of preferring trade with Egypt. For instance, when *al-Ahram* described the Sudanese governor-general's council discussion on easing trade controls, there was no mention of Egypt:

> As for commercial policy which the council acts on today, it is to work on eliminating all restrictions imposed on imports, exports, and local distribution. It is anticipated that [the council] will be

> dismantling supervisory restrictions to a great degree during the coming ten months, although this process will depend to a large extent on economic, financial, and political developments all over the world, and it is specifically not likely to encompass the system set up to control the exchange of currencies.[167]

Trade with Egypt was a secondary concern to Sudanese connections to global economic and financial markets.

More attention for international markets than for Nile Valley relations was not a new orientation for the Condominium administration. This outlook had underpinned development from the start. Certainly, it was maintained during the Second World War, when winning a global conflict trumped developing stronger relations in the Nile Valley. And after the war, to the chagrin of prospective Egyptian merchants, this international orientation continued. In 1947, the president of the Khartoum Chamber of Commerce delivered a speech declaring his hope that the Condominium would allow completely free commercial activity in the country, but stating that he feared that

> the government sees the accelerated removal of the restrictions as encouraging speculation on the general unsettled economic situation, leading to certain dangers. There has been a global deficit of some goods for which there is import demand, and the government intends to continue the original method [of control] at the current time. The import of goods for which there are limited quantities abroad will remain an affair for the hands of importers entrusted with such in the past, although it was not expected that a system of renewing allotments for the Sudan from abroad shall continue more than a few months, with the exception of sugar, cotton textiles, and some foodstuffs.[168]

Preventing speculation and protecting local consumers is commendable, but it should be emphasized that these methods of control harmed Egyptian trade interests more than those of their competitors. Entrusting importation to those traditionally involved, rather than 'fly-by-night' profiteers, is logical, but Egyptians were *not* those established importers, so this policy effectively kept business in their competitors' hands. Also, the speech indicated the probability of longer restrictions on precisely those commodities Egyptians were most capable of providing—textiles, sugar, and other foodstuffs.

With the Sudan continuing controls harmful to Egyptian commercial interests year after year, it is no wonder that Egyptian officials increasingly raised objections. On 6 April 1948, during parliamentary discussion of the economic expert's position, Muhammad Fakri Abaza stated that "numerous difficulties are being erected by the Sudanese government in respect to an Egyptian official undertaking purely economic work, . . . from start to finish this work is intended only to strengthen the commercial and industrial bond between parts of the united nation." Undoubtedly there were political ramifications or intentions behind economic bonds, but when the government responded with a half-hearted promise to investigate alleged political motives behind Sudanese administrative obstructionism, Abaza countered,

> This vagueness is unacceptable, and the government must make us aware of [the information] it has so that we know the difficulties and debate them. And if we have requested of the government that it do all in its power, then it is incumbent upon us to offer it what we have in the way of assistance, and that we declare—collectively—in public that the local government there creates difficulties and erects hurdles between parts of the united nation, and places obstacles in the way of economic officials and to let the entire world know that the behavior of the government there is incompatible with the economic welfare of the countries, indeed it clashes with the most basic rules of human behavior.[169]

Although Abaza targeted the Condominium administration in this particular speech, he was also among the most vociferous in criticizing the failures of the Egyptian expert and his own government's policies.

Egyptian government policies in the aftermath of the Second World War, as during the conflict, deserve at least equal credit for preventing an improvement in trade with the Sudan. For instance, during parliamentary debates about taking the Anglo–Egyptian dispute over the Sudan before the United Nations Security Council, deputies lamented their government's failure to facilitate trade with the Sudan. Mahmud Rashid asked his colleagues, "Why is there no boldness of action at all among us—after we have decided that Egypt and the Sudan are one country—why not lift every obstacle to export and import between the two? Indeed, why is commerce between Egypt and the Sudan not like trade between Lower and Upper Egypt?"[170] There clearly were still Egyptian government controls over trade with the Sudan. On 30 April 1947, Muhammad Samih Musa responded to parliamentary clamor for the elimination of all obstacles to Nile Valley trade by explaining that, "in reality, consideration of the welfare of [our] southern brothers, and ensuring their supply of what they need in the way of Egyptian products and a proper distribution of these goods—all this requires that the Egyptian government attends to commercial affairs of the valley and the shared nationalist ties and interest."[171] The following month the Alexandria Chamber of Commerce published an announcement from the Ministry of Finance that clarified applicable restrictions that had led to this round of complaints. The announcement read:

> It has been customary in the previous years to split the exports of Egypt to the Sudan into four quotas, each of them for three months, and activity has proceeded this year also on this basis.
>
> The authorization for the first quarter of the current year, for the months of January, February, and March, was distributed. And export continued in accordance with this authorization, and the specific quantities of the second quarter quota are still under ministerial consideration.
>
> It is not the intention of the ministry to abandon its policy in the provisioning of the Sudan, and especially from Egyptian products, after having laid down rules which ensure the fairness of the distribution of these products to those in need among the Sudanese population.[172]

Provisioning the Sudan and ensuring a fair distribution of products was well-intentioned, but it also clearly still limited trade.

As a new decade dawned in 1950, there was only a slight lightening of supervision from the Egyptian state. That year the Egyptian General Authority for Exports announced a special system for export to the Sudan.

> 1—The export of Egyptian agricultural products to the Sudan without authorization from the Ministry of Finance is *permissible, provided that this is under the supervision of the customs department.*
> 2—The export to the Sudan of manufactures imported from abroad is *permissible, provided that their price was not paid in hard currency*, and that is due to the illegality of sending this currency from Egypt by indirect means.
> 3—It is necessary that the *export of rice, soap, cement, and tahina paste is subject to a system of quotas*, specific amounts of these goods for export to the Sudan are restricted under the supervision of the imports and

exports office, provided that it distributes to the traders a specific portion proportional to the exports of each of them over the past three years or distributes to the customs branches in proportion to the importance of each port's export of such.

In every case, payment of a surety corresponding to the value of the goods and the tariffs imposed on them was required, and that is to prevent fraudulent acts and sending the goods to another place. And the surety is returned to the exporter only upon presentation of proof of the goods' arrival in the designated location.[173]

Although the export of agricultural produce and manufactures, including textiles, was relatively free of restrictions finally, there was clearly still extensive supervision of Nile Valley trade. Apportioning commodities to merchants on the basis of past activity would limit opportunities for prospective entrepreneurs. Finally, the commodities listed in number three above had been among those singled out for promotion by Egyptian interests since the mid-1930s, yet these regulations in 1950 singled out those same goods for government control.

The basic problem for the improvement of Egyptian–Sudanese commerce in the final years of the Condominium was no different than that of the mid-1930s or the first decades after the reconquest. The Sudan and Egypt functioned as two independent states already. Both remained strongly tied to international markets—exporting largely raw cotton and importing various manufactures, neither of which were sent to or received from one another. During the Second World War the Alexandria Chamber of Commerce concluded that trade with the Sudan was insignificant because the Sudan "depends on importing its manufactured goods requirements from the West and Japan"—an assessment that is fairly accurate for the entire period.[174] Egyptians did raise export levels of some commodities to the Sudan, but in virtually every case these quantities were dwarfed by the amounts and value of exports shipped elsewhere.[175] This study has emphasized the strongly independent nature of the two administrations when discussing Nile water agreements or the transportation infrastructure of the valley. The independent character of each region in respect to commerce was readily apparent in the autonomy of customs regimes. Egypt's customs department described in 1950 the trade situation of the Nile Valley by stating that "commerce between Egypt and the Sudan has special statutes in view of their political circumstances because the Sudan is not an independent nation separated from Egypt by specific political borders, indeed it is a part of Egypt, one of the two halves of the valley detached from the other by well-known historical circumstances."[176] This comment includes the contradictions typical of almost all Egyptian statements concerning the Sudan, which is *not* "independent" or "separated" but is certainly "one of the two halves" and is "detached." Equally typical were statements requesting the "removal of all existing impediments and customs obstacles" or "unifying the customs system in Egypt and the Sudan on a qualitative and quantitative basis."[177] The existence of customs impediments/obstacles or the need to unify systems seem fairly clear indicators that Egypt and the Sudan were separate countries, if not officially independent nations yet.

Egyptian entrepreneurs were aware of the political ramifications of failing to improve commercial relations with the Sudan. Fu'ad Abaza, Talaat Harb, Mr. Kontomichalos, and many others delivered speeches emphasizing economic-political bonds in the years after 1935. After the Second World War Egyptians continued to advocate the same linking of economic development and political aspirations. At a 1946 party honoring a delegation of Sudanese, 'Abd al-Majid al-Rimali, the president of the Cairo Chamber of Commerce, made the following comments on the need to end the British occupation of the valley and its economic future:

> We will live together in true independence, only through virtuous work and friendly effort, in service of our country together, in the interest of its progress and its development, its north and its south, its property owners and its peasants, its agriculturalists and its industrialists, its merchants and its workers.
>
> Furthermore, gentlemen, I must not forget when I am among you to express my feelings as a Sudanese Egyptian, or as an Egyptian Sudanese, or reckoned as a son of the Nile Valley, praying for its unity, demanding its complete independence and its freedom. And I also represent the Cairo Chamber of Commerce that includes all traders of Cairo, and in this last capacity I seek and demand: that there is an economic bulwark for our national unity that holds in check the calamities of the time and vicissitudes of fate and that protects the wealth and abundance of its people. We obtain from you that which exceeds your need of manufactures, and we export to you what you must have of crops and industrial goods. Through these means commercial exchange is lively between Egypt and the Sudan, or between the two halves of the Nile Valley, its north and its south. Each of them is the best customer of the other, in fact the extent of our market and yours expands and becomes one market,

> and a single field in which the surplus plunges madly to where there is need. Agriculture provides industry with what it seeks, and the whole is supported through consistent labor and provisioning, and lively business does not diminish its activities, and prosperity becomes common all about the valley near and far.[178]

In a speech to Sudanese journalists three years later, ‘Abd al-Majid al-Rimali reiterated the link between economic success and political objectives that had inspired Egyptian efforts in the past decades:

> I hope . . . you, Sudanese journalists in the vanguard of public opinion in the Sudan, will be concerned about the economic bonds of the south and north of the valley, and strengthening and completing such, like your concern for political, social, and cultural ties. The former is no less a matter than the latter, since economic issues influence the lives of the people, especially in the modern era.[179]

Most Egyptian officials and entrepreneurs agreed with ‘Abd al-Majid al-Rimali’s premise that economic bonds are just as significant as social, cultural, or other bonds. However, the record of Egyptian exports to the Sudan from the First World War through the 1950s indicates that there was little success in developing commercial ties. Without increased Egyptian exports to the Sudan, and native entrepreneurs or the local population benefiting from the trade, the likelihood of transforming economic bonds into political union was slim.

7 An Economic Lifeline? Egyptian Reliance on Sudanese Imports

> The circumstances of the war have led to Egypt being in great need of the Sudan's excess produce for its domestic markets in order to meet the needs of inhabitants on one hand and to supply some existing industries with a portion of raw materials on the other.
>
> And there is no doubt that if the commercial exchange between Egypt and the Sudan in various crops and goods was progressing in its normal channels, which were customary before the war, that would assist to a great extent in solving many of the problems of provisioning in the two countries. Each of them needs the other and the wartime conditions have made visible the extent of this needed economic cooperation toward which efforts have been directed and which is centered on [mutual] esteem and respect, strengthening economic bonds resulting in mutual prosperity and benefits for Egypt and the Sudan.
>
> We have not drawn nearer to realizing this economic unity.[1]
>
> —'Abdallah Fakri Abaza, general secretary of the Ministry of Trade and Industry, 1944

When the former Egyptian economic expert in the Sudan made these comments, which admitted the failure to draw nearer to economic unity, almost a decade had passed since Fu'ad Abaza's initial visit to the Sudan. That investigative mission on behalf of the Royal Agricultural Society in 1934 focused on Sudanese agricultural production, potentially imported by Egypt. After that time Egyptians had directed most efforts toward economic spheres other than promoting Sudanese agricultural imports. Instead, they attended to increasing their exports to the Sudan, developing transportation facilities, promoting investment there, and engaging in other economic activities that might augur well for an eventually united Nile Valley. However, as 'Abdallah Fakri Abaza stated above, by 1944 Egyptians had not advanced this cause of political union to any great extent, partially because of having failed to frequently and forcefully encourage Sudanese imports. The reasons for this almost lackadaisical attitude toward imports from the south are readily apparent. The main Sudanese export of raw cotton was destined for non-Egyptian markets only. Most other agricultural production was primarily for local consumption, and non-cotton exports to Egypt increased greatly only when there was a significant surplus in the Sudan or superior prices prevailed in Egypt. To a great extent, basic factors of supply and demand dictated import levels from the Sudan. Government measures and the actions of Egyptian entrepreneurs or organizations were ineffective in overcoming these basic market forces.

Furthermore, the failure to improve import levels from the Sudan was doubly detrimental to the hopes of transforming economic bonds into political union. Not only were Egyptians unsuccessful in developing the Sudanese imports market; it was also precisely in this business that local Egyptians and Sudanese merchants were most active. Put another way, the *least* extensive, *least* profitable, *least* easily encouraged commercial sphere offered the *most* opportunity for local entrepreneurs. The Egyptian and Sudanese merchants involved in Sudanese imports were on the periphery of the economy—with their business located away from the most prominent trading centers, not dealing with the most profitable commodities, and often engaged in regionally confined work. They frequently had worked in such a limited capacity for decades. In fact, the same characterization of local merchants would apply to those few actively exporting Egyptian goods to the Sudan. This was hardly a situation likely to win much support for the economic and political union of Egypt and the Sudan.

Raw Materials for Egyptian Manufacturing

In the mid-1930s, a prospective local merchant in the Sudan would have seen greater possible profits in exporting cotton to non–Nile Valley markets, if foreign competitors in this trade could be overcome. However, there were some raw materials that Egypt's budding industrial establishment sought. One resource Egyptians eyed as potentially useful to their industrialization was Sudanese lumber. As early as 1922 editors of *al-Akhbar* reported interest in the Sudan's extensive forests, for supplying Egypt's paper and building industries.[2] Fu'ad Abaza reported dismal results upon the testing of Sudanese lumber for use by the Egyptian railways, but interest in possibilities was sustained through the 1930s.[3] For instance, during the winter of 1938 the Alexandria and Cairo Chambers of Commerce received samples of Sudanese wood, which were then forwarded to government experts for scientific analysis of its manufacturing uses.[4] By March 1939 the government concluded that Sudanese wood "was not less in strength and appearance than the wood imported from abroad, especially for the manufacture of furniture," and that Sudanese supplies might replace foreign imports.[5]

Mahmud Zaki reported that with the outbreak of the Second World War and Egypt's inability to import wood from abroad, interest in possible Sudanese supplies only increased.[6] Furthermore, by this point larger furniture factories in Cairo were heavily involved in determining if Sudanese wood would satisfy their needs.[7] However, the war and the virtual halt of foreign supplies forced consideration of Sudanese wood imports for more than the furniture business alone. In 1943 *al-Jarida al-tijariya al-misriya* reported that the Ministry of Provisions was contacting the pertinent Sudanese departments "in order to help obtain the wood required for the manufacture of match sticks."[8] Wartime manufacture of matchsticks may have required Sudanese wood imports, but this 'industrial' sector was certainly limited and less profitable than others. Wartime restrictions also led to Egyptian discussion of the Sudan's extensive forests being used to provide charcoal supplies—although officials took no action at the time.[9] Even general building-sector needs did not result in greater Sudanese lumber imports to counter local deficits. A 1946 memorandum from the Ministry of Commerce and Industry reported that total Egyptian imports of wood had fallen from 245,000 tons in 1938 to only 3,918 tons by 1943, causing enormous hardships for the unemployed workers of the building sector.[10] Yet no significant increase in Sudanese lumber imports occurred. Egyptians had hoped that increased Sudanese wood supplies might become a profitable trade and useful to local industry, with subsequent employment benefits, but they achieved no real success in this field. Additionally, the development of this 'trade' with the Sudan was less politically useful than other imports from the south. British diplomats could easily portray the development of wood imports to Egypt as 'colonial' exploitation, and this commercial field had little relationship to the lives of most Sudanese.

Many more Sudanese would be affected by changes in the trade of livestock with Egypt. The transport and sale of Sudanese sheep and cattle in Egypt was a hugely important, contentious, and complicated commercial affair that will be examined later in this study. However, animal hides, initially processed in the Sudan, were an especially important raw material imported by the Egyptian leather industry. Table 8 indicates increased import levels of this material from the mid-1930s onward, exceeding 500,000 kilograms annually after 1935.[11] The easing of depressed conditions facilitated the improvement in the later 1930s, as no government measures had specifically aided this trade. Furthermore, the tremendous increases in 1941 and 1942 did not correspond to the actions of interested public or private entities, but rather resulted from increased Egyptian demand given the curtailment of foreign supplies. The economic expert in the Sudan during the war indicated that the normal total consumption needs of Egypt had averaged between 1,600 and 1,800 tons annually, which almost exactly matches the 1941–42 total hide imports from the Sudan.[12] And the decrease of Sudanese hide imports during the last years of the war did result from diminished Egyptian dependence on its southern neighbor.

Table 8. Untanned hides (leather) imported from the Sudan

Year	Kilograms	Value (LE)	Year	Kilograms	Value (LE)
1931	11,243	342	1939	487,744	18,033
1932	13,121	489	1940	580,640	28,915
1933	65,215	2,134	1941	2,118,370	151,218
1934	204,259	6,480	1942	1,563,164	158,569
1935	326,560	13,386	1943	711,223	77,220
1936	616,697	28,642	1944	507,499	57,120
1937	955,641	61,318	1945	744,000	58,444
1938	749,932	33,227	1950–55 (avg.)	1,702,341	265,867

Rather than reduced Egyptian demand for Sudanese animal hide imports, administrative measures caused the decline in trade during the latter war years.[13] Mahmud Zaki reported in 1943 that he had "learned recently that imports of leather from the Sudan to Egypt had in fact stopped as a result of the imposition of certain obstacles on the exports of leather."[14] The Condominium governor-general's wartime report stated that the commerce in hides had been "interrupted in May, 1942, whereby the United Kingdom Commercial Corporation in the Sudan became the sole exporter of hides. Six established exporters were authorised to sell to the Corporation."[15] So the Sudanese government had forced reliance on a limited number and 'foreign' intermediaries, impacting trade levels, but Egyptian demand for animal hides had not changed. *Al-Ahram* reported in 1944 that a "committee of leather traders of Alexandria had appealed to the Ministry of Finances that it permit them to import leather from the Sudan, and the ministry requested that the committee submit a report on what the traders needed in the way of leather."[16] Sudanese wartime controls, and Egyptian acquiescence to them, did not derail the development of a dependent Egyptian–Sudanese relationship in this sphere. Examination of the 1950–55 statistics in table 8 indicates that import levels rebounded to early First World War quantities, when Egypt was obtaining virtually all its needs from the Sudan.

Actually, reliance on Sudanese hide imports occurred even as Egyptians 'failed' to remedy the main problem of this commerce, namely damage caused by poor preparation methods. Fu'ad Abaza summarized the two interconnected problems for hide exports in 1938 as follows:

> First—the lack of supervision on the part of the government of the Sudan over commerce of this product, which is exported to Egypt; thus some Sudanese traders export the bad type *(Iskarto)* instead of the good type agreed upon.
>
> Second—the poorness of the two methods utilized in the initial preparation of raw leather, namely air drying and salt drying. The first method, which is the most widespread, is done by placing the leather on the ground and drying it under the rays of the sun for a specified period, and the outer layer of it is dried while the interior is left, and around 20 percent of it is ruined. [In] the second method, which is less widespread, it is evident that when salting the leather an amount of foreign material is added to the salt, because of the high price of salt, and the percentage of damage is from 10 to 15 percent.[17]

A 1939 study on the possible utilization of Sudanese hides reported that the hides of wild animals for women's shoes found a great market among foreigners, but "the manufacture of purses from Sudanese leather was not successful, because this leather—that is tanned locally—has a great deal of salts."[18] Egypt's importation of large quantities of Sudanese hides by the 1950s was not a result of solving this leather processing problem. Sayyid Ahmad al-Tawil stated in 1951 that Egyptian dependence on Sudanese leather is attributable to the absence of any tariffs between the countries, as Sudanese "leather is not good for anything but the soles of shoes."[19] Since the time of the initial Egyptian complaints, the Sudanese Veterinary Department had encouraged the application of new preparation methods. During the Second World War 'Abdallah Fakri Abaza reported of these efforts that "the presence of a profitable market earlier for bad varieties of cattle leather in Syria and Egypt . . . encourages the people not to apply what they are told in the way of instructions," and "most of the agents of exporters, who tour the markets of the Sudan to collect leather, establish equality in value between the scrawny and the valuable leather."[20] Egyptian import of Sudanese hides increased, but this was clearly not due to improving local processing practices.

Imports of Sudanese hides increased steadily in response to local demand, only rarely interrupted by administrative restrictions. With the Second World War concluded, Egypt's Ministry of Commerce and Industry recommended lifting import restrictions, "knowing full well that the most important region from which it is possible to obtain the leather is the Sudan, and the ministry believes that it is most appropriate to encourage the purchase of leather from the Sudan rather than importing it from abroad."[21] Egyptian dependence on Sudanese supplies was evident, but did this in any way improve the likelihood of the Sudanese favoring union with Egypt? There are indications that Sudanese leather suppliers were actually not tightly bound to Egyptian markets. The 1946 governor-general's report noted a significant drop in exports to Egypt because of "the increased internal demand by tanners for hides."[22] An article of the *Majallat Ghurfat al-Qahira* indicated that Egypt was the natural market for Sudanese leather supplies, but that the Sudanese would sell their product to the highest bidder. This 1952 report stated:

> The Egyptian imports of Sudanese leather this year are few in comparison to imports of previous years. And that is attributable to the rise in raw leather prices in world markets generally, which since June 1950 to today are proportionally between 50 and 80 percent [higher]. Some foreign countries are competition for Egypt as the market of the Sudan, such as England, France, Italy, Sweden, Denmark, and Greece.
>
> And the leather exports of the Sudan to these countries truly increased a lot in the last months of the year, whereas its exports to us continued to drop because of the resistance of Egyptian tanneries initially to match the prices other countries were offering. . . . When the local leather was insufficient for the needs of tanneries they were compelled to accept the prices of some Sudanese leathers.[23]

The situation that had developed in animal hide importation was similar to much Egyptian–Sudanese commerce. The Sudanese population, whether merchants, peasants, or pastoralists, profited from economic ties to Egypt, but they also had few qualms about satisfying their financial interests through relations with other markets.

The financial interests of the Egyptian government undermined possibilities of importing another Sudanese raw material of potential use to local manufacturers. The Sudan produced sufficient tobacco for export to Egypt. Furthermore, attractive, higher prices prevailed in Egypt, resulting in frequent reports of smuggling attempts along the southern Egyptian borders.[24] The cultivation of tobacco in Egypt had been prohibited since 1890, and local manufacturers relied solely on imports of tobacco. Undoubtedly, there was a potential market for this Sudanese raw material among Egyptian manufacturers. However, the Egyptian state had prohibited the import of Sudanese tobacco in 1923 because duties on foreign tobacco imports were a significant share of government revenues. For instance, from April to June in 1922 and in 1923, tobacco alone accounted for 54 percent of total customs receipts.[25] In 1934 Egyptian officials rejected proposals to permit the cultivation of tobacco in Egypt and to tax this crop, explaining to the Chamber of Deputies that revenues from such a tax could not replace the LE6 million currently collected on imports of tobacco.[26] The government strictly controlled the commerce of this product, requiring licensing and registration and establishing penalties for infractions in a 1933 tobacco ordinance.[27]

Dependence on tobacco customs revenues and regulations to prevent Sudanese imports from upsetting this revenue stream did not end with the Second World War. However, there were more frequent expressions of interest—especially from Egyptian sources. Due to shortages of foreign imports, in December 1943 Yusuf Alber, the director of the tobacco section in the customs administration, advocated the import of two Sudanese varieties as substitutes for popular Turkish and Chinese tobaccos.[28] The following year, a group of Egyptian cigarette manufacturers petitioned the Ministry of Finance for permission to import Sudanese tobacco, indicating also their willingness to pay the normal duties on foreign imports.[29] In 1945, with continued problems importing foreign tobacco and its consequent high prices, *al-Jarida al-tijariya al-misriya* reported that Yusuf Alber again "submitted to the Ministry of Finance and the Customs Department a number of proposals in this connection, the most important of which is the permission to import Sudanese tobacco to lessen emphasis on the importation of Turkish tobacco, whose price exceeds the Sudanese by 50 percent."[30] This official emphasized the multiple benefits of the proposed changes. Sudanese cultivators would find a nearby market, probably improving the profit margin for their crop. Higher tobacco prices in the Sudan would be a discouragement to smuggling activities—and the government expenses of stopping them. The Egyptian cigarette industry would procure the raw materials needed during the restricted economic environment of the war. Additionally, Egyptian cigarette exports found a healthy market in the Sudan at this time—with the annual average volume of the Second World War years more than doubling that exported annually during the prior decade. So, this particular commodity would have served as a prime example of a truly mutually beneficial dependency. Although importing Sudanese tobacco seemed an ideal method of strengthening Nile Valley economic relations, the Ministry of Finance rejected the wartime petitions of cigarette manufacturers. Yusuf Alber's proposals fell on deaf ears, and after the war the Egyptian government not only reaffirmed its prohibition of Sudanese tobacco imports but also raised fines for its illegal trafficking.[31]

The traffic in tobacco was infinitesimal in comparison to Sudanese production and trade of cotton, but this was a sphere in which Egypt could have carved out an important, dependent niche. Instead, domestic revenue concerns stymied any possibilities of developing this trade. A report in the March 1952 issue of *Majallat Ghurfat al-Iskandariya*, which was entirely dedicated to the history of Egypt's customs regime, summarized the Sudanese tobacco regulations:

> The reason for the prohibition against importing Sudanese tobacco is . . . because [the Egyptian government] monopolizes this product and because if the imported Sudanese tobacco were offered for sale that would lead to competition for foreign imports of tobacco because there is no import duty collected on [Sudanese imports] to Egypt according to the agreement of 1899, and because if an import duty were imposed on [Sudanese tobacco] that would lead to an increase in its smuggling due to the difficulty of controlling the means of transportation.[32]

Clearly in this economic sector, Egyptians exhibited greater concern for the 'nation' north of Aswan than for improving relations with their southerly national 'brothers.'

Importing Sudanese Cotton Seed

Another example of Egyptian administrative obstruction of a potentially expanding Sudanese agricultural import was commerce in cotton seed. Egypt prohibited the import of all cotton seed throughout the interwar period, and the Sudan had marketed its crop elsewhere for years. However, Second World War developments forced Egypt's leaders to obtain cotton seed from the Sudan to counter deficits in oil-bearing seeds needed for popular consumption and for local oil presses, soap making, and other processing industries. In 1943 a report of the financial committee in the Chamber of Deputies stated that "the government is working on increasing imports from the Sudan, especially oleaginous seeds like cotton seed, sesame, and peanuts."[33]

The statistics in tables 9 and 10 below highlight how wartime circumstances altered some import trends along the Nile Valley. Because of the war, cotton seed imports rose from nothing to a central position in Egyptian markets. Simultaneously, sesame imports, which had developed into a profitable commercial sector before the war, dwindled to levels below those of the worst Depression years. Officials tried to maintain sesame imports from the Sudan to meet local oleaginous seed requirements. Egypt's wartime expert in the Sudan, Mahmud Zaki, stated in an October 1943 interview, "It is expected that an agreement will be concluded on the importation to Egypt of required quantities of sesame for the production of oil to make tahina, considered a victual by the masses."[34] Although the expert informed the governor-general that "Egypt is in great need of all the Sudan's excess [sesame] for the 1943 and 1944 seasons to assist in countering the cotton seed oil deficit," the statistics indicate that cotton seed superseded sesame imports—a situation maintained in the post–Second World War era when cotton seed imports were seven times that of sesame.[35] Ultimately, wartime consumption needs overcame traditional Egyptian fears of harming the local cotton crop by allowing foreign seed or cotton into the country.

Table 9. Sesame imported from the Sudan

Year	Kilograms	Value (LE)	Year	Kilograms	Value (LE)
1931	5,909,803	72,550	1939	10,841,860	123,404
1932	7,437,704	88,828	1940	9,309,618	149,243
1933	5,638,028	54,384	1941	7,802,914	138,448
1934	11,164,557	93,501	1942	5,188,241	232,867
1935	8,829,122	94,672	1943	6,455,728	259,376
1936	12,317,186	163,221	1944	1,066,729	19,993
1937	17,317,186	252,446	1945	889,000	1,597
1938	16,184,996	176,597	1950–55 (avg.)	1,116,622[36]	69,147

Table 10. Cotton seed imported from the Sudan

Year	Tons	Year	Tons
1939	—	1943	109,391
1940	—	1944	135,645
1941	—	1945	124,362
1942	3,216	1950–55 (avg.)	7,633[37]

The wartime substitution of cotton seed imports for sesame supplies was caused purely by rising local demand—Sudanese surpluses, attractive prices, or any specific private-sector plan to augment this trade played no role in the increases. However, as early as 1942 there were clear indications that the Egyptian state would have to take action in response to local shortages. In April of that year officials informed the Chamber of Deputies that "the government had in fact conferred with the government of the Sudan about the purchase of large quantities of Sudanese cotton seed, and these negotiations ended with the agreement on the purchase price [of seed] consigned at Port Sudan."[38] In his July 1942 report Egypt's economic expert explained why the seed shortages had developed: "In view of the restriction of the cultivated area of cotton, a deficit in the cotton seed required for production of necessary oil, whether for the manufacture of soap or for nourishment, has become evident."[39] This basic problem persisted throughout the war years. The *Majallat Ghurfat al-Qahira* reported that demand for Sudanese cotton seed resurfaced in September 1943: "In view of the smallness of the cotton crop this year due to reduction of acreage on which it is cultivated, and desirous of increasing the cotton seed oil necessary for the people's nutritional needs, the Egyptian government has worked to import . . . seed from the Sudan intended for oil presses."[40] A month earlier *al-Ahram* had reported that

> His Excellency [the minister of provisions] was asked about the *difficulties in obtaining edible oil* in some parts of [Cairo]. He responded that the ministry has begun to take measures for the import of 1,500,000 ardeb of cotton seed from the Sudan for oil presses. It forwarded a memorandum to the Council of Ministers on this subject, and [the council] approved it, and the higher committee for provisions will begin studying these issues during its upcoming meeting.[41]

Egyptian reliance on Sudanese cotton seed imports arose because of wartime exigencies, but the statistics above, news reports, and officials' statements all indicate a postwar dependence on these imports.[42]

The growth of a cotton seed market in Egypt began with wartime permission and initial government purchases from the Sudan, but Egyptian officials also imposed extensive controls over this trade. Importers were required to "submit an application to the Agriculture Ministry in order to obtain a permit for [cotton seed importation], and it is required that they submit the application at least three weeks before the importation and they make clear in it the amount they wish to import, the route of its entry into the country, and the mode of transport."[43] These regulations, issued on 3 July 1942, required covered barges only for Nile transport and immediate fumigation upon entering Egypt, and prohibited using Sudanese cotton seed containers for any other purpose within Egypt. Wartime procedures were especially onerous for commerce in cotton seed, but the Egyptian government had actually been advocating regulations that would have affected all foodstuffs imported from the Sudan. In an April 1943 letter to Governor-General Huddleston, Prime Minister Nahhas wrote that "the Ministry of Public Health has been asking ever since 1940 that a health inspection be carried out on all food materials arriving from the Sudan by way of Shellal prior to their admittance into Egypt."[44]

Since restricted wartime conditions had necessitated Egyptian reliance on Sudanese cotton seed imports, available transportation facilities during the conflict logically affected the extent of this commerce.[45] Virtually every report of arrangements to purchase cotton seed ended with comments such as "efforts are being exerted currently for the transportation of these quantities to Egypt at the appropriate time."[46] Egyptian officials could authorize and regulate cotton seed imports, but the cooperation of other authorities was required to obtain means of transport. For instance, after agreeing on the import of certain quantities of Sudanese cotton seed, Egypt's Chamber of Deputies sought "the cooperation of the Allies in finding the shipping necessary for this object, especially since the allied forces persist in obtaining their edible oil requirements from Egypt's [own] cotton seed oil."[47] The Alexandria Chamber of Commerce noted the continued struggle to find shipping space during the final year of the war. It wrote that although Egypt's needs were much greater, "the transport of more than 100,000 tons of [cotton seed] from the Sudan was a difficult problem in itself."[48] Transporting 100,000 tons was difficult, and import levels during the war rarely or barely exceeded this 100,000-ton maximum. Yet there were consistent reports of much higher demand for edible oils in Egypt. It may be that transport capabilities were the most influential factor in wartime cotton seed trade levels.

Finally, although greater reliance had developed along the Nile Valley with respect to the cotton seed trade, how extensively this bound the regions is difficult to fathom. First, the statistics in tables 9 and 10 imply some Egyptian dependence on Sudanese cotton seed and (less so) sesame, but the average imports in the last six years before Sudanese independence fluctuated tremendously. This seems less characteristic of a dependent relationship and more characteristic of a supply source of 'last resort.' Plus, considering most import of Sudanese cotton seed occurred only after government agreement on quantities, prices, and other conditions, this trade did not form a 'free' market capable of attracting additional commercial participants. Finally, although most reports linked cotton seed imports to Egyptian consumption of edible oils, local soap manufacturers also sought Sudanese cotton seed.[49] The economic expert in the Sudan included Egypt's soap industry as a recipient of contracted quantities of Sudanese cotton seed in his 1943 report.[50] In 1950 the Egyptian government formed a committee to investigate solutions to the soap industry's consistent need for oil-bearing seed supplies. Sudanese cotton seed was undoubtedly a possible solution, but members of the committee actually favored other options. For instance, Jalal Husayn Bey stated, "I do not see the dire necessity of importing from the Sudan, even if the prices were reasonable, as there are additional varieties of oil-bearing seeds that can be utilized in the soap industry and that lead to the result we desire."[51] Like the import of hides, tobacco, or lumber, cotton seed never became a raw material with a consistent and growing market among Egyptian manufacturers—and was, subsequently, not a Sudanese import that in any fashion furthered nationalist claims of a united Nile Valley economy.

Sudanese Grain Trade

During and immediately after the First World War, Egypt depended heavily on Sudanese supplies of foodstuffs. A 1919 memorandum from H.P. Harvey, financial advisor to the Egyptian government, urged the allocation of LE400,000 for the development of irrigation projects in Berber and Dongola Provinces in the Sudan. Excess production in these areas would then be directed toward ameliorating Egypt's insufficiencies in cereals.[52] However, Egyptian need for Sudanese grains was not limited to periods of international turmoil. Jean Schatz, head of the statistical department in Egypt's Ministry of Commerce and Industry, wrote that during the second half of the 1920s Egyptian production of the staple crop dhurra was insufficient for consumption requirements and that "it is the Sudan which covers the deficits of Egyptian production."[53] Through the mid-1930s there was no real development of consistent or permanent markets, no creation of new markets for Sudanese produce in Egypt, and no targeting of certain traditional agricultural products—instead, when Egyptian need arose, Sudanese sources filled it.

The beginning of more concerted efforts to strengthen economic ties after 1935 included interest in developing markets for Sudanese agricultural produce. In a speech after the first economic mission, Fu'ad Abaza emphasized Egypt's centrality for Sudanese non-cotton exports. He stated, "We import from the Sudan around 95 percent of its produce (after the exclusion of cotton and gum for which we have no need)."[54] However, in this speech he also admitted to Egypt's failure to target specific Sudanese commodities for promotional efforts. He stated that previous Egyptian governments "had not obtained knowledge of any commodity worthy of encouragement over other commodities."[55] Abaza also mentioned that during a meeting of the permanent committee on 17 February 1935, Sudanese representatives and Condominium officials expressed their willingness to provide Egyptian officials with statistical publications on their agricultural exports to Egypt. During subsequent meetings of the permanent committee, a few commodities were singled out for attention, but most frequently references were to broad categories such as agricultural produce, cereals, grains, and so forth.

The lack of organized, targeted, detailed efforts to promote specific Sudanese imports contrasts markedly with Egyptian encouragement of their own exports to the Sudan. Responsibility for this failure lay in both Egyptian and Sudanese hands. Mustafa Abu al-'Ala, a leading Omdurman merchant, stated at a reception honoring the 1935 mission members that "nothing is more desirable to our souls, we traders, than assistance in finding profitable markets," but failed to identify any commodities explicitly.[56] In 1937, at a party given for Sayyid 'Abd al-Rahman al-Mahdi, both an influential sectarian leader and a wealthy agriculturalist of the Sudan, Fu'ad Abaza stated that "Egypt is a natural market for Sudanese products which encounter customs barriers in Europe."[57] Instead of concentrated efforts focused on a specific crop, the primary determinants of Egyptian reliance on Sudanese foodstuffs were simple factors of supply and demand.

A number of interwar reports from the Sudan indicate that Egyptian demand determined the fortunes of commerce in Sudanese agricultural produce. With the gradual relaxation of depressed conditions by 1934, a governor-general's report noted an "acute shortage of grain in Egypt" and the subsequent rise of dhurra shipments to 10 percent of the Sudan's total exports, "owing to a heavy demand from Egypt."[58] Among the best examples of Egyptian reliance on Sudanese supplies was the regional commerce of northern Sudan with Upper Egypt. Halfa Province reported in

1934 that "demand from the Egyptian inhabitants of the Shellal reach stimulated the cultivation of fruits and vegetables."[59] The Egyptian need for Sudanese agricultural supplies, apparent immediately after the First World War, did not dissipate in the 1930s. In fact, tables 11 and 12 below provide evidence of supply and demand continuing to determine import levels in Egypt. Most apparent from these figures is the lack of steady or explainable increases or decreases in the levels of dhurra and wheat imported by Egypt. Recovery from depressed conditions might explain the rise in imports of both commodities in the 1933–35 period, but this was followed by a precipitous two-year decline for dhurra (less so for wheat imports). There were no administrative measures or private initiatives causing these changes.

Table 11. Dhurra (millet) imported from the Sudan

Year	Kilograms	Value (LE)	Year	Kilograms	Value (LE)
1931	4,636,234	22,867	1939	4,674,588	23,794
1932	1,923	13	1940	10,079,315	58,716
1933	3,752,484	18,494	1941	8,824,336	56,012
1934	88,566,514	417,872	1942	3,264028	29,270
1935	32,082,874	108,998	1943	88,880	694
1936	3,250,254	18,975	1944	1,563,613	14,540
1937	6,103,436	35,565	1945	661,000	5,486
1938	35,658,602	147,116	1950–55 (avg.)	3,053,428	55,074

Table 12. Wheat imported from the Sudan

Year	Kilogram	Value (LE)	Year	Kilogram	Value (LE)
1931	197,413	1,885	1939	291,853	2,246
1932	41,548	364	1940	19,798	217
1933	44,210	374	1941	—	—
1934	414,404	3,686	1942	—	—
1935	189,261	1,584	1943	—	—
1936	276,780	2,718	1944	—	—
1937	14,059	207	1945	—	—
1938	10,710	108	1950–55 (avg.)	—	—

As the Second World War approached, Egyptian demand retained the lead in determining Sudanese agricultural import levels. Before the war, reduced demand for dhurra in Egypt had contributed to decreased imports from the Sudan. In fact, *al-Ahram* reported in 1938 that the export of dhurra to Egypt had come to a temporary standstill, explaining that less need for Sudanese imports was a natural consequence of the beginning of the Egyptian wheat harvest.[60] 'Abdallah Fakri Abaza also emphasized in his study that the extent of Sudanese dhurra imported was largely determined by Egyptian demand. He wrote that "the Egyptian market, in regard to dhurra exported from the Sudan, is not guaranteed and dependence upon it [Egypt's market] is not possible since the Sudan's exports of this crop to Egypt increase sometimes and decrease in others to an extreme degree according to the abundance or scarcity of the Egyptian harvest."[61] The statistical evidence above supports 'Abdallah Fakri Abaza's explanation of the "extreme" fluctuations in import levels. According to him, Sudanese officials confirmed that supply and demand determined grain trade levels. In a late May 1939 meeting of the permanent committee that addressed possible Nile Valley wartime provisioning, the economic expert recounted his earlier conversation with the Condominium's top trade representative. This British official had claimed that if there were conflict, "in every case the yield of each type of produce will depend partially on the prices expected for various necessities. In the clearest terms, the farmer will produce more or less of each crop depending on whether he believes that the return on that crop results in profit or entails loss for him."[62]

However, during the Second World War Sudanese grain imports' response to Egyptian demand became less an issue of profits or not and more one of human survival, especially in Upper Egypt. In 1941 a member of the Chamber of Deputies stated that the people from one district of Aswan were "threatened by starvation," which necessitated larger shipments of dhurra from the Sudan. Egypt's minister of provisions stated in response that "during the past weeks there has arrived from the government of the Sudan indication of their agreeing to increase the quantities from 60 tons a month to 200 tons."[63] In 1943, the economic expert notified the governor-general of the continued need for Sudanese dhurra in the entire region from Halfa to Shellal.[64] The statistical evidence on grain imports during the war does not undermine the argument that basic supply and demand factors controlled trade of these goods. Import levels fluctuated wildly during the war, reflecting periods of extreme need, temporary government arrangements, or short-term excess supplies in the Sudan or better prices in Egypt. A dependent relationship only during the most extraordinary circumstances does not support claims of national unity.

The tremendous fluctuations in annual grain imports during the 1930s and 1940s, evidenced in the tables above, continued in the last years of the Condominium. For example, Egypt imported no dhurra in 1950, yet two years later obtained almost 6 million kilograms from the Sudan. Actually, the most readily explained trend in tables 11 and 12 is the complete stoppage of Sudanese wheat imports. From 1941 on, Egypt imported no wheat from the Sudan—a result of simply switching to foreign suppliers of this commodity. Furthermore, these foreign supplies dwarfed the value of Sudanese dhurra being imported by Egypt at the same time. For example, Egypt imported about LE55,000 of dhurra from the Sudan each year in the early 1950s, but wheat imports from foreign countries were valued at above LE20 million annually. Additionally, while Egypt had relied on Sudanese imports of dhurra only when extraordinary wartime conditions arose, in the following decade Egypt developed a consistent and extensive grain dependency—on foreign countries. From various perspectives, comparing Egyptian relations with the Sudan to those with foreign countries was discouraging for nationalists' hopes. Like Sudanese commerce generally, the Egyptian grain trade had solid ties to the international economy.

Although factors of supply and demand were the most important determinants of Sudanese grain import levels, there were administrative efforts to improve this commerce, beyond the expected responses to extraordinary circumstances. Some government measures assisted grain imports from the Sudan, whether intended or not. According to Charles Issawi, with Egyptian freedom to adjust its customs regime, "in 1930 a prohibitive tariff was imposed resulting in the virtual cutting off of [grain] imports."[65] Even if the statistical record does not indicate an immediate upsurge in Sudanese grain imports, which had no duties imposed on them, such measures encouraged greater Nile Valley interdependency. The 1933–35 rise in grain imports from the Sudan did correspond to administrative measures, but not those of the Egyptian state. Instead, the Sudanese Chamber of Commerce reported that in 1934 "the embargo on dhurra was lifted in the first days of November which permitted the export of large quantities to Egypt."[66] Contributing to this measure's impact was the fact that the Sudanese government had begun during the Depression years "a wide extension of a system of auction markets in which producers were able to have direct dealings with the agents of the main exporters."[67] Prior to the Second World War, both administrations were much more concerned with the cotton trade, import of manufactures, balancing budgets, and so forth—with little direct attention for commerce in grains.

With the onset of the war, administrative supervision of grains came to the forefront. Local provisioning and military needs necessitated this control. The Condominium's promulgation of the Defense of the Sudan Regulations upon the outbreak of war "made all imports and exports subject to licence."[68] These regulations provided justification for a number of decrees limiting agricultural exports to Egypt. In 1941 the Sudanese Chamber of Commerce reported that "the declaration, which the Department of Economics and Trade issued on 9 December last, [stated] that licenses for the export of millet are only permitted in situations of special provisioning of the military authorities or in response to important requests."[69] Condominium officials placed similar limitations on other Sudanese agricultural imports. For instance, the Alexandria Chamber of Commerce reported that the Sudanese government would at least entertain requests for fasulia export licenses, starting in May 1941, because the past "Sudanese government prohibition of requests for the export of fasulia to Egypt and other countries . . . had forced Egypt to import this important foodstuff from abroad."[70] Neither official pronouncements nor the statistical evidence above explicitly link administrative controls and the quantities of Sudanese dhurra imported by Egypt. Imports were generally lower than prewar levels—indirectly indicative of Condominium measures to ensure sufficient grain for local needs or 'foreign' wartime demand, thereby restricting Egyptian markets. Still, even at the lower, administratively restricted wartime levels, a case can still be made for supply and demand being most influential, especially if the widely fluctuating quantities resulted from spikes in Egyptian demand.

Most discussion of grain imports to this point has emphasized the impact of Egyptian demand more than Sudanese supplies. However, prior to the Second World War there were some private initiatives to increase the quantities of Sudanese grains available and marketable—ideally in Egypt. In 1935 *al-Siyasa* reported that the Khartoum Chamber of Commerce believed three steps were essential to increased grain exports. The chamber was convinced increased dhurra and sesame exports to Egypt would occur if the percentage of foreign matter in packages could be limited, if this percentage were included on official certificates accompanying the packages, and if only packages sealed immediately after sieving were exported.[71] Improved sieving of grains became a critical concern, and in the mid-1930s only two sieving machines were operating in Khartoum. Because of the growing pressure to ensure the purity of exported grains, the Sudanese administration "decided to issue special legislation for the regulation of sesame and dhurra, prescribing that exports of these two not contain more than 3 percent foreign particles."[72] Egyptian and Sudanese merchants viewed this decree as a positive development and hoped that such regulation might assist other agricultural exports to Egypt. In February 1936 the Cairo Chamber of Commerce contacted its Khartoum counterpart about remedying the lack of fasulia exports to Egypt by encouraging the sieving of this commodity as well.[73] By 1938 enough sieving establishments had been founded in the Sudan to bring melon seed, chickpeas, and other produce into the process.[74]

Government support for improved sieving of grains was helpful, but private interests, especially Mr. Kontomichalos' commercial company, were centrally involved in the expansion of actual facilities in the Sudan. At the 1938 annual meeting of the Khartoum Chamber of Commerce, George Tutunji praised the "important agreement between the Sudanese Railways Department, Kontomichalos Company, and export merchants" for the establishment of a sieve at Port Sudan.[75] In the same year *al-Ahram* reported an agreement between the Sudanese government and Mr. Kontomichalos' company on the purchase of a new sieve for the Khartoum area, which "the company is using in the sieving of grains exported to Egypt by way of Wadi Halfa."[76] Between 1935 and the start of the Second World War, local entrepreneurs were especially active in improving Sudanese grain processing, ideally producing greater quantities for Egyptian markets. However, the statistical record for dhurra imports above provides no evidence that expanding sieving capabilities was as influential as temporary administrative restrictions or the fluctuations of Egyptian demand.[77]

Overall, despite the efforts of local producers or merchants, basic market forces of supply and demand had the greatest impact on Egyptian import of Sudanese agricultural commodities. The lifting of trade restrictions, imposition of higher duties on foreign imports, transport rate reductions, and other administrative measures caused some transitory increases, but no government initiatives created a permanent, profitable Egyptian market for Sudanese produce. Sudanese dates, *masli* (clarified butter), sesame (later replaced with cotton seed), and other less valuable agricultural products encountered traditionally consistent success in Egyptian markets, and these commodities were generally immune to the promotional efforts of the 1930s and 1940s.[78] Meanwhile, exports of wheat and dhurra rose and fell dramatically during the period under study, with little relationship to administrative measures other than temporary prohibitions against the trade of such grains. Frequently, the most common government role in this trade was arranging the purchase of the quantities needed for popular consumption. In 1951 Egypt's minister of provisions traveled to the Sudan to reconnoiter the local supply situation and meet with Condominium officials to hammer out grain deals. *Al-Jarida al-tijariya al-misriya* reported that "His Excellency dispatched from Khartoum his special secretary, . . . [who] has with him samples of dhurra, large quantities of which His Excellency agreed to purchase, and specialists examined these samples and determined the suitability of this dhurra for popular consumption in Upper Egypt."[79] Clearly, such government involvement in the grain trade was a reaction to supply and demand levels. The ability of Egyptian and Sudanese markets to satisfy each other's needs when conditions necessitated it could buttress claims of political unity, but a consistent, intensified dependency would have been a more diplomatically useful development. Based on this examination of Sudanese agricultural imports, no such intensified dependency developed prior to the mid-1950s.

Import of Sudanese Livestock

Egyptian dependency on Sudanese livestock developed well before the 1950s. In fact, most accounts link Egypt's reliance on Sudanese cattle, and sheep to a lesser degree, with the difficulties arising from the First World War. In 1917 an Egyptian government report on provisions stated that imports from Serbia, Cyprus, and Syria had decreased significantly as a result of the war; therefore, "a very large export to Egypt of Sudanese cattle [had] been arranged."[80] In its discussion of livestock supplies the report concluded that "the Sudan remains the only source of supplying Egypt, [and] it has become necessary to take all measures to aid imports from this country."[81] The number of cattle in Egypt had been so decimated by wartime civilian and military consumption needs that officials feared broad repercussions. In fact, the finance counselor of the Egyptian government, H.P. Harvey, wrote in 1919 that a considerable increase in Sudanese imports was needed to replenish Egypt's stocks, which had dropped to such a level that agricultural production was threatened.[82] In 1919 and 1920 Egyptian imports of Sudanese livestock averaged 29,000 cattle and 154,000 sheep, figures that would not be reached again until the Second World War.[83]

Egyptian reliance on Sudanese livestock was established during the First World War and its immediate aftermath, and the relationship was maintained throughout the interwar period. In the 1920s and 1930s there are consistent references to livestock linkages in the Nile Valley. In the early 1920s the Egyptian Ministry of Finance reported that economic development of the Gash river region in eastern Sudan included the breeding of cattle, from which "a large quantity is exported to Egypt."[84] Both Egyptian and Condominium officials understood that Egyptian demand played a key role in this commerce. The Sudanese governor-general wrote in 1928 that "the cattle and sheep export trade depends entirely upon the Egyptian market, where demand has been poor."[85] In 1931 Egypt's veterinary department director, Ahmad Farid, suggested "the provisioning of workers of the Aswan dam entirely with animals imported from the Sudan."[86] From the First World War, Egyptian livestock consumption was a key determinant of imports from the Sudan, so reduced demand and the onset of the Depression made for some lean years in the early 1930s.

The statistical record for livestock imports from the Sudan, presented in tables 13 and 14 below, supports the importance of Egyptian demand for this trade. A reduced market during the early Depression years corresponds with the lowest levels of livestock import. These levels rose slightly as economic conditions improved in 1934–36 and then dramatically with the outbreak of the Second World War. As with the earlier global conflict, the Second World War created local conditions that propelled Egyptian demand to "crisis" levels. In November 1941 the Cairo Chamber of Commerce wrote that the two governments were discussing "special measures for the import of cattle from the Sudan to alleviate the meat crisis in Egypt."[87] Earlier that year Egyptian senator Ahmad Hanafi Abu al-Fadl claimed that because of civilian and military consumption of meat, the import of Sudanese cattle was required to stave off the elimination of all Egyptian stocks, which would have much wider ramifications. In respect to Egypt's own rapidly dwindling supplies he stated,

> If the government does not perceive this imminent danger for the country and stop this trend, and import from the Sudan the cattle necessary for the consumption of the army as was done before, the consequence of the gradual disappearance of cattle will be realized shortly, and the fellah will not find the necessary cattle for cultivating his land and fertilizing it.[88]

Later in the war, Egypt's economic expert in Khartoum cited a number of reasons for the increased need for Sudanese livestock. Besides the military provisioning, the demands of various government agencies, and requirements for agricultural production, he stated that restaurants and stores (which were selling more meat partially because of the increased foreign presence in Egypt) and local markets offering lower-priced meat to the local population both needed greater supplies of Sudanese cattle.[89] Demand fluctuations of the Depression or the Second World War eras are reflected in the statistics below and explain the rise and fall of livestock import levels.

Table 13. Cattle imported from the Sudan

Year	Number	Value (LE)	Year	Number	Value (LE)
1931	5,246	20,100	1939	8,074	34,070
1932	2,826	8,231	1940	9,691	74,272
1933	5,052	12,541	1941	22,321	155,397
1934	9,026	18,758	1942	51,488	414,156
1935	10,095	32,119	1943	39,730	333,939
1936	10,353	39,493	1944	35,178	310,882
1937	8,379	29,473	1945	36,281	354,059
1938	7,450	32,295	1950–55 (avg.)	31,932	552,119

Table 14. Sheep imported from the Sudan

Year	Number	Value (LE)	Year	Number	Value (LE)
1931	708	663	1939	12,687	11,095
1932	3,705	1,974	1940	35,335	43,433
1933	4,750	3,878	1941	59,954	90,053
1934	16,175	14,571	1942	153,671	270,199
1935	19,005	18,935	1943	88,810	177,287
1936	11,021	11,383	1944	109,306	233,768
1937	5,417	5,359	1945	116,954	263,786
1938	1,656	1,681	1950–55 (avg.)	16,334	63,994

Egyptian demand does not, however, provide a full explanation of the trends in this trade. For instance, the stagnant import levels of the years immediately after 1936 beg an explanation. Although there is no single, undisputed answer to this question, local opinions hinted that availability of livestock was just as critical as Egyptian needs.[90] Top officials in the Condominium administration argued that Sudanese breeders were skilled marketers of their commodities, not always willing to export their livestock if conditions were less than ideal. The governor-general reports of 1936 and 1937 both claimed that livestock breeders treated their animals as a kind of "reserve currency," and many were finding better profits for these "reserves" in Sudanese markets—instead of exporting to Egypt.[91] Other observers corroborated this Condominium assessment. For instance, in early 1939 *al-Ahram* reported that Sudanese traders being pressured to export cattle to Egypt demanded that they be "left to their own devices and they will export the number they want and at the time which they see as most suitable for their export."[92] Egypt's economic expert, 'Abdallah Fakri Abaza, also emphasized local market conditions and their influence on Sudanese livestock imports. He wrote that the lackluster prewar trade in sheep was a result of foreign competition and low prices in Egypt's markets—prices Sudanese suppliers were unwilling to match.[93] With the onset of the Second World War, other obvious determinants of the level of livestock trade with Egypt emerged, but Sudanese willingness to export and ability to profit from it remained a factor. *Al-Ahram* reported on 6 December 1939 that top Egyptian officials had met to discuss the Sudanese cattle trade and the need for cooperation of various departments in this trade, and

> it was decided to hold a meeting this afternoon with the deputy minister [of the Ministry of Commerce and Industry] and with importers of Sudanese cattle and meat sellers in attendance. And that is to establish special regulations for organizing this importation so that *Sudanese producers are guaranteed a reasonable profit* and, at the same time, there is no harm to the interest of the importers or local meat sellers.[94]

Although more extensive collaboration to increase Sudanese cattle imports was necessitated by the war, the influence of Sudanese profit expectations regarding this business cannot be ignored. Furthermore, if the value of imported livestock accurately reflected the prevailing market prices, then the statistics in tables 13 and 14 support the idea that the Sudanese were savvy businesspeople. The value per head for both sheep and cattle practically doubled by the middle of the conflict. Therefore, explanations for increased imports during the war must link rising Egyptian demand with prices sufficiently attractive to overcome Sudanese reluctance to sell their livestock.

Transportation capabilities, costs, and regulations during the war also impacted the level of Sudanese livestock imports. Transportation of cattle had attracted Egyptian attention for some years. In January 1938 the Cairo Chamber of Commerce noted that "the traders who import Sudanese cattle requested that [cattle] be shipped directly to Alexandria [by land] instead of their transport by way of the Red Sea because of the increase in costs of transport and the higher price of meat for the importers of Alexandria."[95] Merchants had not been permitted to ship cattle to Alexandria and the Delta by land as a result of veterinary fears about the spread of cattle disease. Because of this transport restriction, interested parties lobbied for lower port duties in Alexandria to assist the trade. The March 1938 meeting of the permanent committee recorded that "the Sudanese Chamber of Commerce hopes to address the designated authorities at the port of Alexandria for a decrease of the port duties in regard to ships that carry Sudanese cattle only."[96] Although there was some official support for this request, Egypt's Ministry of Transportation refused to lower port duties, claiming there was an "abundance of cattle in Egypt and the lack of needing to import them from the Sudan."[97] In the spring of 1939, *al-Ahram* portrayed a less 'rosy' picture of the situation in Egypt and noted the greater need for cattle from the Sudan.

> It is apparent from a report issued by the Ministry of Commerce and Industry that negotiation between the economic expert for Egypt in the Sudan and Captain Williams, director of the Sudanese veterinary department, revolved around the subject of the cattle trade. The director noted that the number of Sudanese cattle that are exported to Egypt is much less than what it should be. Egypt imports a large number of sheep and cattle from foreign countries, meanwhile Sudanese cattle are not cheap when entering Saidi, Cairo, and Alexandria markets, and that is because transport only takes place by sea, even though it is very expensive, especially port duties.[98]

Whether or not there was an abundance of cattle in Egypt, possibly a result of reliance on foreign suppliers, the Egyptian state had certainly done little to encourage Sudanese cattle imports. Just prior to the Second World War, Egyptian officials received a request from the Sudanese government, in which the latter "expressed its desire to adjust the system dedicated to this trade and the authorization to transport cattle from the Sudan to Egypt by way of Wadi Halfa–Shellal, instead of by way of Port Sudan, and send them directly to Alexandria or any other region of the Egyptian country."[99]

This desire to import cattle by rail directly to Alexandria was not a new development in 1939. The Egyptian administration had debated, conducted technical studies, negotiated with Sudanese officials, and generally dragged its feet in various ways—until the outbreak of the Second World War altered the circumstances. Finally, "the Egyptian Railways Department agreed to designate trains of fifty cars for Sudanese cattle at Shellal without limiting the traders to fixed numbers of cattle that could be shipped in those cars."[100] Officials made similar allowances for the transport of sheep to Lower Egypt. Additionally, the government lowered transport rates for livestock. ‘Abdallah Fakri Abaza wrote that “the Egyptian Railways Department agreed to impose special rates for the movement of trains of animals from Shellal to Cairo or Alexandria, special reduced rates irrespective of the type and quantities of animals transported.”[101] Egyptian demand, market prices, and Sudanese willingness to sell their livestock were still influential in trade levels, but the permissibility of rail transport and the rates levied played an influential short-term role—especially during the war. Egypt’s economic expert during the conflict, Mahmud Zaki, noted that officials had arranged transport facilities for large shipments of Sudanese cattle needed by military forces in Egypt in 1942. Therefore, in his report the following year he argued that “it was within the capability of that [Sudanese] government to increase the means of transport in the following years, or at least preserve what they were in 1942.”[102]

Most restrictions on the transport of cattle resulted not from wartime concerns but from Egyptian veterinary fears. In 1938 the Egyptian Veterinary Department forbade the shipment of Sudanese cattle south of Giza station to prevent the spread of infectious disease in the Delta.[103] In order to supply the markets in this region, the Egyptian state required cattle shipment by sea to Alexandria quarantines. *Al-Ahram* editors explained in 1939 that the existing transport arrangements were caused by “the imposition of quarantine on Sudanese cattle so that diseases are not spread in the Egyptian interior. Moreover the local Egyptian authorities have feared, and still fear, the diffusion of cattle plague caused by the lack of imposing restrictions on cattle imported from abroad.”[104] As noted above, the government managed to accommodate shipping/veterinary concerns during the Second World War in order to meet local demand for Sudanese livestock. However, Egypt’s continued apprehension over maintaining the health of its livestock was apparent in the prohibition of salted meat imports from the Sudan. A September 1943 letter from the Ministry of Public Health to the Council of Ministers on this subject stated that “the Veterinary Department of the Ministry of Agriculture decided to forbid its importation to protect the health of animals in Egypt.”[105] Veterinary concerns about preventing the entry of livestock disease into Egypt and resulting quarantine facilities and regulations negatively impacted import levels of Sudanese livestock, but they were not responsible for annual fluctuations in the trade.

More influential in terms of the amount of livestock imported by Egypt each year were specific government regulations or, more frequently, the supply and demand forces referred to earlier. Egyptian officials and interested traders often criticized Sudanese government restrictions on the export of livestock. Egyptians directed most of their criticism at Second World War measures, but the basis for Condominium control had been established much earlier, through the Animals Export and Import Ordinance of 1913. This ordinance gave the governor-general the power to prohibit the export of livestock or animal products and required certain procedures for export. Among the requirements for export were having a certificate of purchase from a public market or a certificate of export from a provincial governor, using only licensed steamships for export along the Halfa–Shellal route and quarantining livestock along it.[106] The Condominium heightened its control over livestock commerce during the Second World War when it established fixed prices for herds exported at Shellal and limited export "to a small number of reliable merchants."[107] 'Abdallah Fakri Abaza proposed that the Sudanese government ease restrictions and allow market forces to determine trade levels:

> The Sudanese Veterinary Department limits the number of cattle whose export is permitted to Egypt and apportions them to the cattle merchants so that it is not possible for any one of them to increase exports to Egypt above the amount he is licensed to export. Thus, the competition among [the exporters] is less than if this commerce remained free and subject to economic forces.[108]

Egyptians often pointed to the harmful effects of administrative control of the livestock trade, but frequently government measures were critical in satisfying Egyptian demand.

After the Second World War, the Egyptian state often arranged the purchase and transportation of Sudanese livestock. In 1946, responding to a parliamentary question, the Ministry of Commerce and Industry reported that "the government is working on the import of cattle and sheep from Cyrenaica, the Sudan, and Ethiopia, and has imported from them some quantities that have had an influence in reducing the prices of meats."[109] Later that year a government official reported to the Cairo Chamber of Commerce that "there are ten thousand head of calves and great numbers of sheep destined for export from the Sudan to Egypt and it had been decided to send them on the first of September if transportation was not suspended because of the Nile flood."[110] Officials were directly involved in the transport, pricing, and general availability of livestock in Egyptian markets. In 1949 Egypt's Ministry of Provisions was still dispatching agents to the Sudan "in the pursuit of importing the greatest possible number of cattle, until meat is plentiful on a continuous basis."[111] Official efforts to facilitate import of Sudanese cattle after the war allude to the continued primacy of Egyptian demand in determining trade levels. Moreover, the increased import of cattle during the 1950s (see table 13 above) seemingly indicates the successful development of this economic activity.

Before acclaiming Egyptian efforts to increase livestock trade a success, however, one must note that the obstacles to this commerce remained unchanged—and unconquered. In 1935 an *al-Siyasa* article referred to "record numbers of cattle intended for export to Egypt" and reported that Sudanese traders hoped for the assistance of the Egyptian railways and veterinary departments.[112] In the 1950s, the same two issues of transportation and veterinary restrictions were still foremost in the minds of officials hoping to improve cattle imports. A 1950 Ministry of Commerce and Industry report on local meat supply problems addressed the continuing transportation needs. The Alexandria Chamber of Commerce reported that the minister

> had studied the subject with importers of cattle from the Sudan and they proposed:
>
> First—assign two trains with sufficient cars for the shipment of cattle from Shellal twice a week
>
> Second—facilitate the embarkation of cattle from the Bulaq train station immediately to the Cairo slaughterhouse without the necessity of lingering in this station to change trains
>
> Third—designate a piece of empty land in the vicinity of the Cairo slaughterhouse, whose area is 6,800 meters, to the authority of the Ministry of Agriculture in order to build on it with private funds paddocks for sheltering the cattle, provided that ownership of it devolves to the government or it is permissible for [importers] to rent it at a nominal rate for a long period of time.
>
> [The minister] has worked on executing these three proposals, and the director of railways stated that it is possible for the department to transport around nine thousand head of cattle from Shellal to Giza or continuing to the slaughterhouse, on condition that the arrival of cattle is arranged on limited dates and a fixed average, and this practice necessitates allotting three trains returning empty to Shellal, just as the Council of Ministers would have to agree to the project of renting the government land near the Cairo slaughterhouse for building the paddocks.[113]

With increasing Egyptian demand, the means of transporting more Sudanese cattle, and the construction of related infrastructure, were becoming a major undertaking. The same expanding scope of the problem and proposed solutions by the 1950s was apparent in state veterinary concerns. Dr. Abd al-Hamid Dib summarized in 1950 the continued problems associated with disease prevention. After highlighting Egypt's dependence on Sudanese supplies, he stated that among the obstacles to increasing livestock imports was

> the length of the veterinary quarantine in the Halfa and Shellal stations which leads to the emaciation of these animals and increasing the costs of importation, including the importers bearing the costs of guarding and feeding [their livestock], let alone the decrease in weight resulting from losses during the trip and the increase in the costs of transport. And he proposed a remedy to this situation studying the possibility of establishing refrigerated warehouses in the Shellal region. Perhaps these warehouses might be easy after the completion of the electrification project of the Aswan Dam, providing for the slaughter of animals imported from the Sudan as soon as they arrive in the region and storing in these warehouses what veterinary examination has established is safe for consumption, then after that transport by railroad in refrigerated cars to the regions of consumption.[114]

Considering the extent of transportation, storage, veterinary, and other measures the Egyptian state was willing to consider in order to increase imports of Sudanese livestock, the existence of a dependent economic relationship is readily apparent. Whether or not this interdependence can be attributed to Egyptian nationalist efforts is an entirely different question. The statistical and qualitative record indicates that Egyptian actions may have slightly solidified the livestock relationship with the Sudan. However, international events beyond the state's control or the 'invisible hand' of market forces were more likely causes of this improvement. One cannot help but wonder whether Egyptians would have encouraged livestock imports from elsewhere if such supplies were cheaper, consistently available, and more easily acquired than Sudanese stocks.

The Merchants of Egyptian–Sudanese Commerce

The analysis above of selected Sudanese commodities imported by Egypt does not provide a picture of an improving interdependent relationship, and certainly not one likely to further nationalists' hopes of sovereignty over the Nile Valley. The examination of Egyptian exports to the Sudan in the last chapter is even less encouraging. Overall, the statistical record of Egyptian efforts to strengthen trading ties with the Sudan was fairly dismal. However, commercial statistics provide a broad, macro, interregional perspective of economic interdependence—or the lack of it. Also potentially supportive of Egyptian sovereignty aspirations would have been the development of a significant and growing class of merchants dependent on increasingly profitable Egyptian–Sudanese commerce. Such a group would have been more capable of pressuring both the Egyptian administration and British officials for political union. Certainly, an Egyptian economic elite interested in maintaining or expanding Nile Valley commerce would have more direct and influential access to decision makers than the masses who simply purchased Sudanese wheat or meat. Therefore, the question is how extensive, organized, and influential was local merchant involvement in Egyptian–Sudanese trade.

Before answering this question, how might we characterize the prospective local entrepreneurs expected to initiate or expand Egyptian–Sudanese commercial activities? Past scholarship has accurately identified the most active entrepreneurial elements in the Nile Valley as 'foreigners.' Undoubtedly, foreign merchants controlled most trade in the Sudan, a logical outcome of the country's dependence on exporting a commodity—cotton—destined for international markets. In 1947, the Cairo Chamber of Commerce noted this foreign dominance when summarizing the election results of its Khartoum counterpart:

> The elections were held to select the board of directors of the Khartoum Chamber of Commerce and the number of its members is fourteen.
>
> Only four of the Sudanese were successful. They were the notables Mustafa Abu al-'Ala, Mustafa Abu al-Barir, and Yunis and 'Uthman Salih. Three Englishmen, three Syrians, two Greeks, one Indian, and one Armenian were successful. The proportion of Sudanese, which was less than the last elections, has caused agitation among nationalist quarters over the extent of foreign commercial control.[115]

In this article, the Egyptian economic expert at the time, Ahmad 'Abd al-Khaliq, claimed that because of the years of foreign domination and absence of Condominium support for local merchants, very few Sudanese or Egyptians had even stood as candidates. Frustration over the lack of administrative support was not a new development. In 1930 an Omdurman merchant explained this local apathy toward Khartoum chamber activities by stating, "That is because the meetings of the chamber's committee with the [Sudanese government's] economic committee year after year have achieved no success in gaining the assistance requested to improve the commercial situation."[116] Foreign merchants and their concerns dominated the upper echelons of Sudanese commerce and commercial policy.

As in the Sudan, the most prevalent entrepreneurial elements in Egypt were foreign. In his economic study of Egypt, Charles Issawi makes no mention of an Egyptian industrial or commercial middle class because, in his words, "that class was almost entirely foreign."[117] Robert Tignor has also written of the importance of foreign residents in Egypt's commercial/bourgeois sector. In his analysis of the 1919 revolution in Egypt, he notes that the group most forcefully advocating changes to lessen the country's agricultural dependence was the resident foreigners.[118] Many of these foreign residents eventually applied for Egyptian citizenship in the aftermath of the 1937 Montreux convention and later regulations that reduced the advantages of foreign status. In his study of Syrians in Egypt, Thomas Philipp claims that company "directors of Syrian origin almost always held Egyptian citizenship."[119] Whether they officially held foreign or Egyptian citizenship, these individuals were central to local economic development.

The foreign resident community of Egypt was also certainly an integral part of improving economic relations with the Sudan. The most prominent Egyptian firm engaged in Nile Valley trade during the interwar period was the Sudan Import and Export Company, established in 1919.[120] This company was controlled by foreign residents of Syrian origin, its board of directors being dominated by Tutunji family members.[121] The company was founded with a total capital outlay of LE10,000, which was incrementally increased to LE75,000 by 1942. It eventually had branch offices in Khartoum, al-'Ubayd, and Port Sudan for its exports to the Sudan but was also heavily involved in non-cotton exports from the Sudan, including raw materials for its manufacturing plants in Egypt.[122] This 'foreign' Egyptian company was fairly heavily capitalized in comparison to other Egypt-based companies involved specifically in Nile Valley commerce.[123] Besides commercial activities, foreign residents of Egypt were key entrepreneurs in certain manufacturing sectors, often sectors with extensive, lucrative markets in the Sudan specifically—such as sugar refining and cigarette production.[124] Thomas Philipp notes that foreign involvement in Sudanese economic affairs was not confined to large-scale endeavors but also included numerous individual foreign traders. According to this scholar, prior to the First World War, "of the most important Cairo-based merchants carrying on trade with the Sudan," sixteen were Syrian, whereas only six were Egyptian.[125] Whether such merchants remained officially foreign or became Egyptian citizens, their interest, involvement, and influence in Sudanese affairs was critical to Egyptian nationalist aspirations.[126]

The post–First World War Anglo–Egyptian political disputes and the Condominium tendency to discourage all facets of an Egyptian presence in the country further reduced the number of active Egyptian merchants in the Sudan. *Al-Akhbar* published in 1922 a letter from 'Abbas Effendi Mahmud, a resident of the Sudan, that described "methods" used to discourage Egyptian traders from staying in the Sudan. He wrote that "the oppression besetting the Egyptian merchant in the Sudan is very great, to the point that many of them are leaving the Sudan, fleeing the burden of taxes and their mistreatment by the English arbiters."[127] The Sudanese government's hostility toward Egyptians only increased in the aftermath of the 1924 incidents. In 1925 *al-Akhbar* reported that the British inspector of Omdurman had ordered the "beating of one of the Egyptian effendia in the market in the view of the traders and people."[128] Reports of such treatment did little to stimulate new Egyptian commercial ventures, or even their continued presence in the country. When Egyptians began serious efforts to improve that presence in the Sudan during the 1930s, they raised similar accusations of past persecution. *Al-Akhbar* claimed in 1935 that "facing the harassment of the English authorities, the majority of the Egyptian merchants and employers were compelled to leave the Sudan, abandoning their labors and clearing their shops."[129]

During the political turbulence of the early 1920s, Egyptians encountered hostility not only from British administrators but also from some segments of the Sudanese population. For instance, in 1923 a local Sudanese notable, al-Sayyid 'Abdallah al-Tayyib, proposed expelling the Syrians and Greeks from the country, while stating of Egyptians, "If I would explain the degree to which they are useless in the Sudan I would have to speak a long time, but whatever I say, I believe, is well known."[130] With the expulsion of most Egyptians after the 1924 incidents, expressions of anti-Egyptian sentiment became fewer, but the anticipated post-1936 return of Egyptian army units and personnel brought forth renewed concerns from the local population. In September 1936 *al-Balagh* published a telegraphic message sent to the *Times* that stated, "Some of the [Sudanese] merchants fear the intensification of competition, but they believe that it will subside with the spread of commerce and the expected increase of trade between Egypt and the Sudan."[131] Still, if the Sudanese public thought little of Egyptian merchants or feared losing market share to Egyptian competitors, then the prospects of popular support for Nile Valley unity would diminish.

Egyptian economic leaders became increasingly concerned with the reputation of their merchants in the Sudan after the Second World War. In 1947 the Cairo Chamber of Commerce reported on complaints from

Sudanese merchants that some Egyptians were not adhering to the terms of trade agreements, but that "those displaying this sort of conduct in commercial practices, they, praise God, are a very small portion of our traders, but . . . they are at a minimum doing harm to the Egyptian traders collectively."[132] Three years later Egyptians were still concerned about their commercial reputation in Sudanese markets. The economic expert reported:

> There is an issue of great importance that has greatly influenced the weak sales of Egyptian products and the hesitancy of traders to import them. Some of the smaller Egyptian traders, who come to the Sudan intending to conclude contracts with Sudanese traders on the import of goods, have lost their commercial trust because of their poor practices, seeking illegal financial gains.[133]

All reports of such Egyptian commercial misconduct indicated that these transactions were limited in scale and often in more 'remote' markets of the Sudan. Therefore, Egyptians debated the significance of these reported problems. 'Ali al-Barir, an active Egyptian merchant in the Sudan and member of the 1935 mission and later the permanent committee, stated at a January 1951 meeting that "this subject is trivial and really limited in its scope, involving small-time [Sudanese] traders who engage in business with any Egyptian representative, who travels to the Sudan briefly and without any previous activity. It does not merit study and is a waste of time."[134] The poor reputation of some smaller-scale, less experienced Egyptian traders may not have seriously undermined efforts to increase commerce with the Sudan, but such activities certainly would not aid in building popular support for Nile Valley unity. Furthermore, in the analysis below it will be shown that Egyptian merchants were most active in less centrally located regions of the Sudanese economy and were typically engaged in small-scale commerce—precisely where the recurrent poor trading practices of some Egyptian merchants were reportedly occurring.

Despite the poor practices of some traders, Egypt's economic leaders dedicated much time to increasing the number of Egyptian merchants and commercial agents active in the Sudan. At a March 1938 meeting of the permanent committee and the Sudanese Chamber of Commerce, participants recommended a "study of the opinion of the chamber of commerce on the employment of Egyptians in some commercial companies and trading houses of the Sudan."[135] The following month permanent committee members again attended to the question of how to increase the Egyptian commercial presence in the Sudan. At that time they thought it best "to place this task of employing the largest number of Egyptians possible in the Sudan on the shoulders of the Egyptian traders with contacts in the Sudan, like Mr. Ibrahim 'Amir Pasha."[136] Because of the attention various parties gave this issue, the 'normal' numbers of active Egyptians must have been insignificant, or at least not satisfying the hopes of Egypt's nationalists.

The Egyptian Merchants' Presence in the Sudan

If the Egyptian commercial presence by 1938 was not fulfilling the expectations of the interested parties, what exactly was the position of the 'typical' Egyptian merchant in the Sudan? Although a detailed analysis of the varied status of individual traders is beyond the scope of this study, a general characterization of many of the Egyptian merchants in the Sudan is possible. First of all, one must remember that foreign companies dominated large-scale import–export commerce with the Sudan. Based on extensive study of Sudanese economic conditions, 'Ali Mawardi, the exhibition director at the start of the Second World War, confirmed "the scarcity of Egyptian and Sudanese importers in the Sudan."[137] Most opportunities for Egyptian and Sudanese merchants were confined to smaller-scale retail trade.

Unfortunately for Egyptians seeking to establish businesses in the Sudan, many foreign firms and traders had already claimed a foothold in retail activities as well. For instance, based on a review of advertisements in the journals of Egypt's chambers of commerce, it is clear that those merchants and trading houses hoping to increase their Egyptian–Sudanese business were predominantly foreign in origin.[138] A review of the post–Second World War advertisements reveals a litany of Armenian, Greek, Indian, Italian, American, and other foreign merchants and companies. Of twenty-two advertisements specifically targeting Egyptian–Sudanese trade between 1946 and 1953 in the Cairo chamber's journal, there were only four Arabic names listed, and only one of these was definitively Egyptian. Most of the foreign merchants were engaged in retail trade, managing 'general stores,' hoping to import a wide variety of goods from Egypt—and noticeably not the major, valuable imports coming to the Sudan from foreign suppliers. For example, Armenian merchant Haig Topdjian's February 1946 advertisement read, "The shop at the following address in Khartoum wrote us [the journal] indicating its desire to contact exporters and traders of belts, shaving equipment, irons, buttons, games, shoes, underclothing, towels, office supplies, linen, needles, perfumes, and small goods generally."[139] The next month *Majallat Ghurfat al-Qahira* published an advertisement from another Khartoum firm hoping to export Sudanese goods to Egypt. This company, J.C. Bozadjilan-Krikor, was ready to send various goods to Egypt, "especially henna, castor oil seed, herbs, medicinal plants, snake skins, pelts, wool, etc."[140] Not all foreign firms were engaged in the trade of shaving equipment or snake skins, but advertisements requesting cotton textiles, citrus fruits, cigarettes, or other manufactures of Egypt were rare—a further blow to nationalist hopes.[141] Finally, the location of the foreign establishments in these advertisements is important. None of the foreign trading houses was located outside of Khartoum or Port Sudan—the unquestioned centers of the internationally oriented economic system Condominium officials had established in the Sudan.

Equally revealing of the foreign economic dominance in the Sudan is the location of Egyptian merchants in the country. 'Ali Mawardi's study of local commercial conditions, published in the Cairo Chamber of Commerce journal in 1940, provided detailed information on the location of Egyptian merchants' activities.[142] The most readily apparent conclusion is that Egyptian involvement was largely confined to the northern provinces of the Sudan, an area of traditionally extensive interaction with Egypt. Also, these areas were clearly *not* among the most rapidly developing economic regions of the Sudan at the time. Dongola, Berber, Kerima, and Halfa all were noted to have significant Egyptian commercial communities, whereas no Egyptians were active in such major centers as al-'Ubayd, Kassala, Gedaref, and Wad Midani. The exhibition director wrote of Berber Province in the north that "it is the one region of the Sudan in which the foreigners are not found at all."[143] 'Abdallah Husayn, who accompanied the first economic mission to the Sudan, confirmed 'Ali Mawardi's conclusions about the northern regions. He wrote of Halfa that "we found it like the centers of Egypt, and its inhabitants were Egyptians; it was in fact Egyptian."[144] Although Egypt's strong commercial position in this region was maintained, this was not a significant step in strengthening economic ties between the countries.

Another glaring example of Egyptian merchants occupying the 'fringe' positions in Sudanese commerce is found through examination of Red Sea Province, primarily the Port Sudan–Suakin region. Kenneth Perkins notes in his history of Port Sudan that prior to the First World War "Greeks, Syrians, and Egyptians owned all of Port Sudan's dozen or so groceries, outfitters, and general stores."[145] However, Egyptians enjoyed this local commercial importance before Port Sudan became the major import–export center of the country. By the end of the interwar period 'Ali Mawardi mentioned *only* large foreign import–export or shipping companies in his description of the same city. Interestingly, the Red Sea port where Egyptian commercial establishments still conducted business was Suakin, the rapidly declining, former point of entry along the coast. Mawardi wrote of Suakin's port that "no ships enter it except the ships of the [Egyptian] Pharaonic Company, one time per week to transport vegetables and some textiles which are consumed locally, and it takes on coal and salted fish for Suez."[146] In regard to Egyptian merchants of Suakin, the office director singled out Sheikh Muhammad al-Bariri, "who is considered the most important Egyptian trader in the Sudan, and who is among the 'self-made' men, beginning his commercial activity in 1904, while he now possesses around half a million pounds in cash and real property."[147] The claim that Egypt's most important merchant in the Sudan was located in a city in rapid economic decline seems rather significant in the overall assessment of Egyptian trading interests in the Sudan.

In addition to Egyptians' presence being most apparent in regions experiencing less economic growth, the more active Egyptian merchants had been engaged in Sudanese commerce for many years. Hassan Dafalla, in his study of the Nubian community displaced by the construction of the Aswan High Dam, describes the long-term presence of Egyptian merchants in northern Sudan. He notes that one area of Halfa "was occupied by traders of Syrian and Egyptian origin, who had settled there at the close of the nineteenth century."[148] Additionally, he writes of the inhabitants of Basalwa quarter of Halfa, the most populous section of the city, "They were all Egyptians who had emigrated from Upper Egypt and finding life easier in Wadi Halfa had finally settled there and adopted Sudanese nationality."[149] El-Haj Bilal Omer also mentions the presence of commercial groups with Egyptian origins in northern Sudan. Within his ethnically classified groupings of the Dongola area's population were the *falaliyh*, who came to the region as craftsmen and traders with the conquering forces in 1898, and Copts (a subgrouping of the *falaliyh* in Omer's analysis) who "came from Egypt after the Re-Occupation as traders."[150] These early immigrants were critical to commerce in the area "and having former connections with Egypt they geared the trade of the region to that of Egypt."[151] This well-established, pre–First World War presence of Egyptian traders, many of whom later gained Sudanese nationality, is an obvious explanation for why Egyptian merchants were most active in the northern Sudan during the interwar years and beyond.[152]

However, not all Egyptian traders with well-established Nile Valley commercial business were permanent residents of the Sudan. Many of these Egyptians had been active in the Sudan before the interwar period, even though they resided well to the north. 'Abdallah Husayn referred to a number of the more important of these individuals because of their interaction with the 1935 Egyptian economic delegation. These merchants also more frequently conducted business in the major Sudanese centers. Among the first mission's members were Muhammad and Ahmad Hasan Qasim. They had inherited their commercial business with the Sudan from their father, "who had been active in the trade of Sudanese produce all of his life."[153] 'Abdallah Husayn commended these brothers for their efforts to expand trade between the Nile Valley and European commercial centers, as well as for their having learned from their father "not to depend on government officials" in their business.[154] Husayn listed Muhammad 'Abd al-Rahim Samaha as another Egyptian merchant whom "the traders of the Sudan had known for a long time."[155] Finally, Ibrahim 'Amir was another merchant with decades of interaction in the Sudan. He "was an Egyptian who was active in the trade of the Sudan for forty years, had opened a shop for textiles and the sale of manufactures, and had branch offices in the Sudan and Egypt."[156]

Many of the Egyptian merchants residing in the Sudan or particularly active there apparently had strong connections to Upper Egypt. In his Port Sudan tannery, Ibrahim 'Amir employed solely Asyutis. This was not unusual, as most Egyptian laborers in the Sudan came from this area. However, there was also evidence of a more purely commercial connection between Upper Egypt and the Sudan. 'Abdallah Husayn highlighted the activities of the al-Ziq family of Asyut, which was also represented in the 1935 economic mission. He wrote that "the al-Ziq family had an old relationship with the Sudan, having traded in ivory, ostrich feathers, and Asyuti products, and they established commercial centers in the Sudan."[157] 'Abdallah Fakri Abaza also alluded to connections between Upper Egypt and the Sudan, reporting that there were few Egyptians in Khartoum but that "the majority of them were from the people of al-Sa'id."[158] Finally, the commercial activities of the Abu al-'Ala family are representative of the long-established bonds of prominent Upper Egyptian traders with the Sudan. According to Husayn, this family "came from Esna and established offices and commercial warehouses in Khartoum, Port Sudan, Singa, Omdurman, Cairo, and elsewhere."[159] He added that they had "established in the Sudan partnerships with the [Sudanese] merchants 'Abd al-Mon'im Muhammad, Yunis Ahmad, and others; and their company exports the largest quantity of the produce of the Sudan, rivaling the foreign traders."[160] This family's expanding commercial business, including the major Sudanese and Egyptian centers, was the type of development nationalists hoped might be diplomatically useful. Muhammad Husayn al-Rashidi was another excellent example of Egyptian entrepreneurial work well before the post-1935 period of increased Egyptian interest. He owned Cairo's largest sweets and tahina factory, which met 75 percent of the local demand for these products. Husayn wrote of this man that "he obtains a large quantity of the Sudanese sesame crop, and he imports his products to Khartoum, Port Sudan, Omdurman, and the rest of the capitals of the Sudan."[161] The rather extensive business of Muhammad Husayn al-Rashidi and the Abu al-'Ala family, "rivaling foreign traders" and active in the major Sudanese economic centers, was unusual for Egyptian traders. Instead, a fair characterization of the Egyptian entrepreneur in the Sudan would be an individual most active in northern and less developed Sudanese regions, with often long-established business relations and reliant on less lucrative commercial spheres—certainly not an exporter of Sudanese cotton.

Long-standing business relations often depended on the involvement of Sudanese merchants, some of whom independently operated extensive Nile Valley commercial ventures. For instance, the same two merchants specifically noted as partners of the Abu al-'Ala family were also assisting Misr Group's Port Sudan representative in his export and insurance activities.[162] The al-Barir family was another Sudanese group involved in commerce along the Nile Valley. They were from Omdurman and "had businesses in Egypt and the Sudan. Their brother, 'Ali al-Barir Effendi, had established a store in Egypt in which he traded on behalf of his brothers and Sudanese merchants."[163] The more extensive operations of such Sudanese merchants may have strengthened Nile Valley commercial bonds, but the most active Sudanese traders—like their Egyptian counterparts—did not suddenly arise in the interwar years.

The restricted commercial environment during the Second World War did little to inaugurate an era of 'new' Sudanese merchant involvement. In 1943 *al-Ahram* reported that "the well-known trader, Muhammad Hassan Bey, is assuming ownership of two factories, in Khartoum and Omdurman, for the import of Sudanese produce and has selected an accredited agent, Sheikh Azraq Mustafa, the trader of Khartoum and Omdurman who will depart Cairo the evening of next Tuesday to pursue his new activities."[164] Both this merchant and his commercial representative were 'well-known' figures hoping to take advantage of wartime conditions. The Cairo chamber's journal in 1945 included an announcement from Ibrahim Mikha'il Effendi, who stated "his commercial shop lies in the heart of the Arab market of the capital and that he had agents and workers in various regions of the Sudan. He is seeking contacts with Egyptian merchants who are ready to export to the Sudan the following commodities: shoes, perfumes, sweets, biscuits, canned fruits, and vegetables."[165] The number of entrepreneurs like Ibrahim Mikha'il or Muhammad Hassan, with business networks stretching throughout the Nile Valley, was still limited at the end of the Second World War. Even these 'success stories' were not new entrants of the war years, and the general scope and location of Sudanese commercial activity had changed little. Foreign merchants still dominated the economic centers of the Sudan, controlled both wholesale and retail distribution, and traded in the most profitable commodities—often linked to international markets, not Egypt.

Even in regions where Egyptian merchants were traditionally more active and foreign competitors fewer in number, such as the northern Sudanese provinces, the expansion of an Egyptian commercial presence had proceeded slowly. 'Ali Mawardi said of Dongola Province in 1940 that "it is possible to make this country a market for Egyptian commodities if it is given something in the way of importance."[166] 'Abdallah Fakri Abaza also noted potential spheres of commercial activity in the Sudan and the need for Egyptian merchants to take advantage of them. The economic expert hoped to encourage commercial involvement when he described what a Syrian in the Egyptian army had accomplished there. In 1939 he wrote that this man

> left the military service after having accumulated capital not exceeding LE500 and opened a pharmacy, [and] then a shop for the sale of foodstuffs. He worked and persevered until his business is valued [now] in tens of thousands of pounds. . . . There are found, other than him, many conspicuously successful merchants from among Syrians and Greeks, [but] a small number of Egyptians.[167]

Despite decades of general interest and concentrated efforts since the 1936 treaty, both Egypt's economic expert and the Khartoum exhibition director considered the position of Egyptian merchants in the Sudan by the start of the Second World War to be disappointing.

Second World War Opportunities for Local Merchants?

Various administrative restrictions had been a major deterrent to Egyptian–Sudanese trade prior to the Second World War, with consequences for the status of local merchants. Wartime government interference would have a similarly deleterious impact on both Egyptian and Sudanese merchants. For instance, as noted above, both administrations imposed all sorts of restrictions on the plans of the Egypt and Sudan Company to export Egyptian textiles to the Sudan. Despite the controls, many Egyptians viewed this company's activities as an improvement in their commercial position in the Sudan, but analysis of the investors in the company prevents its acclamation as a truly 'new' development. First of all, many of the investors were members of the 1930s economic missions and permanent committee, such as Fu'ad Abaza, 'Ali Shukri Khamis, and Yusuf Nahhas.[168] Second, foreign residents (the Tutunjis, Cicurels, and others) were well represented in the list of initial investors. Finally, many of the Egyptian and Sudanese merchants with traditional commercial connections between the two countries were also prominent investors. Among the shareholders were Muhammad al-Bariri, Muhammad 'Abd al-Rahim Samaha, Muhammad 'Abd al-Mon'im, and the Abu al-'Ala and al-Bariri families, all of whom had been active in Egyptian–Sudanese commerce for decades. The formation of this company appears to have been a reaction by well-established commercial interests to potentially profitable wartime conditions rather than a truly significant improvement of the position of local merchants and entrepreneurs.

The Condominium administration worked diligently to ensure that traders were not able to exploit wartime conditions. As discussed in the last chapter, the 1935 Defense of Sudan Regulations formed the basis for administrative control of the economy during the Second World War—controls equally applicable to both imports and exports. British officials also periodically issued declarations more specifically targeted at Sudanese exports and opportunities for local merchants. In 1941 *al-Ahram* reported that the Sudanese government not only "abolished the general permission to export dhurra" and decreed a "halt in the exporting of cotton or cotton seed," but also "demanded of exporters and importers that they submit to an official of the provisions committee the permit that confirms surety payment for exports and imports."[169] Cotton seed and dhurra exports to Egypt during the war were among the most attractive commercial fields for local merchants—in contrast to raw cotton, gum Arabic, and other Sudanese commodities destined solely for foreign markets. A 1943 memorandum from the Aswan Chamber of Commerce explained the problems facing local merchants and their traditional activities because of Condominium supervision:

> Aswan was distinguished by its geographic location as a means of connecting Egypt and the Sudan and the majority of its traders had worked before the war in importation of Sudanese goods and their sale in regions of the country and the exportation of some Egyptian goods to the Sudan. Therefore exchange proceeded in an excellent manner. Since the war began the relations have begun to weaken and split, and that is not because of the traders, but rather results

> from the system that has been mandated, preventing the Egyptian trader from importing and exporting, and monopolizing this business in other hands.[170]

This memorandum, sent to the Ministry of Commerce and Industry, listed numerous items Egypt desperately needed from the Sudan during the war and claimed that "all of these are prohibited from exportation to Egypt, whereas they are exported to Palestine and other areas."[171] Furthermore, the Aswan chamber memorandum complained of trade being monopolized by "other hands," an indirect reference to the wartime activities of the United Kingdom Commercial Corporation (UKCC).

This British commercial company handled Sudanese wartime commerce in order to prevent exploitation of local market conditions and to ensure satisfaction of regional/wartime needs. The prominent historian of the modern Sudan M.W. Daly states of this company that "the export of commodities in great demand elsewhere in the region was managed by the United Kingdom Commercial Corporation: the difference between high foreign market prices and the lower local prices was passed to a stabilization fund," which Sudanese authorities then used to subsidize expensive imports.[172] As one would expect, Egyptians portrayed the UKCC in less flattering terms. Mahmud Zaki explained the rationale behind the UKCC's monopoly by stating that the "painful truth" is "that the government of the Sudan administers the excess of its produce according to the instructions of the Middle East Supply Center without taking the opinion of the Egyptian government."[173] The Cairo Chamber of Commerce was less acrimonious in its annual report on 1943 commercial activities, actually complimenting the government's work with the UKCC and Sudanese authorities to provision Egypt with needed agricultural goods, but the chamber did advocate lifting the requirement that all Sudanese produce pass through UKCC hands.[174]

Difficulty obtaining needed Sudanese foodstuffs was not the sole problem created by the UKCC's wartime monopoly. The company's position effectively eliminated any real opportunities for local merchants' advancement during the war. By granting the UKCC a monopoly over local commerce, the Condominium administration was also—intentionally or not—preserving foreign dominance in the Sudan. This concern with essentially 'freezing' the local commercial situation during the Second World War was also mentioned earlier in the discussion of restrictions placed on the Egypt and Sudan Company that hoped to export Egyptian textiles to the Sudan. Whether restricting Egyptian companies or facilitating the UKCC monopoly, the Sudanese government maintained the prewar foreign-dominated status quo. In August 1941, the Alexandria Chamber of Commerce reported that "the Sudanese government gave two companies, and no others, the right to trade with Eritrea and Abyssinia."[175] Although this article did not identify the two companies involved, they were apparently foreign firms since the author expressed his hope that Sudanese authorities would open this commerce to Egyptian companies soon. Furthermore, although this was obviously not Egyptian–Sudanese trade, it is reflective of the extensive control enjoyed by an essentially 'anti-Egyptian' administration. In March 1944, during a parliamentary discussion of provision concerns and grain imports from the Sudan, deputy Muhammad al-Farnawani Bey noted the poor results for Egyptian merchants due to Sudanese officials' interference. This deputy acknowledged the more frequent and adequate shipments of Sudanese grains recently, but also stated, "As for the true Egyptians, they are still in need of our concern because they have not seen anything from the wartime commerce, and the proof is in their hands, for they are *forbidden from the trade in grains* and this is estimated at thirty million ardebs (annually)."[176] Justifications for tight administrative control of commerce during the war were numerous and well founded, but this control also prevented any potential improvement in Egyptian merchants' position.

Egyptian complaints that Condominium wartime controls discouraged development of commercial bonds or the position of local merchants were mild criticism. Some Egyptians argued that the UKCC monopoly of Sudanese exports was outright exploitation of wartime conditions. The enormous price differences and profits of the UKCC particularly rankled Egyptians. Egypt's wartime economic expert wrote that

> the United Kingdom Commercial Corporation . . . requisitions these products [sesame, peanuts, and other agricultural products] at the prices which the government of the Sudan fixes, then it sells them in foreign countries for raised prices; just as occurred for example with sesame, when this organization purchased it in the Sudan at a price fluctuating between LE18 and LE19.50 per ton and sold it in Egypt at a price of LE42 per ton.[177]

Al-Ahram reported in February 1944 that such exploitation was not occurring through UKCC trade with Egypt alone. It reported in February 1944 that "this company purchased last season 17,728 tons of sesame at a price of LE18.75 pounds per ton and sold this quantity to the government of

Palestine for around LE25 per ardeb, which yielded for the government of the Sudan a profit estimated at LE150,000."[178] Sudanese merchants joined their Egyptian colleagues in complaining of the UKCC's exploitation of wartime conditions, with one trader claiming that the price of a jerry can of sesame oil in the Sudan was 80 piasters, while the same commanded a price of LE4 in the Arabian Peninsula.[179] Egyptian officials knew of the tremendous profits accumulated by the UKCC (and the Sudan's stabilization fund) during the war, but they had no power to end the monopoly. After the war, on 3 December 1945, Sayyid Jalal pointedly asked the minister of commerce and industry, "Is His Excellency the minister aware that the consolidated British association known as UKCC has requisitioned Sudanese crops such as sesame, peanuts, green beans, and others at very reduced prices and sold these in Egypt at much higher prices, reaching at times three times the original price?"[180] The minister countered that the war had necessitated UKCC's monopoly of Sudanese trade, but that he was happy to report receipt of written assurance that trade with the Sudan would now be free of UKCC interference. During the war the Egyptian government's argument had been that the UKCC should sell its goods in Egyptian markets at the Sudanese purchase price, with the addition of transport costs and a reasonable profit, in order to allow Egypt to take measures for the orderly distribution and sale of these goods.[181] The perceived exploitation of wartime conditions by the UKCC was the most glaring facet of widespread Egyptian frustration with this foreign company that had "control over the Sudanese market and all markets which do business with the Sudan."[182]

Conclusion

The UKCC monopoly during the Second World War simply continued the Condominium's tight control of commerce, which had been in place since the nineteenth-century reconquest. In fact, continuity is the dominant theme in assessing the position of local merchants engaged in Nile Valley trade. Utilizing the UKCC or specific wartime policies, the Sudanese administration prevented any significant increase in the number of local traders or the scope of their activities. Condominium measures preserved foreign commercial dominance, while Egyptian and Sudanese merchants were largely confined to outlying regions, less profitable commodities, and smaller volumes. Furthermore, many of the most prominent local traders of the 1930s and 1940s were continuing business ventures, and relying on local connections, inaugurated generations earlier. Despite the efforts of Egyptian nationalists from the mid-1930s, there was no evidence of major shifts in the status of Egyptian or Sudanese merchants in Nile Valley commerce—certainly no changes with obvious utility to claims of a united nation.

This theme of continuity is equally applicable in assessing Egyptian importation of Sudanese commodities during the first half of the twentieth century. Foreign manufactures were a substantial portion of Egyptian imports and, with little manufacturing base, the Sudan certainly could not compete in this commerce. However, Egypt also imported various foodstuffs for decades—a phenomenon that only increased at this time because of continued population growth and limited domestic food production. Depending on a combination of Egyptian annual needs and a Sudanese willingness or desire to export, Sudanese grains, oil-bearing seeds/nuts, and livestock traditionally found their way to Egyptian markets. This relationship continued right through the final years of the Condominium. For instance, articles in the Alexandria Chamber of Commerce journal highlighted Egypt's continued dependence on its southern neighbor in combatting a local meat market crisis in 1950. Merchants and officials met in January and "the prevailing opinion was to work mainly on importing lamb and beef by all means, especially Sudanese and Ethiopian types."[183] By August 1950 the minister of commerce and industry was able to announce "that large quantities of cattle and frozen meat will arrive in Egypt in the middle of the coming month and . . . that the ministry is serious in working to extend the enclosures for cattle imported from Ethiopia and the Sudan."[184] In a similar vein, Egyptian Minister of Provisions Ahmad Hamza Bey visited the Sudan in 1951 and concluded agreements that would deliver Sudanese cotton seed and dhurra to Egyptian markets over the following two years. In a subsequent interview, the minister clearly indicated Egypt's continuing need for Sudanese foodstuffs when he stated that "the most important achievement of the trip was organizing the exchange of various goods between the halves of the valley, and we made known our willingness to purchase *all the surplus* of Sudanese goods."[185]

Despite Egyptian willingness or desire for a more dependent commercial relationship, there had been little success in permanently increasing Sudanese imports or the position of local merchants in Nile Valley trade. Most of the local merchants involved in Nile Valley trade during the 1930s through the 1950s were not new to the business. The failure to attract new commercial ventures was probably due to both the absence of a noteworthy increase in the volume of trade and government measures that discouraged potential entrepreneurs (some might say profiteers) during the more auspicious Second World War years. Government measures also contributed to

Egypt's inability to boost imports from the Sudan, especially Egyptian veterinary concerns about Sudanese livestock. Although attributing Egyptian 'failure' to a specific regulation or two might be alluring, the true determinants of Egyptian imports from the Sudan were simply local supply and demand. Unfortunately for Egyptian nationalists, supply, demand, price levels, and profits also largely determined Sudanese commercial relations with other areas of the world. Therefore, just as Sudanese markets treated Egypt as simply one among many suppliers of needed imports, Sudanese exporters viewed Egypt as only one of many potential global destinations for their commodities. This was a commercial relationship of independent states, not regions of a single nation.

Conclusion

> You had nothing whatsoever to do with the Sudan before your occupation of Egypt. The Sudan then formed Egypt's southern part and you took advantage of your occupation of Egypt to set your feet in the Sudan. *You never claimed* that you act for yourselves there or that you have obligations toward the Sudanese but *you have always said* that you are acting in the name of Egypt and for Egypt. We do not, therefore, recognize what *you claim now* about your obligations toward the Sudanese.[1]
>
> —Salah al-Din Bey, Egyptian minister of foreign affairs, conversation with British ambassador, Cairo, 6 July 1951

> It is *no longer the time* for words but for deeds, for productive and permanent deeds, deeds not made in noise and anger, but which have as their basis a careful consideration, the ordering and bringing together of all ranks to face all eventualities and to demonstrate that the people of Egypt and the Sudan are not among those that can be compelled to accept what they do not desire and that do not demand their right to live.[2]
>
> —Mustafa Nahhas, Egyptian Chamber of Deputies, 8 October 1951

The words of these Egyptian officials are particularly relevant in concluding this study. Salah al-Din Bey and Mustafa Nahhas were both speaking during the last decade in which Egyptians would be able to make any claims to governing the Sudan. They voiced their opinions amid the slow course of negotiations leading to the 1953 agreement that permitted Sudanese independence three years later. Additionally, their statements identified two of the most influential, yet basic, causes for the failed efforts to strengthen Egyptian–Sudanese economic bonds. Mustafa Nahhas argued in 1951 that it was no longer the time for mere words or plans and that Egyptians must undertake concrete and productive actions. Unfortunately for the nationalist cause, such exhortations needed a response decades earlier. Concerted economic activities of Egyptians were absent for far too long. Besides the late start—virtually an aborted start—another broad cause for the failure to develop Nile Valley economic bonds was administrative opposition. Salah al-Din's criticism of British vacillation in justifying their control of the Sudan did not explicitly mention Condominium opposition, but he and others believed firmly that the Sudanese administration had stymied Egyptian activities in the country for decades.

Actually, neither the Egyptian nor the Sudanese administration viewed unified economic development as their charge, or even worthy of much attention. Egyptian nationalists' hopes of uniting the Nile Valley were doomed by the administrative division of the region since the reconquest in 1898–99. Hugh Seton-Watson, in *Nation and States*, notes the importance of bureaucratic structures in delineating the scope of nationalist movements. He states, "In colonial Africa, state boundaries arbitrarily fixed by imperial governments largely determined the units within which the attempt was made to create modern nations."[3] Egyptians consistently denied all accusations of an "imperial" character to their presence in the Sudan, but the Anglo–Egyptian conquest certainly created the "state boundaries" to their south. Like Seton-Watson, Eric Hobsbawm also links the establishment of administrative boundaries to national development, stating that "the unity imposed by conquest and administration might sometimes, in the long run, produce a people that saw itself as a 'nation.'"[4] Egyptians claimed their reconquest in 1899 was actually unifying a historical, natural nation, but the fact remains that they acquiesced (under duress or not) to the establishment of a separate administrative structure in the Sudan—one maintained thereafter.

The Sudanese administration's independence from Egyptian influence and its general opposition to strengthening bonds along the Nile Valley certainly inhibited economic progress that might have assisted Egyptian sovereignty claims—ideally with Sudanese support for such. Egyptians considered the Condominium among the most serious impediments to their hopes of a united nation. Mahmud Rashid, a parliamentary deputy of the Nationalist Party in 1947, not only was critical of the Egyptian administration but also highlighted the detrimental local impact of the Condominium government:

> [The Egyptian government] is doing nothing—it is incumbent upon the ministry to prepare a program aimed at convincing the people of the Sudan of the legitimacy of Egypt and the Sudan being one country, and to establish a wide-ranging political and economic program in the Sudan, and to undertake financial assistance for our hard-working brothers. And we are aware that the Sudanese today believe that every Sudanese who works for the sake of unity is met with suffering and contempt from the government of the Sudan, and every Sudanese working for Sudanization encounters only welcome, cooperation, and approval from [that] government.[5]

Most Egyptians believed that the Sudanese government purposefully undermined Egypt's national interests, and they attributed this opposition to the British dominance of the Condominium administration. The policies of these British officials may have been motivated by genuine concern for Sudanese welfare or unspoken British imperial interests. Assessing British motivations matters little, while great significance lies in the fact that Egyptians controlled no top decision-making positions in the Condominium. This absence of an Egyptian presence only solidified the independent nature of the Sudanese administration. Since the events of 1924 resulted in the expulsion of many Egyptians from Sudanese service, politicians advocated the necessity of a recovered Egyptian administrative presence, most importantly at influential levels of that government. Makram 'Ubayd Pasha, parliamentary deputy and former Egyptian minister, railed against the governor-general's announcement in 1946 that there would be no increase in the number of Egyptian personnel:

> How many Egyptian employees are in the Sudan now?! You will not find [Egyptian] employees other than those delegated by us. As for the governor-general, he is English, as is his deputy, and the secretaries, who function like ministers among us, and the directors of departments and their deputies, and provincial governors and their deputies. As for the district commissioners, they are Sudanese. Therefore, *there is not found a single Egyptian employee in a position of responsibility*.[6]

Because of the lack of sympathetic Egyptian officials within the Condominium administration, Egyptians could confidently complain of obstructionist measures by the Sudanese state.

Egyptian charges of Sudanese obstructionism ranged widely, from emigration and travel restrictions to bureaucratic interference in religious, educational, or cultural affairs. Nationalists with economic concerns raised numerous complaints, but most heated criticism revolved around Sudanese customs policies and landholding restrictions. As examined in chapter four, Egyptians believed that Article 7 of the Condominium agreement had established a unified customs regime—one that would provide the entire valley with equal protection from the depredations of unchecked foreign intrusions. British authorities, holding all influential positions as Makram 'Ubayd Pasha noted above, concluded that this article provided them with tremendous leeway to alter tariffs for the benefit of the Sudan alone. The Condominium authorities established a level playing field for all 'foreign' merchants in the Sudan—including Egyptian merchants. Egyptians most frequently complained that British officials had not raised tariffs on foreign imports to correspond with the level of Egyptian duties, thereby failing to provide Egyptian merchants with a properly protected market in the Sudan. Actually, some tariff changes of the Condominium can be directly linked to Egyptian commercial successes. Chapter six includes examination of artificial silk–cotton textile mixes produced in Upper Egypt, and these Egyptian goods benefited tremendously from the Sudanese government imposing higher duties on foreign imports of silk products. Similarly, Egyptian leather shoes incurred no duties upon shipment to Sudanese markets and found an expanded market after 1938, when Condominium administrators had raised tariffs on foreign imports.[7] Some success in limited commercial spheres did little to mollify Egyptian interests claiming that Condominium opposition was holding back their expansion of market share in lucrative fields, like cotton textiles.

Condominium officials justified this customs regime, which treated Egyptian interests as simply one of many 'foreign' parties involved in Sudanese markets, by maintaining that such markets should be managed with the local inhabitants' well-being in mind. Egyptian exports to the Sudan were already exempt from all customs charges. The Condominium administration was under no obligation to impose duties on potentially less expensive, higher-quality foreign imports just to improve Egyptian market share in the Sudan. The same concern for Sudanese interests lay behind agricultural landholding policies. The Condominium administration planned and executed the huge Gezira project, designed to develop agricultural potentials, raise revenues, and improve Sudanese farmers' lives, but British interests running the scheme also clearly pocketed profits in the process. Egyptians reasoned they might also engage in such agricultural ventures and therefore railed against Condominium regulations restricting their ability to obtain, develop, and profit from landholding.

As examined in chapter five, British officials imposed conditions on agricultural concessions to prevent land speculation, despite such conditions possibly discouraging well-intentioned Egyptian investors. Egyptian nationalists and Condominium officials simply differed in their assessments of Sudanese administrative intentions. British officials claimed government measures were protecting their Sudanese charges from predatory northern neighbors. Egyptians argued that Condominium commercial, landholding, transport, and other policies, supposedly protecting the Sudanese, were actually British imperial measures designed to divide their nation.

Egyptians maintained that the British-dominated Condominium administration was the chief obstacle to their economic initiatives in the Sudan, and their hopes of uniting the Nile Valley, but the Egyptian administration itself prioritized issues that undermined progress toward economic unity. Among the best examples of this 'self-inflicted' harm to the nationalist economic cause was evident from the analysis of Nile Valley transportation in chapter four. Like the Condominium administration, the Egyptian government was most concerned with protecting revenue streams and the interests of its population. Reduced transport rates might have encouraged greater trade with the Sudan, but lowered rates threatened incoming revenues. Additionally, there were more extensive and influential Egyptian interests, who traded with non-Sudanese regions and would not be supportive of favoring Nile Valley commerce in this manner. Plus, throughout the period under study the Egyptian government decided not to fund costly infrastructure projects, such as a railroad connection along the Shellal–Halfa stretch or facilities for the movement and marketing of Sudanese livestock in Egypt. The Egyptian government had to balance the interests of local businessmen, those of the general population, and the desire to strengthen ties with the Sudan—and Sudanese ties were often the last priority.

Tobacco cultivation and processing provide a good, short synopsis of how Egyptian government measures undermined efforts to unify the valley. Tobacco manufactures, specifically cigarettes, did find profitable markets within the Sudan. In fact, cigarette exports remained among the more lucrative exports to the Sudan throughout the period.[8] Moreover, Condominium administrative measures actually helped this trade, with duties increased on foreign imports of cigarettes in November 1935 and June 1936.[9] The Egyptian state was not always as correspondingly supportive of the tobacco/cigarette trade. For instance, in August 1935, "the Post and Telegraph Department of the government of the Sudan proposed . . . as a reflection of the great desire for the strengthening of economic and commercial relations between Egypt and the Sudan, the lowering of duties on packages exchanged between the two countries."[10] Cigarette manufacturers relied on the parcel post for their export business, but the Egyptian state did not agree to the Sudanese proposal, claiming its "share of the profits from these [new] duties will decline at a rate of 20.5 percent annually."[11] When the Egyptian state finally reduced parcel rates in 1937, the quantity of cigarettes exported to the Sudan increased immediately. Parcel rates, like Egyptian government measures both to prohibit local tobacco cultivation and to prevent the importation/smuggling of Sudanese tobacco, were largely determined by revenue collection concerns. Any fair assessment of the dismal results in Egyptian–Sudanese tobacco and cigarette trade would have to place most blame on the Egyptian administration's actions or priorities.

Although in certain economic fields either the Egyptian or the Sudanese administration is deserving of greater blame, the development of stronger bonds actually necessitated collective responsibility or a common desire to see this economic unity to fruition. Many of the participants from the mid-1930s forward emphasized this need for cooperation in solving the economic problems facing the Nile Valley nationalists. In a 1950 interview, Ahmad al-Tawil, a member of the earlier Egyptian economic missions and an active merchant in the Sudan, listed numerous specific needs for commercial development, ranging from transport rates and facilities to specific taxes on salt and raw cattle hides. This trader also alluded to the most basic problem for merchants:

> Yes, indeed, there are some existing obstacles facing commercial interchange between the halves of the valley, and the most important of them are:
>
> First—The lack of a *unified government policy* between the north and south of the valley in respect to customs, as we have previously stated the duties imposed on foreign imports to the Sudan are considerably reduced, and Egyptian commerce is undermined by most serious competition.[12]

The absence of a unified customs regime in the Nile Valley remained a major obstacle to the development of a common commercial market—and responsibility for this absence lay with *both* administrations. However, local merchants, and entrepreneurs generally, needed more than administrative collaboration on just customs policies. Through transport, travel/emigration, taxation, financial, and other policies, both governments needed to demonstrate a consistent desire to favor the local economy—potentially at the expense of external markets. Neither administration consistently did this.

Besides the problems posed by two independent and often antagonistic administrations, Egyptians also had to counter accusations that their goals in the Sudan were more imperialistic than nationalistic. Egyptians investing in an irrigated agricultural scheme could improve the livelihood of Sudanese peasants, yet Egyptian investors stood to profit more than the local farmers. Development of the Nile River's hydraulic system would better utilize this precious resource of Sudanese and Egyptian peasants, but the agreements reached awarded a greater share of waters to the latter. The Egyptian government provided significant monies for the early development of Sudanese infrastructure, but that same government would later forcefully call for the repayment of the debts.[13] Despite Egyptian claims of common interests and 'brotherly' concerns for the Sudanese, British officials could easily portray these interests and activities in the Sudan as imperialist, profit-seeking, or certainly favoring Egyptians more than Sudanese.

Additionally, Egyptian entrepreneurs were engaged in much more profitable undertakings beyond the confines of the Nile Valley. Egyptian–Sudanese commercial statistics for 1950 illustrate this point. There are always specific conditions that cause fluctuations in trade levels, but 1950 qualifies as a typical post–Second World War economic year for the Nile Valley. Moreover, 1950 was a decade and a half after serious efforts to unite the economies began and a few years after the 'gains' made during wartime conditions might have been solidified. The Ministry of Finance's report on financial and economic policies in the country stated that "among its most important concerns perpetually is the strengthening of commercial relations between halves of the valley in every way possible."[14] In 1950 Egyptian imports from the Sudan amounted to little more than LE2.5 million, with Egypt relying on the United Kingdom (LE41.3 million), France (LE20.8 million), Italy (LE15.4 million), Australia (LE12.9 million), the United States (LE12.6 million), and others to satisfy the bulk of its needs.[15] Obviously, since the Sudan exported primarily raw cotton, there was little congruence between Sudanese supplies and Egyptian demand—which ultimately says a great deal about the likelihood of economic unification generally. The ministry's report included similarly discouraging results for Egyptian exports to the Sudan. Egypt exported much more to international markets, while the Sudan was the destination for only 1.8 percent of Egypt's exports. Furthermore, the traditional, hand-crafted, silk–cotton mixed textiles from Upper Egypt accounted for over one-third the value of all Egyptian goods sent to the Sudan that year. Cotton export dependence, Egypt's in this case, once again skews the results. Still, considering how extensive Egyptian trade with regions beyond the Nile Valley was, it is difficult to believe that local entrepreneurs would consistently and seriously give priority to economic development with the Sudan.

Commercial results, such as those of 1950, can be utilized in multiple ways. For instance, as stated above, such import–export figures might lead one to conclude that despite their rhetoric Egyptian economic leaders may not have been deeply concerned about relations with the Sudanese. On the other hand, the paltry import–export figures might allow one to claim that Egyptians were less imperialistic, profit-seeking, or exploitative than others trading with the Sudan. Egypt was importing little from the Sudan because British imperialists had constructed a local economy designed principally to produce cotton for British textile mills. At the same time, British, Japanese, and other manufactures were flooding and exploiting unprotected Sudanese markets. Egyptian nationalists chose to interpret the statistics in this manner, even if their own entrepreneurs only sought to replace the foreign competition in the same activities. However one chooses to interpret trade statistics, it is clearly difficult to make any claims of Nile Valley economic unity by the 1950s. The absence of any significant progress in strengthening economic bonds during the period of this study is the most telling evidence of Egyptian nationalists' failures.

During the first decades of Condominium rule, although the Egyptian government was providing developmental loans and balancing the Sudanese budget, there was hardly a word spoken about strengthening economic ties. In 1924, when the expulsion of Egyptian personnel solidified the administrative division of the Nile Valley, Sa'd Zaghlul and other leaders repeatedly emphasized the historical rights of Egypt and the irrefutable unity of Egyptian and Sudanese lands. In June of that year the Egyptian prime minister stated to his colleagues in the Chamber of Deputies, "Monies we have spent, blood we have shed, hardships we have endured and our fathers endured hardships before us, we derive our life from that river which pours forth from the upper Sudan . . . it is inconceivable that we leave one speck of the Sudan to others."[16] Like other politicians at the time and afterward, Sa'd Zaghlul made virtually no mention of any economic relationship with the Sudan other than Nile water concerns. Also, the tone of such statements was fairly imperialistic, stressing the Egyptian expectations of a 'return' in water rights and political control for the blood and money expended in the Sudan. Plus, Egyptians had resolved their main 'economic' concern in the Sudan with the signing of the 1929 Nile waters agreement—an agreement that only helped divide the valley.

More than a decade passed between Sa'd Zaghlul's complaints over the expulsion of Egyptian personnel and the beginning of organized economic development efforts in the Sudan by Egyptian entrepreneurs and officials. These later economic initiatives, with clearly enunciated nationalist objectives, roughly coincided with the negotiation and conclusion of the 1936 Anglo–Egyptian treaty. The Ministry of Foreign Affairs' report on the proposed treaty noted that it would allow Egypt real participation in the administration of the Sudan, rights to emigrate and own property, and the possibility that "Egypt can strengthen economic ties between the two countries without restraint or condition."[17] However, even at this time, with economic endeavors in the Sudan permissible and some underway already, there were indications that Egyptians still gave Sudanese affairs secondary importance. Muhammad 'Aziz Abaza was among those deputies critical of the proposed treaty during debate of the ministry's report. He stated, "It has been said that Egypt obtained the rights to emigrate, to own property, and equality in commerce, and we are thankful for the negotiators' efforts in returning these preexisting rights to us, however [these rights] appear paltry when compared to the price we paid for them."[18] Muhammad 'Aziz Abaza and his ilk were pleased with Sudanese improvements, but this improved relationship with the Sudan was too costly if the 'price' paid was the continued British occupation of Egypt. Israel Gershoni and James Jankowski's study of Egyptian nationalism notes that such opinions on the 'costs' paid were typical, as "Egyptian leaders tended to view the independence of Egypt as taking priority over the question of Egyptian–Sudanese unity."[19] Certainly, other nationalist objectives may have trumped economic development with the Sudan, but at least by the mid-1930s such activities were finally underway.

Almost two decades later, in the mid-1950s, with negotiations underway that would eventually permit the Sudanese to choose their sovereign future, what sort of economic bonds had developed? The past two chapters have highlighted the sorrowful statistical results of Nile Valley trade through the 1950s, and the Egyptian government's own statements confirm this lack of improvement. In 1953 the Egyptian Ministry of Commerce and Industry's annual report on foreign trade noted that Egypt's share of Sudanese imports and exports had increased but Egypt's share of total Sudanese imports and exports had actually declined. Furthermore, the reliance on certain limited-market items of trade was still apparent. For the 1951–52 trade year, Egyptian exports of silk–cotton textile mixes constituted 40 percent of the total exports to the Sudan, while cotton textiles were only 10 percent of that total. After recitation of similarly dismal results, the ministry recommended the following:

> Therefore we must work to realize the objective of all in Egypt and the Sudan in respect to strengthening ties between the two and encouraging commercial exchange between their markets.
>
> In order to arrive at this goal the detailed study of these markets to understand the possibilities of goods exchanged is necessary. Likewise, it is incumbent upon merchants and entrepreneurs in both Egypt and the Sudan that they cooperate together in the trade of goods, giving preference to the products of Egypt or the Sudan—when possible—over the products of foreign countries.[20]

For almost two decades Egyptian delegations, economic experts, staff of the exhibition in Khartoum, and other officials conducted and published results of extensive studies on Sudanese market conditions. Giving preference to local producers and merchants was among the first issues taken up by Egypt's permanent committee on the Sudan. That the Ministry of Commerce and Industry was still advocating preferential treatment of locals and recommending market studies in 1953 is clear evidence of little progress in unifying the Egyptian–Sudanese economy. At roughly the same time, Egyptian officials were arguing before British and other diplomatic audiences that their rightful sovereignty over the Sudan was buttressed by historical, geographic, and various long-standing cultural bonds. Nationalists' hopes of a strengthened union had not been realized—and provided no support for their cause.

This study has claimed that Egyptians failed to grasp opportunities for greater economic unity with the Sudan because of poor planning and policy choices, antagonistic administrations, international market forces, late initiation of activities, and various other factors. Whatever specific causes may have led to this failure, the likelihood of Egyptian nationalists ever truly unifying the Egyptian and Sudanese economies was always extremely low. The problem Egyptians faced was at least partially definitional—basically, what actually constitutes a unified economy. Should regions of a unified economy trade more with each other than with external entities? Does a unified economy rely more heavily on internal investors and expertise? Must a unified economy include some ideal balance of agricultural, industrial, and commercial activities? The answer to these questions seemed to be "yes," based on Egyptian initiatives during the period of this study. Just like in the first decades of Condominium rule, the Sudan in the 1950s continued to trade more with foreign countries, rely on foreign investment and expertise, and rely predominantly on exporting raw cotton. The Sudanese economy remained unchanged.

The Egyptian economy in the 1950s remained virtually identical to its Sudanese counterpart. Certainly there had been more diversification and development, but Egypt also relied on cotton production, foreign investment, and commerce beyond the Nile Valley. If both regions were still largely the classical 'dependent' economies, why not one larger, instead of two smaller, dependent economies? Historically, there have been both territorially large and small dependent economies. Although Egyptians during the first half of the twentieth century would not have put it this way, why not one larger, agriculturally dependent Nile Valley nation? The answer seems to be that neither the British nor the Sudanese wanted it.

Egyptians claimed sovereignty over the Sudan, but the British and Sudanese enjoyed the greatest powers in deciding the region's fate.[21] One of the most glaring omissions in Egyptian records concerning efforts to unify the Nile Valley economy is indications of Sudanese popular support for these efforts. This study has identified the occasional Sudanese merchant or newspaper editor who spoke glowingly of Egyptian–Sudanese union, but there was no broad indication of true popular support for this cause. Egyptians could claim religious, linguistic, geographic, historical, and various cultural bonds with the Sudanese, but Sudanese claims of the same needed some fostering. The development of these bonds—and economic ties—would be most easily and successfully fostered through state institutions. Unfortunately for Egyptians, the British firmly held the administrative reins of the Sudanese state. Therefore, one of the most effective means of unifying a nation, what Benedict Anderson labeled "official nationalism," remained out of Egyptians' reach. In his work with this label Anderson emphasizes reactionary attempts by threatened imperial/dynastic states to counter more revolutionary nationalists, but the concept is particularly relevant to our study. He notes that "the model of official nationalism assumes its relevance above all at the moment when revolutionaries successfully take control of the state, and are for the first time in a position to use the power of the state in pursuit of their visions."[22] Egyptians never controlled the Condominium state, in fact they rarely had serious influence in that state. Without an administrative presence in the Sudan, Egyptian efforts to strengthen economic or other bonds were futile. They may have claimed the unity of the Nile Valley for decades, but they had also permitted the establishment of two independent states in 1899. The Sudanese simply confirmed those independent nations some fifty years later.

NOTES

Notes to Introduction

1 Peter Woodward, *Condominium and Sudanese Nationalism* (London: Rex Collings, 1979); Heather J. Sharkey, *Living with Colonialism: Nationalism and Culture in the Anglo–Egyptian Sudan* (Berkeley, CA: University of California Press, 2003). Tim Niblock's study, like that of Mansour Khalid, differs only in the chronological time span examined—ranging well beyond the Condominium's end. Tim Niblock, *Class and Power in Sudan: The Dynamics of Sudanese Politics, 1898–1985* (Albany: State University of New York Press, 1987); Mansour Khalid, *The Government They Deserve: The Role of the Elite in Sudan's Political Evolution* (London: Kegan Paul, 1990).

2 Studies from virtually every discipline on the modern Sudan pay great attention to the two *sayyids*. Analysis of the Graduates Congress, other than in nationalist movement analyses, tends to receive rather cursory coverage. For a more extensive investigation of this influential political body, see Ahmad Khayr, *Kifahjil: tarikh harakat al-Khirrijin wa-tatawwuriha fi al-Sudan* (Khartoum: Dar al-Sudaniya li-l-Kutub, 2002).

3 M.W. Daly, *Empire on the Nile: The Anglo–Egyptian Condominium, 1898–1934* (Cambridge: Cambridge University Press, 1986); M.W. Daly, *Imperial Sudan: The Anglo–Egyptian Condominium, 1934–1956* (Cambridge: Cambridge University Press, 1991); Muddathir 'Abd al-Rahim, *Imperialism and Nationalism in the Sudan: A Study in Constitutional and Political Development, 1899–1956* (London: Oxford University Press, 1969); Gabriel R. Warburg, *Islam, Sectarianism, and Politics in Sudan since the Mahdiyya* (Madison, WI: University of Wisconsin Press, 2003). These historical works were also a significant improvement upon the earlier studies of the Condominium era produced by former colonial administrators. The following are representative of such works by former administrators, often top members of the Sudan Political Service: K.D.D. Henderson, *The Making of*

the Modern Sudan: The Life and Letters of Sir Douglas Newbold, K.B.E. of the Sudan Political Service (Westport, CT: Greenwood, 1974); Sir Harold MacMichael, *The Anglo–Egyptian Sudan* (London: Faber and Faber, 1934).

4 Although not always stated in western histories of the Condominium era, clearly implied in such works is the rapaciousness of Egyptians in dealing with the Sudan, contrasted with the altruism and self-sacrifice of British diplomats and members of the Sudan Political Service.

5 Alexander Scholch, *Egypt for the Egyptians* (Reading: Ithaca Press, 1981); Afaf Lutfi Sayyid-Marsot, *Egypt's Liberal Experiment, 1922–1936* (Berkeley, CA: University of California Press, 1977); Charles Wendell, *The Evolution of the Egyptian National Image* (Berkeley, CA: University of California Press, 1972); Jacques Berque, *Egypt: Imperialism and Revolution* (New York: Praeger, 1972); Mahmud Zayid, *Egypt's Struggle for Indepedence* (Beirut: Khayats, 1965); Jamal Mohammed Ahmed, *The Intellectual Origins of Egyptian Nationalism* (Oxford: Oxford University Press, 1960); Magda Baraka, *The Egyptian Upper Class between Revolutions, 1919–1952* (Reading: Ithaca Press, 1998); James Jankowski, *Egypt's Young Rebels: "Young Egypt," 1933–1952* (Stanford, CA: Hoover Institution Press, 1975); Israel Gershoni and James Jankowski, *Egypt, Islam, and the Arabs: The Search for Egyptian Nationhood, 1900–1930* (New York: Oxford University Press, 1986); Israel Gershoni and James Jankowski, *Redefining the Egyptian Nation, 1930–1945* (New York: Cambridge University Press, 1995). Some of the scholars mentioned here span the boundaries between the more 'traditional' historians and their successors, cited next.

6 Eve Marie Troutt Powell, *A Different Shade of Colonialism: Egypt, Great Britain and the Mastery of the Sudan* (Berkeley, CA: University of California Press, 2003); Joel Beinin, *Workers on the Nile: Nationalism, Communism, Islam, and the Egyptian Working Class, 1882–1954* (Princeton, NJ: Princeton University Press, 1987); Lisa Pollard, *Nurturing the Nation: The Family Politics of Modernizing, Colonizing, and Liberating Egypt (1805–1923)* (Berkeley, CA: University of California Press, 2005); Beth Baron, *Egypt as a Woman: Nationalism, Gender, and Politics* (Cairo: American University in Cairo Press, 2005); Donald M. Reid, *Whose Pharaohs? Archaeology, Museums, and Egyptian National Identity from Napoleon to World War I* (Berkeley, CA: University of California Press, 2003); Margot Badran, *Feminists, Islam, and Nation: Gender and the Making of Modern Egypt* (Princeton, NJ: Princeton University Press, 1995); Malak Badrawi, *Isma'il Sidqi, 1875–1950: Pragmatism and Vision in Twentieth Century Egypt* (London: Routledge, 1996); Ellis Goldberg, *Tinker, Tailor, and Textile Worker: Class and Politics in Egypt, 1930–1952* (Berkeley, CA: University of California Press, 1986); Christina Phelps Harris, *Nationalism and Revolution in Egypt: The Role of the Muslim Brotherhood* (Westport, CT: Hyperion, 1981); Amy J. Johnson, *Reconstructing Rural Egypt: Ahmed Hussein and the History of Egyptian Development* (Syracuse, NY: Syracuse University Press, 2004).

7 Charles Issawi, *Egypt: An Economic and Social Analysis* (Oxford: Oxford University Press, 1947); Marius Deeb, "Bank Misr and the Emergence of the Local Bourgeoisie in Egypt," *Middle Eastern Studies* 12, no. 3 (1976): 69–86; Marius Deeb, "The Socioeconomic Role of the Local Foreign Minorities in Modern Egypt, 1805–1961," *International Journal of Middle East Studies* 9, no. 1 (1978): 11–22; Robert L. Tignor, *State, Private Enterprise, and Economic Change in Egypt, 1918–1952* (Princeton, NJ: Princeton University Press, 1984); Eric Davis, *Challenging Colonialism: Bank Misr and Egyptian Industrialization, 1920–1941* (Princeton, NJ: Princeton University Press, 1983); Robert Vitalis, *When Capitalists Collide: Business Conflict and the End of Empire in Egypt* (Berkeley, CA: University of California Press, 1995).

8 Although a majority of studies on the Egyptian economy focus on late nineteenth- and early twentieth-century 'capitalist' transformations occurring, important works by Peter Gran and Nelly Hanna have argued that the beginning of economic changes—even if not of a 'nationalist' nature—should be located in earlier periods.

9 Troutt Powell, *A Different Shade of Colonialism.*

10 Among the many works by Yunan Labib Rizq, two that directly address Egyptian hopes for a united Nile Valley and the resultant troubles with British officials are *Qadiyat wihdat Wadi al-Nil bayna al-mu'ahada wa-taghyir al-waqi' al-isti'mari, 1936–1946* (Cairo: Ma'had al-Buhuth wa-l-Dirasat al-'Arabiya, 1975), and *al-Sudan fi al-mufawadat al-misriya al-baritaniya, 1930–1936* (Cairo: Ma'had al-Buhuth wa-l-Dirasat al-'Arabiya, 1974). The scholarship on the Anglo–Egyptian dispute over the Sudan differs from that on either Sudanese or Egyptian nationalism individually. The dispute scholarship is composed almost solely of diplomatic/political studies of Egypt's claimed sovereignty over the Sudan and British opposition to such. These works certainly address the Egyptian nationalist movement at points, but the emphasis is on diplomatic negotiations—and, invariably, little attention is given to economic relationships of the Nile Valley. In addition to numerous monographs on this topic from Egyptian scholars, the works of Mekki Abbas, J.A. Hail, and Travis Hanes are among the more noteworthy English-language contributions to the field. Mekki Abbas, *The Sudan Question: The Dispute over the Anglo–Egyptian Condominium, 1884–1951* (New York: Praeger, 1952); J.A. Hail, *Britain's Foreign Policy in Egypt and Sudan, 1947–1956* (Reading: Ithaca Press, 1996); W. Travis Hanes III, *Imperial Diplomacy in the Era of Decolonization: The Sudan and Anglo–Egyptian Relations, 1945–1956* (Westport, CT: Greenwood, 1995).

11 Terence Walz, *Trade between Egypt and Bilad as-Sudan, 1700–1820* (Cairo: Institut Français d'Archéologie Orientale du Caire, 1978).

12 Chapter one of this book addresses the differing opinions of both Egyptian leaders at the time and subsequent scholarship with respect to the 'normal' relationship between sections of the Nile Valley.

13 Although many scholars employ these labels, or similar constructions, in their works, among the more succinct descriptions of the scholarly groups is that provided by Anthony Smith. Anthony D. Smith, *The Ethnic Origins of Nations* (New York: Blackwell, 1986), 7–13.

14 Ernest Gellner, *Nations and Nationalism* (Ithaca, NY: Cornell University Press, 1983), 13.

15 Benedict Anderson is probably the most influential theorist who maintains that nations are modern creations but also culturally based phenomena. Anderson argues that the combination of an expanding vernacular print capitalism, new conceptions of time and space, and the decline of traditional social bonds (religious or dynastic) facilitated the modern-era emergence of culturally united nations. Benedict Anderson, *Imagined Communities: Reflections on the Origin and Spread of Nationalism*, rev. ed. (New York: Verso, 2006).

16 Smith, *The Ethnic Origins of Nations*; John A. Armstrong, *Nations before Nationalism* (Chapel Hill, NC: University of North Carolina Press, 1982). Although Anderson included examination of a nation's literature and local press in his study, he linked this cultural production to specifically modern-era developments.

17 Charles Beard, *An Economic Interpretation of the Constitution of the United States* (New Brunswick, NJ: Transaction Publishers, 1998).

18 Although virtually all scholars make brief mention of the economic and financial concerns of nationalist movements, they commonly award these concerns a secondary role. Economic grievances may inspire the members of a nation to take action, but cultural attributes, administrative activities, or other non-economic factors are deemed to be what makes the nation. Marxist scholars have expectedly placed greater attention on the economic foundations of nationalist movements. Michael Hechter and Tom Nairn are two scholars who have emphasized economic connections in movements. Probably the clearest and most concise statement of economic components of nationalism is Joseph Stalin's requirement that a nation include "an internal economic bond which welds the various parts of a nation into a single whole." Joseph Stalin, *Marxism and the National and Colonial Question* (New York: International Publishers, n.d.), 6–7.

19 United Nations Security Council, *Verbatim Records of Anglo–Egyptian Dispute, 5th August 1947–10th September 1947* (Cairo: Government Press, 1947), 25.

Notes to Chapter 1

1 al-Dawla al-Misriya, Majlis al-Nuwwab, *Majmu'at Madabit dawr al-in'iqad al-'adi al-awwal* (15 March–10 July 1924) (Cairo: al-Matba'a al-Amiriya, 1924), 714.

2 al-Dawla al-Misriya, Majlis al-Nuwwab, *Majmu'at Madabit dawr al-in'iqad al-'adi al-thalith*, vol. 1 (18 November 1939–12 March 1940) (Cairo: al-Matba'a al-Amiriya, 1940), 5.

3 al-Dawla al-Misriya, Majlis al-Nuwwab, *Majmu'at Madabit dawr al-in'iqad al-'adi al-awwal*, vol. 1 (18 January–5 June 1945) (Cairo: al-Matba'a al-Amiriya, 1946), 70.

4 al-Dawla al-Misriya, Majlis al-Shuyukh, *Majmu'at Madabit dawr al-in'iqad al-'adi al-'ashrin* (18 January–7 August 1945) (Cairo: al-Matba'a al-Amiriya, 1946), 718.

5 Israel Gershoni, "Geographers and Nationalism in Egypt: Huzayyin and the Unity of the Nile Valley, 1945–1948," in *The Nile: Histories, Cultures, Myths*, ed. Haggai Erlich and Israel Gershoni (Boulder, CO: Lynne Rienner, 2000), 204.

6 Gershoni, "Geographers and Nationalism in Egypt," 204.

7 Gershoni, "Geographers and Nationalism in Egypt," 204 (emphasis added).

8 Steven Serels, "Famines of War: The Red Sea Grain Market and Famine in Eastern Sudan, 1889–1891," *Northeast African Studies* 12, no. 1 (2012): 73–94.

9 Huddleston to Nahhas, 18 May 1944, File Majlis al-Wuzara'–al-Fatra ba'd 1923, no. 3D, Dar al-Watha'iq (hereinafter "DW"), 2.

10 *al-Ahram*, 2 August 1939.

11 Gabriel Warburg, *Historical Discord in the Nile Valley* (Evanston, IL: Northwestern University Press, 1992), 19.

12 *Majallat Ghurfat al-Iskandariya*, September 1937, 10 (emphasis added).

13 al-Dawla al-Misriya, Majlis al-Nuwwab, *Majmu'at Madabit dawr al-in'iqad al-'adi al-thalith*, vol. 1 (18 November 1939–12 March 1940), 33–34.

14 *al-Jarida al-tijariya al-misriya*, 9 May 1947.

15 Undoubtedly the most extensive study of the manner in which Sudanese were portrayed within Egyptian culture is Troutt Powell's *A Different Shade of Colonialism*. While this description greatly simplifies her work, she convincingly argues that the portrayal of Sudanese in Egyptian media was a key element in the development of an Egyptian national identity. An earlier study from Dr. Powell additionally demonstrated that Egyptian political leaders like Mustafa Kamil and historians examining the Sudan, namely Na'um Shuqayr in his 1903 work, viewed themselves as racially distinct from and superior to Sudanese. Eve Marie Troutt Powell, "Brothers along the Nile: Egyptian Concepts of Race and Ethnicity, 1895–1910," in *The Nile: Histories, Cultures, Myths*, ed. Haggai Erlich and Israel Gershoni (Boulder, CO: Lynne Rienner, 2000), 178.

16 Although this study acknowledges the role of southern Sudanese regions in historical trends of the era—and will briefly address the regions when appropriate—the central focus is the relationship of Egyptian nationalists and their non-southern Sudanese counterparts. The opportunities for strengthened economic bonds clearly lay in northern/central Sudan, plus British officials denied Egyptians access to the south.

17 Abd el-Fattah Ibrahim el-Sayed Baddour, *Sudanese–Egyptian Relations: A Chronological and Analytical Study* (The Hague: Martinus Nijhoff, 1960), 16–17.

18 Although emphasizing twentieth-century changes in education, Mohamed Omer Beshir's study provides a clear summary of traditional Sudanese education. Mohamed Omer Beshir, *Educational Development in the Sudan, 1898–1956* (Oxford: Clarendon, 1969).

19 James Currie, "The Educational Experiment in the Anglo–Egyptian Sudan, 1900–33," Part 2, *Journal of the Royal African Society* 34, no. 134 (1935): 46.

20 Currie, "The Educational Experiment in the Anglo–Egyptian Sudan, 1900–33," Part 1, *Journal of the Royal African Society* 33, no. 133 (1934): 365–66.

21 Beshir, *Educational Development in the Sudan*, 80.

22 Beshir, *Educational Development in the Sudan*, 46.

23 *al-Ahram*, 8 March 1939.

24 "Graduates Congress Note on Education," submitted to Civil Secretary on 5 July 1939, quoted in Beshir, *Educational Development in the Sudan*, 237.

25 Beshir, *Educational Development in the Sudan*, 159.

26 al-Dawla al-Misriya, Majlis al-Nuwwab, *Majmu'at Madabit dawr al-in'iqad al-'adi al-thalith*, vol. 1 (14 November 1946–3 March 1947) (Cairo: al-Matba'a al-Amiriya, 1948), 495.

27 *Majallat Ghurfat al-Qahira*, April 1937, 69. Frequently, Egyptian comments on the need for greater attention to Sudanese education—or cultural unity generally—were attached to much longer diatribes on the latest British transgressions in the Sudan or the need for economic projects there. For a good example of such, see the Egyptian economic expert's comments just prior to the Second World War: *Majallat Ghurfat al-Iskandariya*, July 1939, 11–12.

28 *al-Ahram*, 26 July 1939.

29 Beshir, *Educational Development in the Sudan*, 160–61.

30 The centrality of Egyptian teachers, and civil servants generally, is attested to by all sources, but these sources do not always describe Egyptians as "enthusiastic" officials of the Sudan. For instance, Beshir writes of a "modern" Egyptian school in which "the majority of army officers employed as teachers were persons who had *committed offences in Egypt* and were appointed to the school in Khartoum as a *punishment*." Beshir, *Educational Development in the Sudan*, 14 (emphasis added).

31 *al-Ahram*, 5 August 1939.

32 al-Dawla al-Misriya, Majlis al-Nuwwab, *Majmu'at Madabit dawr al-in'iqad al-'adi al-thalith*, vol. 1 (18 November 1939–12 March 1940), 30.

33 Beshir, *Educational Development in the Sudan*, 157.

34 Beshir, *Educational Development in the Sudan*, 165. Egypt had developed a presence within non-traditional, higher education in the Sudan, although non-Egyptian schools were much more numerous—eighty-four for boys and thirteen for girls.

35 al-Dawla al-Misriya, Majlis al-Nuwwab, *Majmu'at Madabit dawr al-in'iqad al-'adi al-thalith*, vol. 3 (26 May–18 June 1947) (Cairo: al-Matba'a al-Amiriya, 1948), 2821.

36 al-Dawla al-Misriya, Majlis al-Nuwwab, *Majmu'at Madabit dawr al-in'iqad al-'adi al-rabi'*, vol. 1 (12 November 1947–9 February 1948) (Cairo: al-Matba'a al-Amiriya, 1949), 9. Also, in the entire Egyptian liberal parliamentary era,

from 1924 to the 1952 revolution, these statements were undoubtedly the most extensive treatment of Sudanese education in an opening speech.

37 Eiman el-Nour, "Nationalism and the Rise of the Sudanese Novel," in *The Road Less Traveled: Reflections on the Literatures of the Horn of Africa*, ed. Ali Jimale Ahmed (Trenton, NJ: Red Sea Press, 2007), 376–77.

38 el-Nour, "Nationalism and the Rise of the Sudanese Novel," 383. Like others, this author acknowledged Egyptian literary influences, but he argued for an eventual independent Sudanese literary scene. The styles or trends among Sudanese novelists may have come from Egypt or beyond—but the topics and themes were uniquely Sudanese.

39 el-Nour, "Nationalism and the Rise of the Sudanese Novel," 399–400.

40 *al-Jarida al-tijariya al-misriya*, 26 May 1947.

41 *al-Ahram*, 10 March 1943.

42 The term 'Mahdiya' is usually associated with the revolt against Egyptian rule and the subsequent period of Sudanese independence in the late nineteenth century. The Ansar are literally the followers or helpers of the Mahdi in this revolutionary period—and subsequently the followers of the Mahdi's successors.

43 Frederick de Jong, "The Sufi Orders in Egypt during the 'Urabi Insurrection and the British Occupation (1882–1914): Some Societal Factors Generating Aloofness, Support, and Opposition," in *Sufi Orders in Ottoman and Post-Ottoman Egypt and the Middle East: Collected Studies* (Istanbul: Isis Press, 2000), 157.

44 John Voll's work on the Khatmiya order in the Sudan notes the longer-term ties of the order with the Egyptian government—bonds established between the earliest Mirghani leaders and the Egyptian dynasty founded by Muhammad Ali, who administered the Hijaz region where the Mirghani family was originally located. John Voll, "A History of the Khatmiyyah Tariqah in the Sudan" (PhD diss., Harvard University, 1969).

45 Gabriel Warburg, "Some Social and Economic Aspects of Turco-Egyptian Rule in the Sudan," *Belleten* 53, no. 49 (1989): 793–94.

46 Representative of these British claims was a letter from Sudanese Governor-General Huddleston to Egyptian Prime Minister Mustafa Nahhas in 1944. Huddleston to Nahhas, 18 May 1944, 7.

47 Fadwa Abd al-Rahman Ali Taha, *The Anglo–Egyptian Dispute over the Sudan, 1937–1947* (Khartoum: Khartoum University Press, 2006), 35.

48 Gabriel Warburg, "Religious Policy in the Northern Sudan: Ulama and Sufism, 1899–1918," *Asian and African Studies* 7 (1971): 99.

49 *al-Ahram*, 30 November 1939.

50 *al-Ahram*, 16 February 1940.

51 Ali Taha, *The Anglo-Egyptian Dispute*, 34.

52 *al-Jarida al-tijariya al-misriya*, 16 November 1951.

53 al-Dawla al-Misriya, Majlis al-Shuyukh, *Majmu'at Madabit dawr al-in'iqad al-'adi al-thani wa-l-'ashrin* (14 November 1946–10 July 1947) (Cairo: al-Matba'a al-Amiriya, 1948), 54.

54 al-Dawla al-Misriya, Majlis al-Nuwwab, *Majmu'at Madabit dawr al-in'iqad al-'adi al-thalith*, vol. 1 (14 November 1946–3 March 1947), 359.

55 al-Dawla al-Misriya, Majlis al-Nuwwab, *Majmu'at Madabit dawr al-in'iqad al-'adi al-awwal* (15 March–10 July 1924), 345.

56 This study refers to Muhammad Ali, his successors, and the general Egyptian political/economic elite of the pre-1952 revolution era as 'Egyptians,' while recognizing that 'Turco-Egyptian,' 'Turco-Circassian,' or some other label might more accurately describe their ethnic origins. This study uses 'Egyptian' simply for convenience and the fact that these leaders resided in Egypt, based their economic/political power in the valley, and generally linked their personal interests with Egyptian nationalist interests.

57 al-Dawla al-Misriya, Majlis al-Nuwwab, *Majmu'at Madabit dawr al-in'iqad al-'adi al-awwal* (15 March–10 July 1924), 345.

58 Warburg, "Some Social and Economic Aspects," 795.

59 John Voll, "Unity of the Nile Valley: Identity and Regional Integration," *Journal of African Studies* 3, no. 2 (1976): 207.

60 Warburg, "Some Social and Economic Aspects," 793–94.

61 Warburg, *Historical Discord in the Nile Valley*, 59.

62 al-Dawla al-Misriya, Majlis al-Nuwwab, *Majmu'at Madabit dawr al-in'iqad ghayr al-'adi li nazar mu'ahadat al-sadaqa wa-l-tahaluf bayna Misr wa-Baritanya al-'Uzma* (2–19 November 1936) (Cairo: al-Matba'a al-Amiriya, 1937), 68.

63 Warburg, *Historical Discord in the Nile Valley*, 19–36.

64 al-Dawla al-Misriya, Majlis al-Nuwwab, *Majmu'at Madabit dawr al-in'iqad al-'adi al-awwal* (15 March–10 July 1924), 714.

65 Heather Sharkey-Balasubramanian, "The Egyptian Colonial Presence in the Anglo–Egyptian Sudan, 1898–1932," in *White Nile, Black Blood: War, Leadership, and Ethnicity from Khartoum to Kampala*, edited by Jay Spaulding and Stephanie Beswick (Lawrenceville, NJ: Red Sea Press, 2000), 288–89.

66 Hassan Ahmad Ibrahim, "Mahdist Risings against Condominium Government in the Sudan," *International Journal of African Historical Studies* 2, no. 3 (1979): 440–71.

67 "Notes on the Kitchener Memorial Medical School" (n.d.), in Beshir, *Educational Development in the Sudan*, 217–18 (emphasis added).

68 Voll, "Unity of the Nile Valley," 215. Although Voll argues convincingly that Sudanese opinion is the ultimate factor in eventual sovereignty decisions, this was not a foregone conclusion early in the twentieth century—or earlier. Furthermore, the implication of this argument is that Egyptians had very little impact in determining the Sudan's fate, which is precisely the perspective that this study hopes to counter with its analysis of economic developments.

69 Sharkey-Balasubramanian, "The Egyptian Colonial Presence," 303.
70 al-Dawla al-Misriya, Majlis al-Nuwwab, *Majmu'at Madabit dawr al-in'iqad al-'adi al-rabi'*, vol. 1 (12 November 1947–9 February 1948), 5.
71 al-Dawla al-Misriya, Majlis al-Nuwwab, *Majmu'at Madabit dawr al-in'iqad al-'adi al-thani*, vol. 4 (16 July–20 August 1951) (Cairo: al-Matba'a al-Amiriya, 1952), Session 38, 6.
72 Baddour, *Sudanese–Egyptian Relations*, 242.

Notes to Chapter 2

1 Winston Churchill, *The River War: An Account of the Reconquest of the Sudan* (London: Eyre and Spottiswoode, 1951), 363–64.
2 Berque, *Egypt*, 415.
3 *al-Akhbar*, 11 September 1922.
4 Muhammad Shafiq Pasha, "Note sur les Travaux de Contrôle du Nil," 21 April 1921, File Majlis al-Wuzara'–al-Sudan, Maslahat al-Riyy, no. 10, DW, 6.
5 al-Dawla al-Misriya, Majlis al-Nuwwab, *Majmu'at Madabit dawr al-in'iqad al-'adi al-thani*, vol. 2 (12 April–8 June 1932) (Cairo: al-Matba'a al-Amiriya, 1932), 812.
6 al-Dawla al-Misriya, Majlis al-Nuwwab, *Majmu'at Madabit dawr al-in'iqad al-'adi al-awwal* (15 March–10 July 1924), 188.
7 Fu'ad Abaza, "Mushahidat 'an zira'at al-qutn fi Wadi al-Nil," *al-Siyasa*, 1 May 1935 (emphasis added).
8 *al-Ahram*, 21 November 1938.
9 *al-Jarida al-tijariya al-misriya*, 8 May 1930.
10 Hassan Ramzi al-Arna'udi, "al-Sudan!! al-Sudan!!" *al-Akhbar*, 28 January 1930.
11 Allenby to Zaghlul, 22 November 1924, File Majlis al-Wuzara'–al-Fatra ba'd 1923, no. 3B, DW, 2.
12 *al-Akhbar*, 1 September 1931.
13 al-Dawla al-Misriya, Majlis al-Nuwwab, *Majmu'at Madabit dawr al-in'iqad al-'adi al-thani*, vol. 2 (12 April–8 June 1932), 838.
14 al-Dawla al-Misriya, Majlis al-Shuyukh, *Majmu'at Madabit dawr al-in'iqad al-'adi al-thani wa-l-'ashrin* (14 November 1946–10 July 1947), 119 (emphasis added).
15 Actually, the one major dissension in these commissions' reports came from H.T. Cory of the United States, who was a member of the group appointed in January 1920. He was in agreement with his colleagues on the projects proposed, but wrote that giving Egypt a considerably larger share of future increases of water storage capacity would be harmful to Sudanese economic development.
16 "Report of the Nile Projects Commission," 1920, File Majlis al-Wuzara'–Nizarat al-Ishgal, no. 2/4/B/2, DW, 5.
17 Husayn Rushdi, "Mashru' mu'ahada bi-sh'an al-Sudan," File Majlis al-Wuzara'–al-Sudan, no. 3A, DW, 2.

18 The Sudan Irrigation Service was not only independent of Egypt's Ministry of Public Works but also headed by British officials until 1938. In that year, an Egyptian, 'Abd al-Qawi Ahmad Bey, was appointed inspector general of the service for the first time.

19 *al-Akhbar*, 12 November 1924.

20 Amin al-Rafi'i, "al-Hala al-siyasiya al-yawm," *al-Akhbar*, 11 January 1925.

21 al-Dawla al-Misriya, Majlis al-Shuyukh, *Majmu'at Madabit dawr al-in'iqad al-'adi al-rabi'*, vol. 2 (18 November 1926–14 July 1927) (Cairo: al-Matba'a al-Amiriya, 1927), 910.

22 Muhammad Mahmud to Residency, 7 May 1929, Number 66.1/3, File Majlis al-Wuzara'–al-Fatra ba'd 1923–al-Sudan, no. 3J, DW, 1 and 3.

23 al-Dawla al-Misriya, Majlis al-Nuwwab, *Majmu'at Madabit dawr al-in'iqad al-'adi al-thani*, vol. 2 (12 April–8 June 1932), 756.

24 al-Dawla al-Misriya, Majlis al-Nuwwab, *Majmu'at Madabit dawr al-in'iqad al-'adi al-thani*, vol. 2 (12 April–8 June 1932), 789.

25 al-Dawla al-Misriya, Majlis al-Nuwwab, *Majmu'at Madabit dawr al-in'iqad al-'adi al-thani*, vol. 2 (12 April–8 June 1932), 789.

26 al-Dawla al-Misriya, Majlis al-Nuwwab, *Majmu'at Madabit dawr al-in'iqad al-'adi al-thani*, vol. 2 (12 April–8 June 1932), 788. Although Hafiz Ramadan and others were concerned about overall Egyptian control of Nile River developments, and British officials in the Sudan did have some top-echelon influence, Egyptians retained supervisory roles over the actual functioning and monitoring of major projects in the Sudan. In the early 1950s, the Egyptian Ministry of Works could still unequivocally state that Egyptian personnel were in charge of water usage in the Sudan and that all hydraulic activities in the Sudan were still adhering to the 1929 or subsequent agreements. Al-Dawla al-Misriya, Majlis al-Nuwwab, *Majmu'at Madabit dawr al-in'iqad al-'adi al-thani*, vol. 5 (28 August–17 October 1951) (Cairo: al-Matba'a al-Amiriya, 1952), Session 43, 5.

27 al-Dawla al-Misriya, Majlis al-Nuwwab, *Majmu'at Madabit dawr al-in'iqad al-'adi al-thani*, vol. 2 (12 April–8 June 1932), 851.

28 "Mesures à prendre contre l'insuffisance des céréales en Egypte," 9 August 1914, File Majlis al-Wuzara' al-Tamwin, no. 10/4, DW, 1.

29 al-Dawla al-Misriya, Majlis al-Nuwwab, *Majmu'at Madabit dawr al-in'iqad al-'adi al-awwal* (15 March–10 July 1924), 119.

30 Muhammad As'ad Wilaya, "Muzahamat al-qutn al-sudani li-Misr," *al-Jarida al-tijariya al-misriya*, 2 April 1925.

31 *al-Akhbar*, 5 February 1925.

32 al-Ghurfa al-Tijariya al-Misriya bi-l-Iskandariya, *Taqrir al-Ghurfa al-Tijariya al-misriya li-madinat al-Iskandariya 'an a'maliha fi sanat 1925–1926* (Alexandria: Matba'at al-Jarida al-Tijariya al-Misriya, 1926), 69–70.

33 al-Dawla al-Misriya, Majlis al-Shuyukh, *Majmu'at Madabit dawr al-in'iqad al-'adi al-rabi'*, vol. 1 (18 November 1926–14 July 1927), 113. During the Second

World War Egyptians would again complain of too much Sudanese land being used for cotton cultivation, although not because of this crop rivaling Egyptian cotton in international markets. Instead, Egyptians believed Sudanese agriculturalists were doing less than their part in meeting the region's urgent need for essential foodstuffs at that time.

34 *al-Jarida al-tijariya al-misriya*, 20 March 1929.

35 *al-Akhbar*, 17 May 1930.

36 al-Dawla al-Misriya, Majlis al-Nuwwab, *Majmu'at Madabit dawr al-in'iqad al-'adi al-thalith*, vol. 1 (15 December 1932–28 February 1933) (Cairo: al-Matba'a al-Amiriya, 1933), 429.

37 *al-Akhbar*, 12 January 1931.

38 al-Dawla al-Misriya, Majlis al-Shuyukh, *Majmu'at Madabit dawr al-in'iqad al-'adi al-thamin* (17 December 1931–7 July 1932) (Cairo: al-Matba'a al-Amiriya, 1932), 418.

39 A. Hechmat, "Note au Conseil des Ministres," 2 October 1909, Number 288, File Majlis al-Wuzara', no. 10, DW.

40 al-Dawla al-Misriya, Majlis al-Shuyukh, *Majmu'at Madabit dawr al-in'iqad al-'ashir* (14 December 1933–28 June 1934) (Cairo: al-Matba'a al-Amiriya, 1934), 319–20.

41 The Sennar dam is the obvious omission from this list of Nile projects, but this facility was financed by the Condominium administration through a loan guaranteed by the British government.

42 al-Dawla al-Misriya, Majlis al-Nuwwab, *Majmu'at Madabit dawr al-in'iqad al-'adi al-thani*, vol. 2 (12 April–8 June 1932), 856.

43 al-Dawla al-Misriya, Majlis al-Nuwwab, *Majmu'at Madabit dawr al-in'iqad al-'adi al-thani*, vol. 2 (12 April–8 June 1932), 774.

44 al-Dawla al-Misriya, Majlis al-Nuwwab, *Majmu'at Madabit dawr al-in'iqad al-'adi al-thani*, vol. 2 (12 April–8 June 1932), 758.

45 al-Dawla al-Misriya, Majlis al-Shuyukh, *Majmu'at Madabit dawr al-in'iqad al-tasi'* (15 December 1932–27 June 1933) (Cairo: al-Matba'a al-Amiriya, 1933), 710.

46 al-Dawla al-Misriya, Majlis al-Shuyukh, *Majmu'at Madabit dawr al-in'iqad al-'adi al-sadis 'ashara*, vol. 2 (22 April–18 October 1941) (Cairo: al-Matba'a al-Amiriya, 1942), 385.

47 F. Newhouse to Inspector General of Projects, 22 May 1921, Number 15.10/6N/09214, File Majlis al-Wuzara', no. 2/4/B/2, 1, DW.

48 al-Dawla al-Misriya, Majlis al-Nuwwab, *Majmu'at Madabit dawr al-in'iqad al-'adi al-awwal* (15 March–10 July 1924), 188.

49 *al-Akhbar*, 6 August 1931.

50 al-Dawla al-Misriya, Majlis al-Nuwwab, *Majmu'at Madabit dawr al-in'iqad al-'adi al-thani*, vol. 2 (12 April–8 June 1932), 743.

51 al-Dawla al-Misriya, Majlis al-Nuwwab, *Majmu'at Madabit dawr al-in'iqad al-'adi al-thani*, vol. 2 (12 April–8 June 1932), 750.

52 al-Dawla al-Misriya, Majlis al-Nuwwab, *Majmu'at Madabit dawr al-in'iqad al-'adi al-thani*, vol. 1 (17 December 1931–11 April 1932) (Cairo: al-Matba'a al-Amiriya, 1932), 46.

53 al-Dawla al-Misriya, Majlis al-Nuwwab, *Majmu'at Madabit dawr al-in'iqad al-'adi al-thani*, vol. 2 (12 April–8 June 1932), 755.

54 al-Dawla al-Misriya, Majlis al-Nuwwab, *Majmu'at Madabit dawr al-in'iqad al-'adi al-thani*, vol. 2 (12 April–8 June 1932), 786.

55 "Report of the Nile Projects Commission," 1920, File Majlis al-Wuzara', no. 2/4/B/2, 54, DW.

56 Amin al-Rafi'i, "al-Hala al-siyasiya al-yawm—madha yarjri fi al-Sudan wa-ma hiya siyasat al-wizara," *al-Akhbar*, 11 April 1925.

57 al-Dawla al-Misriya, Majlis al-Nuwwab, *Majmu'at Madabit dawr al-in'iqad al-'adi al-thani*, vol. 2 (12 April–8 June 1932), 790.

58 al-Dawla al-Misriya, Majlis al-Shuyukh, *Majmu'at Madabit dawr al-in'iqad al-'adi al-thamin* (17 December 1931–7 July 1932), 386–87.

59 Jean Schatz, "Aperçu général sur les principales cultures égyptiennes," *L'Egypte Contemporaine* 23, no. 138 (1932): 615.

60 'Abdallah Husayn, *al-Sudan min tarikh al-qadim ila rihlat al-ba'tha al-misriya*, vol. 3 (Cairo: al-Matba'a al-Rahmaniya, 1935), 203–204.

61 *al-Siyasa*, 14 June 1937.

62 al-Dawla al-Misriya, Majlis al-Shuyukh, *Majmu'at Madabit dawr al-in'iqad al-'adi al-sadis 'ashar*, vol. 2 (22 April–18 October 1941), 385.

63 Sudan, *Report on the Administration, Finances and Condition of the Sudan in 1933* (London: His Majesty's Stationery Office, 1934), 13.

64 F. Newhouse to Inspector General of Projects, 22 May 1921, File Majlis al-Wuzara', no. 2/4/B/2, 4, DW.

65 "Taqrir nashat al-ghurfa al-tijariya bi-l-Sudan," 12 April 1934, File 'Abdin no. 105, DW, 2.

66 New York Times Company, "Summary of British Argument," 1927, File Majlis al-Wuzara'–al-Fatra ba'd 1923, no. 3A, DW, 2.

67 al-Dawla al-Misriya, Majlis al-Nuwwab, *Majmu'at Madabit dawr al-in'iqad al-'adi al-thalith*, vol. 1 (17 November 1927–27 March 1928) (Cairo: al-Matba'a al-Amiriya, 1928), 39.

68 *al-Akhbar*, 13 July 1935. In addition to the Ethiopian studies and the contradictory earlier reports, in the following year Dr. 'Abd al-Hamid Sa'id encouraged the government to become more interested in the region because of the danger of Italian control there and the potential threat to Egypt's water supplies. al-Dawla al-Misriya, Majlis al-Nuwwab, *Majmu'at Madabit dawr al-in'iqad al-'adi al-awwal*, vol. 1 (23 May–24 August 1936) (Cairo: al-Matba'a al-Amiriya, 1936), 41.

69 Egypt, Ministry of Foreign Affairs, 22 July 1929, Number 1/4/42, File Majlis al-Wuzara'–al-Fatra ba'd 1923, no. 3A, DW, 2.

70 Egyptian Consulate of Addis Ababa to Ministry of Foreign Affairs, 1 June 1935, Number 499, File Majlis al-Wuzara'–al-Fatra ba'd 1923, no. 3A, DW, 2.

71 Abbas, *The Sudan Question*, 82.

72 al-Dawla al-Misriya, Majlis al-Nuwwab, *Majmu'at Madabit dawr al-in'iqad al-'adi al-thalith*, vol. 3 (17 May–27 June 1933) (Cairo: al-Matba'a al-Amiriya, 1933), 1712.

73 al-Dawla al-Misriya, Majlis al-Nuwwab, *Majmu'at Madabit dawr al-in'iqad al-'adi al-thalith*, vol. 3 (17 May–27 June 1933), 1718.

74 *al-Siyasa*, 14 May 1936.

75 The potential of lessening the impact of rising population levels and restricted agricultural resources in Egypt through emigration to the Sudan is explored more fully in chapter five. The present analysis concentrates solely on Egyptian laborers employed on hydraulic works in the Sudan.

76 Sudan, *Report by the Governor-General on the Administration, Finances and Conditions of the Sudan in 1938* (London: His Majesty's Stationery Office, 1939), 126.

77 Sudan, *Report on the Administration, Finances and Conditions of the Sudan in 1937* (London: His Majesty's Stationery Office, 1938), 101.

78 Sudan, *Report on the Finances, Administration and Condition of the Sudan in 1929* (London: His Majesty's Stationery Office, 1930), 116.

79 al-Dawla al-Misriya, Majlis al-Nuwwab, *Majmu'at Madabit dawr al-in'iqad al-'adi al-awwal* (15 March–10 July 1924), 634.

80 *al-Akhbar*, 7 October 1924.

81 Husayn, *al-Sudan*, vol. 3, 220.

82 Muhammad Shafiq Pasha, "Note sur les travaux de contrôle du Nil," 21 April 1921, 9 and 19.

83 Sudan, *Report on the Administration in 1933*, 112.

84 *al-Siyasa*, 14 June 1937.

85 Ahmad Ziwar to Allenby, 12 March 1925, File 'Abdin no. 105, DW.

86 al-Dawla al-Misriya, Majlis al-Nuwwab, *Majmu'at Madabit dawr al-in'iqad al-'adi al-thalith*, vol. 2 (1 March–16 May 1933) (Cairo: al-Matba'a al-Amiriya, 1933), 671.

87 al-Dawla al-Misriya, Majlis al-Shuyukh, *Majmu'at Madabit dawr al-in'iqad al-'adi al-rabi'*, vol. 2 (18 November 1926–14 July 1927), 1134.

88 al-Dawla al-Misriya, Majlis al-Nuwwab, *Majmu'at Madabit dawr al-in'iqad al-'adi al-thalith*, vol. 2 (1 March–16 May 1933), 672.

89 al-Dawla al-Misriya, Majlis al-Shuyukh, *Majmu'at Madabit dawr al-in'iqad al-'ashir* (14 December 1933–28 June 1934), 374.

90 al-Dawla al-Misriya, Majlis al-Nuwwab, *Majmu'at Madabit dawr al-in'iqad al-'adi al-rabi'*, vol. 2 (11 April–29 May 1934) (Cairo: al-Matba'a al-Amiriya, 1934), 905.

91 al-Dawla al-Misriya, Majlis al-Nuwwab, *Majmu'at Madabit dawr al-in'iqad al-'adi al-rabi'*, vol. 2 (11 April–29 May 1934), 906.

92 al-Dawla al-Misriya, Majlis al-Nuwwab, *Majmu'at Madabit dawr al-in'iqad al-'adi al-awwal*, vol. 1 (11 January–17 April 1930) (Cairo: al-Matba'a al-Amiriya, 1931), 581.

93 al-Dawla al-Misriya, Majlis al-Nuwwab, *Majmu'at Madabit dawr al-in'iqad al-'adi al-thalith*, vol. 2 (1 March–16 May 1933), 662.

94 al-Dawla al-Misriya, Majlis al-Nuwwab, *Majmu'at Madabit dawr al-in'iqad al-'adi al-rabi'*, vol. 2 (11 April–29 May 1934), 928.

95 al-Dawla al-Misriya, Majlis al-Nuwwab, *Majmu'at Madabit dawr al-in'iqad al-'adi al-thani*, vol. 2 (27 April–10 June 1937) (Cairo: al-Matba'a al-Amiriya, 1937), 1076.

96 *al-Balagh*, 6 January 1937.

97 al-Dawla al-Misriya, Majlis al-Nuwwab, *Majmu'at Madabit dawr al-in'iqad al-'adi al-thani*, vol. 2 (27 April–10 June 1937), 1082.

98 al-Dawla al-Misriya, Majlis al-Nuwwab, *Majmu'at Madabit dawr al-in'iqad al-'adi al-thani*, vol. 2 (27 April–10 June 1937), 1084.

99 al-Dawla al-Misriya, Majlis al-Nuwwab, *Majmu'at Madabit dawr al-in'iqad ghayr al-'adi li-nazar mu'ahadat al-sadaqa wa-l-tahaluf bayna Misr wa-Baritaniya al-'Uzma* (2–19 September 1936) (Cairo: al-Matba'a al-Amiriya, 1937), 70.

100 H.E. Fass to Makram 'Ubayd Pasha, 3 November 1936, File Majlis al-Wuzara'–al-Fatra ba'd 1923, no. 3J, DW.

101 Miles Lampson to Muhammad Mahmud, 14 April 1938, Number 133/22/38, File Majlis al-Wuzara'–al-Fatra ba'd 1923, no. 3J, DW.

102 al-Dawla al-Misriya, Majlis al-Nuwwab, *Majmu'at Madabit dawr al-in'iqad al-'adi al-awwal*, vol. 1 (12 April–12 July 1938) (Cairo: al-Matba'a al-Amiriya, 1939), 1000–1001.

103 The 1936 treaty had permitted the return of the Egyptian army to the Sudan, but most of the military clauses in the treaty dealt with the British forces in Egypt itself, primarily the movement of units from Cairo to the Suez Canal region. This reassignment of British forces, as well as sending Egyptian units to the Sudan, necessitated construction of new barracks, supply facilities, means of transportation, and so forth. In his study of Egypt's independence movement, Mahmud Zayid wrote that Egypt paid three-quarters of the total expenses associated with barracks construction in these military transfers. Zayid, *Egypt's Struggle for Independence*, 176. Although most of the expenses were a result of repositioning forces within Egypt, the total financial commitments to the military became increasingly burdensome. Charles Issawi noted of Egypt's military budget, "Since the Treaty of 1936 it has risen from under £E 2,000,000 to over £E 7,000,000." Issawi, *Egypt*, 142.

104 al-Dawla al-Misriya, Majlis al-Nuwwab, *Majmu'at Madabit dawr al-in'iqad ghayr al-'adi li-nazar mu'ahadat al-sadaqa wa-l-tahaluf bayna Misr wa-Baritanya al-'Uzma* (2–19 September 1936), 84.

105 al-Dawla al-Misriya, Majlis al-Nuwwab, *Majmu'at Madabit dawr al-in'iqad al-'adi al-thalith*, vol. 3 (17 May–27 June 1933), 1266.

106 Kenneth J. Perkins, *Port Sudan: The Evolution of a Colonial City* (Boulder, CO: Westview Press, 1993), 48.

107 Sir John Carmichael, "Economic Development in the Sudan, 1899–1956," in *The Condominium Remembered: Proceedings of the Durham Sudan Historical Records Conference*, Vol. 2: *The Transformation of the Old Order in the Sudan*, edited by Deborah Lavin (Durham: Centre for Middle Eastern and Islamic Studies, 1993), 4.

108 al-Dawla al-Misriya, Majlis al-Shuyukh, *Majmu'at Madabit dawr al-in'iqad al-'adi al-khamis* (17 November 1927–28 June 1928) (Cairo: al-Matba'a al-Amiriya, 1928), 303.

109 al-Dawla al-Misriya, Majlis al-Shuyukh, *Majmu'at Madabit dawr al-in'iqad al-'adi al-rabi'*, vol. 2 (18 November 1926–14 July 1927), 706.

110 Abbas, *The Sudan Question*, 66–67.

111 *al-Siyasa*, 1 July 1936.

112 Daly, *Imperial Sudan*, 54.

113 H.E. Fass to Makram 'Ubayd Pasha, 3 November 1936.

114 H.E. Fass to Makram 'Ubayd Pasha, 3 November 1936.

115 al-Dawla al-Misriya, Majlis al-Nuwwab, *Majmu'at Madabit dawr al-in'iqad ghayr al-'adi li-nazar mu'ahadat al-sadaqa wa-l-tahaluf bayna Misr wa-Baritanya al-'Uzma* (2–19 September 1936), 70.

116 al-Dawla al-Misriya, Majlis al-Nuwwab, *Majmu'at Madabit dawr al-in'iqad ghayr al-'adi li-nazar mu'ahadat al-sadaqa wa-l-tahaluf bayna Misr wa-Baritanya al-'Uzma* (2–19 September 1936), 69.

117 H.E. Fass to Makram 'Ubayd Pasha, 3 November 1936.

118 *al-Ahram*, 24 November 1939.

119 The Second World War delayed the beginning of debt repayments, but even just prior to the 1953 agreement, which gave the Sudan the right to political self-determination (and eventually independence), only LE150,000 of the roughly LE5 million total debt had been repaid. L.A. Fabunmi, *The Sudan in Anglo-Egyptian Relations: A Case Study of Power Politics 1800–1956* (Westport, CT: Greenwood, 1973), 135.

120 al-Dawla al-Misriya, Majlis al-Nuwwab, *Majmu'at Madabit dawr al-in'iqad ghayr al-'adi li-nazar mu'ahadat al-sadaqa wa-l-tahaluf bayna Misr wa-Baritanya al-'Uzma* (2–19 September 1936), 70. Makram 'Ubayd, a key figure among the Wafdist leadership for years, played the leading role in debt resolution negotiations with British officials of the Condominium administration. In this role, he became the object of much criticism in the local press. For a good summary of the various criticisms, see especially articles of 4–5 November 1938 in *al-Ahram*.

121 al-Dawla al-Misriya, Majlis al-Shuyukh, *Majmu'at Madabit dawr al-in'iqad ghayr al-'adi li-nazar mu'ahadat al-sadaqa wa-l-tahaluf bayna Misr wa-Baritanya al-'Uzma* (2–19 September 1936) (Cairo: al-Matba'a al-Amiriya, 1937), 74.

122 *al-Ahram*, 22 May 1939.

Notes to Chapter 3

1 al-Dawla al-Misriya, Majlis al-Nuwwab, *Majmu'at Madabit dawr al-in'iqad al-'adi al-thani*, vol. 4 (1–25 July 1946) (Cairo: al-Matba'a al-Amiriya, 1947), 3220.
2 Ahmad Ziwar to Allenby, 25 January 1925, File 'Abdin no. 104, DW, 2.
3 C.W. Spinks, inspector general, Ministry of War, 3 January 1925, File Majlis al-Wuzara' al-Sudan, no. 3J, DW.
4 Fabunmi, *The Sudan in Anglo–Egyptian Relations*, 99.
5 al-Dawla al-Misriya, Majlis al-Nuwwab, *Majmu'at Madabit dawr al-in'iqad al-'adi al-thani*, vol. 3 (30 May–8 August 1939) (Cairo: al-Matba'a al-Amiriya, 1940), 3350.
6 Although the 'official' reason for staff reductions at this time was the deteriorating financial situation of the Sudanese government, the results of these measures meshed well with the Condominium administration's goal of greater reliance on 'native administration.' This policy had been increasingly pursued since 1924 and was designed to encourage greater reliance on the 'traditional,' rural, tribal/religious leaders of the country rather than the urban, educated, civil servant class, who British officials feared were more susceptible to Egyptian political 'intriguers.'
7 al-Dawla al-Misriya, Majlis al-Nuwwab, *Majmu'at Madabit dawr al-in'iqad al-'adi al-thani*, vol. 1 (17 December 1931–11 April 1932), 448.
8 *al-Siyasa*, 28 July 1936.
9 al-Dawla al-Misriya, Majlis al-Nuwwab, *Majmu'at Madabit dawr al-in'iqad al-'adi al-thani*, vol. 1 (19 November 1938–27 February 1939) (Cairo: al-Matba'a al-Amiriya, 1940), 1061.
10 al-Dawla al-Misriya, Majlis al-Nuwwab, *Majmu'at Madabit dawr al-in'iqad al-'adi al-thani*, vol. 1 (19 November 1938–27 February 1939), 1061–62.
11 *al-Siyasa*, 18 August 1936.
12 al-Dawla al-Misriya, Majlis al-Nuwwab, *Majmu'at Madabit dawr al-in'iqad al-'adi al-awwal*, vol. 1 (30 March–27 July 1942) (Cairo: al-Matba'a al-Amiriya, 1942), 308.
13 There is plenty of evidence in Egyptian media and government reports that the Egyptian officials working in the Sudan constituted an important market. For example, see *al-Akhbar*, 19 January 1935; *al-Akhbar*, 30 November 1935; Ahmad 'Abd al-Wahhab, "al-Nata'ij al-iqtisadiya li-l-mu'ahada," *Majallat Ghurfat al-Qahira*, June 1937, 18; Husayn, *al-Sudan*, vol. 3, 168.
14 al-Dawla al-Misriya, Majlis al-Nuwwab, *Majmu'at Madabit dawr al-in'iqad al-'adi al-awwal*, vol. 1 (18 January–5 June 1945), 63.
15 Ali Taha, *The Anglo–Egyptian Dispute over the Sudan*, 19.
16 Berque, *Egypt*, 655.
17 Huddleston to Nahhas, 18 May 1944, 3.
18 Egypt, *Egypt–Sudan: Collection of Documents* (Cairo: Government Press, 1947), 49.

19 *Majallat Ghurfat al-Iskandariya*, April 1939, 27.
20 *Majallat Ghurfat al-Qahira*, September 1938, 124.
21 al-Dawla al-Misriya, Majlis al-Shuyukh, *Majmu'at Madabit dawr al-in'iqad ghayr al-'adi li nazar mu'ahadat al-sadaqa wa-l-tahaluf bayna Misr wa-Baritanya al-'Uzma* (2–19 November 1936) (Cairo: al-Matba'a al-Amiriya, 1937), 36.
22 *al-Ahram*, 13 January 1939.
23 al-Dawla al-Misriya, Majlis al-Shuyukh, *Majmu'at Madabit wa-malahiq dawr al-in'iqad al-'adi*, vol. 25 (16 January–15 May 1950) (Cairo: al-Matba'a al-Amiriya, 1951), 80.
24 al-Dawla al-Misriya, Majlis al-Nuwwab, *Majmu'at Madabit dawr al-in'iqad al-'adi al-awwal*, vol. 1 (18 January–5 June 1945), 398.
25 *al-Ahram*, 20 November 1939.
26 al-Dawla al-Misriya, Majlis al-Shuyukh, *Majmu'at al-malahiq li-madabit dawr al-in'iqad al-'adi*, vol. 17 (10 November 1941–9 September 1942) (Cairo: al-Matba'a al-Amiriya, 1951), 58.
27 Tussun to Nahhas, 10 September 1942, File Majlis al-Wuzara'–al-Fatra ba'd 1923, no. 3D, DW, 1.
28 *al-Ahram*, 6 October 1943.
29 Huddleston to Nahhas, 18 May 1944, 5.
30 Nahhas to Huddleston, 1 January 1944, File Majlis al-Wuzara'–al-Fatra ba'd 1923, no. 3D, DW, 3.
31 Huddleston to Nahhas, 18 May 1944, 5.
32 *al-Ahram*, 4 July 1939 and 17 August 1939.
33 al-Dawla al-Misriya, Majlis al-Nuwwab, *Majmu'at Madabit dawr al-in'iqad al-'adi al-awwal*, vol. 2 (11 June–6 August 1945) (Cairo: al-Matba'a al-Amiriya, 1946), 1640.
34 *al-Ahram*, 15 August 1939.
35 *al-Ahram*, 14 December 1938.
36 *al-Ahram*, 3 February 1939.
37 *al-Jarida al-tijariya al-misriya*, 20 April 1941. Additionally, there was a separate facility for the permanent exhibition of Egyptian manufactures established prior to the Second World War, with a director who more consistently resided in the Sudan. These institutional arrangements designed to encourage Egyptian–Sudanese commercial exchange are addressed separately later in this chapter.
38 *al-Jarida al-tijariya al-misriya*, 30 July 1938.
39 *al-Ahram*, 28 July 1939.
40 *al-Ahram*, 31 July 1939.
41 *al-Ahram*, 26 August 1943.
42 *al-Ahram*, 26 August 1943.
43 al-Dawla al-Misriya, Majlis al-Shuyukh, *Majmu'at al-malahiq li-madabit dawr al-in'iqad al-'adi*, vol. 24 (18 November 1948–1 November 1949) (Cairo: al-Matba'a al-Amiriya, 1950), 77.

44 Ministry of Commerce and Industry to Council of Ministers, "Mudhakkirat marfu'a li-Majlis al-Wuzara'," May 1946, File 'Abdin no. 26–Wizarat al-Tijara wa-l-Sina'a, DW.

45 al-Dawla al-Misriya, Wizarat al-Tijara wa-l-Sina'a, *al-Sudan, a'mal al-ba'athat al-misriya wa-l-lajna al-da'ima li-l-Sudan min sanat 1935 ila sanat 1938* (Cairo: al-Matba'a al-Amiriya, 1938), 13.

46 Daly, *Imperial Sudan*, 58.

47 al-Dawla al-Misriya, Wizarat al-Tijara wa-l-Sina'a, *A'mal al-ba'athat al-misriya*, 12.

48 The following biographical information on Fu'ad Abaza and his family is derived from the work of 'Abdallah Husayn, a member of the 1935 Egyptian economic mission to the Sudan. Husayn published his detailed study of conditions in the Sudan, the mission's activities, and extensive narratives on the members of this mission shortly after completion of its work. Husayn, *al-Sudan*, vol. 3, 35–44.

49 Fu'ad Abaza, "al-Ba'tha al-misriya fi al-Sudan, sanat 1935," speech at the Royal Geographical Society in Cairo, 25 April 1935 (Cairo, 1937), 4.

50 The minute details of all of the mission's activities in the Sudan can be found in Husayn's *al-Sudan*, vol. 3. His description of the mission's activities encompasses almost the entire third volume of the work.

51 Abaza, "al-Ba'tha al-misriya fi al-Sudan, sanat 1935," 5.

52 Sudan, *Report on the Administration, Finances and Condition of the Sudan in 1935* (London: His Majesty's Stationery Office, 1936), 11.

53 *al-Akhbar*, 13 February 1935.

54 *al-Siyasa*, 27 November 1937.

55 Most analyses of the interwar years include the Egyptian government as an integral—extremely influential—participant in economic developments. For instance, Davis's *Challenging Colonialism* explores the origins, composition, objectives, and success—or not—of the Misr group's role in Egypt's progress. His study appropriately highlights the extensive state involvement in this conglomerate's nationalist economic pursuits. Similarly, a central element of Robert Vitalis' analysis of the Abbud group and its interactions with the Misr and Yahya groups in *When Capitalists Collide* was the competition for state 'favors,' especially the struggle over government concessions.

56 Abaza, "Mudhakkira," 19.

57 *al-Jarida al-tijariya al-misriya*, 12 January 1939. The first chair of the committee was Ahmad 'Abd al-Wahab, a known advocate of protectionist policies, who died after only four meetings had been held. Davis, *Challenging Colonialism*, 153.

58 *Majallat Ghurfat al-Iskandariya*, February 1939, 20.

59 Deeb, "Bank Misr," 75.

60 Hiroshi Shimizu, *Anglo-Japanese Trade Rivalry in the Middle East in the Interwar Period* (Reading: Ithaca Press, 1986), 78.

61 *al-Ahram*, 9 February 1939.
62 *al-Ahram*, 26 March 1939.
63 *al-Jarida al-tijariya al-misriya*, 11 February 1939.
64 *Majallat Ghurfat al-Iskandariya*, February 1939, 25–26.
65 *al-Ahram*, 27 February 1939 (emphasis added).
66 *al-Ahram*, 8 February 1939. Since January 1938 the committee had been a part of the government, but *al-Ahram*'s use of the phrase "government committee" simply reflected the apparent diminution of private-sector representation.
67 *al-Ahram*, 10 February 1939 (emphasis added).
68 *al-Ahram*, 2 May 1939 (emphasis added).
69 *al-Ahram*, 12 May 1939.
70 *al-Ahram*, 23 February 1939.
71 Abaza, "Mudhakkira," 20.
72 *Majallat Ghurfat al-Iskandariya*, October 1938, 15–16.
73 *al-Ahram*, 13 July 1941 (emphasis added).
74 *al-Ahram*, 16 June 1939.
75 *Majallat Ghurfat al-Qahira*, September 1939, 939.
76 'Abdallah Fakri Abaza, *Buhuth iqtisadiya 'an al-Sudan*, Cairo, [1940], 19.
77 "Mahdar jalsat al-lajna al-da'ima li-l-Sudan al-mun'aqada fi 4 Yunyu sanat 1938," File 'Abdin no. 105, DW, 3.
78 *Majallat Ghurfat al-Qahira*, March 1938, 123–24.
79 *al-Akhbar*, 7 March 1935.
80 Abaza, "Mudhakkira," 12.
81 "Mahdar jalsat al-lajna al-da'ima li-l-Sudan al-mun'aqada fi 31 Yanayir sanat 1938," 2.
82 Abaza, *Buhuth iqtisadiya 'an al-Sudan*, 10.
83 Tutunji to Permanent Committee, 26 June 1938, File 'Abdin no. 105, DW, 1–2. In the following discussion and in subsequent references, the 'Khartoum office' is the term most often given to the office of the director of the exhibition of Khartoum, whose duties were broader than merely managing the exhibition.
84 *Majallat Ghurfat al-Qahira*, May 1937, 87.
85 Tutunji to Permanent Committee, 26 June 1938, 2.
86 "Mahdar jalsat al-lajna al-da'ima li-l-Sudan al-mun'aqada fi 31 Yunyu sanat 1938," 4.
87 *al-Ahram*, 4 December 1938.
88 *al-Ahram*, 16 July 1939.
89 Abaza, *Buhuth iqtisadiya 'an al-Sudan*, 15.
90 *al-Ahram*, 10 July 1939.
91 *Majallat Ghurfat al-Qahira*, May 1938, 71.
92 *al-Ahram*, 26 July 1940.
93 *al-Ahram*, 17 July 1941.

94 *al-Jarida al-tijariya al-misriya*, 15 March 1942.

95 *Majallat Ghurfat al-Iskandariya*, January 1943, 14.

96 Based on statistics from the February issues of *Majallat Ghurfat al-Qahira*, the value of exhibit sales for 1938 was LE1,648, which rose to LE3,453 by 1941.

97 *al-Ahram*, 29 March 1944.

98 *Majallat Ghurfat al-Qahira*, June 1944, 456–57.

99 Mahmud Zaki, "Taqrir," File Majlis al-Wuzara'–al-Fatra ba'd 1923, no. 3D, DW, 18.

100 Rushdi, "Mashru' mu'ahada bi-sh'an al-Sudan," 1.

101 *al-Akhbar*, 19 October 1935.

102 *al-Akhbar*, 1 May 1935.

103 al-Dawla al-Misriya, Majlis al-Nuwwab, *Majmu'at Madabit dawr al-in'iqad al-'adi al-awwal*, vol. 1 (12 April–12 July 1938), 565.

104 *Majallat Ghurfat al-Qahira*, September 1936, 89.

105 *Majallat Ghurfat al-Iskandariya*, January 1939, 15.

106 "Mahdar jalsat al-lajna al-da'ima li-l-Sudan al-mun'aqada fi 4 Yunyu sanat 1938," 1.

107 al-Dawla al-Misriya, Majlis al-Nuwwab, *Majmu'at Madabit dawr al-in'iqad al-'adi al-awwal*, vol. 1 (12 April–12 July 1938), 935.

108 "Mahdar jalsat al-lajna al-da'ima li-l-Sudan al-mun'aqada fi 31 Yanayir sanat 1938," 4.

109 *al-Jarida al-tijariya al-misriya*, 26 January 1939.

110 al-Dawla al-Misriya, Majlis al-Nuwwab, *Majmu'at Madabit dawr al-in'iqad al-'adi al-awwal*, vol. 1 (12 April–12 July 1938), 935.

111 Abaza, *Buhuth iqtisadiya 'an al-Sudan*, 13.

112 'Abd al-Rahman Fakri, "Mawdu' al-tamwin," 19 September 1938, File 'Abdin no. 105, DW, 1.

113 Abaza, *Buhuth iqtisadiya 'an al-Sudan*, 178.

114 *Majallat Ghurfat al-Qahira*, February 1940, 207.

115 Hamid Sultan, "Masa'il mutannawi'a 'an al-Sudan," File Majlis al-Wuzara', no. 3H, DW, 16.

116 Zaki, "Taqrir," 2–3.

117 Sudan, *Report on the Administration of the Sudan, for the Years 1939–1941* (Khartoum: McCorquodale and Co., 1950), 30.

118 Sudan, *Report on the Administration of the Sudan in 1946* (Khartoum: McCorquodale and Co., 1948), 86.

119 Sudan, *Annual Report of the Department of Economics and Trade, 1945* (Khartoum: McCorquodale and Co., 1945), 4.

120 Zaki, "Taqrir," 6.

121 Mahmud Zaki, "Kitab ila al-hakim al-'am," File Majlis al-Wuzara'–al-Fatra ba'd 1923, no. 3D, DW, 2.

122 Sultan, "Masa'il mutannawi'a 'an al-Sudan," 16.

123 Abaza, *Buhuth iqtisadiya 'an al-Sudan*, 177.

124 Zaki, "Taqrir," 2.

125 al-Dawla al-Misriya, Majlis al-Nuwwab, *Majmu'at Madabit dawr al-in'iqad al-'adi al-awwal*, vol. 1 (30 March–27 July 1942), 481.

126 Zaki, "Taqrir," 3.

127 Sudan, *Annual Report of the Department of Economics and Trade, 1945*, 5.

128 Zaki, "Taqrir," 2.

129 Zaki, "Taqrir," 2.

130 Huddleston to Nahhas, 18 May 1944, 3.

131 Zaki, "Kitab ila al-hakim al-'am," 4. Transportation restrictions, specifically what maritime or rail/road facilities were available, were critical in the level of Nile Valley commercial interdependence during the Second World War. This aspect of Egyptian–Sudanese economic relations merits its own analysis—included in the next chapter.

132 *al-Jarida al-tijariya al-misriya*, 27 June 1944.

133 Sudan, *Reports by His Majesty's High Commissioner on the Finances, Administration, and Condition of Egypt and the Soudan for the Year 1920* (London: His Majesty's Stationery Office, 1921), 51.

134 Hasan Saqr, "al-Sudan—Tijarat al-'aqmisha wa-l-mansujat al-qutniya fi al-aswaq al-sudaniya," *Majallat Ghurfat al-Qahira*, June 1939, 755.

135 'Ali Mawardi, "al-Tabadul al-tijari bayna Misr wa-l-Sudan," *Majallat Ghurfat al-Qahira*, April 1940, 361.

136 United Nations Security Council, *Verbatim Records*, 33.

137 *al-Majalla al-tijariya al-nubiya*, 3 April 1924, 182.

138 *al-Akhbar*, 13 February 1935.

139 *al-Siyasa*, 21 June 1935.

140 *Majallat Ghurfat al-Iskandariya*, January 1940, 17–18.

141 Mawardi, "al-Tabadul al-tijari bayna Misr wa-l-Sudan," 367.

142 For instance, in 1920 the Sudanese administration doubled the "postal registration fee on inland and Egyptian traffic." Sudan, *Reports by His Majesty's High Commissioner for the Year 1920*, 115. During the post-1935 era of increased Egyptian involvement in the Sudan these duties were raised again. *al-Balagh*, 29 January 1937, 1.

143 *al-Majalla al-tijariya al-nubiya*, 17 July 1921, 10–12.

144 *al-Siyasa*, 24 August 1936.

145 *al-Siyasa*, 28 April 1935.

146 *al-Siyasa*, 14 October 1935.

147 *al-Ahram*, 23 April 1938.

148 "Taqrir al-Ghurfa al-Tijariya al-Sudaniya 'an al-mawdu'at wa-l-muqtarahat al-lati tanawalaha al-bahth athna'a ziyarat al-lajna al-da'ima li-l-Khartum fi Maris sanat 1938," File 'Abdin no. 105, DW, 3. In the minutes of the 4 June meeting of the permanent committee, it was determined that the committee would subscribe to four Sudanese papers.

149 Abaza, *Buhuth iqtisadiya 'an al-Sudan*, 109.
150 *al-Jarida al-tijariya al-misriya*, 3 December 1939.
151 *Majallat Ghurfat al-Qahira*, September 1938, 124.
152 *al-Jarida al-tijariya al-misriya*, 3 December 1939.
153 *Majallat Ghurfat al-Qahira*, February 1939, 196.
154 "Mahdar al-ijtima' al-awwal li-lajnat al-Sudan al-Musafira," File 'Abdin no. 105, DW, 1.
155 Abaza, "al-Ba'tha al-misriya fi al-Sudan, sanat 1935," 16.
156 *al-Jarida al-tijariya al-misriya*, 17 June 1939.
157 "Mahdar jalsat al-lajna al-da'ima li-l-Sudan al-mun'aqada fi 28 Yunyu sanat 1938," 5.
158 *al-Jarida al-tijariyh al-misriya*, 8 December 1938.
159 Abaza, "al-Ba'tha al-misriya fi al-Sudan, sanat 1935," 19.
160 "Mahdar jalsat al-lajna al-da'ima li-l-Sudan al-mun'aqada fi 4 Yunyu sanat 1938," 4.
161 Abaza, *Buhuth iqtisadiya 'an al-Sudan*, 13.
162 *Majallat Ghurfat al-Qahira*, October 1937, 73–74.
163 Mawardi, "al-Tabadul al-tijari bayna Misr wa-l-Sudan," 369.
164 *Majallat Ghurfat al-Qahira*, February 1947, 172. Although the Cairo chamber publication rarely delved into the political struggles over the Sudan, in this article Mahmud Haykal Bey, director of the commercial section of the chamber, commented that some of the more harmful recent incidents were perpetrated by "elements hostile to the economic reputation of Egypt" and that trade relations were still subject to political intrigues in the Sudan. *Majallat Ghurfat al-Qahira*, August 1950, 850.
165 *Majallat Ghurfat al-Qahira*, August 1951, 199.
166 *Majallat Ghurfat al-Qahira*, December 1947, 1274; *Majallat Ghurfat al-Qahira*, May 1952, 510.
167 Allenby to Zaghlul, 12 May 1924, Number 14327/17, File Majlis al-Wuzara'–al-Fatra ba'd 1923, no. 3J, DW, 2.
168 *al-Siyasa*, 22 August 1935.
169 Sudan, *Report on the Administration, Finances and Condition of the Sudan in 1936* (London: His Majesty's Stationery Office, 1937), 41.
170 *Majallat Ghurfat al-Iskandariya*, December 1948, 11.
171 *Majallat Ghurfat al-Iskandariya*, December 1948, 14.
172 *Majallat Ghurfat al-Iskandariya*, March 1949, 95 (emphasis added). This report does acknowledge that the exhibition at least stimulated general interest in the Sudan.

Notes to Chapter 4

1 Abaza, *Buhuth iqtisadiya 'an al-Sudan*, 11.
2 Gouvernement Égyptien, Rapport de la Commission du Commerce et de l'Industrie (Edition Provisoire Confidentielle) (Cairo: Imprimerie Nationale, 1917), File Majlis al-Wuzara', no. 19, DW 19.

3 al-Dawla al-Misriya, Wizarat al-Tijara wa-l-Sina'a, *A'mal al-ba'athat al-misriya*, 14.
4 Sudan, *The Revised Edition of the Laws of the Sudan, from 1899 to 1926 (1st June)* (London: McCorquodale and Co., 1926), 559.
5 *al-Akhbar*, 18 September 1922.
6 Sudan, *The Revised Edition of the Laws*, 562–63.
7 "Taqrir nashat al-Ghurfa al-Tijariya bi-l-Sudan," 16.
8 *al-Akhbar*, 7 March 1935.
9 "Mahdar jalsat al-lajna al-da'ima li-l-Sudan al-mun'aqada fi 26 Fibrayir sanat 1938," 3.
10 "Mahdar jalsat al-lajna al-da'ima li-l-Sudan al-mun'aqada fi 26 Fibrayir sanat 1938," 3.
11 *al-Ahram*, 22 July 1940.
12 No fees were imposed on individuals obtaining transit visas from the Condominium administration, but the Egyptian government was collecting duties on some travel documentation. The Cairo Chamber of Commerce reported in 1942 that it had assigned a subcommittee the task of investigating the possibility of lifting travel restrictions and "the lowering of fees of passports." *Majallat Ghurfat al-Qahira*, March 1942, 290.
13 Ahmad Zaki Sa'd, "Mudhakkira," July 1943, File Majlis al-Wuzara'–al-Fatra ba'd 1923, no. 3D, DW, 1.
14 *Majallat Ghurfat al-Iskandariya*, January 1949.
15 *Majallat Ghurfat al-Qahira*, June/July 1950, 701.
16 Huddleston to Nahhas, 18 May 1944, 1.
17 "Taqrir al-ghurfah," 2.
18 Zaki, "Taqrir," 20–21. It should also be noted that these foreign residents were mainly Levantines, requesting easier travel to and from Palestine and Syria.
19 Zaki, "Taqrir," 21.
20 *al-Akhbar*, 30 April 1927.
21 Sudan, *Report on the Administration in 1946*, 17. The governor-general reported that 200 of 631 passports issued that year had been given to foreign residents.
22 Abaza, *Buhuth iqtisadiya 'an al-Sudan*, 105.
23 Abaza, *Buhuth iqtisadiya 'an al-Sudan*, 106.
24 Abaza, *Buhuth iqtisadiya 'an al-Sudan*.
25 For a listing of the transport rates during this period of most intensive Egyptian efforts to increase trade with the Sudan (1935–39), see Husayn, *al-Sudan*, vol. 3, 313; al-Dawla al-Misriya, Majlis al-Nuwwab, *Majmu'at madabit dawr al-in'iqad al-'adi al-awwal*, vol. 1 (23 May–24 August 1936), 364. Additionally, if passenger rates were too steep the result would be not only less trade with and travel to and from the Sudan, but also less use of government transportation facilities generally—with subsequently less revenue produced. Local merchants made precisely this argument shortly after the First World War, when the Egyptian government raised railroad and telegraph rates. In

1922 merchants informed the Council of Ministers that these changes would force them to rely on foreign transport companies. Al-Ghurfa al-Tijariya al-Misriya bi-l-Iskandariya, *Taqrir al-Ghurfa al-Tijariya al-Misriya li-madinat al-Iskandariya 'an a'maliha fi sanat 1922–1923* (Alexandria: Imprimerie Publicité Égyptienne, 1923), 18–19.

26 "Taqrir al-Ghurfa," 3. This report noted the desire for reductions specifically for traders, yet the need for seasonal reductions may imply that their travel to Egypt was for other than commercial purposes, possibly escaping the Sudan's inclement summer weather.

27 *Majallat Ghurfat al-Iskandariya*, October 1938, 19.

28 *Majallat Ghurfat al-Qahira*, September 1939, 892. A later report from the economic expert elaborated on the various passenger rate reductions. He stated that the Egyptian railroad authorities were granting Sudanese students and government employees larger reductions, while Sudanese Railways was "granting traders who do business with it (the Sudan) of at least 500LE per year a reduction of 50 percent of the costs of travel to Egypt." *al-Ahram*, 25 December 1939.

29 Sudan, *The Revised Edition of the Laws*, 563.

30 Sudan, *The Sudan: A Record of Progress, 1898–1947* (Khartoum: Sudan Surveys Department, 1947), 12.

31 Sultan, "Masa'il mutannawi'a 'an al-Sudan," 2–3.

32 Sudan, *The Revised Edition of the Laws*, 571.

33 Sudan, *The Revised Edition of the Laws*, 569–70.

34 Sudan, *The Revised Edition of the Laws*, 565–68.

35 Sudan, *The Revised Edition of the Laws*, 564.

36 *al-Ahram*, 30 April 1938.

37 Sudan, *The Revised Edition of the Laws*, 287.

38 *Majallat Ghurfat al-Iskandariya*, January 1941, 23.

39 *al-Ahram*, 21 May 1939; *al-Ahram*, 31 July 1940 (emphasis added).

40 *al-Ahram*, 23 September 1933.

41 *Majallat Ghurfat al-Qahira*, September 1937, 106.

42 *al-Ahram*, 29 August 1939.

43 Zaki, "Taqrir," 22. In comparison to the two days spent traveling in steamships between Wadi Halfa and Shellal, the much greater distances from Cairo to Shellal and from Wadi Halfa to Khartoum took approximately sixty hours total by railroad.

44 *al-Ahram*, 11 December 1939.

45 *Majallat Ghurfat al-Iskandariya*, June 1941, 9.

46 *al-Ahram*, 24 February 1946.

47 Sudan Agency to Under Secretary of State, Ministry of Agriculture, 16 February 1915, File Majlis al-Wuzara', no. 3A, DW.

48 *al-Jarida al-tijariya al-misriya*, 11 June 1934.

49 *al-Ahram*, 23 May 1939.

50 *Majallat Ghurfat al-Qahira*, June/July 1950, 703.

51 Also in 1937, Law No. 14, a tax reform measure, was adopted, which allowed taxes on interest and dividends, commercial or industrial wages/salaries, and inheritances. Tignor, *State*, 152.

52 "The Traders' Tax Ordinance, 1913," File Majlis al-Wuzara', al-Sudan–al-Qawanin, no. 11W, DW, 1–2. It is interesting to note that Sudanese economic activities that were exempt from taxation were precisely those to which Egyptians had least access, such as land ownership or cultivation. The next chapter examines the difficulties for Egyptians in obtaining control of land, the rental profits from which were exempt under the Traders' Tax Ordinance. In addition, profits under LE24 were exempt, but the major commercial undertakings desired by Egyptians would not have fallen into this category.

53 *al-Akhbar*, 7 October 1924.

54 Sudan, *Report on the Finances, Administration and Conditions of the Sudan in 1928* (London: His Majesty's Stationery Office, 1929), 57.

55 Sudan, *Report on the Administration of the Sudan for the Years 1942–1944* (Khartoum: McCorquodale and Co., 1950), 22.

56 *Laws of the Sudan*, vol. 2, 919.

57 Sudan, *Report on the Finances, Administration and Condition of the Sudan in 1930* (London: His Majesty's Stationery Office, 1931), 84.

58 Emphasis in the analysis above has been mainly on Condominium administrative measures, as Egyptians most frequently complained of these policies and procedures. However, the Egyptian government also rarely instituted changes that assisted economic relations with the Sudan at the expense of its own treasury.

59 Egypt, *Egypt–Sudan: Collection of Documents*, 5.

60 Fabunmi, *The Sudan in Anglo–Egyptian Relations*, 55.

61 Sudan, *Reports by His Majesty's High Commissioner for the Year 1920*, 120.

62 Sudan, *Reports by His Majesty's High Commissioner for the Year 1920*, 120.

63 This 30 percent figure is an underestimate based on figures in the annual reports of the governor-general of the Sudan. M.W. Daly has given a 33 percent figure for the same items during the Depression years. Daly, *Imperial Sudan*, 87.

64 United Nations Security Council, *Verbatim Records*, 122.

65 Egypt, *Egypt–Sudan: Collection of Documents*, 5.

66 Abbas, *The Sudan Question*, 51.

67 Sudan, *The Revised Edition of the Laws*, 264.

68 Egypt, *Egypt–Sudan: Collection of Documents*, 5.

69 Taha al-Sa'id Nasr, "al-Nizam al-hali li-idarat al-Sudan," Number 43, File Majlis al-Wuzara', no. 3H, DW, 10.

70 al-Dawla al-Misriya, Majlis al-Nuwwab, *Majmu'at Madabit dawr al-in'iqad al-'adi al-awwal*, vol. 1 (23 May–24 August 1936), 610.

71 al-Dawla al-Misriya, Majlis al-Nuwwab, *Majmu'at Madabit dawr al-in'iqad al-'adi al-awwal* (15 March–10 July 1924), 864. Taha al-Sa'id Nasr also made note of the Condominium's lack of adherence to Article 7 when he was preparing documents for Egypt's presentation before the United Nations Security Council in 1947. He wrote that "the jurisdiction of this article has been violated when import duties were imposed in the Sudan higher than those imposed in Egypt. And duties were imposed on commodities sent from Egypt to the Sudan." Taha al-Sa'id Nasr, "al-Nizam al-hali li-idarat al-Sudan," 10.

72 Abaza, *Buhuth iqtisadiya 'an al-Sudan*, 199–200.

73 This percentage was determined from the ratio of the total adjustment payments sent to the Sudan over the previous four years to the total value of all goods sent to the Sudan during the same period. For instance, in 1924 Egypt paid 43 millièmes on every one pound worth of goods sent to the Sudan, according to this formula. al-Dawla al-Misriya, Majlis al-Nuwwab, *Majmu'at Madabit dawr al-in'iqad al-'adi al-awwal*, vol. 1 (15 March–10 July 1924), 864.

74 al-Dawla al-Misriya, Majlis al-Nuwa, *Majmu'at Madabit dawr al-in'iqad al-'adi al-awwal*, vol. 1 (12 April–12 July 1938), 622.

75 *al-Jarida al-tijariya al-misriya*, 5 May 1925.

76 al-Dawla al-Misriya, Majlis al-Nuwwab, *Majmu'at Madabit dawr al-in'iqad al-'adi al-awwal*, vol. 1 (15 March–10 July 1924), 668.

77 al-Dawla al-Misriya, Majlis al-Nuwwab, *Majmu'at Madabit dawr al-in'iqad al-'adi al-awwal*, vol. 1 (15 March–10 July 1924), 864.

78 al-Dawla al-Misriya, Majlis al-Nuwwab, *Majmu'at Madabit dawr al-in'iqad al-'adi al-awwal*, vol. 1 (15 March–10 July 1924), 616.

79 Sudan, *The Revised Edition of the Laws*, 312.

80 Sudan, *The Revised Edition of the Laws.*

81 Sudan, *Report on the Administration, Finances and Condition of the Sudan in 1938* (London: His Majesty's Stationery Office, 1939), 36–37.

82 A. Landhof to Said Zulficar Pasha, 19 September 1919, al-Maliya–Jamarik, File 'Abdin no. 257, DW, 1.

83 Tignor, *State*, 110.

84 Sudan, *Reports by His Majesty's High Commissioner for the Year 1920*, 41. At times payment of duties in kind left the government with quantities of commodities the value of which was falling.

85 M. el-Darwish, "Index Numbers of Wholesale Prices in Egypt," *L'Égypte Contemporaine* 35, no. 132 (1932): 18.

86 Davis, *Challenging Colonialism*, 138.

87 Sudan, *Report on the Administration in 1930*, 48.

88 *al-Jarida al-tijariya al-misriya*, 31 March 1930.

89 In the following analysis, frequent reference will be made to the lack of a Halfa–Shellal connection, but some Egyptian sources mention the absence of

a railroad between Aswan and Wadi Halfa. The discrepancy is minor, as Shellal was just a few kilometers south of Aswan and consisted of little more than the railroad station. The dates and technical information on the construction of specific segments of Egypt's railways between Asyut and Shellal can be found in al-Dawla al-Misriya, Wizarat al-Maliya, Maslaht 'Umum al-Ihsa' al-Amiriya, *al-Ihsa' al-sanawi al-'amm li-l-qutr al-misri 1923–1924* (Cairo: al-Matba'a al-Amiriya, 1925), 269.

90 M. Abani to Council of Ministers, 10 June 1900, Number 38a, File Majlis al-Wuzara'–al-Sudan–Sikak Hadid al-Sudan, no. 8, DW.

91 Reginald Wingate to Mustafa Fahmi Pasha, 2 April 1901, File Majlis al-Wuzara'–al-Sudan–Sikak Hadid al-Sudan, no. 8, DW, 2.

92 Abbas, *The Sudan Question*, 4.

93 Mason Bey, "Note sur la communication par voie ferrée avec le Soudan," 1 September 1883, File Majlis al-Wuzara'–al-Sudan–Sikak Hadid al-Sudan, no. 8, DW, 6. For a detailed history of the technical studies carried out in the early Condominium period concerning the eventual decision to establish a railroad link to Port Sudan, see E.W.C. Sandes, *The Royal Engineers in Egypt and the Sudan* (Chatham: MacKays, 1937).

94 K.M. Barbour, *The Growth, Location, and Structure of Industry in Egypt* (New York: Praeger, 1972), 90.

95 Fabunmi, *The Sudan in Anglo–Egyptian Relations*, 158.

96 al-Dawla al-Misriya, Majlis al-Shuyukh, *Majmu'at Madabit dawr al-in'iqad al-'adi al-hadi 'ashar* (23 May–20 September 1936) (Cairo: al-Matba'a al-Amiriya, 1936), 122.

97 *al-Jarida al-tijariya al-misriya*, 5 October 1941.

98 al-Dawla al-Misriya, Majlis al-Nuwwab, *Majmu'at Madabit dawr al-in'iqad al-'adi al-thalith*, vol. 3 (5 June–28 June 1928) (Cairo: al-Matba'a al-Amiriya, 1928), 1369.

99 al-Dawla al-Misriya, Lajnat al-Naql, "Taqrir muqaddam ila majlis idarat sikak hadid wa-talighrafat wa-talifunat al-hukuma al-misriya 'an fasl mizaniyat maslahat al-sikak al-hadidiya wa-talighrafat wa-talifunat 'an mizaniyat al-dawla," 15 May 1933, File 'Abdin no. 324–Maslahat al-Sikak al-Hadidiya, DW, 4.

100 Issawi, *Egypt*, 28. Issawi's comment on Egyptian "isolation" here is clearly concerned with economic interactions, but the interwar-era Egyptian state is sometimes characterized as uninvolved generally in its neighbors' affairs. It is certainly the contention of this study that Egyptian leaders were vitally interested in regional developments, whether they involved the Sudanese areas or its neighbors, such as the Ethiopian activities along the Blue Nile examined in chapter two. Fred Lawson's 2005 article, addressing Egyptian resolution of its territorial dispute with Libya/Italy and its diplomatic role in a Yemeni–Saudi border dispute, also undermines the contention that Egypt had little to do with regional affairs. Fred Lawson, "Reassessing Egypt's Foreign Policy

during the 1920s and 1930s," in *Re-Envisioning Egypt, 1919–1952*, edited by Arthur Goldschmidt, Amy J. Johnson, and Barak A. Salmoni (Cairo: American University of Cairo Press, 2005), 46–67.

101 *al-Ahram*, 21 January 1939.

102 Zaki, "Taqrir," 23.

103 Sudan, Wizarat al-Naql wa-l-Muwasalat, *Laws of the Sudan*, vol. 2 (Khartoum: McCorquodale and Co., 1941), 767.

104 *Rapport de la Commission du Commerce*, 50.

105 *al-Majalla al-tijariya al-nubiya*, 13 August 1922.

106 *al-Majalla al-tijariya al-nubiya*, 28 April 1929, 12.

107 Sudan, *Report on the Administration, Finances and Condition of the Sudan in 1934* (London: His Majesty's Stationery Office, 1935), 110.

108 Hassan Dafalla, *The Nubian Exodus* (London: C. Hurst & Co., 1975), 24.

109 For instance, Muhammad Husayn Haykal recalled in 1935 a trip he had taken through the region on the Cook company's steamers in 1926 (Muhammad Husayn Haykal, "Hadith al-Yawm," *al-Siyasa*, 4 February 1935). References to Cook company steamers in the region indicate the firm was largely confined to passenger traffic, because almost all references to altering rates for commodities identify the Sudanese government as the responsible party.

110 "Mahdar jalsat al-lajna al-da'ima li-l-Sudan al-mun'aqada fi 11 Abril sanat 1938," 2.

111 Abaza, *Buhuth iqtisadiya 'an al-Sudan*, 10–11.

112 Henderson, *The Making of the Modern Sudan*, 168.

113 Abaza, *Buhuth iqtisadiya 'an al-Sudan*, 138.

114 Sudan, *Report on the Finances, Administration and Condition of the Sudan in 1932* (London: His Majesty's Stationery Office, 1933), 120.

115 *al-Siyasa*, 31 July 1936.

116 *Majallat Ghurfat al-Qahira*, February 1941, 163.

117 Sudan, *Report on the Administration the Years 1942–1944*, 33.

118 *Majallat Ghurfat al-Qahira*, October 1946, 1005.

119 al-Dawla al-Misriya, Majlis al-Nuwwab, *Majmu'at Madabit dawr al-in'iqad al-'adi al-Awwal*, vol. 1 (18 January–5 June 1945), 814.

120 Zaki, "Taqrir," 22.

121 Jean Schatz, "Le Soudan et ses relations commerciales avec l'Égypte," *L'Égypte Contemporaine* 31, no. 190 (1940): 283.

122 al-Dawla al-Misriya, Majlis al-Nuwwab, *Majmu'at Madabit dawr al-in'iqad al-'adi al-Awwal*, vol. 1 (18 January–5 June 1945), 492.

123 *al-Ahram*, 21 May 1939.

124 *al-Ahram*, 28 July 1939.

125 *al-Ahram*, 8 January 1946.

126 *al-Siyasa*, 28 February 1938.

127 al-Dawla al-Misriya, Wizarat al-Tijara wa-l-Sina'a, *A'mal al-ba'athat al-misriya wa-l-lajna al-da'ima*, 81.

128 Abaza, "Mudhakkira," 12.
129 Tamam Hamam Tamam, "al-Siyasa al-misriya tujaha al-Sudan 1936–1953" (M.A. thesis, University of Cairo, 1971), 23.
130 Issawi, *Egypt*, 28.
131 *al-Siyasa*, 12 October 1936.
132 Abaza, *Buhuth iqtisadiya 'an al-Sudan*, 11.
133 Sultan, "Masa'il mutannawi'a 'an al-Sudan," 17.
134 *al-Siyasa*, 1 April 1937.
135 Saqr, "al-Sudan—Tijarat al-aqmisha wa-l-mansujat al-qutniya fi al-aswaq al-sudaniya," 756.
136 Sudan, *Report on the Administration for the Years 1939–1941*, 37.
137 *al-Ahram*, 25 May 1939.
138 *Majallat Ghurfat al-Qahira*, December 1939, 1286.
139 Henderson, *The Making of the Modern Sudan*, 223.
140 *al-Ahram*, 5 November 1939.
141 Abaza, *Buhuth iqtisadiya 'an al-Sudan*, 166.
142 al-Dawla al-Misriya, Majlis al-Nuwwab, *Majmu'at Madabit dawr al-in'iqad al-'adi al-thalith*, vol. 2 (13 March–30 April 1940) (Cairo: al-Matba'a al-Amiriya, 1940), 1366.
143 Abaza, *Buhuth iqtisadiya 'an al-Sudan*, 11.
144 *al-Jarida al-tijariya al-misriya*, 26 November 1945.
145 *Majallat Ghurfat al-Iskandariya*, June 1949.
146 *al-Ahram*, 28 June 1943.
147 *al-Ahram*, 8 February 1946.
148 al-Dawla al-Misriya, Majlis al-Nuwwab, *Majmu'at Madabit dawr al-in'iqad al-'adi al-rabi'*, vol. 1 (12 November 1947–9 February 1948), 5 (emphasis added). Although the government claimed to have started studying the project, earlier that year only LE20,000 had been added to the Ministry of Transportation's budget for the dispatch of a commission to the Halfa–Shellal region. Considering estimated costs in the LE4–5 million range for the entire project, this seems like a rather paltry financial commitment. al-Dawla al-Misriya, Majlis al-Nuwwab, *Majmu'at madabit dawr al-in'iqad al-'adi al-thalith*, vol. 3 (26 May–18 June 1947), 2232.
149 *al-Ahram*, 2 December 1939.
150 *al-Ahram*, 20 February 1946.
151 al-Dawla al- Misriya, Majlis al-Nuwwab, *Majmu'at madabit dawr al-in'iqad al-'adi al-rabi'*, vol. 1 (12 November 1947–9 February 1948), 302.
152 Huddleston to Nahhas, 18 May 1944, 4.
153 Sudan, *Report on the Administration of the Sudan in 1949* (Khartoum: McCorquodale and Co., 1950), 153.
154 Issawi, *Egypt*, 104.
155 *Majallat Ghurfat al-Qahira*, November 1953, 41.

156 Sudan, *Report on the Finances in 1932*, 120.

157 Sudan, *Report on the Finances in 1928*, 54.

158 Sudan, *Report on the Finances in 1929*, 44.

159 al-Dawla al-Misriya, Majlis al-Nuwwab, *Majmu'at madabit dawr al-in'iqad al-'adi al-rabi'*, vol. 2 (11 April–29 May 1934), 664.

160 al-Dawla al-Misriya, Majlis al-Nuwwab, *Majmu'at madabit dawr al-in'iqad al-'adi al-thani*, vol. 3 (9 June–7 July 1932) (Cairo: al-Matba'a al-Amiriya, 1932), 1223.

161 This law was revised in 1944 because of a perceived need to increase the annual fees on vehicles. The text of the original 1934 law and the adjustments made in 1944, as well as the fees charged in both cases, can be found in al-Dawla al-Misriya, Majlis al-Nuwwab, *Majmu'at madabit dawr al-in'iqad al-'adi al-thalith*, vol. 3 (27 June–9 August 1944) (Cairo: al-Matba'a al-Amiriya, 1945), 2482–83.

162 Sudan, *The Revised Edition of the Laws*, 524.

163 One facet of the control over motor transport that was an obstacle to increased use of vehicles between the two countries was that the legislation passed by each administration, especially the collection of fees, was applicable to vehicles working within each country's boundaries. Therefore, it appears that those interested in Halfa–Shellal motor transport service would have been required to spend more on the necessary fees. Since Wadi Halfa was just barely within the Sudanese area of administration, a local arrangement to eliminate this problem may have been reached, although no evidence of such was found.

164 Sudan, *Report on the Administration in 1934*, 45.

165 al-Dawla al-Misriya, Majlis al-Nuwwab, *Majmu'at madabit dawr al-in'iqad al-'adi al-thani*, vol. 2 (27 April–10 June 1937), 1255.

166 al-Dawla al-Misriya, Majlis al-Nuwwab, *Majmu'at madabit dawr al-in'iqad al-'adi al-thani*, vol. 2 (27 April–10 June 1937), 1255.

167 al-Dawla al-Misriya, Majlis al-Nuwwab, *Majmu'at madabit dawr al-in'iqad al-'adi al-thani*, vol. 3 (14 June–14 July 1937) (Cairo: al-Matba'a al-Amiriya, 1937), 1457.

168 al-Dawla al-Misriya, Majlis al-Nuwwab, *Majmu'at madabit dawr al-in'iqad al-'adi al-thani*, vol. 3 (14 June–14 July 1937), 1462.

169 "Mahdar Jalsat al-Lajna al-Da'ima li-l-Sudan al-Mun'aqada fi 26 Fabrayir Sanat 1938," 2.

170 al-Dawla al-Misriya, Wizarat al-Tijara wa-l-Sina'a, *A'mal al-ba'athat al-misriya wa-l-lajna al-da'ima*, 23.

171 Abaza, *Buhuth iqtisadiya 'an al-Sudan*, 11.

172 *al-Ahram*, 11 May 1939.

173 *al-Ahram*, 16 May 1939.

174 *al-Ahram*, 25 July 1939.

175 Abaza, *Buhuth iqtisadiya 'an al-Sudan*, 110.

176 al-Dawla al-Misriya, Majlis al-Nuwwab, *Majmu'at madabit dawr al-in'iqad al-'adi al-thani*, vol. 2 (28 February–29 May 1939) (Cairo: al-Matba'a al-Amiriya, 1940), 1797.

177 *al-Ahram*, 28 October 1940.

178 Sultan, "Masa'il mutannawi'a 'an al-Sudan," 17.

179 *al-Ahram*, 25 July 1939.

180 *al-Ahram*, 3 February 1939.

181 *al-Ahram*, 20 June 1939. Debate over railroad and road options among permanent committee members eventually led to the formation of a special committee, headed by the economic expert, mandated to compose a report with the details on all options. *al-Ahram*, 10 July 1939.

182 al-Dawla al-Misriya, Majlis al-Nuwwab, *Majmu'at madabit dawr al-in'iqad al-'adi al-thani*, vol. 1 (12 November 1945–19 Febraury 1946) (Cairo: al-Matba'a al-Amiriya, 1946), 97.

183 During the Second World War, Egyptian authorities had apparently seriously begun examining the possibility of constructing a more permanent road than that maintained by the British. However, the Alexandria Chamber of Commerce reported in September 1942 that due to the lack of asphalt and total costs estimated at LE1.25 million the government had decided to stop construction of this road. *Majallat Ghurfat al-Iskandariya*, September 1942, 19.

184 al-Dawla al-Misriya, Majlis al-Nuwwab, *Majmu'at madabit dawr al-in'iqad al-'adi al-thalith*, vol. 1 (14 November 1946–2 March 1947) (Cairo: al-Matba'a al-Amiriya, 1948).

185 al-Dawla al-Misriya, Majlis al-Nuwwab, *Majmu'at madabit dawr al-in'iqad al-'adi al-Rabi'*, vol. 3 (12 April–8 June 1948) (Cairo: al-Matba'a al-Amiriya, 1949), 1748 (emphasis added).

186 Fabunmi, *The Sudan in Anglo-Egyptian Relations*, 149.

187 Fabunmi, *The Sudan in Anglo-Egyptian Relations*, 149.

188 Certainly interior caravan routes had been utilized for centuries in the transport of livestock and small-volume commercial goods. Regular exchange of bulk goods relied on water transport—either via the Nile or the Red Sea.

189 Perkins, *Port Sudan*, 64. Suakin was one of the few remaining places in the Sudan where Egyptian merchants were the dominant entrepreneurial element. Suakin's decline is directly attributable to the establishment of Port Sudan. Kenneth Perkins notes that Port Sudan's growth resulted in the traffic of pilgrims across the Red Sea being "virtually the only economic enterprise of significance in Suakin by the mid-1920s" (186). Typical of Egyptian opinions that the British had undermined Suakin was a lecture delivered by 'Abd al-Fattah al-Bishari Bey of the Egyptian military in the Sudan. His 1946 lecture on the history of the Sudan "concluded by talking about the city of Suakin and described how it had been the first commercial port on the Red Sea, and how its affairs were neglected afterwards." *al-Ahram*, 6 February 1946.

190 *al-Jarida al-tijariya al-misriya*, 26 January 1939.
191 *al-Ahram*, 18 November 1938.
192 In his summary of the 1935–38 activities of Egyptian missions to the Sudan and the permanent committee, Fu'ad Abaza wrote that the Bank Misr companies had been contacted from the beginning and that "a delegation of its officials traveled to the Sudan in order to become familiar with the commercial situation there from close at hand." Abaza, "Mudhakkira," 7.
193 Davis, *Challenging Colonialism*, 180.
194 *al-Siyasa*, 26 March 1935.
195 *al-Jarida al-tijariya al-misriya*, 29 November 1935.
196 *al-Siyasa*, 24 February 1935.
197 Davis, *Challenging Colonialism*, 181.
198 *al-Ahram*, 17 June 1938.
199 *al-Ahram*, 17 June 1938.
200 *Majallat Ghurfat al-Iskandariya*, January 1939, 15–16.
201 *Majallat Ghurfat al-Qahira*, March 1936, 100.
202 Abaza, "Mudhakkira," 8.
203 Abaza, *Buhuth iqtisadiya 'an al-Sudan*, 120.
204 al-Dawla al-Misriya, Wizarat al-Tijara wa-l-Sina'a, *A'mal al-ba'athat al-misriya wa-l-lajna al-da'ima*, 42.
205 Abaza, *Buhuth iqtisadiya 'an al-Sudan*, 17–18.
206 Zaki, "Taqrir," 24.
207 *al-Ahram*, 30 March 1940.
208 *al-Ahram*, 6 January 1940.
209 Abaza, *Buhuth iqtisadiya 'an al-Sudan*, 177.
210 *Majallat Ghurfat al-Qahira*, November 1939, 1164. Additionally, officials did not require sureties from all traders, but only merchants who had not previously been actively exporting to the Sudan.
211 al-Dawla al-Misriya, Majlis al-Nuwwab, *Majmu'at Madabit dawr al-in'iqad al-'adi al-thani*, vol. 1 (19 November 1942–19 April 1943) (Cairo: al-Matba'a al-Amiriya, 1943), 1017. Egyptian concern about Red Sea shipping space specifically, rather than using other means of transportation for this commodity, existed because exporters normally sent Sudanese cotton and cotton seed through Port Sudan, and because the shipment of such via the Nile route required extraordinary precautions to protect Egyptian cotton quality.
212 Nahhas to Huddleston, 1 January 1944.

Notes to Chapter 5

1 al-Dawla al-Misriya, Majlis al-Nuwwab, *Majmu'at Madabit dawr al-in'iqad al-'adi al-awwal*, vol. 2 (11 June–6 August 1945), 1045.
2 *Majallat Ghurfat al-Qahira*, October 1936, 5 (emphasis added).
3 Salvatore Cicurel, "al-Ta'awun al-iqtisadi bayna Misr wa-l-Sudan," *Majallat*

Ghurfat al-Qahira, June 1937, 50.

4 Eric Hobsbawm, *Nations and Nationalism since 1780: Programme, Myth, Reality* (Cambridge: Cambridge University Press, 1990), 78.

5 Walker Connor, "When Is a Nation?" in *Nationalism*, ed. John Hutchinson and Anthony D. Smith (Oxford: Oxford University Press, 1994), 157.

6 Gellner, "Nationalism and Modernization," in *Nationalism*, ed. John Hutchinson and Anthony D. Smith (Oxford: Oxford University Press, 1994), 63.

7 Rupert Emerson, *From Empire to Nation* (Cambridge, MA: Harvard University Press, 1962), 174.

8 In addition to gaining the support of the general population and the cooperation of the elite, Egyptian investors needed to win over the British-staffed Sudan Political Service. Prior to 1953, it was never precisely clear how much, if any, input the Sudanese population would have in determining their future, but it was always obvious that Britain would be one of the primary participants when decisions were made. Egyptians believed that a much stronger claim of sovereignty could be laid before British negotiators if Egyptians could portray increased investment initiatives as beneficial to the Sudanese population and could couple such with traditional claims of cultural unity.

9 British officials claimed Egyptian agricultural involvement would certainly be exploitative, but some Sudanese organizations noted that general economic improvement would ultimately come through precisely the type of agricultural schemes that Egyptians sought. In an April 1930 meeting, the Khartoum Chamber of Commerce's president provided extensive details concerning northern agricultural schemes, including tremendous potential profits for investors. However, like the Egyptians, he emphasized the broad economic impact of such investments:

> We must not forget that this country is primarily agricultural and it is impossible that trade develops without the progress of agriculture and an increase in population, and I reiterate the concern expressed to you last year that we must not set our hopes on any spectacular success and we must be satisfied with slow steady increases now and in the near future. . . . [omission of extensive section on details of how agricultural schemes would be managed]
>
> If agricultural schemes like these are established in other provinces and the Gezira, the purchasing power of native inhabitants will increase by LE500,000 or 750,000 and this will produce comparable progress in the commercial situation. (*al-Jarida al-tijariya al-misriya*, 8 May 1930)

10 Gabriel Baer, *A History of Landownership in Modern Egypt, 1800–1950* (Oxford: Oxford University Press, 1962), 139–40.

11 Abaza, *Buhuth iqtisadiya 'an al-Sudan*, 61.

12 *al-Akhbar*, 7 July 1922.

13 *al-Akhbar*, 8 September 1922.

14 The Gezira agricultural scheme was established on a cooperative basis, with the Sudanese government, the Sudan Plantations Syndicate (a private British company that functioned as the scheme's 'managers'), and the local farmers sharing the profits. Due to the confused landholding situation in

the region, largely because of the agricultural policies imposed during the Mahdiya, determining ownership was difficult, but those Sudanese with definite ownership claims were paid an annual rent for the forced inclusion of their lands in the scheme. Although somewhat dated, two very good works on the planning, establishment, functioning, and results of the scheme are Arthur Gaitskell, *Gezira: A Story of Development in the Sudan* (London: Faber and Faber, 1959); Tony Barnett, *The Gezira Scheme: An Illusion of Development* (London: Frank Cass, 1977).

15 Steven Serels, "Political Landscaping: Land Registration, the Definition of Ownership and the Evolution of Colonial Objectives in the Anglo–Egyptian Sudan, 1899–1924," *African Economic History* 35 (2007): 72.

16 al-Dawla al-Misriya, Majlis al-Shuyukh, *Majmu'at Madabit dawr al-in'iqad ghayr al-'adi li-nazar mu'ahadat al-sadaqa wa-l-tahaluf bayna Misr wa-Baritaniya al-'Uzma* (2–19 November 1936), 55.

17 *al-Akhbar*, 25 October 1931.

18 al-Dawla al-Misriya, Wizarat al-Tijara wa-l-Sina'a, *A'mal al-ba'athat al-misriya wa-l-lajna al-da'ima*, 64.

19 Assessments of the Gezira scheme were tremendously subjective. Egyptians had consistently questioned the Sudan Plantation Syndicate's management, but when greater local supervision of the scheme was implemented after the Second World War, the foreign president of the Khartoum Chamber of Commerce advised "to wait and see if the previously achieved *success* in this business will accompany the new organization." *Majallat Ghurfat al-Qahira*, May 1945, 467 (emphasis added).

20 Isma'il Sidqi, "Note sur une Excursion au Soudan," 10 February 1918, File 'Abdin no. 104, DW, 5.

21 al-Dawla al-Misriya, Majlis al-Nuwwab, *Majmu'at madabit dawr al-in'iqad al-'adi al-awwal* (15 March–10 July 1924), 345.

22 Davis, *Challenging Colonialism*, 180.

23 *Majallat Ghurfat al-Iskandariya*, March 1939, 22.

24 Rashed el-Barawy, *Egypt, Britain and the Sudan* (Cairo: Renaissance Bookshop, 1952), 17.

25 Husayn Kamil Salim, "Unity of the Nile Valley, The Economic Aspect," Lecture at the Royal Society of Engineers in Cairo, 17 April 1947, File Majlis al-Wuzara', no. 3H, DW, 1.

26 el-Haj Bilal Omer, *The Danagla Traders of Northern Sudan* (Reading: Ithaca Press, 1985), 4.

27 I.S.G. Matthews, "Irrigation Development in the Sudan, 1898–1955," in Deborah Lavin, *The Condominium Remembered: Proceedings of the Durham Historical Records Conference 1982*, vol. 2: *The Transformation of the Old Order in the Sudan* (Durham: Centre for Middle Eastern and Islamic Studies, 1993), 26–27.

28 Sudan, *Report on the Finances in 1929*, 69.

29 *al-Jarida al-tijariya al-misriya*, 3 December 1939.
30 *Majallat Ghurfat al-Qahira*, September 1939, 938.
31 Sultan, "Masa'il mutannawi'a 'an al-Sudan," 16.
32 Fabunmi, *The Sudan in Anglo–Egyptian Relations*, 157.
33 *al-Ahram*, 12 April 1938.
34 al-Dawla al-Misriya, Wizarat al-Tijara wa-l-Sina'a, *A'mal al-ba'athat al-misriya wa-l-lajna al-da'ima*, 12.
35 Fu'ad Abaza, "al-Ba'athat al-misriya fi al-Sudan," *al-Siyasa*, 20 February 1935, 4.
36 *al-Siyasa*, 12 August 1935.
37 *al-Siyasa*, 7 November 1935.
38 The information on this meeting comes from two sources that published summaries of the proceedings: Husayn, *al-Sudan*, vol. 3, 300–301; *al-Akhbar*, 7 March 1935.
39 Husayn, *al-Sudan*, vol. 3, 301.
40 Husayn, *al-Sudan*, vol. 3, 300.
41 *al-Siyasa*, 25 March 1935.
42 *al-Balagh*, 4 February 1937.
43 *Majallat Ghurfat al-Qahira*, October 1939, 1018–20.
44 Zaki, "Taqrir," 19.
45 *al-Ahram*, 10 October 1939.
46 *al-Ahram*, 9 October 1940.
47 *al-Jarida al-tijariya al-misriya*, 26 February 1935.
48 al-Dawla al-Misriya, Wizarat al-Tijara wa-l-Sina'a, *A'mal al-ba'athat al-misriya wa-l-lajna al-da'ima*, 14.
49 Abaza, *Buhuth iqtisadiya 'an al-Sudan*, 66.
50 *al-Ahram*, 10 January 1946.
51 Abaza, *Buhuth iqtisadiya 'an al-Sudan*, 66.
52 Hasan Sabri to Stewart Symes, October 1943, File Majlis al-Wuzara'–al-Fatra ba'd 1923, no. 3D, DW, 1.
53 Saeed M.A. el-Mahdi, *A Guide to Land Settlement and Registration* (Khartoum: Khartoum University Press, 1971), 1.
54 Gaitskell, *Gezira*, 44.
55 The Land Acquisition Ordinance of 1903 and the Notice in Connection with the Natives Disposition of Lands Restriction Ordinance of 1918 can be found in Sudan, *The Revised Edition of the Laws*, 13–19, 435–36.
56 Another critical aspect of the 1925 land ordinance was that it allowed the government to register lands as 'public' if the claims of either Sudanese or foreigners over them were less than full ownership. This policy of increasingly registering lands in the government's name meant fewer problems for the administration when it needed extensive tracts of land for the implementation of irrigation schemes or when awarding concessions.
57 *al-Ahram*, 18 January 1946.
58 *Majallat Ghurfat al-Qahira*, June 1946, 811.

59 *Majallat Ghurfat al-Iskandariya*, June 1946, 24.
60 *al-Akhbar*, 14 May 1922.
61 Husayn, *al-Sudan*, vol. 3, 301.
62 *Majallat Ghurfat al-Iskandariya*, June 1946, 24.
63 Ending the multifaceted occupation of their country was clearly the nationalist objective. However, some early proposals, such as that offered by Husayn Rushdi in 1921, included an explicit desire for the free movement of Egyptians to the Sudan. Husayn Rushdi, "Mashru' mu'ahada bi-sh'an al-Sudan," File Majlis al-Wuzara', no. 3A, DW, 1.
64 al-Dawla al-Misriya, Majlis al-Shuyukh, *Majmu'at Madabit dawr al-in'qad ghayr al-'adi li-nazar mu'ahadat al-sadaqa wa-l-tahaluf bayna Misr wa-Baritanya al-'Uzma* (2–19 November 1936), 28.
65 Abbas, *The Sudan Question*, 67.
66 Fabunmi, *The Sudan in Anglo–Egyptian Relations*, 431.
67 *al-Jarida al-tijariya al-misriya*, 26 January 1939.
68 Sidqi, "Note sur une Excursion au Soudan," 12–13. In a 1919 editorial, Sidqi claimed of the Sudan that "any progress there was achieved largely through Egypt's expenditure." He maintained that a remedy to the Sudan's lack of productive agricultural schemes would be the emigration of Egyptian fellaheen. Badrawi, *Isma'il Sidqi*, 21.
69 Taraf 'Ali, "al-Sudan," *al-Akhbar*, 11 September 1922.
70 *al-Akhbar*, 17 March 1927.
71 al-Dawla al-Misriya, Majlis al-Nuwwab, *Majmu'at Madabit dawr al-in'iqad al-'adi al-thalith*, vol. 1 (15 December 1932–28 February 1933), 163.
72 *al-Siyasa*, 14 May 1936.
73 Prince 'Amr Tussun was intimately involved in the economic efforts after 1935 since the Royal Agricultural Society, which he headed at the time, was the primary initiator of the efforts. Local papers and journals consistently reported on Prince Tussun's speeches when Sudanese dignitaries or economic delegations visited Egypt. Additionally, he wrote a number of works during the interwar years, some of which dealt with Egypt's nationalist struggle and the Sudan problem. One example of his publications on the Sudan is *al-Mas'ala al-sudaniya* (Alexandria: Matba'at al-Mustaqbal, 1936), which sought to demonstrate that Britain's involvement in the Sudan was unsupportable according to accepted principles of international law.
74 Husayn, *al-Sudan*, vol. 2, 557.
75 *al-Jarida al-tijariya al-misriya*, 15 November 1935.
76 al-Dawla al-Misriya, Majlis al-Nuwwab, *Majmu'at Madabit dawr al-in'iqad al-'adi al-thalith*, vol. 1 (18 November 1939–12 March 1940), 59.
77 al-Dawla al-Misriya, Majlis al-Nuwwab, *Majmu'at Madabit dawr al-in'iqad al-'adi al-thalith*, vol. 1 (19 November 1942–19 April 1943) (Cairo: al-Matba'a al-Amiriya, 1943), 926.
78 *al-Ahram*, 3 December 1939.

79 *al-Ahram*, 2 March 1940.
80 *al-Akhbar*, February 1935.
81 *al-Jarida al-tijariya al-misriya*, 10 May 1938.
82 *al-Akhbar*, 19 October 1935.
83 Egypt's economic expert in the Sudan, Mahmud Zaki, highlighted the way Condominium officials equated educated Egyptian employees with political troubles. He stated in 1943 that "the Sudan is in need of our money and our efforts. The Sudan is not in need of [our] employees." *Majallat Ghurfat al-Iskandariya*, February 1943, 44.
84 'Abd al-Halim Ilyas Nasir, "al-Sudan—Ihtiyajuh li-ayadi al-'Amila," *al-Akhbar*, 27 October 1922.
85 *al-Akhbar*, 1 September 1931.
86 *al-Akhbar*, 1 September 1931.
87 al-Dawla al-Misriya, Majlis al-Shuyukh, *Majmu'at Madabit dawr al-in'qad ghayr al-'adi li-nazar mu'ahadat al-sadaqa wa-l-tahaluf bayna Misr wa-Baritanya al-'Uzma* (2–19 November 1936), 55.
88 Abaza, "Mudhakkira," 4.
89 Abaza, "Mudhakkira," 4.
90 Husayn, *al-Sudan*, vol. 3, 244.
91 Husayn, *al-Sudan*, vol. 3, 163.
92 Husayn, *al-Sudan*, vol. 2, 551.
93 Ali al-Barir, "Misr wa-l-Sudan ba'd al-Mu'ahada," *Majallat Ghurfat al-Qahira*, April 1937, 69.
94 Abaza, *Buhuth iqtisadiya 'an al-Sudan*, 65.
95 Determining the exact level of Egyptian emigration to the Sudan specifically is a difficult process, one which I hope to carry further in later research. Egyptian statistical compilations provide extensive information on population levels but little indication of whether or not emigration occurred and, if so, to what destinations. A more precise understanding of Egyptian emigration to the Sudan could possibly be achieved through consultation of the Sudanese documentation, which was not possible in the preparation of the present study. The estimate of four thousand emigrants was derived from population statistics on the Sudan in *al-Siyasa*, 13 September 1935; "Statistics, Civil Populations of Provinces, 1945," Number 48, File Majlis al-Wuzara', no. 3H, DW.
96 Sultan, "Masa'il mutannawi'a 'an al-Sudan," 15.
97 Abbas, *The Sudan Question*, 92.
98 Fabunmi, *The Sudan in Anglo–Egyptian Relations*, 431.
99 Zaki, "Taqrir," 20.
100 Huddleston to Nahhas, 10 August 1943, Number E.15 (97-H-1), File Majlis al-Wuzara'–al-Fatra ba'd 1923, no. 3D, DW, 2.
101 Another travel expense that Egyptian interests felt prevented emigration was the Sudanese Railways Department restricting third-class travel to Sudanese

passengers only. Permission for Egyptian laborers to purchase third-class tickets was among the objectives of an economic mission planned for 1939. *Majallat Ghurfat al-Iskandariya*, December 1938, 12.

102 Sudan, *Report on the Administration in 1933*, 111.

103 Virtually all studies of Sudanese agricultural development during the Condominium period noted that the need for seasonal laborers was of the utmost importance for the irrigation schemes.

104 Charles Issawi, *Egypt at Mid-Century: An Economic Survey* (Oxford: Oxford University Press, 1954), 59.

105 *al-Akhbar*, 19 October 1935.

106 *al-Ahram*, 15 August 1939.

107 *Majallat Ghurfat al-Iskandariya*, June 1946, 24.

108 *Majallat Ghurfat al-Iskandariya*, May 1947, 21.

109 Abbas, *The Sudan Question*, 47.

110 United Nations Security Council, *Verbatim Records*, 24.

111 Sidqi, "Note sur une Excursion au Soudan," 5, 12–13.

112 *al-Akhbar*, 11 September 1922.

113 *al-Akhbar*, 20 February 1935.

114 *Majallat Ghurfat al-Qahira*, October 1936, 3.

115 *Majallat Ghurfat al-Qahira*, October 1936, 5–6.

116 Cicurel, "al-Ta'awun al-iqtisadi bayna Misr wa-l-Sudan," 50.

117 Cicurel, "al-Ta'awun al-iqtisadi bayna Misr wa-l-Sudan," 55.

118 Abaza, *Buhuth iqtisadiya 'an al-Sudan*, 87–94.

119 Abaza, *Buhuth iqtisadiya 'an al-Sudan*, 92.

120 al-Dawla al-Misriya, Majlis al-Nuwwab, *Majmu'at Madabit dawr al-in'iqad al-'adi al-Rabi'*, vol. 2 (15 April–8 July 1941) (Cairo: al-Matba'a al-Amiriya, 1941), 852.

121 *al-Ahram*, 5 January 1940.

122 *al-Jarida al-tijariya al-misriya*, 21 February 1935.

123 Virtually every Egyptian publication that summarized industrial potentials in the Sudan from 1935 forward lists the same fields. Isma'il Sidqi's speech about Egypt's industrial resurgence in 1940 specifically mentioned leather, lumber, and oil-seed-processing industrial possibilities in the Sudan. *al-Ahram*, 5 January 1940. The Condominium administration itself mentioned at the start of the Second World War not only its concern for production of various agricultural crops but also encouragement of tomato processing and dehydration of onions—exactly the sort of processing industries Egyptians constantly highlighted. *al-Ahram*, 9 October 1940.

124 Zaki, "Taqrir," 19.

125 al-Dawla al-Misriya, Majlis al-Nuwwab, *Majmu'at Madabit dawr al-in'iqad al-'adi al-awwal*, vol. 2 (11 June–6 August 1945), 1045.

126 al-Dawla al-Misriya, Majlis al-Nuwwab, *Majmu'at Madabit dawr al-in'iqad al-'adi al-awwal*, vol. 2 (11 June–6 August 1945), 1045.

127 *Majallat Ghurfat al-Qahira*, June 1946, 811.
128 *Majallat Ghurfat al-Qahira*, June 1947, 798. Although the ministry claimed the breadth of expertise needed in the Sudan necessitated shorter appointments for more specialists, one must wonder if this decision was also predicated on Egyptian officials' lack of enthusiasm for appointments in the Sudan.
129 Davis, *Challenging Colonialism*, 4.
130 *al-Akhbar*, 30 November 1935.
131 Husayn, *al-Sudan*, vol. 3, 93.
132 Husayn, *al-Sudan*, vol. 3, 93–94.
133 Davis, *Challenging Colonialism*, 181.
134 Davis, *Challenging Colonialism*, 169.
135 Gabriel Giet Jal, *The Sudan Question in the Anglo–Egyptian Treaty of 1936: An Historical Study of Conflict in Anglo–Egyptian Relations in the Sudan, 1899–1936* (Juba: Juba University Press, 1989), 62.
136 *al-Jarida al-tijariya al-misriya*, 12 February 1952.
137 *al-Jarida al-tijariya al-misriya*, 12 February 1952.
138 Khalid, *The Government They Deserve*, 62.

Notes to Chapter 6

1 al-Dawla al-Misriya, Majlis al-Nuwwab, *Majmu'at Madabit dawr al-in'iqad al-'adi al-thani*, vol. 3 (1 May–9 July 1951) (Cairo: al-Matba'a al-Amiriya, 1952), 14.
2 Fabunmi, *The Sudan in Anglo–Egyptian Relations*, 115.
3 Fabunmi, *The Sudan in Anglo–Egyptian Relations*, 157.
4 With the onset of the Second World War, western imports were curtailed, but this did not result in Egypt making up the difference entirely. Increasingly the Sudan relied on imports from the east and south. For instance, after heavier reliance early in the war, by 1944 Egypt's share of Sudanese imports had already dropped to 23 percent, while India supplied 35 percent of the total. Furthermore, readers should not equate Sudanese imports from Egypt entirely with imported manufactures. A significant portion of Egyptian commodities sent to the Sudan were agricultural goods or the products of agribusiness. Rice, onions, and refined sugar—along with home-spun textiles—were among the most important exports to the Sudan.
5 The table is based on Sudan, *Annual Report of the Department of Economics and Trade, 1938* (Khartoum: McCorquodale, 1939); Sudan, *Annual Report of the Department of Economics and Trade, 1945* (Khartoum: McCorquodale, 1945); *Majallat Ghurfat al-Qahira*, October 1953, 114.
6 *al-Akhbar*, 3 December 1935 (emphasis added).
7 al-Dawla al-Misriya, Majlis al-Nuwwab, *Majmu'at Madabit dawr al-in'iqad al-'adi al-awwal* (11 January–17 April 1930), 77.
8 al-Dawla al-Misriya, Majlis al-Nuwwab, *Majmu'at Madabit dawr al-in'iqad al-'adi al-awwal* (12 April–12 July 1938), 89.

9 *Majallat Ghurfat al-Qahira*, October 1939, 1016.

10 Issawi, *Egypt*, 115.

11 *al-Akhbar*, 13 July 1931. Egypt's first expert would write of the Nile Valley fruit seasons that "the Sudanese fruit become ripe in a different season than Egyptian fruit, which ripen usually around two months earlier on average." Abaza, *Buhuth iqtisadiya 'an al-Sudan*, 16–17.

12 *Majallat Ghurfat al-Qahira*, June 1939, 800–801. The Ministry of Commerce and Industry hoped to export preserved fruits from Asyut to various markets, and Egypt's railway department had agreed to reduce rates on citrus transport that year to encourage exportation.

13 *al-Jarida al-tijariya al-misriya*, 11 November 1935.

14 *al-Siyasa*, 28 February 1938.

15 *Majallat Ghurfat al-Qahira*, April 1940, 399.

16 *Majallat Ghurfat al-Qahira*, December 1939, 1290–91.

17 *Majallat Ghurfat al-Qahira*, May 1938, 70.

18 *al-Ahram*, 27 December 1938.

19 *al-Ahram*, 1 January 1939.

20 Abaza, "Mudhakkira," 11.

21 Abaza, "Mudhakkira," 11.

22 *Majallat Ghurfat al-Qahira*, May 1938, 73.

23 *al-Ahram*, 31 October 1939.

24 "Mahdar jalsat al-lajna al-da'ima li-l-Sudan al-mun'aqada fi 11 Abril sanat 1938," 3. The lower rate applied to "entirely fruit" shipments was granted if no less than 7,500 kilograms of a ten-ton railroad car was used for fruit shipment. al-Dawla al-Misriya, Wizarat al-Tijara wa-l-Sina'a, *A'mal al-ba'athat al-misriya wa-l-lajna al-da'ima*, 27.

25 *al-Akhbar*, 13 March 1941.

26 Abaza, *Buhuth iqtisadiya 'an al-Sudan*, 156.

27 Abaza, *Buhuth iqtisadiya 'an al-Sudan*, 156.

28 In fact, the average export levels from 1950 to 1955 in table 2 actually disguise improved export levels. Less than 3,000 kilograms exported to the Sudan in 1951 drove down average annual exports of citrus fruit, which were otherwise well in excess of 1 million kilograms per year. Furthermore, the Sudan was clearly the primary destination of this commodity, with total Egyptian exports to all other countries during this period averaging about 200,000 kilograms annually.

29 *Majallat Ghurfat al-Qahira*, March 1936, 98–99.

30 "Mahdar jalsat al-lajna al-da'ima li-l-Sudan al-mun'aqada fi 31 Yanayir sanat 1938," 2.

31 *al-Ahram*, 4 December 1938.

32 Actually, the only other problem for citrus exports noted by Egyptian sources before the Second World War was the expansion of local Sudanese fruit production. Abaza, *Buhuth iqtisadiya 'an al-Sudan*, 51; *al-Ahram*, 25 April 1940.

However, the fruits cultivated in the Sudan were mainly different varieties than in Egypt and matured at different times of the year.

33 Abaza, *Buhuth iqtisadiya 'an al-Sudan*, 157.

34 *al-Ahram*, 4 February 1940.

35 *al-Jarida al-tijariya al-misriya*, 30 August 1943.

36 al-Dawla al-Misriya, Wizarat al-Tijara wa-l-Sina'a, *A'mal al-ba'athat al-misriya wa-l-lajna al-da'ima*, 26.

37 Abaza, "Mudhakkira," 9–10.

38 *Majallat Ghurfat al-Qahira*, March 1936, 100.

39 Abaza, "Mudhakkira," 13.

40 *Majallat Ghurfat al-Iskandariya*, October 1938, 18.

41 Abaza, *Buhuth iqtisadiya 'an al-Sudan*, 159.

42 Abaza, *Buhuth iqtisadiya 'an al-Sudan*, 160.

43 *al-Ahram*, 16 June 1940.

44 *al-Ahram*, 29 March 1944.

45 Discussion of postwar exports to the Sudan below indicates that the necessity of severe controls on rice export to ensure local consumption needs were satisfied did not end with the war's conclusion in 1945.

46 Obviously, the anomaly in this assertion is 1942. A review of commerce-related documentation for this year provided no detailed explanations for the lack of exports.

47 Sudan, *Report on the Administration in 1949*, 44, 49.

48 Export figures during the war fluctuated because of Egyptian supply, Sudanese demand, transportation, or other factors, and similar variability continued in the 1950s. For instance, in 1953 Egypt exported only 256,554 kilograms worth LE9,196 to the Sudan.

49 The figures cited in this paragraph are based on statistics from Sudan, *Annual Report of the Department of Economics and Trade, 1938*; Sudan, *Annual Report of the Department of Economics and Trade, 1945*; Egypt, *Annual Statement of Foreign Trade* [1918–55].

50 *al-Jarida al-tijariya al-misriya*, 22 August 1934.

51 *al-Jarida al-tijariya al-misriya*, 31 July 1935.

52 *Majallat Ghurfat al-Qahira*, June 1939, 755–56.

53 *al-Jarida al-tijariya al-misriya*, 25 November 1939.

54 'Abdallah Fakri Abaza and others reported that Egyptian silks were well received by upper-class women frequenting the permanent exhibition of Egyptian products at Khartoum, but there is no documentation that silk exports to the Sudan ever increased dramatically prior to independence. *Majallat Ghurfat al-Iskandariya*, January 1939, 16; *al-Ahram*, 25 February 1939; *Majallat Ghurfat al-Qahira*, March 1939, 390–91. Ultimately, both silk and artificial silk textiles either could not find a sufficient market in the Sudan or could not compete in those markets without government assistance similar to that provided in Egyptian markets.

55 *Rapport de la Commission du Commerce*, 10.

56 Berque, *Egypt*, 329. Most histories of Egypt during the first half of the twentieth century do not mention Naqqada or this textile, largely because it was only exported to the Sudan. Robert Tignor briefly notes that there were some one thousand looms producing this textile in Naqqada during the 1930s, but, other than these two scholars, reference to the product is found only in very specialized studies. Robert L. Tignor, *Egyptian Textiles and British Capital, 1930–1956* (Cairo: American University in Cairo Press, 1989), 10.

57 *Majallat Ghurfat al-Qahira*, September 1940, 680.

58 *Majallat Ghurfat al-Qahira*, January 1939, 35.

59 Abaza, *Buhuth iqtisadiya 'an al-Sudan*, 148.

60 *Majallat Ghurfat al-Qahira*, April 1940, 367–68.

61 Prior to 1928, the annual statements of the foreign trade of Egypt included mixed textiles within the cotton textile category. Although one year is not sufficient indication of earlier trends, in 1928, before the Depression, over 300,000 kilograms of mixed textiles were exported to the Sudan—a volume little different from that recorded in the following decades.

62 *Majallat Ghurfat al-Qahira*, April 1952, 471.

63 This Sudanese customs duty seemingly also would have encouraged Egyptian exports of purely silk or artificial silk products, but it never did. By 1939 Egypt's share of the Sudanese silk textile market did rise to 26.9 percent, but the total value of this trade was a mere LE1,375. Additionally, 'Abdallah Fakri Abaza noted of textiles made entirely of artificial silk that "in spite of the tangible progress of this industry, the abundance of its production in Egypt, and the duties imposed on this type of silk imported from [countries] other than Egypt . . . Egypt does not export to the Sudan other than minuscule amounts." Abaza, *Buhuth iqtisadiya 'an al-Sudan*, 149.

64 al-Dawla al-Misriya, Majlis al-Nuwwab, *Majmu'at Madabit dawr al-in'iqad al-'adi al-thani*, vol. 3 (1 May–9 July 1951), 61.

65 Sudan, *Report on the Administration in 1949*, 49; Sudan, *Annual Report of the Department of Economics and Trade* [1945], 121–22. Similarly discouraging results emerge if one looks at Egypt's proportion of *total* textile imports of the Sudan. From 1934 to 1939, Egypt provided only 14.9 percent of the value of all textiles imported by the Sudan, plus 99.2 percent of that 14.9 percent consisted of cotton–artificial silk mixes and cotton textiles dyed after weaving. Abaza, *Buhuth iqtisadiya 'an al-Sudan*, 147.

66 Cotton piece goods shipped to the Sudan totaled over 1 million kilograms every year during this period—so the average here is a fairly accurate measure of the trade at that time.

67 Shimizu, *Anglo–Japanese Trade Rivalry*, 61.

68 Sudan, *Annual Report of the Department of Economics* [1945], 121–22.

69 *al-Jarida al-tijariya al-misriya*, 16 August 1943.

70 If Japan's share is determined according to value of imports, the percentage is still 91. *Majallat Ghurfat al-Qahira*, June 1939, 753.

71 *Majallat Ghurfat al-Qahira*, April 1940, 362–63. 'Ali Mawardi further explained that Japanese textiles were handled locally by Syrian, Greek, and especially Indian merchants residing in the Sudan. The director was highlighting the importance of well-established local marketing networks—something else Egyptians would have to address for success.

72 *al-Ahram*, 16 July 1939.

73 *al-Ahram*, 7 March 1939.

74 Sudan, *Reports of His Majesty's High Commissioner for the Year 1920*, 120.

75 Egypt, *Egypt–Sudan: Collection of Documents*, 5.

76 In his study of the development of Bank Misr, Eric Davis argues that the protective tariffs were, "without doubt, the single most important factor" in the expansion of the Misr companies after 1930. Davis, *Challenging Colonialism*, 138.

77 el-Darwish, "Index Numbers of Wholesale Prices in Egypt," 68.

78 al-Dawla al-Misriya, Majlis al-Nuwwab, *Majmu'at Madabit dawr al-in'iqad al-'adi al-thani*, vol. 2 (28 February–29 May 1939), 1798.

79 *Majallat Ghurfat al-Qahira*, March 1937, 68.

80 *Majallat Ghurfat al-Qahira*, June 1937, 51. The editors of the Alexandria Chamber of Commerce's journal also noted Condominium budgetary concerns when they reported in April 1939 that the Sudanese government collected roughly LE80,000 on Japanese imports, and it was in such need of this revenue that it was reluctant to tamper with the system. *Majallat Ghurfat al-Iskandariya*, April 1939, 22.

81 "'Alaqat Misr bi-l-Sudan iqtisadiyan," 19 September 1938, File 'Abdin 105, 1. Muhammad Shahin Hamza also alluded to potential Anglo–Egyptian cooperation in countering foreign textile competition, stating in the Chamber of Deputies that "the Sudanese and English authorities in the Sudan are annoyed by the cheapness of foreign commodities, especially the Japanese," caused by insufficient tariffs. al-Dawla al-Misriya, Majlis al-Nuwwab, *Majmu'at Madabit dawr al-in'iqad al-'adi al-thani*, vol. 2 (28 February–29 May 1939), 1798. The British press, in this case the *Manchester Guardian*, also expected Anglo–Egyptian coorperation, claiming "every step Britain takes in fighting the Japanese competition will probably receive the support of the Egyptian authorities and their approval." *al-Ahram*, 25 June 1938.

82 *Majallat Ghurfat al-Qahira*, June 1939, 755.

83 *al-Ahram*, 26 November 1939.

84 *al-Ahram*, 1 January 1940.

85 *al-Ahram*, 12 February 1940.

86 *al-Ahram*, 10 August 1941.

87 *al-Ahram*, 25 January 1944. The importation of Indian textiles increased dramatically during the war but the elevated levels were maintained in

subsequent years. The Khartoum Chamber of Commerce president stated in a postwar speech that the Sudan imported four times as many cotton textiles from India as from Egypt. *Majallat Ghurfat al-Qahira*, April 1947.

88 Tignor, *State*, 103.

89 Davis, *Challenging Colonialism*, 162.

90 *Majallat Ghurfat al-Qahira*, September 1940, 681.

91 *Majallat Ghurfat al-Qahira*, August 1947 (emphasis added).

92 *Majallat Ghurfat al-Qahira*, March 1948.

93 *Majallat Ghurfat al-Qahira*, January 1948.

94 *Majallat Ghurfat al-Qahira*, August 1948.

95 *Majallat Ghurfat al-Qahira*, December 1948.

96 *Majallat Ghurfat al-Qahira*, October 1951.

97 *al-Jarida al-tijariya al-misriya*, 17 November 1952.

98 Some Egyptian textile exports were affected by a greater variety of factors. For instance, Egypt had enjoyed a profitable role in providing the *ziraq* or 'blue' cotton piece good in the Sudan. Actually, this textile was produced in England or Japan, imported to the Sudan, shipped to Upper Egyptian dye works typically, and then returned to the Sudan. By the Second World War Egypt was rapidly losing its role in this commerce because of high transport and insurance costs, as well as the complicated process of applying for customs drawbacks when the goods were returned to the Sudan. Khartoum permanent office director 'Ali Mawardi provided details on this trade and its problems in the Cairo Chamber of Commerce's journal. *Majallat Ghurfat al-Qahira*, April 1940.

99 *Majallat Ghurfat al-Iskandariya*, July 1950.

100 Only Egyptian export of shoes, and specifically rubber-soled shoes, was able to overcome foreign competition and significantly improve its market in the Sudan. Egyptians had sent significant quantities of leather boots and shoes to the Sudan for years (and this field remained the most valuable of the products mentioned here), but rubber-soled shoes only found a market when Japanese supplies were cut off in the Second World War—albeit without any government assistance in the war or afterwards. Shoes, both leather and rubber-soled, remained valuable exports to the Sudan, but these and other 'minor' fields were dwarfed by the value of textiles.

101 Abaza, *Buhuth iqtisadiya 'an al-Sudan*, 145.

102 Egypt and the Sudan placed excise duties on sugar production, but the duties imposed were included in the details of sugar trade agreements reached, which meant increased duties had virtually no impact on export volume. Sudan, *Report on the Administration in 1936*, 42; *al-Siyasa*, 12 March 1936. Transportation rates also did not influence export levels, although the costs were noticeably higher when trade proceeded by rail southward, rather than by ship via Alexandria or Cairo. "Exercice 1931–1932," 31 January 1933, File Maslahat al-Sharikat no. 111, DW, 6.

103 It should be noted that exports of 1955 alone constituted the volume of virtually the entire period. If 1955 is omitted, the average is only 5,498 kilograms annually.

104 "Rapport sur les Travaux de la Commission d'Approvisionnement du Gouvernement Égyptien," File Majlis al-Wuzara', no. 10/4, DW, 16.

105 "Rapport sur les Travaux de la Commission d'Approvisionnement," 19.

106 Daly, *Imperial Sudan*, 105. The Khartoum Chamber of Commerce reported in 1937 that even when the Condominium lowered the sales price of sugar significantly, the monopoly still contributed over a half million pounds to government revenues. *Majallat Ghurfat al-Qahira*, April 1937, 74.

107 *al-Akhbar*, 25 June 1922.

108 Husayn, *al-Sudan*, vol. 3, 297.

109 Sudan, *Report on the Finances, Administration and Condition of the Sudan in 1931* (London: His Majesty's Stationery Office, 1932), 95.

110 Abaza, *Buhuth iqtisadiya 'an al-Sudan*, 144.

111 *al-Jarida al-tijariya al-misriya*, 8 May 1930.

112 *al-Jarida al-tijariya al-misriya*, 25 May 1934.

113 *al-Ahram*, 2 December 1939. An earlier report from *al-Ahram* stated that the government had raised the price of sugar by 25 piasters, a 16 percent increase. *al-Ahram*, 27 November 1939.

114 "al-Tamwin al-Sukr," Majlis al-Wuzara', no. 10/5, DW.

115 "Sharikat Wadi Kom Ombo," File Maslahat al-Sharikat, no. 111, DW.

116 *al-Ahram*, 20 June 1939. The negotiations over sugar provisions from Egypt lasted a number of months, and in December 1939 officials were still debating details, particularly how long the guaranteed provisioning of the Sudan would last. *al-Ahram*, 6 December 1939.

117 *al-Ahram*, 9 October 1940.

118 Tignor, *State*, 54.

119 Zaki, "Taqrir," 17.

120 Not only did the statistics support Egypt's fulfilling its provisionary role in the Nile Valley, but local journals also reported that "the Sudan imported *all that was necessary* in the way of sugar from Egypt . . . *according to the agreement* completed recently." *Majallat Ghurfat al-Qahira*, September 1940 (emphasis added).

121 United Nations Security Council, *Verbatim Records*, 122.

122 Abbas, *The Sudan Question*, 93.

123 Sudan, *Report on the Administration in 1937*, 25–26.

124 Abaza, *Buhuth iqtisadiya 'an al-Sudan*, 146.

125 al-Dawla al-Misriya, Majlis al-Nuwwab, *Majmu'at Madabit dawr al-in'iqad al-'adi al-thani*, vol. 4 (1–25 July 1946), 3743–44; *Majallat Ghurfat al-Qahira*, December 1949.

126 Egypt, *Annual Statement of Foreign Trade* [1943–45]. At times in the documentary record there are hints of Egyptian interest in different non-

Sudanese markets during the war. For instance, in December 1939 the Cairo Chamber of Commerce reported sugar shipments to Iraq and Palestine, and official interest in Transjordan as well, but the government's own statistics reveal only small quantities exported anywhere besides the Sudan. *Majallat Ghurfat al-Qahira*, December 1939.

127 H. Naus to Husayn Rushdi, September 1914, Majlis al-Wuzara', no. 10/5, DW.

128 A significant drop in cotton prices and difficulties marketing this crop were also a dominant concern of leaders of the Egyptian economy during the Depression.

129 *Majallat Ghurfat al-Iskandariya*, January 1941, 24.

130 *Majallat Ghurfat al-Qahira*, April 1940, 360. An earlier article from the Khartoum permanent office director emphasized the possibility of Egyptians supplanting the Japanese as the primary supplier of textiles to the Sudan during the war. *Majallat Ghurfat al-Qahira*, February 1940, 301.

131 Tignor, *State*, 176.

132 *al-Jarida al-tijariya al-misriya*, 14 January 1941.

133 During the war, Egyptian and Sudanese customs administrations agreed to duty-free transit of goods through either country to the other. Sudan, *Report on the Administration for the Years 1939–1941*, 37. Also, officials reached agreement in 1941 on means of facilitating Sudanese exports through Egypt to the states of the Middle East. *Majallat Ghurfat al-Qahira*, May 1941.

134 Abaza, *Buhuth iqtisadiya 'an al-Sudan*, 144.

135 *al-Jarida al-tijariya al-misriya*, 14 January 1941.

136 *al-Ahram*, 23 July 1940.

137 Huddleston to Nahhas, 11 November 1943, File Majlis al-Wuzara'–al-Fatra ba'd 1923, no. 3D, DW, 1 (emphasis added)..

138 *al-Ahram*, 14 October 1939.

139 *al-Jarida al-tijariya al-misriya*, 25 October 1943.

140 Zaki, "Taqrir," 1.

141 al-Dawla al-Misriya, Majlis al-Nuwwab, *Majmu'at Madabit dawr al-in'iqad al-'adi al-thalith*, vol. 1 (13 March–30 April 1940), 1710–12.

142 *Majallat Ghurfat al-Qahira*, July 1943, 7.

143 *Majallat Ghurfat al-Qahira*, June 1944.

144 *al-Jarida al-tijariya al-misriya*, 27 June 1944.

145 Zaki, "Taqrir," 15.

146 Zaki, "Taqrir," 16. The exports permitted for 1943 included three hundred tons of *firka*-type mixed textiles, 1.9 million yards of cotton textiles to meet Sudanese government requests, twelve thousand garments destined for the Khartoum exhibition, and 120,000 cotton garments of other types (split evenly between artisanal and industrial manufactures).

147 *al-Jarida al-tijariya al-misriya*, 25 October 1943.

148 *Majallat Ghurfat al-Iskandariya*, July 1942, 20.

149 *al-Ahram*, 26 July 1940.

150 *Majallat Ghurfat al-Qahira*, January 1944. Later in 1944, Ahmad 'Abd al-Khaliq, the newly appointed economic expert, summarized the company's acquisition of the Khartoum office and confirmed that "its guiding principle is the building of economic foundations, for which the office had been established under the control and supervision of the economic expert." *al-Ahram*, 29 March 1944.

151 *al-Jarida al-tijariya al-misriya*, 16 August 1943 (emphasis added).

152 *al-Jarida al-tijariya al-misriya*, 30 August 1943.

153 *al-Ahram*, 2 January 1944.

154 *al-Jarida al-tijariya al-misriya*, 25 October 1943. Despite these restrictions, the expert still maintained that the company was "an encouragement to the establishment of other companies with commercial, agricultural and industrial intentions between Egypt and the Sudan." Zaki, "Taqrir," 17.

155 Undoubtedly, a major objective for Condominium administration price fixing was to prevent inflation—and the impact this would have on the local population. Inflation also lay behind some of the wartime statistical 'success' of Egyptian imports in the Sudan. Egyptians were certainly aware that this played a part in their improved commercial record during the conflict. A parliamentary report noted of tremendous trade levels with the Sudan during 1941–42 that "a large part of this increase stems from the rise of prices of commodities imported from it [the Sudan] and sent to it." al-Dawla al-Misriya, Majlis al-Nuwwab, *Majmu'at Madabit dawr al-in'iqad al-'adi al-thani*, vol. 1 (19 November 1942–19 April 1943), 670.

156 *al-Ahram*, 18 December 1939.

157 *Majallat Ghurfat al-Iskandariya*, August 1941, 10.

158 *Majallat Ghurfat al-Iskandariya*, June 1941, 10.

159 Mahmud Zaki, "Kitab ila al-Hakim al-'Am," File Majlis al-Wuzara'–al-Fatra ba'd 1923, no. 3D, DW, 3. In this letter, the expert made specific reference to complaints raised by the Egyptian Federation of Industries in respect to the permits needed and the impact this had on the Egyptian economy generally—not just commercial relations.

160 "Mulakhkhas Hadith bayn Nahhas wa Huddleston," 11 November 1943, File Majlis al-Wuzara'–al-Fatra ba'd 1923, no. 3D, DW, 3.

161 Nahhas to Huddleston, 1 January 1944, 2.

162 Huddleston to Nahhas, 18 May 1944, 3–4. In addition to import controls, the Condominium government had forbidden the export of many foodstuffs earlier that Egypt would desperately need during the war. *Majallat Ghurfat al-Qahira*, October 1939.

163 *al-Ahram*, 4 October 1939.

164 Sudan, *The Sudan: A Record of Progress*, 68.

165 al-Dawla al-Misriya, Majlis al-Nuwwab, *Majmu'at Madabit dawr al-in'iqad al-'adi al-Awwal*, vol. 1 (30 March–27 July 1942), 150.

166 Sudan, *Report on the Administration for the Years 1942–1944*, 9 (emphasis added).
167 *al-Ahram*, 17 February 1946.
168 *Majallat Ghurfat al-Qahira*, April 1947.
169 al-Dawla al-Misriya, Majlis al-Nuwwab, *Majmu'at Madabit dawr al-in'iqad al-'adi al-rabi'*, vol. 2 (16 February–6 April 1948) (Cairo: al-Matba'a al-Amiriya, 1949), 1602.
170 al-Dawla al-Misriya, Majlis al-Nuwwab, *Majmu'at Madabit dawr al-in'iqad al-'adi al-thalith*, vol. 2 (10 March–21 May 1947) (Cairo: al-Matba'a al-Amiriya, 1948), 1746.
171 al-Dawla al-Misriya, Majlis al-Nuwwab, *Majmu'at Madabit dawr al-in'iqad al-'adi al-thalith*, vol. 2 (10 March–21 May 1947), 1792.
172 *Majallat Ghurfat al-Iskandariya*, May 1947.
173 *Majallat Ghurfat al-Qahira*, June 1950 (emphasis added).
174 *Majallat Ghurfat al-Iskandariya*, January 1941, 24.
175 For instance, Egypt's most profitable year of exporting rice to the Sudan came in 1950, with a total value of LE150,630. That same year Egypt shipped LE7,635,650 worth of rice to other countries. Egypt, *Annual Statement of Foreign Trade, 1950 & 1951* (Cairo: Government Press, 1953).
176 *Majallat Ghurfat al-Iskandariya*, July 1950.
177 *Majallat Ghurfat al-Iskandariya*, June 1946.
178 *Majallat Ghurfat al-Qahira*, May 1946.
179 *Majallat Ghurfat al-Qahira*, May 1949.

Notes to Chapter 7

1 *Majallat Ghurfat al-Qahira*, April 1944.
2 *al-Akhbar*, 11 September 1922.
3 Abaza, "Mudhakkira," 9.
4 *Majallat Ghurfat al-Iskandariya*, December 1938, 12.
5 *al-Jarida al-tijariya al-misriya*, 9 March 1939.
6 Zaki, "Kitab ila al-hakim al-'am," 3.
7 *Majallat Ghurfat al-Qahira*, February 1940, 183.
8 *al-Jarida al-tijariya al-misriya*, 27 September 1943.
9 al-Dawla al-Misriya, Majlis al-Shuyukh, *Majmu'at madabit dawr al-in'iqad al-'adi al-tas'ia 'ashara*, vol. 1 (18 November 1943–25 April 1944) (Cairo: al-Matba'a al-Amiriya, 1944), 732.
10 Ministry of Commerce and Industry, "Mudhakkira marfu'a li-Majlis al-Wuzara' bi-sha'n mukafahat al-batala 'an tariq tashji' sina'at al-bina'," June 1946, File 'Abdin no. 26, DW, 1.
11 Rarely during the 1920s did Sudanese imports to Egypt exceed 150,000 kilograms, apparently because the latter's capacity to process untanned hides was not extensive during this earlier era. Berque, *Egypt*, 326.
12 Zaki, "Taqrir," 10.

13 Veterinary concerns and quarantine measures that greatly influenced livestock imports played little role in the hide trade. There were occasional reports that untanned leather had to be surrendered by traders at quarantine facilities, rather than customs houses, but there are no indications of these requirements significantly undermining trade. *al-Jarida al-tijariya al-misriya*, 17 February 1930.
14 Zaki, "Taqrir," 10.
15 Sudan, *Report on the Administration for the Years 1942–1944*, 72.
16 *al-Ahram*, 22 March 1944.
17 Abaza, "Mudhakkira," 10. Fu'ad Abaza noted also that the permanent committee had sought the assistance of the Sudanese Chamber of Commerce in lowering the price of 'industrial' salt sold by the Port Sudan salt company to discourage this contamination.
18 *al-Ahram*, 19 April 1939.
19 *Majallat Ghurfat al-Qahira*, November 1951, 962.
20 Abaza, *Buhuth iqtisadiya 'an al-Sudan*, 124.
21 *Majallat Ghurfat al-Qahira*, December 1947.
22 Sudan, *Report on the Administration in 1946*, 86.
23 *Majallat Ghurfat al-Qahira*, August 1952.
24 Reports of smuggling on Egypt's southern border are included in newspapers and government records throughout the period of this study—most commonly small groups of Bedouin having been apprehended attempting to smuggle silks and tobacco into Egypt. Reflective of these typically short news items was a 1938 report in *al-Ahram*, stating simply that "large quantities of Sudanese tobacco are smuggled into Egypt and distributed to customers." *al-Ahram*, 4 December 1938. The following spring this newspaper reported that Berber smugglers were caught carrying 500 kilograms of tobacco and twenty bolts of Japanese silk bound for Egypt. *al-Ahram*, 27 May 1939.
25 "Provisional Statement of the Customs Receipts for the Month of June 1922, 1923," File 'Abdin no. 258–Maliya–Jamarik, DW.
26 al-Dawla al-Misriya, Majlis al-Nuwwab, *Majmu'at Madabit dawr al-in'iqad al-'adi al-Rabi'*, vol. 2. (11 April–29 May 1934), 988.
27 "Tobacco Ordinance, 1933," File Majlis al-Wuzara'–al-Fatra ba'd 1923, no. 5H, DW.
28 *al-Jarida al-tijariya al-misriya*, 6 December 1943.
29 *Majallat Ghurfat al-Qahira*, June 1944, 467.
30 *al-Jarida al-tijariya al-misriya*, 24 September 1945.
31 *Majallat Ghurfat al-Qahira*, January 1945, 82; al-Dawla al-Misriya, Majlis al-Nuwwab, *Majmu'at Madabit dawr al-in'iqad al-'adi al-rabi'*, vol. 1 (11 April–29 May 1934), 335.
32 *Majallat Ghurfat al-Iskandariya*, March 1952, 72.
33 al-Dawla al-Misriya, Majlis al-Nuwwab, *Majmu'at Madabit dawr al-in'iqad al-'adi al-thani*, vol. 1 (19 November 1942–19 April 1943), 687.

34 *al-Jarida al-tijariya al-misriya*, 25 October 1943.

35 Zaki, "Kitab ila al-hakim al-'am," 2. Furthermore, it should be noted that in addition to the decrease in sesame imports from the Sudan, peanuts (another key oil-producing commodity) dropped from roughly 6,000 tons in 1940 to none for 1944 and 1945.

36 During 1950–55, sesame imports from the Sudan fluctuated dramatically, with zero imports in 1950 and 1951 to over 6 million kilograms imported in 1955 alone.

37 During 1950–55, there were tremendous fluctuations, from zero imports in 1950 to over 24,000 tons in 1955.

38 al-Dawla al-Misriya, Majlis al-Nuwwab, *Majmu'at Madabit dawr al-in'iqad al-'adi al-thani*, vol. 1 (19 November 1942–19 April 1943), 1017.

39 Zaki, "Taqrir," 4.

40 *Majallat Ghurfat al-Qahira*, September 1943, 501.

41 *al-Ahram*, 19 August 1943 (emphasis added).

42 The Egyptian press reported major government purchases of cotton seed from the Sudan in 1947, 1949, and 1951. Plus, the prohibition of cotton seed imports was not reestablished during the postwar years. *Majallat Ghurfat al-Qahira*, April 1949, 525; *al-Jarida al-tijariya al-misriya*, 19 March 1951. Occasionally there were complaints concerning the price of Sudanese cotton seed, but this did not lead to agreements being nullified. For instance, in 1947, with heightened Anglo–Egyptian tensions over British military forces in Egypt and the continued 'occupation' of the Sudan, Mawris Fakhri 'Abd al-Nur claimed in the Chamber of Deputies that "the English Sudanese government is irritated with the Egyptian government, and I saw that they raised, with the stroke of a pen, the price of cotton seed from LE6 to LE18 for 1 ton, . . . and this is a military fine upon Egypt, or a fine for the killing of another *sirdar*." al-Dawla al-Misriya, Majlis al-Nuwwab, *Majmu'at Madabit dawr al-in'iqad al-'adi al-thalith*, vol. 3 (26 May 1947–18 June 1947), 2440.

43 *Majallat Ghurfat al-Qahira*, December 1942, 971.

44 Nahhas to Huddleston, 13 April 1943, Number 5/3–2, File Majlis al-Wuzara'–al-Fatra ba'd 1923, no. 3D, DW, 1.

45 Obviously, transportation facilities, regulations, and rates impacted all commodities traded between Egypt and the Sudan, regardless of the direction in which goods were shipped. Cotton seed was a critical transport concern of the Second World War, but Egyptian officials participating in earlier economic missions to the Sudan had reported that reducing transport charges on Sudanese produce was essential—whether there was a global conflict or not. *Majallat Ghurfat al-Qahira*, February 1937, 138.

46 *Majallat Ghurfat al-Qahira*, September 1943, 501.

47 al-Dawla al-Misriya, Majlis al-Nuwwab, *Majmu'at Madabit dawr al-in'iqad al-'adi al-thani*, vol. 1 (19 November 1942–19 April 1943), 1017.

48 *Majallat Ghurfat al-Iskandariya*, December 1944, 19.

49 Egyptian interests had attempted to promote common soap exports to the Sudan since 1935, but soap producers and traders never transformed the Sudan into a major market. Exports to the Sudan between 1932 and 1938 were never less than 1.2 million kilograms per year, but the 1950–55 average export level was just over 300,000 kilograms.

50 Zaki, "Taqrir," 4.

51 *Majallat Ghurfat al-Qahira*, December 1950, 1199.

52 H.P. Harvey, "Note au Conseil des Ministres," 1 December 1919, File Majlis al-Wuzara', no. 10, DW, 1.

53 Schatz, "Aperçu Général," 656. The author noted other commodities as well in which the Sudan covered the deficits of Egyptian harvests. For example, in regard to groundnuts, "it is the Anglo–Egyptian Sudan which completes the supplies of Egypt." Schatz, "Aperçu Général," 704.

54 *al-Siyasa*, 28 April 1935.

55 *al-Siyasa*, 28 April 1935.

56 Husayn, *al-Sudan*, vol. 3, 244.

57 *Majallat Ghurfat al-Iskandariya*, September 1937, 15.

58 Sudan, *Report on the Administration in 1934*, 8–9.

59 Sudan, *Report on the Administration in 1934*, 109. The reliance of Upper Egyptian regions on Sudanese agricultural supplies was especially evident during the Second World War. An important component of this trade relationship was Sudanese export of dates to Egypt. Date imports enjoyed a traditional, consistent market in Egypt, exceeding well over 3 million kilograms annually (except for 1943). Even in this stable trade, Egyptian demand remained a critical factor. For instance, in 1931 Halfa Province reported that "trade is generally bad and cannot improve until Egypt buys the commodities the province exports," and the province depended mainly on date exports. Sudan, *Report on the Finances in 1931*, 112.

60 *al-Ahram*, 13 June 1938.

61 Abaza, *Buhuth iqtisadiya 'an al-Sudan*, 128.

62 *al-Ahram*, 5 June 1939.

63 al-Dawla al-Misriya, Majlis al-Nuwwab, *Majmu'at Madabit dawr al-in'iqad al-'adi al-rabi'*, vol. 2 (15 April–8 July 1941), 1390.

64 Zaki, "Kitab ila al-hakim al-'am," 3. Although the survival of certain regions of Egypt depended on Sudanese grain imports during the war, there are some indications of a reciprocally dependent relationship. For instance, the 1942 report of the Northern Province of the Sudan stated that "the export to Egypt at high prices of haricot, horse beans, and chick peas . . . kept the [local] market alive." So, some Sudanese markets and merchants had *self*-interest in the wartime grain trade, instead of merely meeting Egyptian needs. Sudan, *Report on the Administration for the Years 1942–1944*, 137.

65 Issawi, *Egypt*, 69.

66 "Taqrir nashat al-Ghurfa al-Tijariya bi-l-Sudan," 4.
67 Sudan, *The Sudan: A Record of Progress*, 67.
68 Sudan, *The Sudan: A Record of Progress*, 68.
69 *Majallat Ghurfat al-Iskandariya*, June 1941, 10.
70 *Majallat Ghurfat al-Iskandariya*, August 1941, 10–11.
71 *al-Siyasa*, 18 September 1935.
72 *al-Siyasa*, 18 September 1935.
73 *Majallat Ghurfat al-Qahira*, March 1936, 30.
74 *Majallat Ghurfat al-Qahira*, October 1938, 99. This article reported specifically that the recent founding of a sieve at Wadi Halfa would encourage exports of such produce.
75 *al-Ahram*, 17 April 1938.
76 *al-Ahram*, 18 August 1938.
77 The other commodity to which the Sudanese state applied purity requirements in 1935, sesame, seems to have been more positively affected. The value of sesame imports, which had never surpassed LE100,000 annually, averaged over LE175,000 annually between 1936 and 1940. Wartime restrictions and the allowance of Sudanese cotton seed imports led to a serious reduction in sesame imports after 1940, and these developments mitigate consideration of the mid-1930s efforts to improve sieving capabilities in the Sudan as successful.
78 In addition to their immunity to promotional efforts, these commodities were also less responsive to exceptional circumstances. Egyptian import of Sudanese dates demonstrated this tendency. For instance, the Halfa Province governor reported in 1932 bright export prospects with "the approaching submersion of over a million date trees on the Egyptian side of the boundary by the heightening of the Assouan Dam." Sudan, *Report on the Finances in 1932*, 119. Despite hopes of increased date exports with this hydraulic project, the volume of this trade invariably fell between 3.5 and 4.5 million kilograms annually throughout the 1930s and 1940s. Even potentially harmful measures, such as 1935 regulations that compelled "the Sudanese government to inspect all shipments intended for export to Egypt at that time," did little to alter such traditional imports from the Sudan. Abaza, *Buhuth iqtisadiya 'an al-Sudan*, 139.
79 *al-Jarida al-tijariya al-misriya*, 19 March 1951.
80 "Rapport sur les Travaux de la Commission Approvisionnement," 26. Among the scholars who identified the war as the turning point in Egyptian reliance on Sudanese livestock was Waldo Glanville. He stated of Sudanese livestock trade that "Egypt could obtain better quality cattle from adjacent Mediterranean countries up to the outbreak of World War I." Waldo Glanville, "Livestock Development in the Sudan, 1899–1956," in Lavin, *The Condominium Remembered*, vol. 2, 57.
81 "Rapport sur les Travaux de la Commission Approvisionnement," 27.
82 Harvey, "Note au Conseil des Ministres," 1.

83 Egypt, Customs Administration, *Annual Statement of the Foreign Trade of Egypt during 1919* (Cairo: al-Matba'a al-Amiriya, 1920), 410; Egypt, Customs Administration, *Annual Statement of the Foreign Trade of Egypt during 1920–1924* (Cairo: al-Matba'a al-Amiriya, 1925), 584.

84 E.M. Dowson, Ministry of Finance, 19 December 1922, Number 50.H.10/4, File Majlis al-Wuzara'–al-Fatra ba'd 1923, no. 3A, DW, 1.

85 Sudan, *Report on the Finances in 1928*, 49.

86 *al-Akhbar*, 10 June 1931.

87 *Majallat Ghurfat al-Qahira*, November 1941, 757.

88 al-Dawla al-Misriya, Majlis al-Shuyukh, *Majmu'at Madabit dawr al-in'iqad al-'adi al-sadis 'ashara*, vol. 2 (22 April–18 October 1941), 552.

89 Zaki, "Taqrir," 9–10.

90 Although analysis at this point concentrates on transportation capabilities, sales prices, Sudanese willingness to sell, and other factors that influenced the availability of Sudanese livestock in Egyptian markets between 1936 and 1940, there were certainly also references to Egyptian demand still being critical to this trade. For instance, in 1939 Sudanese authorities implied that sufficient demand existed in Egyptian markets when they complained that "Egypt imports small quantities of cattle, even though the doubling of the quantities imported and the replacement of what it imports from abroad is within Egypt's capabilities." *Majallat Ghurfat al-Iskandariya*, June 1939, 22.

91 Sudan, *Report on the Administration in 1936*, 106; Sudan, *Report on the Administration in 1937*, 48–49.

92 *al-Ahram*, 30 April 1939.

93 Abaza, *Buhuth iqtisadiya 'an al-Sudan*, 117. Although he emphasized Egyptian market influences, this author did mention the Sudanese Department of Economics and Trade's reference "to the improvement of the economic situation in the Sudan which has led to increased demand of the necessary sheep for local consumption—those for slaughter in the Sudan—at considerable prices, and a diminished scope for what can be exported at reasonable prices."

94 *al-Ahram*, 6 December 1939 (emphasis added).

95 *Majallat Ghurfat al-Qahira*, January 1938, 134.

96 "Taqrir al-Ghurfah," 2.

97 *Majallat Ghurfat al-Qahira*, May 1939, 648. During the Second World War officials finally lowered Alexandria port fees—from LE32 to LE13 per ship. Abaza, *Buhuth iqtisadiya 'an al-Sudan*, 17.

98 *al-Ahram*, 20 March 1939.

99 *al-Ahram*, 23 May 1939.

100 Abaza, *Buhuth iqtisadiya 'an al-Sudan*, 17.

101 Abaza, *Buhuth iqtisadiya 'an al-Sudan*, 73.

102 Zaki, "Taqrir," 9.

103 *al-Ahram*, 26 June 1938.

104 *al-Ahram*, 23 May 1939.

105 Ministry of Public Health, "al-Mawad al-ghidha'iya al-warida min al-Sudan," 26 September 1943, File Majlis al-Wuzara'–al-Fatra ba'd 1923, no. 3D, DW, 1.

106 Animals Export and Import Ordinance, 1913, File Majlis al-Wuzara', no. 11W, DW, 2.

107 Sudan, *Report on the Administration for the Years 1939–1941*, 68.

108 Abaza, *Buhuth iqtisadiya 'an al-Sudan*, 119–20.

109 al-Dawla al-Misriya, Majlis al-Nuwwab, *Majmu'at madabit dawr al-in'iqad al-'adi al-thani*, vol. 3 (7 May–26 June 1946), 2706.

110 *Majallat Ghurfat al-Qahira*, October 1946.

111 *Majallat Ghurfat al-Qahira*, June 1949.

112 *al-Siyasa*, 3 September 1935.

113 *Majallat Ghurfat al-Iskandariya*, April 1950.

114 *Majallat Ghurfat al-Qahira*, June 1950.

115 *Majallat Ghurfat al-Qahira*, April 1947.

116 *al-Jarida al-tijariya al-misriya*, 13 May 1930.

117 Issawi, *Egypt at Mid-Century*, 42.

118 Robert L. Tignor, "The Egyptian Revolution of 1919: New Directions in the Egyptian Economy," *Middle Eastern Studies* 12, no. 3 (1976): 48. Issawi and Tignor are not alone in their assessment of foreign commercial activities, as all scholars (Davis, Vitalis, Owen, and others) of interwar economic development acknowledge resident foreigners' critical entrepreneurial roles.

119 Thomas Philipp, *The Syrians in Egypt 1725–1975* (Stuttgart: Steiner, 1985), 137. Despite this author's claims that Syrian directors tended to take Egyptian citizenship, he also notes that no Syrians were included in the directorships of the "purely" Egyptian Misr companies. Additionally, there is plenty of evidence that foreign residents retained other citizenship as long as this was beneficial. Gudrun Kramer certainly makes this point in her study of the Egyptian Jewish community, arguing that despite simple procedures for gaining Egyptian citizenship, few Jews applied for it until after Montreux. Gudrun Kramer, *The Jews in Modern Egypt, 1914–1952* (London: I.B. Tauris, 1989), 34. Additionally, the records of specific companies support this trend of foreign residents' hesitancy in acquiring Egyptian citizenship. For instance, the Syrian residents of Egypt who managed the Sudan Import Export Company, a firm heavily involved in Sudanese exports to Egypt, delayed obtaining citizenship. In 1940 only one individual from the board of directors and higher-salaried officials had acquired Egyptian citizenship, although most would apply for it by 1948. This change was a result of the post–Second World War passage of Law No. 138, which mandated more stringent citizenship requirements for Egyptian companies. Document Number 30, Sharikat al-Waridat wa-l-Sadirat al-Sudaniya, File Maslahat al-Sharikat no. 87, DW.

120 Most of the information on this firm is drawn from company records compiled in Egypt and found in File Maslahat al-Sharikat, no. 87, DW.

121 Thomas Philipp notes the inclusion of some local Jews on the company's board of directors until after the Second World War, but the Tutunji family consistently represented the majority of board members. Philipp, *The Syrians in Egypt*, 138.

122 Company-owned factories that were specifically referred to in the records include a soap-making plant and a wood-working establishment.

123 An example of early commercial ventures with little capital outlay would be the Company of Egyptian-Nubian Treasures, founded in 1920 with capital amounting to only LE500. *Al-Majalla al-tijariya al-nubiya*, 28 August 1921, 95. Even companies founded over two decades later, designed specifically to take advantage of Second World War conditions, like the Egyptian–Sudanese Company for Commerce, were lightly capitalized ventures. This company began activities with only LE4,000 in capital. *Al-Jarida al-tijariya al-misriya*, 10 April 1944. Although this financial outlay was an improvement on the earlier Nubian undertaking, it certainly does not compare to the investment of the Tutunji family undertaking by that time.

124 Although not an example in the earlier analysis of Egyptian exports to the Sudan, Egyptian cigarettes were a consistently valuable commodity traded with the Sudan, and early meetings of the permanent committee of the Sudan included discussion of means of improving this export performance. Egyptian cigarette manufacture had been controlled by Greeks of Egypt since the introduction of modern processes. Roger Owen, "The Study of Middle Eastern Industrial History: Notes on the Interrelationship between Factories and Small-Scale Manufacturing with Special References to Lebanese Silk and Egyptian Sugar, 1900–1930," *International Journal of Middle East Studies* 16, no. 4 (1984): 482–83.

125 Philipp, *The Syrians in Egypt*, 120.

126 Like other scholars, Robert Tignor makes precisely this point in his 1984 study of Egyptian interwar economic development, namely that long-resident foreigners must be included in analysis of economic developments of this period and that they were an integral part of the local entrepreneurial class—including that class's pursuit of Egyptian 'nationalist' objectives in the Sudan.

127 *al-Akhbar*, 14 May 1922.

128 *al-Akhbar*, 1 March 1925. In addition to this public beating, a 3 January 1925 article from the same newspaper reported that the Condominium administration had imprisoned a number of Egyptians, including some merchants.

129 *al-Akhbar*, 30 November 1935.

130 al-Sayyid 'Abdallah al-Tayyib, "Rapport," 10 September 1923, File 'Abdin no. 104, DW, 8. Such especially venomous opinions of Egyptians should not be viewed necessarily as the prevailing position among all Sudanese. Sudanese groups tended to favor one or the other of the co-domini during this period,

and therefore one's approval or not of an Egyptian commercial presence was often a reflection of such allegiances.

131 *al-Balagh*, 1 September 1936.

132 *Majallat Ghurfat al-Qahira*, February 1947, 172.

133 *Majallat Ghurfat al-Qahira*, August 1950, 850.

134 *Majallat Ghurfat al-Qahira*, February 1951, 199.

135 "Mahdar jalsat al-lajna al-da'ima li-l-Sudan al-mun'aqada fi 5 Maris sanat 1938," File 'Abdin no. 105, DW, 1.

136 "Mahdar jalsat al-lajna al-da'ima li-l-Sudan al-mun'aqada fi 11 Abril sanat 1938," 4.

137 *Majallat Ghurfat al-Qahira*, February 1940, 300.

138 Undoubtedly there are various reasons why local traders may have been underrepresented in the advertising sections of these journals, but these publications were directed toward precisely the audience that nationalist leaders hoped might become more engaged in Egyptian–Sudanese commerce.

139 *Majallat Ghurfat al-Qahira*, February 1946, 230.

140 *Majallat Ghurfat al-Qahira*, March 1946, 393.

141 Although there were few advertisements requesting specifically textiles from Egypt, those few confirmed the arguments of other sources that foreign textiles had well-established distribution networks in the Sudan that were foreign-controlled. For instance, from the same review of postwar advertisements, the only merchant specifically seeking cotton and wool textiles was an Indian, Harilal Motichand of Port Sudan. *Majallat Ghurfat al-Qahira*, November 1948, 1278. In contrast to this most lucrative sphere of trade, the Tutunji advertisement focused on the much less profitable commercial activity of importing from the Sudan "edible oils, seeds, grain, white and red sesame, and others." *Majallat Ghurfat al-Qahira*, February 1953, 125.

142 The Cairo Chamber of Commerce published a two-part report by the exhibition director in April and May 1940. The article was part of the general effort to raise awareness of Sudanese economic conditions and to encourage greater Egyptian activity. However, from secondary-source corroboration it appears that his description of the situation in the Sudan, and especially Egyptian merchants' position, was both accurate and reasonably objective. Much of the general description in this and the following paragraphs is based on his article and the book published by 'Abdallah Husayn.

143 *Majallat Ghurfat al-Qahira*, May 1940, 471.

144 Husayn, *al-Sudan*, vol. 3, 282. More recent scholarship has also mentioned a stronger Egyptian presence in northern Sudan. For instance, in his study of northern Sudanese traders, el-Haj Bilal Omer notes "the penetration of Egyptian petty traders in Dongola region: they exchanged food crops for new kinds of items they imported from Egypt." Omer, *The Danagla Traders of Northern Sudan*, 8.

145 Perkins, *Port Sudan*, 75.

146 *Majallat Ghurfat al-Qahira*, May 1940, 468–69.

147 *Majallat Ghurfat al-Qahira*, May 1940, 469.
148 Dafalla, *The Nubian Exodus*, 15.
149 Dafalla, *The Nubian Exodus*, 17.
150 Omer, *The Danagla Traders of Northern Sudan*, 21–22.
151 Omer, *The Danagla Traders of Northern Sudan*, 80.
152 El-Haj Bilal Omer wrote that these Egyptian residents of the northern regions "continued to dominate in both the wholesale and retail trade until the beginning of the forties." Omer, *The Danagla Traders of Northern Sudan*, 81.
153 Husayn, *al-Sudan*, vol. 3, 62, 67.
154 Husayn, *al-Sudan*, vol. 3, 62, 67.
155 Husayn, *al-Sudan*, vol. 3, 267.
156 Husayn, *al-Sudan*, vol. 3, 267. Husayn also reported that the permanent committee hoped that merchants as well established as Ibrahim 'Amir would be capable of employing more Egyptian merchants in their business.
157 Husayn, *al-Sudan*, vol. 3, 68.
158 *Majallat Ghurfat al-Qahira*, October 1939, 1020.
159 Husayn, *al-Sudan*, vol. 3, 130.
160 Husayn, *al-Sudan*, vol. 3, 243.
161 Husayn, *al-Sudan*, vol. 3, 65.
162 Husayn, *al-Sudan*, vol. 3, 93.
163 Husayn, *al-Sudan*, vol. 3, 268.
164 *al-Ahram*, 29 November 1943.
165 *Majallat Ghurfat al-Qahira*, September 1945, 721.
166 *Majallat Ghurfat al-Qahira*, May 1940, 472.
167 *Majallat Ghurfat al-Qahira*, October 1939, 1020.
168 The following information on the various shareholders was taken from the documents that officially established the company, published in the local newspaper. *al-Jarida al-tijariya al-misriya*, 16 April 1944.
169 *al-Ahram*, 1 August 1941.
170 *Majallat Ghurfat al-Qahira*, March 1943.
171 *Majallat Ghurfat al-Qahira*, March 1943.
172 Daly, *Imperial Sudan*, 173.
173 Zaki, "Taqrir," 10.
174 *Majallat Ghurfat al-Qahira*, January 1944.
175 *Majallat Ghurfat al-Iskandariya*, August 1941, 11.
176 *Majallat Ghurfat al-Qahira*, May 1944, 352 (emphasis added).
177 Zaki, "Taqrir," 23–24.
178 *al-Ahram*, 24 February 1944.
179 *al-Jarida al-tijariya al-misriya*, 27 September 1943.
180 al-Dawla al-Misriya, Majlis al-Nuwwab, *Majmu'at Madabit dawr al-in'iqad al-'adi al-thani*, vol. 1 (12 November 1945–19 February 1946) (Cairo: al-Matba'a al-Amiriya, 1946), 35.

181 Zaki, "Kitab ila al-hakim al-'am," 1.

182 al-Dawla al-Misriya, Majlis al-Nuwwab, *Majmu'at Madabit dawr al-in'iqad al-'adi al-awwal*, vol. 1 (30 March–27 July 1942), 481.

183 *Majallat Ghurfat al-Iskandariya*, February 1950.

184 *Majallat Ghurfat al-Iskandariya*, August 1950.

185 *al-Jarida al-tijariya al-misriya*, 26 March 1951 (emphasis added).

Notes to Conclusion

1 United Kingdom, *Anglo–Egyptian Conversations on the Defense of the Suez Canal and on the Sudan, December 1950–November 1951* (London: His Majesty's Stationery Office, 1951), 33 (emphasis added).

2 Egypt, Ministry of Foreign Affairs, *Records of Conversations, Notes, and Papers Exchanged between the Royal Egyptian Government and the United Kingdom Government, (March 1950–November 1951)* (Cairo: Government Press, 1951), 178 (emphasis added).

3 Hugh Seton-Watson, *Nations and States: An Enquiry into the Origins of Nations and the Politics of Nationalism* (Boulder, CO: Westview Press, 1977), 9.

4 Hobsbawm, *Nations and Nationalism*, 138.

5 al-Dawla al-Misriya, Majlis al-Nuwwab, *Majmu'at Madabit dawr al-in'iqad al-'adi al-tabi'*, vol. 1 (12 November 1947–9 February 1948), 639.

6 al-Dawla al-Misriya, Majlis al-Nuwwab, *Majmu'at Madabit dawr al-in'iqad al-'adi al-thalith*, vol. 1 (14 November 1946–3 March 1947), 356 (emphasis added).

7 Sudan, *Annual Report of the Department of Economics* [1938], 65. Even this success in shoe importation must be tempered by consideration of the different levels of leather and stuck rubber-soled shoes. 'Abdallah Fakri Abaza reported that even with increased imports, Egypt's share of total Sudanese shoe imports only amounted to 21 percent in 1939, with most Sudanese imports coming from Japan and being of the stuck rubber-soled variety. Finally, improved leather shoe imports were not only due to Condominium assistance in the form of customs changes but also to the Sudan's stores department contracting to buy shoes from one of the larger Egyptian shoe manufacturers. *Majallat Ghurfat al-Qahira*, September 1940, 682.

8 The value of Egyptian cigarette exports did not rival that of textiles, but levels remained above LE200,000 annually in the 1920s and recovered from the Depression-era downturn by the Second World War. This statistical claim is based on the same combination of Egyptian and Sudanese official publications used to compile commercial data in earlier chapters.

9 Sudan, *Report on the Administration in 1935*, 41; Sudan, *Report on the Administration in 1936*, 42.

10 *al-Akhbar*, 7 August 1935.

11 *al-Akhbar*, 7 August 1935.

12 *Majallat Ghurfat al-Qahira*, June 1950 (emphasis added).

13 Egyptian and British officials debated how to fairly calculate and arrange the repayment of Sudanese debts to Egypt from the time of the 1936 Anglo–Egyptian treaty. Most of the controversy revolved around precisely what monies were provided to the Condominium government as loans that had to be repaid. Egyptian and British officials came up with different estimates—ranging between LE5.1 and LE5.4 million. A comprehensive summary of the issues debated at the time Governor-General Symes visited Cairo is provided in *al-Ahram*, 24 November 1939.

14 al-Dawla al-Misriya, Majlis al-Nuwwab, *Majmu'at Madabit dawr al-in'iqad al-'adi al-thani*, vol. 3 (1 May–9 July 1951), 59–61. All statistics in this paragraph are based on the Ministry of Finance's report from this source.

15 Sudanese imports constituted only 1.2 percent of total Egyptian imports by value that year.

16 al-Dawla al-Misriya, Majlis al-Nuwwab, *Majmu'at Madabit dawr al-in'iqad al-'adi al-awwal* (15 March–10 July 1924), 714.

17 al-Dawla al-Misriya, Majlis al-Nuwwab, *Majmu'at Madabit dawr al-in'qad ghayr al-'adi li-nazar mu'ahadat al-sadaqa wa-l-tahaluf bayna Misr wa-Baritanya al-'Uzma* (2–19 November 1936), 21.

18 al-Dawla al-Misriya, Majlis al-Nuwwab, *Majmu'at Madabit dawr al-in'qad ghayr al-'adi li-nazar mu'ahadat al-sadaqa wa-l-tahaluf bayna Misr wa-Baritanya al-'Uzma* (2–19 November 1936), 52.

19 Gershoni and Jankowski, *Egypt, Islam, and the Arabs*, 53.

20 *Majallat Ghurfat al-Qahira*, October 1953, 119.

21 John Voll and many other scholars have made this point—essentially that "developing Sudanese attitudes were crucial in either opening or closing the door to unity." Voll, "Unity of the Nile Valley," 207.

22 Anderson, *Imagined Communities*, 159.

Selected Bibliography

Unpublished Government Sources from Dar al-Watha'iq, Cairo, Egypt

The following collections were relied on extensively in this monograph. Folder, file, and document numbers are cited in footnotes.

Majlis al-Wuzara'
Maslahat al-Sharikat
'Abdin

Published Government Sources—Arabic

al-Dawla al-Misriya. Majlis al-Nuwwab, *Majmu'at Madabit*. Cairo: al-Matba'a al-Amiriya, 1924–55.

———. Majlis al-Shuyukh, *Majmu'at Madabit*. Cairo: al-Matba'a al-Amiriya, 1924–55.

———. Maslahat 'Umum al-Ihsa' al-Amiriya. *al-Ihsa' al-sanawi al-'amm li-l-qutr al-misri*. Cairo: al-Matba'a al-Amiriya, 1914–29, 1931–55.

———. Wizarat al-Tijara wa-l-Sina'a, Lajnat al-Sudan al-Da'ima. *al-Sudan, a'mal al-ba'athat al-misriya wa-l-lajna al-da'ima li-l-Sudan min sanat 1935 ila sanat 1938*. Cairo: al-Matba'a al-Amiriya, 1938.

al-Hukuma al-Misriya. Wizarat al-Maliya. Maslahat al-Jamarik al-Misriya. *Taqrir 'an tijarat Misr al-kharijiya 'amm 1945*. Cairo: al-Matba'a al-Amiriya, 1947.

———. Wizarat al-Maliya wa-l-Iqtisad. Maslahat al-Jamarik al-Misriya. *Taqrir 'an tijarat Misr al-kharijiya 'amm 1951*. Cairo: al-Matba'a al-Amiriya, 1952.

Jumhuriya Misr. Ri'asat Majlis al-Wuzara'. *al-Sudan min 13 Fabrayir 1841 ila 12 Fabrayir 1953*. Cairo: al-Matba'a al-Amiriya, 1953.

Published Government Sources—English and French

Egypt. *Annual Statement of Foreign Trade*. Cairo: Government Press, [1918–55.]

———. *Egypt–Sudan: Collection of Documents*. Cairo: Government Press, 1947.

Egypt, Ministry of Foreign Affairs. *Records of Conversations, Notes and Papers Exchanged between the Royal Egyptian Government and the United Kingdom Government (March 1950–November 1951)*. Cairo: Government Press, 1951.

Gouvernement Égyptien. *Rapport de la Commission du Commerce et de l'Industrie (Edition Provisoire Confidentielle)*. File Majlis al-Wuzara', no. 19, DW. Cairo: Imprimerie Nationale, 1917.

Sudan. *Annual Report of the Department of Economics and Trade, 1938*. Khartoum: McCorquodale and Co., 1939.

———. *Annual Report of the Department of Economics and Trade, 1945*. Khartoum: McCorquodale and Co., 1945.

———. *Reports by His Majesty's High Commissioner on the Finances, Administration, and Condition of Egypt and the Soudan for the Year 1920*. London: His Majesty's Stationery Office, 1921.

———. *Report on the Finances, Administration and Condition of the Sudan in 1928*. London: His Majesty's Stationery Office, 1929.

———. *Report on the Finances, Administration and Condition of the Sudan in 1929*. London: His Majesty's Stationery Office, 1930.

———. *Report on the Finances, Administration and Condition of the Sudan in 1930*. London: His Majesty's Stationery Office, 1931.

———. *Report on the Finances, Administration and Condition of the Sudan in 1931*. London: His Majesty's Stationery Office, 1932.

———. *Report on the Finances, Administration and Condition of the Sudan in 1932*. London: His Majesty's Stationery Office, 1933.

———. *Report on the Administration, Finances and Condition of the Sudan in 1933*. London: His Majesty's Stationery Office, 1934.

———. *Report on the Administration, Finances and Condition of the Sudan in 1934*. London: His Majesty's Stationery Office, 1935.

———. *Report on the Administration, Finances and Condition of the Sudan in 1935*. London: His Majesty's Stationery Office, 1936.

———. *Report on the Administration, Finances and Condition of the Sudan in 1936*. London: His Majesty's Stationery Office, 1937.

———. *Report on the Administration, Finances and Condition of the Sudan in 1937*. London: His Majesty's Stationery Office, 1938.

———. *Report on the Administration, Finances and Condition of the Sudan in 1938*. London: His Majesty's Stationery Office, 1939.

———. *Report on the Administration of the Sudan, for the Years 1939–1941*. Khartoum: McCorquodale and Co., 1950.

———. *Report on the Administration of the Sudan, for the Years 1942–1944*. Khartoum: McCorquodale and Co., 1950.

———. *Report on the Administration of the Sudan in 1946*. Khartoum: McCorquodale and Co., 1948.

———. *Report on the Administration of the Sudan in 1949*. Khartoum: McCorquodale and Co., 1950.

———. *The Revised Edition of the Laws of the Sudan, from 1899 to 1926 (1st June)*. London: McCorquodale and Co., 1926.

———. *The Sudan: A Record of Progress, 1898–1947*. Khartoum: Sudan Surveys Department, 1947.

———. Wizarat al-Naql wa al-Muwasalat. *Laws of the Sudan*. 2 vols. Khartoum: McCorquodale and Co., 1941.

Sudan, Commission of Inquiry into the Disturbances in the Southern Sudan during August, 1955. *Report of the Commission of Inquiry into the Disturbances in the Southern Sudan during August, 1955*. Khartoum: McCorquodale and Co., 1956.

United Kingdom. *Reports by His Majesty's High Commissioner on the Finances, Administration, and Condition of Egypt and the Soudan for the Year 1920*. London: His Majesty's Stationery Office, 1921.

———. *Anglo–Egyptian Conversations on the Defence of the Suez Canal and on the Sudan, December 1950–November 1951*. London: His Majesty's Stationery Office, 1951.

United Nations Security Council. *Verbatim Records of Anglo–Egyptian Dispute, 5th August 1947–10th September 1947*. Cairo: Government Press, 1947.

Periodicals—Arabic

al-Ahram

al-Akhbar

al-Balagh

al-Ikhwan al-Muslimin

al-Jarida al-tijariya al-misriya

Majallat Ghurfat al-Iskandariya

Majallat Ghurfat al-Qahira

al-Majalla al-tijariya al-nubiya

Sahifat al-tijara wa-l-sina'a

al-Siyasa

Secondary Sources—English and French

Abbas, Mekki. *The Sudan Question: The Dispute over the Anglo–Egyptian Condominium, 1884–1951*. New York: Praeger, 1952.

Abbas, Raouf, and Assem el-Dessouky. *The Large Landowning Class and the Peasantry in Egypt, 1837–1952*. Edited by Peter Gran. Translated by Amer Mohsen with Mona Zikri. Syracuse, NY: Syracuse University Press, 2011.

'Abd al-Rahim, Muddathir. *Imperialism and Nationalism in the Sudan: A Study in Constitutional and Political Development, 1899–1956*. London: Oxford University Press, 1969.

Abdin, Hasan. *Early Sudanese Nationalism, 1919–1925*. Khartoum: University of Khartoum, 1985.

Abu Hasaba, Afaf Abdel Majid. *Factional Conflict in the Sudanese National Movement, 1918–1948*. Khartoum: University of Khartoum, 1985.

Ahmed, Jamal Mohammed. *The Intellectual Origins of Egyptian Nationalism*. Oxford: Oxford University Press, 1960.

Ali Taha, Fadwa Abd al-Rahman. *The Anglo–Egyptian Dispute over the Sudan, 1937–1947*. Khartoum: Khartoum University Press, 2006.

el-Amin, Mohammed Nuri. "Britain, the 1924 Sudanese Uprising, and the Impact of Egypt on the Sudan." *International Journal of African Historical Studies* 19, no. 2 (1986): 235–60.

Anderson, Benedict. *Imagined Communities: Reflections on the Origin and Spread of Nationalism*. Rev. ed. New York: Verso, 2006.

Anderson, J.N.D. "Law Reform in Egypt: 1850–1950." In *Political and Social Change in Modern Egypt*, edited by P.M. Holt, 209–30. Oxford: Oxford University Press, 1968.

Armstrong, John A. *Nations before Nationalism*. Chapel Hill, NC: University of North Carolina, 1982.

Askari, Hassein, and John Thomas Cummings. *Middle East Economies in the 1970s: A Comparative Approach*. New York: Praeger, 1976.

Awad, Mohamed. "Egypt, Great Britain, and the Sudan: An Egyptian View." *Middle East Journal* 1, no. 3 (1947): 281–91.

Ayubi, Nazih N. *Distant Neighbors: The Political Economy of Relations between Europe and the Middle East/North Africa*. Reading: Ithaca Press, 1995.

Baddour, Abd el-Fattah Ibrahim al-Sayed. *Sudanese–Egyptian Relations: A Chronological and Analytical Study*. The Hague: Martinus Nijhoff, 1960.

Badran, Margot. "Dual Liberation: Feminism and Nationalism in Egypt, 1870s–1925." *Feminist Issues* 8, no. 1 (1988): 15–34.

———. *Feminists, Islam, and Nation: Gender and the Making of Modern Egypt*. Princeton, NJ: Princeton University Press, 1995.

Badrawi, Malak. "Financial Cerberus? The Egyptian Parliament, 1924–1952." In *Re-Envisioning Egypt, 1919–1952*, edited by Arthur Goldschmidt, Amy J. Johnson, and Barak A. Salmoni, 94–122. Cairo: American University in Cairo Press, 2005.

———. *Isma'il Sidqi, 1875–1950: Pragmatism and Vision in Twentieth Century Egypt*. London: Routledge, 1996.

Baer, Gabriel. *Studies in the Social History of Modern Egypt*. Chicago: Chicago University Press, 1969.

———. *A History of Landownership in Modern Egypt, 1800–1950*. Oxford: Oxford University Press, 1962.

Bakheit, G.M.A. "British Administration and Sudanese Nationalism, 1919–1939." PhD diss., Cambridge University, 1965.

Balibar, Etienne. "The Nation Form: History and Ideology." In *Race, Nation, Class: Ambiguous Identities*, edited by Etienne Balibar and Immanuel Wallerstein, 86–106. London: Verso, 1991.

Baraka, Magda. *The Egyptian Upper Class between Revolutions, 1919–1952*. Reading: Ithaca Press, 1998.

el-Barawy, Rashed. *Egypt, Britain and the Sudan*. Cairo: Renaissance Bookshop, 1952.

Barbour, K.M. *The Growth, Location, and Structure of Industry in Egypt*. New York: Praeger, 1972.

Barnett, Tony. *The Gezira Scheme: An Illusion of Development*. London: Frank Cass, 1977.

Baron, Beth. *Egypt as a Woman: Nationalism, Gender, and Politics*. Cairo: American University in Cairo Press, 2005.

Beard, Charles. *An Economic Interpretation of the Constitution of the United States*. New Brunswick, NJ: Transaction Publishers, 1998.

Berque, Jacques. *Egypt: Imperialism and Revolution*. New York: Praeger, 1972.

Bein, F.L. "Land Use Patterns along the Nile." *Sudan Notes and Records* 59 (1978): 180–89.

Beinin, Joel. *Workers on the Nile: Nationalism, Communism, Islam and the Egyptian Working Class, 1882–1954*. Princeton, NJ: Princeton University Press, 1987.

Beshir, Mohamed Omer. *Educational Development in the Sudan, 1898–1956*. Oxford: Clarendon, 1969.

Binder, Leonard. *In a Moment of Enthusiasm: Political Power and the Second Stratum in Egypt*. Chicago: University of Chicago Press, 1978.

Birch, Anthony H. *Nationalism and National Integration*. London: Unwin Hyman, 1989.

Botman, Selma. *Egypt from Independence to Revolution, 1919–1952*. Syracuse, NY: Syracuse University Press, 1991.

———. *Engendering Citizenship in Egypt*. New York: Columbia University Press, 1999.

———. *The Rise of Egyptian Communism, 1939–1970*. Syracuse, NY: Syracuse University Press, 1988.

Breuilly, John. "Approaches to Nationalism." In *Mapping the Nation*, edited by Gopal Balakrishnan, 146–74. London: Verso, 1996.

———. *Nationalism and the State*. Manchester: Manchester University Press, 1985.

Carmichael, Sir John. "Economic Development in the Sudan, 1899–1956." In *The Condominium Remembered: Proceedings of the Durham Sudan Historical Records Conference*, Vol. 2: *The Transformation of the Old Order in the Sudan*, edited by Deborah Lavin. Durham: Centre for Middle Eastern and Islamic Studies, 1993.

Chase-Dunn, Christopher, and Thomas D. Hall. *Core/Periphery Relations in Precapitalist Worlds*. Boulder, CO: Westview, 1991.

Chatterjee, Partha. *Nationalist Thought and the Colonial World: A Derivative Discourse?* Minneapolis, MN: University of Minnesota Press, 1986.

———. "Whose Imagined Community." In *Mapping the Nation*, edited by Gopal Balakrishnan, 214–25. London: Verso, 1996.

Churchill, Winston. *The River War: An Account of the Reconquest of the Sudan*. London: Eyre and Spottiswoode, 1951.

Cleland, Wendell. "A Population Plan for Egypt." *L'Égypte Contemporaine* 30, no. 185 (1939): 461–84.

Collins, Jeffrey G. *The Egyptian Elite under Cromer, 1882–1907*. Berlin: Klaus Schwarz, 1984.

Collins, Robert O. "History, Hydropolitics and the Nile: Nile Control—Myth or Reality." In *The Nile, Resource Evaluation, Resource Management, Hydropolitics and Legal Issues*, edited by P.P. Howell and J.A. Allan, 153–80. London: Centre for Near and Middle Eastern Studies, 1990.

———. *The Southern Sudan in Historical Perspective*. New Brunswick, NJ: Transaction Publishers, 2006.

———. *The Waters of the Nile: Hydropolitics and the Jonglei Canal, 1900–1988*. Oxford: Clarendon, 1990.

Collins, Robert O., and Robert L. Tignor. *Egypt and the Sudan*. Englewood Cliffs, NJ: Prentice Hall, 1967.

Connor, Walker. "When is a Nation?" In *Nationalism*, edited by John Hutchinson and Anthony D. Smith, 154–59. Oxford: Oxford University Press, 1994.

Coury, Ralph. *The Making of an Egyptian Arab Nationalist: The Early Years of 'Azzam Pasha, 1893–1936*. Reading: Garnet, 1998.

Cromer, Earl of [Evelyn Baring]. "The Capitulations in Egypt." In *Political and Literary Essays, 1908–1913*. London: MacMillan, 1913.

Crouchley, A.E. "A Century of Economic Development, 1837–1937." *L'Égypte Contemporaine* 30, no. 182–83 (1939): 133–55.

Currie, James. "The Educational Experiment in the Anglo–Egyptian Sudan, 1900–33," Part 1. *Journal of the Royal African Society* 33, no. 133 (1934): 361–71.

———. "The Educational Experiment in the Anglo–Egyptian Sudan, 1900–33," Part 2. *Journal of the Royal African Society* 34, no. 134 (1935): 41–59.

Dafalla, Hassan. *The Nubian Exodus*. London: C. Hurst & Co., 1975.

Daly, M.W. *Empire on the Nile: The Anglo–Egyptian Condominium, 1898–1934*. Cambridge: Cambridge University Press, 1986.

———. *Imperial Sudan: The Anglo–Egyptian Condominium, 1934–1956*. Cambridge: Cambridge University Press, 1991.

Daly, M.W., and P.M. Holt. *A History of the Sudan: From the Coming of Islam to the Present Day*. London: Longman, 1988.

el-Darwish, M. "Index Numbers of Wholesale Prices in Egypt." *L'Égypte Contemporaine* 23, no. 132 (1932): 18–34.

Davis, Eric. *Challenging Colonialism: Bank Misr and Egyptian Industrialization, 1920–1941*. Princeton, NJ: Princeton University Press, 1983.

Deeb, Marius. "Bank Misr and the Emergence of the Local Bourgeoisie in Egypt." *Middle Eastern Studies* 12, no. 3 (1976): 69–86.

———. *Party Politics in Egypt: The Wafd and Its Rivals, 1919–1939*. London: Ithaca Press, 1979.

———. "The Socioeconomic Role of Local Foreign Minorities in Modern Egypt, 1805–1961." *International Journal of Middle East Studies* 9, no. 1 (1978): 11–22.

Deutsch, Karl W. *Nationalism and Social Communication: An Inquiry into the Foundations of Nationality*. 2nd ed. Cambridge: MIT Press, 1966.

Doran, Michael. *Pan-Arabism before Nasser: Egyptian Power Politics and the Palestine Question*. Oxford: Oxford University Press, 1999.

Egger, Vernon. *A Fabian in Egypt: Salamah Musa and the Rise of the Professional Classes in Egypt, 1909–1939*. Lanham, MD: University Press of America, 1986.

Emerson, Rupert. *From Empire to Nation*. Cambridge, MA: Harvard University Press, 1962.

Eran, Oded. "Negotiating the Anglo–Egyptian Relationship between the World Wars." In *Imperialism and Nationalism in the Middle East*, edited by Keith Wilson, 56–75. London: Mansell, 1983.

Erlich, Haggai. *Students and University in 20th Century Egyptian Politics*. London: Frank Cass, 1989.

EzzelArab, AbdelAzziz. *European Control and Egypt's Traditional Elites—A Case Study in Elite Economic Nationalism*. Lewiston: Edwin Mellon, 2002.

Fabunmi, L.A. *The Sudan in Anglo–Egyptian Relations: A Case Study of Power Politics 1800–1956*. Westport, CT: Greenwood, 1973.

Fahim, Hussein M. *Egyptian Nubians, Resettlement and Years of Coping*. Salt Lake City, UT: University of Utah, 1983.

Fahmy, Ziad. *Ordinary Egyptians: Creating the Modern Nation through Popular Culture*. Stanford, CA: Stanford University Press, 2011.

Fluehr-Lobban, Carolyn, and Kharyssa Rhodes, eds. *Race and Identity in the Nile Valley: Ancient and Modern Perspectives*. Trenton, NJ: Red Sea Press, 2004.

Gaddi, L., and I.G. Levi. "Observations Générales sur le Nouveau Tarif Douanier." *L'Égypte Contemporaine* 23, no. 133–34 (1932): 200–39.

Gaitskell, Arthur. *Gezira: A Story of Development in the Sudan*. London: Faber and Faber, 1959.

Gellner, Ernest. "Nationalism and Modernization." In *Nationalism*, edited by John Hutchinson and Anthony D. Smith. Oxford: Oxford University Press, 1994.

———. *Nations and Nationalism*. Ithaca, NY: Cornell University Press, 1983.

Gershoni, Israel. "Geographers and Nationalism in Egypt: Huzayyin and the Unity of the Nile Valley, 1945–1948." In *The Nile: Histories, Cultures, Myths*, edited by Haggai Erlich and Israel Gershoni, 199–215. Boulder, CO: Lynne Rienner, 2000.

Gershoni, Israel, and Meir Hatina, eds. *Narrating the Nile: Politics, Cultures, Identities*. Boulder, CO: Lynne Rienner, 2008.

———. *Nations and Nationalism*. Ithaca, NY: Cornell University Press, 1983.

Gershoni, Israel, and James Jankowski. *Commemorating the Nation: Collective Memory, Public Commemoration, and National Identity in Twentieth-Century*

Egypt. Chicago: Middle East Documentation Center, 2004.
———. *Egypt, Islam, and the Arabs: The Search for Egyptian Nationhood, 1900–1930*. New York: Oxford University Press, 1986.
———. *Redefining the Egyptian Nation, 1930–1945*. New York: Cambridge University Press, 1995.
Glanville, Waldo. "Livestock Development in the Sudan, 1899–1956." In *The Condominium Remembered*, edited by Deborah Lavin, vol. 2, 57–64. Durham: Centre for Middle Eastern and Islamic Studies, 1993.
Goldberg, Ellis. *Tinker, Tailor, and Textile Worker: Class and Politics in Egypt, 1930–1952*. Berkeley, CA: University of California, 1986.
Goldschmidt, Arthur, Jr. "The Egyptian Nationalist Party: 1892–1919." In *Political and Social Change in Modern Egypt*, edited by P. M. Holt, 308–33. Oxford: Oxford University Press, 1968.
———. *Modern Egypt: The Formation of a Nation-State*. Boulder, CO: Westview, 1988.
Gorman, Anthony. *Historians, State and Politics in Twentieth Century Egypt: Contesting the Nation*. London: Routledge, 2003.
Gran, Peter. *Islamic Roots of Capitalism: Egypt, 1760–1840*. Austin, TX: University of Texas Press, 1979.
Hail, J.A. *Britain's Foreign Policy in Egypt and Sudan, 1947–1956*. Reading: Ithaca Press, 1996.
Hall, John A. *The State of the Nation: Ernest Gellner and the Theory of Nationalism*. Cambridge: Cambridge University Press, 1998.
Hanes, W. Travis, III. *Imperial Diplomacy in the Era of Decolonization: The Sudan and Anglo–Egyptian Relations, 1945–1956*. Westport, CT: Greenwood, 1995.
Hanna, Nelly. *Artisan Entrepreneurs in Cairo and Early-Modern Capitalism (1600–1800)*. Syracuse, NY: Syracuse University Press, 2011.
Harlen, Christine M. "A Reappraisal of Classical Economic Nationalism and Economic Liberalism." *International Studies Quarterly* 43, no. 4 (1999): 733–44.
Harris, Christina Phelps. *Nationalism and Revolution in Egypt: The Role of the Muslim Brotherhood*. Westport, CT: Hyperion, 1981.
Hearn, Jonathan. *Rethinking Nationalism: A Critical Introduction*. New York: Palgrave Macmillan, 2006.
Henderson, K.D.D. *The Making of the Modern Sudan: The Life and Letters of Sir Douglas Newbold, K.B.E. of the Sudan Political Service*. Westport, CT: Greenwood, 1974.
———. *Sudan Republic*. New York: Praeger, 1965.
Hershlag, Z.Y. *Introduction to the Modern Economic History of the Middle East*. 2nd rev. ed. Leiden: Brill, 1980.
Hill, Richard. *Egypt in the Sudan 1820–1881*. Oxford: Oxford University Press, 1959.

———. *Sudan Transport: A History of Railway, Marine, and River Services in the Republic of the Sudan*. Oxford: Oxford University Press, 1965.

Hobsbawm, Eric. *Nations and Nationalism since 1780: Programme, Myth, Reality*. Cambridge: Cambridge University Press, 1990.

Hobsbawm, Eric, and Terence Ranger, eds. *The Invention of Tradition*. Cambridge: Cambridge University Press, 1984.

Hroch, Miroslav. *Social Preconditions of National Revival in Europe: A Comparative Analysis of the Social Composition of Patriotic Groups among the Smaller European Nations*. Translated by Ben Fowkes. Cambridge: Cambridge University Press, 1985.

Hurriez, Sayyid H., and Elfatih A. Abdel Salam. *Ethnicity, Conflict and National Integration in the Sudan*. Khartoum: University of Khartoum Press, 1989.

Hutchinson, John. *Modern Nationalism*. London: Fontana, 1994.

———. "Moral Innovators and the Politics of Regeneration: The Distinctive Role of Cultural Nationalists in Nation-Building." *International Journal of Comparative Sociology* 33, no. 1–2 (1992): 101–17.

Hutchinson, John, and Anthony D. Smith, eds. *Nationalism*. Oxford: Oxford University Press, 1994.

Ibrahim, Abdel Rahman A. "Trade and Regional Underdevelopment in Sudan." In *Trade and Traders in the Sudan*, edited by Leif O. Manger, 109–38. Bergen: University of Bergen, 1984.

Ibrahim, Hassan Ahmed. *The 1936 Anglo–Egyptian Treaty*. Khartoum: Khartoum University Press, 1976.

———. "Imperialism and Neo-Mahdism in the Sudan: A Study of British Policy towards Neo-Mahdism, 1924–1927." *International Journal of African Historical Studies* 13, no. 2 (1980): 214–39.

———. "Mahdist Risings against Condominium Government in the Sudan." *International Journal of African Historical Studies* 2, no. 3 (1979): 440–71.

Ismail, Mahmoud Ismail Mohamed. "Nationalism in Egypt before Nasser's Revolution." PhD diss., University of Pittsburgh, 1966.

Issawi, Charles. *Egypt: An Economic and Social Analysis*. Oxford: Oxford University Press, 1947.

———. *Egypt at Mid-Century: An Economic Survey*. Oxford: Oxford University Press, 1954.

———. *Egypt in Revolution: An Economic Analysis*. Oxford: Oxford University Press, 1963.

———. "The Entrepreneur Class." In *Social Forces in the Middle East*, edited by S.N. Fisher, 116–36. Ithaca, NY: Cornell University Press, 1955.

Jal, Gabriel Giet. *The Sudan Question in the Anglo–Egyptian Treaty of 1936: An Historical Study of Conflict in Anglo–Egyptian Relations in the Sudan, 1899–1936*. Juba: Juba University Press, 1989.

Jankowski, James. *Egypt's Young Rebels: "Young Egypt," 1933–1952*. Stanford, CA: Hoover Institution Press, 1975.

Jankowski, James, and Israel Gershoni, eds. *Rethinking Nationalism in the Arab Middle East*. New York: Columbia University Press, 1997.

Johnson, Amy J. *Reconstructing Rural Egypt: Ahmed Hussein and the History of Egyptian Development*. Syracuse, NY: Syracuse University Press, 2004.

de Jong, Frederick. *Sufi Orders in Ottoman and Post-Ottoman Egypt and the Middle East: Collected Studies*. Istanbul: Isis Press, 2000.

Kamenka, Eugene, ed. *Nationalism: The Nature and Evolution of an Idea*. Canberra: Australian National University Press, 1973.

Karrar, Ali Salih. "The Sufi Brotherhoods in the Sudan until 1900, with Special Reference to the Shayqiyya Region." PhD diss., University of Bergen, 1985.

Keddie, Nikki R. *An Islamic Response to Imperialism: Political and Religious Writings of Sayyid Jamal ad-Din "al-Afghani."* Berkeley, CA: University of California Press, 1968.

Kedourie, Elie. "The Genesis of the Egyptian Constitution of 1923." In *Political and Social Change in Modern Egypt*, edited by P.M. Holt, 347–61. Oxford: Oxford University Press, 1968.

———. *Nationalism*. New York: Praeger, 1960.

Kedourie, Elie, ed. *Nationalism in Asia and Africa*. New York: Meridian, 1970.

Khalid, Mansour. *The Government They Deserve: The Role of the Elite in Sudan's Political Evolution*. London: Kegan Paul, 1990.

Kitroeff, Alexander. *The Greeks in Egypt, 1919–1937*. Reading: Ithaca Press, 1989.

Kohn, Hans. *The Idea of Nationalism: A Study in Its Origins and Background*. New York: Macmillan, 1944.

Kramer, Gudrun. *The Jews in Modern Egypt, 1914–1952*. London: I.B. Tauris, 1989.

Landes, David S. *Bankers and Pashas: International Finance and Economic Imperialism in Egypt*. Cambridge, MA: Harvard University Press, 1979.

Laqueur, Walter Z. *Communism and Nationalism in the Middle East*. New York: Praeger, 1956.

Larson, Barbara K. "The Rural Marketing System of Egypt over the Last Three Hundred Years." *Comparative Studies in Society and History* 27, no. 3 (1985): 494–530.

Laskier, Michael M. *The Jews of Egypt, 1920–1970: In the Midst of Zionism, Anti-Semitism, and the Middle East Conflict*. New York: New York University Press, 1992.

Lavin, Deborah, ed. *The Condominium Remembered: Proceedings of the Durham Historical Records Conference 1982*. Vol. 1: *The Making of the Sudanese State*. Durham: Centre for Middle Eastern and Islamic Studies, 1991.

———. *The Condominium Remembered: Proceedings of the Durham Historical Records Conference 1982*. Vol. 2: *The Transformation of the Old Order in the Sudan*. Durham: Centre for Middle Eastern and Islamic Studies, 1993.

Lawson, Fred H. "Reassessing Egypt's Foreign Policy during the 1920s and 1930s." In *Re-Envisioning Egypt, 1919–1952*, edited by Arthur Goldschmidt, Amy

J. Johnson, and Barak A. Salmoni, 46–67. Cairo: American University in Cairo Press, 2005.

———. *The Social Origins of Egyptian Expansionism during the Muhammad 'Ali Period.* New York: Columbia University Press, 1992.

Lesch, Ann Mosely. *The Sudan: Contested National Identities*. Bloomington: Indiana University Press, 1998.

Levi, I.G. "Aperçu Historique du Commerce et de l'Industrie." *L'Égypte Contemporaine* 24, no. 152 (1933): 671–92.

———. "Le Commerce Extérieur et l'Industrialization de l'Égypte." *L'Égypte Contemporaine* 30, no. 186–87 (1939): 595–632.

———. "Le Commerce Extérieur et l'Industrialization de l'Égypte." *L'Égypte Contemporaine* 31, no. 193 (1940): 505–34.

Mabro, Robert, and Samir Radwan. *The Industrialization of Egypt, 1939–1973: Policy and Performance*. Oxford: Clarendon, 1976.

MacMichael, Sir Harold. *The Anglo-Egyptian Sudan*. London: Faber and Faber, 1934.

el-Mahdi, Saeed M.A. *A Guide to Land Settlement and Registration*. Khartoum: Khartoum University Press, 1971.

Mahmud, Fatma B. *The Sudanese Bourgeoisie: Vanguard of Development?* London: Zed Books, 1984.

Mayall, James. *Nationalism and International Society*. Cambridge: Cambridge University Press, 1990.

Melamid, Alexander. "Egypt and the Gezira Irrigation Scheme of the Sudan." *Middle Eastern Affairs* 4, no. 3 (1953): 87–90.

Mills, David E. "The Development of the Sudanese Economy under Condominium Rule." MA thesis, University of Utah, 1993.

———. "Dividing the Nile: The Failure to Strengthen Egyptian–Sudanese Economic Bonds, 1918–1945." PhD diss., University of Utah, 1997.

Mitchell, Timothy. *Colonising Egypt*. Cambridge: Cambridge University Press, 1990.

Mohammed, Ahmed el-Awad. "Militarism in the Sudan: The Colonial Experience." *Sudan Notes and Records* 61 (1980): 15–26.

Mondal, Anshuman Ahmed. *Nationalism and Post-Colonial Identity: Culture and Ideology in India and Egypt*. London: Routledge, 2003.

Musrey, Alfred G. *An Arab Common Market: A Study in Inter-Arab Trade Relations, 1920–67*. New York: Praeger, 1969.

Nairn, Tom. *The Break-Up of Britain, Crisis and Neo-Nationalism*. London: Humanities Press, 1977.

Nasser, Hoda Gamal Abdel. *Britain and the Egyptian Nationalist Movement, 1936–1952*. Reading: Ithaca Press, 1994.

Niblock, Tim. *Class and Power in Sudan: The Dynamics of Sudanese Politics, 1898–1985*. Albany: State University of New York Press, 1987.

el-Nour, Eiman. "Nationalism and the Rise of the Sudanese Novel." In *The Road Less Traveled: Reflections on the Literatures of the Horn of Africa*, edited by Ali Jimale Ahmed, 369–404. Trenton, NJ: Red Sea Press, 2007.

O'Brien, Patrick. "The Long-Term Growth of Agricultural Production in Egypt: 1821–1962." In *Political and Social Change in Modern Egypt*, edited by P.M. Holt, 162–95. Oxford: Oxford University Press, 1968.

O'Leary, Brendan. "On the Nature of Nationalism: An Appraisal of Ernest Gellner's Writings on Nationalism." *British Journal of Political Science* 27, no. 2 (1997): 191–222.

Omer, el-Haj Bilal. *The Danagla Traders of Northern Sudan*. Reading: Ithaca Press, 1985.

Owen, E.R.J. "Agricultural Production in Historical Perspective: A Case Study of the Period 1890–1939." In *Egypt since the Revolution*, edited by P.J. Vatikiotis, 50–65. New York: Praeger, 1968.

———. "The Attitudes of British Officials to the Development of the Egyptian Economy, 1882–1922." In *Studies in the Economic History of the Middle East*, edited by M.A. Cook, 485–500. Oxford: Oxford University Press, 1970.

Owen, Roger. *State, Power, and Politics in the Making of the Modern Middle East*. 3rd ed. London: Routledge, 2004.

———. "The Study of Middle Eastern Industrial History: Notes on the Interrelationship between Factories and Small-Scale Manufacturing with Special References to Lebanese Silk and Egyptian Sugar, 1900–1930." *International Journal of Middle East Studies* 16, no. 4 (1984): 475–87.

Owen, Roger, and Bob Sutcliffe. *Studies in the Theory of Imperialism*. London: Longman, 1972.

Perkins, Kenneth J. *Port Sudan: The Evolution of a Colonial City*. Boulder, CO: Westview Press, 1993.

Philipp, Thomas. *The Syrians in Egypt, 1725–1975*. Stuttgart: Steiner, 1985.

Pollard, Lisa. *Nurturing the Nation: The Family Politics of Modernizing, Colonizing and Liberating Egypt (1805–1923)*. Berkeley, CA: University of California Press, 2005.

Radwan, Samir Muhammad. *Capital Formation in Egyptian Industry and Agriculture, 1882–1967*. London: Ithaca, 1974.

Rahman, H. *A British Defence Problem in the Middle East: The Failure of the 1946 Anglo–Egyptian Negotiations*. Reading: Ithaca Press, 1994.

Rajani, Kanth, ed. *Paradigms in Economic Development*. New York: M.E. Sharpe, 1993.

Reid, Donald M. *Whose Pharaohs? Archaeology, Museums, and Egyptian National Identity from Napoleon to World War I*. Berkeley, CA: University of California Press, 2003.

Reynolds, Nancy Y. "National Socks and the 'Nylon Woman': Materiality, Gender, and Nationalism in Textile Marketing in Semicolonial Egypt, 1930–1956." *International Journal of Middle East Studies* 43, no. 1 (2011): 49–74.

Royal Institute of International Affairs. *Great Britain and Egypt 1914–1951: Information Papers Number 19*. London: Broadwater, 1952.
Ruay, Deng D. Akol. *The Politics of Two Sudans: The South and the North, 1821–1969*. Uppsala: Nordiska Afrikainstitutet, 1994.
Sabit, Adel M. *A King Betrayed: The Ill-Fated Reign of Farouk of Egypt*. London: Quartet, 1989.
Sabry, Hussein Zulfakar. *Sovereignty for Sudan*. Reading: Ithaca Press, 1982.
Safran, Nadav. *Egypt in Search of Political Community: An Analysis of the Intellectual and Political Evolution of Egypt, 1804–1952*. Cambridge, MA: Harvard University Press, 1961.
Sandes, E.W.C. *The Royal Engineers in Egypt and the Sudan*. Chatham: MacKays, 1937.
Sayyid-Marsot, Afaf Lutfi. *Egypt's Liberal Experiment, 1922–1936*. Berkeley, CA: University of California Press, 1977.
Schatz, Jean. "Aperçu général sur les principales cultures égyptiennes." *L'Égypte Contemporaine* 23, no. 138 (1932): 611–735.
———. "Le développement du commerce de l'Égypte." *L'Égypte Contemporaine* 24, no. 145 (1933): 651–695; *L'Égypte Contemporaine* 24, no. 146–147 (1933): 43–104; *L'Égypte Contemporaine* 24, no. 148–149 (1933): 283–332.
———. "La guerre et ses conséquences sur le commerce extérieur de l'Égypte." *L'Égypte Contemporaine* 31, no. 193 (1940): 547–71.
———. "Le Soudan et ses relations commerciales avec l'Égypte." *L'Égypte Contemporaine* 31, no. 190 (1940): 233–84.
Scholch, Alexander. *Egypt for the Egyptians*. Reading: Ithaca Press, 1981.
Sconyers, David. "Servant or Saboteur? The Sudan Political Service during the Crucial Decade: 1946–1956." *Bulletin* (British Society of Middle Eastern Studies) 14, no. 1 (1987): 42–51.
Seers, Dudley, Bernard Schaffer, and Marja-Liisa Kiljunen, eds. *Underdeveloped Europe: Studies in Core–Periphery Relations*. Atlantic Highlands, NJ: Humanities, 1979.
Serels, Steven. "Famines of War: The Red Sea Grain Market and Famine in Eastern Sudan, 1889–1891." *Northeast African Studies* 12, no. 1 (2012): 73–94.
———. "Political Landscaping: Land Registration, the Definition of Ownership and the Evolution of Colonial Objectives in the Anglo–Egyptian Sudan, 1899–1924." *African Economic History* 35 (2007): 59–75.
Seton-Watson, Hugh. *Nations and States: An Enquiry into the Origins of Nations and the Politics of Nationalism*. Boulder, CO: Westview, 1977.
al-Shahi, Ahmed. *Themes from Northern Sudan*. Reading: Ithaca Press, 1986.
Shamir, Shimon, ed. *The Jews of Egypt: A Mediterranean Society in Modern Times*. Boulder, CO: Westview, 1987.
Sharkey, Heather J. "A Century in Print: Arabic Journalism and Nationalism in Sudan, 1899–1999." *International Journal of Middle East Studies* 31 (1999): 531–49.

———. *Living with Colonialism, Nationalism and Culture in the Anglo–Egyptian Sudan*. Berkeley, CA: University of California Press, 2003.

Sharkey-Balasubramanian, Heather. "The Egyptian Colonial Presence in the Anglo–Egyptian Sudan, 1898–1932." In *White Nile, Black Blood: War, Leadership, and Ethnicity from Khartoum to Kamapala*, edited by Jay Spaulding and Stephanie Beswick, 279–314. Lawrenceville, NJ: Red Sea Press, 2000.

Shimizu, Hiroshi. *Anglo-Japanese Trade Rivalry in the Middle East in the Interwar Period*. Reading: Ithaca Press, 1986.

Smith, Anthony D. *The Ethnic Origins of Nations*. New York: Blackwell, 1986.

———. "Nationalism and Classical Social Theory." *British Journal of Sociology* 34, no. 1 (1983): 19–38.

———. *Nationalism and Modernism: A Critical Survey of Recent Theories of Nations and Nationalism*. London: Routledge, 1998.

———. *Theories of Nationalism*. London: Harper and Row, 1971.

Smith, Anthony D., ed. *Nationalist Movements*. New York: St. Martins, 1977.

Stalin, Joseph. *Marxism and the National and Colonial Question*. New York: International Publishers, n.d.

Terry, Janice. *The Wafd: 1919–1952*. London: Third World Centre for Research and Publishing, 1982.

Tignor, Robert L. "Bank Misr and Foreign Capitalism." *International Journal of Middle East Studies* 8, no. 2 (1977): 161–81.

———. "The Egyptian Revolution of 1919: New Directions in the Egyptian Economy." *Middle Eastern Studies* 12, no. 3 (1976): 41–67.

———. *Egyptian Textiles and British Capital, 1930–1956*. Cairo: American University in Cairo Press, 1989.

———. *Modernization and British Colonial Rule in Egypt*. Princeton, NJ: Princeton University Press, 1966.

———. *State, Private Enterprise, and Economic Change in Egypt, 1918–1952*. Princeton, NJ: Princeton University Press, 1984.

Tilley, Charles. "Reflections on the History of European State-Making." In *The Formation of National States in Western Europe*, edited by Charles Tilley, 3–83. Princeton, NJ: Princeton University Press, 1975.

Tivey, Leonard, ed. *The Nation-State: The Formation of Modern Politics*. New York: St. Martins, 1981.

Troutt Powell, Eve M. "Brothers along the Nile: Egyptian Concepts of Race and Ethnicity, 1895–1910." In *The Nile: Histories, Cultures, Myths*, edited by Haggai Erlich and Israel Gershoni, 171–81. Boulder, CO: Lynne Rienner, 2000.

———. *A Different Shade of Colonialism: Egypt, Great Britain and the Mastery of the Sudan*. Berkeley, CA: University of California Press, 2003.

Vitalis, Robert. *When Capitalists Collide: Business Conflict and the End of Empire in Egypt*. Berkeley, CA: University of California Press, 1995.

Voll, John. "A History of the Khatmiyyah Tariqah in the Sudan." PhD diss., Harvard University, 1969.

———. "Unity of the Nile Valley: Identity and Regional Integration." *Journal of African Studies* 3, no. 2 (1976): 205–28.

Wahbah, Murad. *The Role of the State in the Egyptian Economy, 1945–1981*. Reading: Ithaca Press, 1994.

Wallerstein, Immanuel. *Africa, the Politics of Independence: An Interpretation of Modern African History*. New York: Vintage, 1971.

———. "The Construction of Peoplehood: Racism, Nationalism, Ethnicity." In *Race, Nation, Class: Ambiguous Identities*, edited by Etienne Balibar and Immanuel Wallerstein, 71–85. London: Verso, 1991.

Walz, Terence. "The Paper Trade of Egypt and the Sudan in the Eighteenth and Nineteenth Centuries." In *Modernization in the Sudan*, edited by M.W. Daly, 29–48. New York: Lilian Barber, 1985.

———. *Trade between Egypt and Bilad as-Sudan, 1700–1820*. Cairo: Institut Français d'Archéologie Orientale du Caire, 1978.

Warburg, Gabriel R. *Egypt and the Sudan: Studies in History and Politics*. London: Frank Cass, 1985.

———. "From Ansar to Umma: Sectarian Politics in the Sudan, 1914–1945." *Asian and African Studies* 9 (1973): 101–53.

———. *Historical Discord in the Nile Valley*. Evanston, IL: Northwestern University Press, 1992.

———. *Islam, Nationalism, and Communism in a Traditional Society: The Case of Sudan*. London: Frank Cass, 1978.

———. *Islam, Sectarianism, and Politics in Sudan since the Mahdiyya*. Madison: University of Wisconsin Press, 2003.

———. "Religious Policy in the Northern Sudan: Ulama and Sufism, 1899–1918." *Asian and African Studies* 7 (1971): 89–119.

———. "Some Social and Economic Aspects of Turco-Egyptian Rule in the Sudan." *Belleten* 53, no. 49 (1989): 769–95.

Warburg, Gabriel, and Uri M. Kupferschmidt, eds. *Islam, Nationalism and Radicalism in Egypt and the Sudan*. New York: Praeger, 1983.

Wendell, Charles. *The Evolution of the Egyptian National Image*. Berkeley, CA: University of California Press, 1972.

Wingate, Sir Ronald. *Wingate of the Sudan: The Life and Times of General Sir Reginald Wingate, Maker of the Anglo–Egyptian Sudan*. Westport, CT: Greenwood, 1975.

Wondimneh, Tilahun. *Egypt's Imperial Aspirations over Lake Tana and the Blue Nile*. Addis Ababa: Addis Ababa University Press, 1979.

Woodward, Peter. *Condominium and Sudanese Nationalism*. London: Rex Collings, 1979.

Zayid, Mahmud. *Egypt's Struggle for Independence*. Beirut: Khayats, 1965.

———. "The Origins of the Liberal Constitutional Party in Egypt." In *Political and Social Change in Modern Egypt*, edited by P.M. Holt, 334–46. Oxford: Oxford University Press, 1968.

Secondary Sources—Arabic

Abaza, 'Abdallah Fakri. *Buhuth iqtisadiya 'an al-Sudan*. Cairo, [1940].

Abaza, Fu'ad. "al-Ba'tha al-misriya fi al-Sudan, sanat 1935." Speech at the Royal Geographical Society in Cairo, 25 April 1935. Cairo, 1937.

Ahmad, Nabil 'Abd al-Hamid Sayyid. *al-Nashat al-iqtisadi li-l-ajanib wa atharuhu fi al-mujtama' al-misri min sanat 1922 ila sanat 1952*. Cairo: al-Hay'a al-Misriya al-'Amma li-l-Kitab, 1982.

'Ali Taha, Fadwa 'Abd al-Rahman. *Kayfa nala al-Sudan istiqlalahu: dirasa tarikhiya li-ittifaqiyat 12 Fibrayir 1953 al-misriya al-baritaniya hawla al-hukm al-dhati wa taqrir al-masir li-l-Sudan*. Khartoum: Sharikat Dar al-Khartum, 1997.

al-Buhayra, Zaki. *al-Tatawwur al-iqtisadi al-ijtima'i fi al-Sudan, min al-azma al-'alamiya hatta al-istiqlal 1930–1956*. Cairo: Maktabat al-Nahda al-Misriya, 1987.

Diyab, Ahmad Ibrahim. *al-'Alaqat al-misriya al-sudaniya, 1919–1924*. Cairo: al-Hay'a al-Misriya al-'Amma li-l-Kitab, 1985.

Ghurbal, Muhammad Shafiq. *Tarikh al-mufawadat al-misriya al-baritaniya*. Cairo: Maktabat al-Nahdah al-Misriya, 1952.

al-Ghurfa al-Tijariya al-Misriya bi-l-Iskandariya. *Taqrir al-Ghurfa al-Tijariya al-Misriya li-madinat al-Iskandariya 'an a'maliha fi sanat 1922–1923*. Alexandria: Imprimerie Publicité Égyptienne, 1923.

———. *Taqrir al-Ghurfa al-Tijariya al-Misriya li-Madinat al-Iskandariya 'an a'maliha fi sanat 1925–1926*. Alexandria: Matba'at al-Jarida al-Tijariya al-Misriya, 1926.

———. *Taqrir al-Ghurfa al-Tijariya al-Misriya li-madinat al-Iskandariya 'an a'maliha fi sanat 1927–1928*. Alexandria: Matba'at al-Taqaddum, 1928.

———. *Taqrir al-Ghurfa al-Tijariya al-Misriya li-madinat al-Iskandariya, sanat 1937*. Alexandria: Matba'at al-Mustaqbal, 1938.

Habib, 'Aziz Muhammad. *al-Sudan, Dirasat tabi'iya wa iqtisadiya*. Cairo: al-Anglo al-Misriya, 1972.

al-Hamamdi, Jalal al-Din. *Madha fi al-Sudan?* Cairo: Dar al-Ma'arif, 1945.

Hamid, Musa 'Abdallah. *Istiqlal al-Sudan bayna al-waqi'iya wa-l-rumansiya*. Khartoum: Manshurat al-Khartum 'Asimat al-Thaqafa al-'Arabiya, 2005.

Hamzah, Sa'd Mahir. *al-Sina'a wa mashakilha fi al-Sudan*. Cairo: Maktabat al-Nahda al-Misriya, 1958.

Hannawi, Muhammad 'Abd al-Hamid Ahmad. *Ma'rikat al-Jala' wa wihdat Wadi al-Nil, 1945–1954*. Cairo: al-Hay'a al-Misriya al-'Amma li-l-Kitab, 1998.

Husayn, 'Abdallah. *al-Sudan min al-tarikh al-qadim ila rihlat al-ba'tha al-misriya*. 3 vols. Cairo: al-Matba'a al-Rahmaniya, 1935.

Ibrahim, 'Abdallah A. *Tarikh Misr wa-l-Sudan al-hadith wa-l-mu'asir*. Cairo: Dar al-Thaqafa, 1997.

Kamil, Mustafa. *al-Maqalat*. Edited by Yuwaqim Rizq Murqus. Cairo: al-Hay'a al-Misriya al-'Amma li-l-Kitab, 1986.
Khayr, Ahmad. *Kifahjil: tarikh harakat al-Khirrijin wa-tatawwuriha fi al-Sudan*. Khartoum: al-Dar al-Sudaniya li-l-Kutub, 2002.
Mansur, 'Abd al-Fattah 'Abd al-Samad. *al-'Alaqat al-misriya al-sudaniya, fi zill al-ittifaq al-thuna'i, 1899–1924*. Cairo: al-Hay'a al-Misriya al-'Amma li-l-Kitab, 1993.
Maqqar, Nasim. *al-Usus al-tarikhiya li-l-takamul al-iqtisadi bayna Misr wa-l-Sudan: dirasa fi al-'alaqat al-iqtisadiya al-misriya al-sudaniya, 1821–1848*. Cairo: al-Hay'a al-Misriya al-'Amma li-l-Kitab, 1985.
Muhammad, Zahir Jasim. *Tatawwur al-hay'a al-siyasiya fi al-Sudan, 1899–1969*. Cairo: al-Maktab al-Misri li-Tawzi' al-Matbu'at, 2003.
Murqus, Yuwaqim Rizq. *al-Sudan fi al-barlaman al-misri, 1924–1936*. Cairo: al-Hay'a al-Misriya al-'Amma li-l-Kitab, 1989.
Mustafa, Muhammad al-Makkawi. *Bina' al-iqtisad al-sudani al-hadith: fatrat al-takwin wa-dawr al-ma'unat wa-l-qurud al-misriya*. Cairo, 2004.
Najib, Muhammad. *Risala 'an al-Sudan*. Cairo: al-Matba'a al-Amiriya, 1954.
Radi, Nawal 'Abd al-'Aziz. *Sidwi wa-l-Ikhwan wa Wafd al-Sudan, 'Am 1946*. Cairo: al-Matba'a al-Tijariya al-Haditha, 1988.
Riyad, Zahir. *al-Sudan al-mu'asir mundhu al-fath al-misri hatta al-istiqlal*. Cairo: Maktab al-Anglo al-Misriya, 1966.
Rizq, Yunan Labib. *Qadiyat wihdat Wadi al-Nil bayna al-mu'ahada wa taghyir al-waqi' al-isti'mari, 1936–1946*. Cairo: Ma'had al-Buhuth wa-l-Dirasat al-'Arabiya, 1975.
———. *al-Sudan fi 'ahd al-hukm al-thana'i al-awwal, 1899–1924*. Cairo: Ma'had al-Buhuth wa-l-Dirasat al-'Arabiya, 1976.
———. *al-Sudan fi al-mufawadat al-misriya al-baritaniya, 1930–1936*. Cairo: Ma'had al-Buhuth wa-l-Dirasat al-'Arabiya, 1974.
———. *al-Thawabit wa-l-mutaghayyirat fi al-'alaqat al-misriya al-sudaniya*. Cairo: Dar al-Hilal, 1994.
Salih, Mahmud 'Abidin. *al-'Alaqat al-sudaniya al-misriya: wa-afaq tatawwuriha*. Cairo, 2004.
Salim, Latifah Muhammad. *al-Sahafa wa-l-haraka al-wataniya al-misriya, 1945–1952: min malaffat al-kharijiya al-baritaniya*. Cairo: al-Hay'a al-Misriya al-'Amma li-l-Kitab, 1987.
al-Shahid, Muhammad Labib. *Mudhakkiratan: li-l-marhumayn Amir al-Liwa' Muhammad Basha Labib al-Shahid wa Amir al-Alay Ahmad Bak Rif'at 'an a'mal al-jaysh al-misri fi al-Sudan wa ma'sat khurujihi minhu*. Alexandria: Matba'at al-Mustaqbal, 1936.
al-Shami, Salah al-Din 'Ali. *al-Muwasalat wa-l-tatawwur al-iqtisadi fi al-Sudan*. Cairo: Dar al-Tiba'a al-Haditha, 1959.
Taha, Faysal 'Abd al-Rahman 'Ali. *al-Haraka al-siyasiya al-sudaniya wa-l-sira' al-misri al-baritani bi-sha'n al-Sudan, 1936–1953*. Cairo: Dar al-Amin, 1998.

Tamam, Tamam Hamam. "Mawaqif hizb al-Wafd al-misri min mas'alat al-Sudan fi al-fatra 1919–1951." PhD diss., Cairo University, 1974.

———. "al-Siyasa al-misriya tujaha al-Sudan 1936–1953." MA thesis, Cairo University, 1971.

Tussun, 'Amr. *al-Mas'ala al-sudaniya*. Alexandria: Matba'at al-Mustaqbal, 1936.

Index